DEFENDING THE REALM

Inside MI5 and the
War on Terrorism

Mark Hollingsworth and Nick Fielding

André Deutsch

This new edition published in 2003
First published in 1999, 2000
by André-Deutsch Ltd
An imprint of the
Carlton Publishing Group
20 Mortimer Street
London W1T 3JW

A catalogue record for this book is available from the British Library

ISBN 0 233 00010 0

Printed and bound in Great Britain by
Mackays of Chatham plc

CONTENTS

Preface   v

Chapter One: Into the Fire: New Threats and Targets   1

Chapter Two: Joining the Twilight Zone   39

Chapter Three: The Spying Game   67

Chapter Four: Subversion and the X Files   93

Chapter Five: The Secret War Against the IRA   131

Chapter Six: Terrorism in the UK: How MI5
        Failed to Counter the Al Qaeda Threat   165

Chapter Seven: Bombings, Assassination and the
        Bugging of a Journalist   182

Chapter Eight: The Whistleblower   204

Chapter Nine: Exile, Arrest and the Great Escape   240

Chapter Ten: Who Watches the Watchers?   282

Appendix One: Structure of MI5   320

Appendix Two: David Shayler's Submission
        to the Cabinet Office Review   322

Notes and References   338

Bibliography   353

Index   355

'The purpose of the Security Service is the Defence of the Realm and nothing else.'

Brigadier Sir Findlay Stewart, chairman of the Security Executive, in his secret report on MI5 commissioned by Prime Minister Clement Attlee, 1947

PREFACE

It all started with a phone call. One day Nick Fielding was telephoned at the *Mail on Sunday* office by a source. 'Would you like to meet an MI5 officer?' he said cautiously.

Fielding was at first sceptical. Journalists rarely receive offers to meet intelligence operatives willing to talk about the secret world. It might be a set-up. The officer might be part of a clandestine plot to plant some disinformation. This, however, was different. After meeting him several times, Fielding realised that he was genuine. The MI5 officer knew too much detail and he was desperate for an outlet for his frustrations. He had repeatedly spoken to his managers and raised his concerns inside the Security Service, but to no avail. All he received were blank stares and indifferent responses. The 'appropriate authorities' expressed no interest in investigating the issues. Disillusioned, the officer was looking for a vehicle to inform the public.

His name was David Shayler, and that phone call started a chain of events that led to the publication of this book. Its catalyst was the publication in the *Mail on Sunday*, on 24 August 1997, of a series of revelations about MI5, based on Shayler's testimony and written by the authors of this book.

This book is largely due to the courage of Shayler, who has been punished by the New Labour establishment for speaking out. Gagged by an injunction and threatened with prosecution, he fled to France. His long-standing girlfriend, Annie Machon, also a former MI5 officer, was arrested by six Special Branch detectives at Gatwick airport; and his friends were arrested and then released.

Shayler himself was arrested in Paris after the French Secret Service were falsely told by their UK counterparts that he was 'a terrorist'. After languishing in jail for three-and-a-half months, he was released after the French court ruled he had been motivated by political and public interest considerations.

Shayler and his partner Annie Machon were forced into exile purely because he refused to remain silent about abuses of power by MI5. Democracy has been enhanced by the revelation of some of the truths behind the façade at MI5's HQ at Thames House, but Shayler is paying a heavy price for revealing them. Machon deserves no less credit for the sacrifices she has made in supporting the cause.

Unlike past MI5 whistleblowers and 'defectors', Shayler is not motivated by political, ideological or even moral factors. His primary concern is what he witnessed as the lack of accountability, excessive secrecy and the bungling incompetence of Security Service operations.

Two other factors impress us about Shayler. Unlike some other former intelligence officers, he is not prone to confirming or encouraging wild conspiracy theories. And he understands the importance of not releasing genuine security and state secrets. He never disclosed to the authors, not even privately, names of MI5 agents or ongoing sensitive operations.

If this book was born out of Shayler's revelations, it was conceived by the courage of the *Mail on Sunday* in publishing them. Credit for that must go to Jonathan Holborow, then editor, who showed remarkable fortitude, despite immense legal and political pressures. He was supported by our colleagues at the *Mail on Sunday*, who worked on different aspects of the investigation, notably Peter Dobbie and Joe Murphy, and photographers David O'Neill and Philip Ide.

We are also grateful to John Wadham, director of the human rights organisation Liberty, who has fought selflessly on Shayler's behalf from the very beginning. This is despite the exasperation of negotiating with Whitehall. He was instrumental in preparing the complex, but successful, court defence that prevented Shayler's extradition from France.

The legal aspects of this story have far-reaching implications for press freedom. We were fortunate in the formidable legal team of Harvey Kass and Eddy Young at Associated Newspapers, Geoffrey Robertson, QC, David Smyth of Kingsley Napley (representing Nick Fielding) and Brian Spiro of Simons Muirhead and Burton (acting for Mark Hollingsworth).

Advised by Andrew Monson, QC, and André Deutsch, we reluctantly submitted this manuscript to the Defence, Press and Broadcasting Advisory Committee (commonly known as the D-Notice Committee). This is the voluntary system, administered by a Ministry of Defence official, which provides 'guidance to the media about defence and counter-terrorist information, the publication of which would be damaging to national security'.

Although the D-Notice Committee has no legal authority, the underlying implication for authors is that more censorious legal action may occur if they do not comply. We regarded the submitting of our book for pre-publication vetting by the state authorities as pernicious – not least because they themselves have a vested interest in censoring its contents. In our case, the irony is that the Special Branch investigation into the Shayler affair admitted that our *Mail on Sunday* articles 'did not cause serious damage to the work of the Security Service or national security'.

However, as the Official Secrets Act prohibits disclosure of every single aspect of MI5 (regardless of whether or not it damages national security), we co-operated with the D-Notice Committee. Our decision was based on legal prudence. It should not be misconstrued as an approval of a system we view as both repressive and undemocratic. The authorities asked us to make some small changes to the contents of the manuscript, none of which we believe reduced or undermined its central thrust.

This book was written at immense speed and we very much appreciate the support we received. The history of MI5 was researched and written by Mary Ann Nicholas, who contributed a first-rate and perceptive analysis. Richard Norton-Taylor, the *Guardian*'s security editor, generously allowed us access to his files. We are also indebted to Lisa Pereira, Hazel Armstrong and a young woman who wishes only to be known as 'MM' for their diligent and efficient research in libraries.

As ever, Olga Sheppard was speedy and ultra-accurate in her transcribing of taped interviews. And we were privileged that our manuscript was edited by Hazel Orme, whose forensic eye and wider strategic appraisal improved the book immeasurably. Thanks also to Louise Dixon, Miranda Filbee and Chris Hawkes, our commissioning editors, and Jonathan Bloom, André Deutsch's head of legal and business affairs, for their expert and intelligent handling of the legal negotiations.

Finally, our most persistent and determined supporter was our agent Robert Kirby, of Peters, Fraser and Dunlop. He never lost faith in the project, despite the monumental legal obstacles that confronted it.

Since the publication of the paperback edition of this book in September 2000, the world has changed in a profound and perhaps permanent way. A year later, 3,000 people died after hijacked aircraft crashed into the twin towers of the World Trade Centre in New York City and the Pentagon in Washington DC. The shockwaves from these Al Qaeda attacks are still reverberating around the world. They reveal that America and Britain's much-vaunted intelligence agencies were completely unprepared for an attack of such magnitude. In Britain, Islamist radicals were able to organise and operate for years with impunity. The consequence, according to some estimates, is that there are now several hundred people at liberty in the UK who have been trained at Al Qaeda camps in Afghanistan and elsewhere.

In the wake of 11 September 2001, the intelligence community has been turned upside down on both sides of the Atlantic. New organisations have come into being and a new urgency has influenced the activities of MI5, MI6 and its American counterparts. But it will take them years to build up the expertise and contacts needed to combat the new terrorist threats, in particular the possibility that such groups may one day gain access to nuclear, chemical or biological weapons. An even greater challenge facing legislators is ensuring a balance between security and human rights. Already there are signs of a new intolerance threatening hard-won democratic freedoms.

That is the primary reason for this new, updated edition of *Defending the Realm*. It includes a substantial amount of new information and revelations, notably a new chapter by Nick Fielding on MI5's monitoring and operations against Al Qaeda in the UK. Now, more than ever, MI5's activities need to be scrutinised and held to account as we enter an era dominated by concerns about international terrorism.

Mark Hollingsworth
Nick Fielding
March 2003

1

INTO THE FIRE:
NEW THREATS AND TARGETS

'Loyalty to whoever you work for is extremely important. The only problem is, it is not *the* most important thing. And when it comes to not admitting mistakes or covering up or not rectifying things only to save face, that's a problem.'

Coleen Rowley, an FBI agent who has been critical of how intelligence agencies have investigated terrorism,
Time magazine, 30 December 2002

Two Metropolitan Police Special Branch officers sit patiently and pensively in their specially rented apartment in Bickenhall Street, Marylebone, central London. It is December 1992 and they are monitoring two Chechen men suspected of being involved in organised crime who have bought a four-bedroom £1 million flat across the street. It is part of a wider, top-secret surveillance operation against the activities of Chechen militant extremists based in the UK.

For many years, support for the Chechen rebels has been co-ordinated in London, where funds are raised for the holy war in their 'homeland' from Islamic sympathisers and via dissident websites. A group called Al Muhajiroun, based in north London, is reported to have recruited Muslim students and sent them to Chechnya to fight in a jihad against the Russian army. Under pressure from President Putin, MI5 has been given the task of investigating such activists in the UK who are suspected of backing violent insurrection in Chechnya. It believes that up to 100 young British-born Muslims have left the country to fight and train in Chechnya.

MI5's operation is run in parallel with MI6 and the CIA who provide Russian forces with satellite reconnaissance photographs and telephone intercepts.

The Special Branch officers are aware of the extreme sensitivity and danger of their stake-out. The Chechens across the street, Ruslan Utsyev, 39, and his brother Nasabek, 21, are suspected of running a multi-million dollar aluminium fraud and money-laundering scam. But there is a more important factor: one of them is an MI5 informant.

For several weeks the surveillance is successful. The Chechens openly and brazenly live the high life, going on drinking sprees and bring home prostitutes. People entering the luxury flat are photographed and intelligence is gathered. But suddenly the Special Branch officers receive a phone call from Scotland Yard. They are ordered to withdraw immediately as a specialist MI5 team will be taking over. Bemused, they vacate the premises. But a catastrophic error is made during the hand-over: MI5 delay moving in their surveillance unit.

Soon after Special Branch depart, two Chechens evade security, break into the flat and shoot the two men three times in the head. They die instantly. One is placed in a cardboard box and the other is left in the penthouse. The murders are only discovered after a delivery man notices a strong smell from the box while he is driving across London to take it to a house in Harrow. The police are then alerted.

The brutal killings occur after Special Branch withdraw and before MI5 move in across the street. One of the victims is the MI5 informant. The rebel Chechen government claim their compatriots were not gangsters and were killed by the KGB. 'We believe their murder was political,' said Charles Tchkotoua, the Chechen Ambassador-at-large in London. He also complains that the two men should have been given better security protection.[1]

The Special Branch officers, now working in the private sector, are enraged and furious by the blunder. They complain to their Commander that not only did a brave MI5 informant lose his life, but securities worth millions of pounds aimed at financing a terrorist campaign in the UK are stolen and lost. 'It was an appalling blunder and tragedy,' one of the Special Branch officers told us. 'Those people died purely because MI5 wanted to take over the operation, so they could demonstrate to Whitehall that they could cope with such tasks. But it just showed how ill-equipped and laid-back they are. By the time they got their act together, it was too late.'

There is no love lost between the two agencies. The Special Branch officers feel that they are often forced to hand over the intelligence to the 'glory boys' of MI5, while the latter perceive Special Branch as plodding policemen with a fancy name. Such a damaging turf war encapsulates the current turmoil at the heart of British Intelligence. For MI5 faces the biggest challenge in its 94-year history: international terrorism on an unprecedented scale.

The devestating attack on 11 September 2001 has been widely regarded as a massive failure of intelligence. The CIA and western intelligence agencies were not snoozing at their desks as the hijacked planes crashed into the twin towers, but even its most fervent supporters admit the absence of a detailed warning is an indictment. 'I don't think even Pearl Harbour matches this one,' said a loyal former CIA officer. 'How often do you lose half a division in a day? Nothing has ever happened on this scale before.' And its executive director, A.B. 'Fuzzy' Krongard, admitted that the CIA had been far too concerned with weapons of mass destruction.[2]

At an operational level, the criticism by former officers is that the CIA has become increasingly bureaucratic; reduced its reliance on human intelligence from agents; become too insular and preoccupied with political turf wars; and too risk-averse and obsessed with analyis and technology, producing far too much intelligence which is often examined too late. It is this 'fatal malaise', as former CIA officer Robert Baer calls it, which has undermined the effectiveness of western intelligence agencies. 'The only way to defeat terrorism is for the CIA to once again go out and start talking to people,' wrote Baer in his memoir *See No Evil*. 'To people who can go where it can't, see what it can't and hear what it can't.'[3]

Over at the FBI, veteran agent and whistleblower Coleen Rowley issued a similar damning indictment. She revealed how in the weeks preceeding 11 September 2001, the FBI in Washington DC prevented agents in Minneapolis from further investigating Zacarias Moussaoui, one of the conspirators. Specific warnings were ignored, agents were drowning in paperwork and lived in fear of offending the hierachy, she told *Time* magazine. 'There's a certain pecking order and it's pretty strong. It's rare that someone picks up the phone and calls a rank or two above themselves.'[4]

This critique is an uncanny mirror-image of MI5 as revealed by former officers David Shayler and Jestyn Thirkell-White. They accept that the Service is staffed by dedicated and competant people. They know that their technical expertise and surveillance teams are first-rate. But the dissidents also say that MI5 has failed to adapt from the cosy, rarefied atmosphere of the Cold War, where human intelligence could be caricatured as sidling up to the right people at the embassy cocktail party. Instead, the Service's attempts to infiltrate Islamic militant cells in the UK has been handicapped by bureaucratic inertia, by wrongly distributed resources and slow, inflexible procedures. According to Shayler, human intelligence is the most useful weapon against terrorism. 'You can spend £1 million putting a bug in a front room, but once your target has left the room you've lost them,' said the MI5 whistleblower. 'The Service is used to dealing with static targets, but now you've got fast-moving terrorist organisations and it hasn't adapted its systems to keep up.'[5]

Shayler also claims that an elitist recruitment policy has meant a failure to infiltrate Middle East terrorist groups. Until 1994, new MI5 officers were required to have grandparents born in the UK. This ruled out a range of ethnic minorities who could have proved invaluable in penetrating extremist Islamic cells. The first black officer did not join MI5 until the mid-1990s and they still only represent 3.2 per cent of the staff, with none of them at senior level.

Hiring officers from ethnic minority backgrounds is a crucial asset in countering Middle East terrorism. For infiltrating an agent into an organisation is complicated by a language barrier which involves many diverse dialects. Even Arabic-speakers speak differently, depending on their origins. Eventually, in 1998, MI5 woke up and openly advertised in newspapers to recruit British Muslims in a new policy to increase surveillance on Islamic groups linked to terrorism. The adverts said that employees would 'contribute to work of national importance' and would be 'interpreting cryptic remarks'.[6] This was expanded in 2000 to include job advertisements in ethnic newspapers like *Eastern Eye* and *New Nation* under the slogan – 'A Life Less Ordinary'.

Responding to criticism from Muslim leaders that MI5 was trying to recruit informers, a Home Office spokesperson said: 'There has been an upsurge in terrorism from the Middle East. It would be irresponsible not to have experts who can speak languages associated with such people. In the past it was necessary to have Gaelic speakers to deal with Irish terrorists. There are many groups in this country associated with the Middle East and many are legitimate. Nevertheless, it is important that we monitor terrorist threats.'[7]

Countering terrorism has long been a problem for MI5. When the phenomena first exploded on the world stage in the 1970s, MI5 was barely involved and struggled to cope. Traditionally, it was viewed as a criminal matter and dealt with by the police and Special Branch. But by the early 1990s, state-sponsored violence and militant Islamic fundamentalism presented a far greater security threat.

Britain had become both a magnet and a haven for political and religious exiles from the Middle East. They were attracted by the freedom to speak out and publish their views – a right that few had experienced in their homeland. But these lively debates often spilled over into fractious disputes at public meetings and in university student unions. Britain was fast becoming a battleground for Middle East conflicts.

MI5 responded by pouring resources into G Branch, responsible for counter-terrorism in the UK. However, it was impeded by the same weaknesses it faced while investigating the IRA: a management that preferred bureaucratic rather than operational solutions and ponderous internal methods once the intelligence had arrived.

MI5's lack of expertise on Middle Eastern groups in Britain was highlighted by the fiasco surrounding the outbreak of the Gulf War in January 1991. The Security Service and Special Branch were mobilised in a major anti-terrorist alert. An assessment by the Joint Intelligence Committee suggested that Iraqi sympathisers loyal to Saddam Hussein might carry out attacks in Britain, possibly involving chemical or biological weapons. In the run-up to the Gulf War, nearly 800 Iraqis were deported from Britain. At the outbreak of hostilities, eight Iraqi diplomats were expelled almost immediately, along with 67 other Arabs. A further 35 were held in a camp on Salisbury Plain, while 33 were held in a prison near York.

But many of those detained were not supporters of Saddam Hussein. Many had been long-time opponents. A Home Office panel set up to hear appeals for some of those due to be deported found that most of them posed no threat to national security. Most were postgraduate students completing research in engineering and science at universities such as Manchester, Salford, Keele,

Cardiff and Liverpool. One, a Kuwaiti who had a wife and British-born child, thought he had been arrested because of an argument he had had with a Saudi in a local mosque.

On their eventual release, many said there had been no attempt to interrogate them. Yet when Home Secretary Kenneth Baker had announced that 88 Palestinians and Iraqis were to be deported in January 1991 he said that no evidence of the 'terrorist links' could be published because such information would endanger national security. Yet if they really were terrorists, went the argument, why weren't they questioned?

They included people like Bedford computer salesman Ali al-Saleh, who had lived peacefully in Britain for 20 years. 'We only learnt the police had been at our house when we phoned the next-door neighbour to remind her to feed the cat,' he said.[8] 'They thought I was working for the Saudi embassy. I left that job two years ago. They [the police] also did not know that we had two British-born children. When they saw them they decided not to arrest my wife and allowed her to stay at home with the kids.' It got worse. 'The policemen who drove me to London didn't know where the jail was. I used to live off the Caledonian Road [in north London, close to Pentonville Prison], so I directed them.' It later emerged that one of the reasons Mr Saleh had been arrested was that his wife's sister had married a man whose uncle was the Palestinian terrorist Abu Nidal.

Another of those arrested was Abbas Shiblak, a moderate and highly respected Palestinian author. Mahmood Ayyad, who worked at the Qatar embassy, was also picked up, even though he had previously been given security clearance to drive on to the runways at Heathrow airport to pick up diplomats. He even produced pictures of the Queen walking past him with a group of Arab diplomats.

The reason MI5 made so many mistakes in deciding who should be taken in by Special Branch was because of the way in which it processed the information it had at its disposal. The MI5 officer in charge did the security assessment very quickly and based it on the security summary and printouts, which did not include actual evidence. Neither did he consult the database of terrorist targets. That was the blunder.

The Home Office responded by appointing MI5's in-house staff counsellor, Sir Phillip Woodfield, to examine the way in which it had handled the affair. Within a few months Woodfield had cleared the

Service, accepting their 'arguments that it was right to err on the side of caution'[9] when drawing up lists of suspects. He concluded that Special Branch and MI5 should not be criticised in any way.

The fiasco over the Gulf War detainees was not the only failure by G Branch. Three years later another investigation highlighted serious problems in the organisation. It concerned the bomb attacks on the Israeli embassy and other Jewish offices in north London in July 1994. According to David Shayler, an officer in G Branch at the time, MI5 was warned that an attack on the embassy was imminent. Despite receiving specific information from a highly reliable source, it did nothing. The MI5 officer who received the warning failed to act on it and after the bombing, which injured 13 people, it was found 'buried' in a cupboard by another officer, leading to speculation of a cover-up by the officer who had received it.

The woman concerned was not even disciplined, said Shayler, despite an immediate inquiry headed by the section chief. As a result, morale in MI5's international terrorism section dropped alarmingly, particularly when senior management failed to institute new procedures to prevent a similar event occurring.

The bomb at the embassy, in Kensington Palace Gardens, had been timed to do maximum damage to the Middle East peace negotiations. It exploded just 24 hours after Jordan's King Hussein shook hands with Israeli Prime Minister Yitzhak Rabin at the White House. It was followed by a second bomb at Balfour House, a north London office block used by Jewish charities, which injured a further six people. As a result of the bombings, more than a hundred Israeli and Jewish buildings in Britain were placed under 24-hour armed guard.

Indirect confirmation of the story came from a 1994 *Sunday Times* article,[10] published just after the attack, which stated that a top Israeli secret service delegation had visited London three weeks before the bombing. The Mossad officers had told MI5 that Hezbollah was planning to attack two targets in London. They correctly identified the Israeli embassy and Balfour House. But Scotland Yard's Anti-terrorist Squad told the paper that the tip-off was not passed on to them. Further warnings were passed on by the Jewish Board of Deputies and by Dr Jonathan Sacks, the Chief Rabbi, who also said they were ignored.

Shayler's story seemed to be the missing piece of the jigsaw. Now it was clear why Scotland Yard had not been informed. The MI5 officer who had been given the warning had simply ignored it, then sought to cover it up when the bomb exploded. Without information from MI5, the police, already preoccupied with the discovery the previous week of a suspected IRA plot to bomb the Conservative Party conference, were reluctant to act and place extra guards on potential Jewish/Israeli targets.

In 1996, two young Palestinians, Jawad Botmeh and Samar Alami, were convicted of a conspiracy to carry out the Israeli embassy bombing and sentenced to 20-year prison sentences. Yet both had a cast-iron alibi and the case against them was riddled with inconsistencies.

Botmeh and Alami were found guilty because they had been trying to discover ways of making simple explosive devices, with mainly household ingredients, for use as a form of basic self-defence by Palestinians in the West Bank and the Gaza Strip. Both were scientists from well-known Palestinian families. The judge at their trial accepted that they had no links with any terrorist organisation. Their amateurish activities were also in sharp contrast to the bombings, which had been carried out professionally, so much so that the police forensics team could not even establish what explosive had been used.

The police accept that the case remains unsolved and that the actual bombers have never been caught. Botmeh and Alami believe that they were duped by one of the bombers, but information they provided to police has not been followed up. In particular, they were never asked for a detailed description of the man they believe was involved in planning and carrying out the bombings – Ridd Mughrabi. Mughrabi had asked them to accompany him to Milton Keynes to buy one of the cars used in the bombings and also asked them to store material for him. He has never been found by police, but when their solicitor, Gareth Pierce, arranged for a sketch artist to see Botmeh and Alami separately, a year after the trial, the resultant pictures were almost identical.[11]

The information provided by Shayler on the bomb warning surfaced unexpectedly in the case that solicitors are now mounting to gain an appeal for Botmeh and Alami. In November 1997, Gareth Pierce – a highly respected solicitor who represented the Guildford Four – wrote to the Crown Prosecution Service asking for any information relevant to Shayler's allegations. Sixteen months later, in

March 1999, it was revealed that Home Secretary Jack Straw had signed two Public Interest Immunity Certificates, which meant that his officials did not have to release information on the case. The Home Office has not contended that the information is irrelevant, simply that its grounds for non-disclosure are connected to national security. Gareth Pierce has stated: 'I am totally, absolutely and one hundred per cent sure, as sure as of any person that I have ever represented, that these two have no involvement whatsoever in the bombing of the Israeli embassy.'[12]

In early 2000, the status of Botmeh and Alami as high-security category A prisoners was removed after lobbying by the Lebanese government and Palestinian community, notably a 200,000-signature petition from the West Bank and Lebanon.

Their Appeal was based mainly on Shayler's revelations and that two key MI5 documents about the case were not made available to the court. This included an MI5 report concluding that the Israelis blew up their own embassy to persuade the British to increase security on Israeli property in the UK. The prosecution lawyers admitted that this material was not made available and said this was due to seven cases of 'human error'.

The MI5 documents are crucial to Botmeh and Alami's defence because of what the police admitted was 'an intelligence vacuum'. Cross-examined at the original trial, Det Supt William Emerton, the officer in charge of the investigation into the bombings, acknowledged: 'I have asked the Security Services whether they are aware of anybody from any source; and one of the big things about this investigation, frankly, is the intelligence vacuum that surrounds it. There was nobody anywhere in the world who can give any indication of any clue about anybody doing anything. This is a straightforward police investigation.'

It was this 'intelligence vacuum' that helped persuade the jury that the bombings were carried out by a small amateurish group in west London. MI5 later admitted that there had been a warning about an attack on Israeli targets in London at that time by a group which had nothing to do with Botmeh and Alami.

The prosecution also rejected detailed information and documents handed to police in 1994 about a suspect unrelated to Botmeh and Alami who had a map of the Israeli embassy and an ammunition list. The Court of Appeal was also not persuaded and, in November 2001, it refused to quash their convictions.

Confronted by the Al Qaeda threat of suicide bombing, MI5 plans to increase its staff by 25 per cent to about 2,400 and has expanded its role into protective security. It is not only advising government departments but also the private sector. Based on covertly obtained intelligence from GCHQ and the US National Security Agency, MI5 provides regular threat assessments. These are sent by secure e-mail to relevant ministries and to some major corporations, notably BP and Shell, because of the potential for terrorist attacks on refineries and tankers.[13] At a meeting at MI5's headquarters at Thames House, in March 2003, security advisors to leading multi-national companies were warned to expect a wave of terrorist attacks if the war in Iraq proceeded. MI5 directors said this could include attempted assassinations of individual expatriate staff or suicide bomb attacks on the premises of their companies in Saudi Arabia, Kuwait, Jordan and Bahrain, as well as raising the risk of terrorism in the UK.[14]

Specific threat assessments, including leads MI5 is pursuing in covert operations, are circulated to a much smaller audience. This inner circle comprises of 10 Downing Street, key Cabinet ministers and permanent secretaries, notably at the Home Office, Ministry of Defence, the Cabinet Office and the Foreign Office. If the information is particularly sensitive, it is sent in a hand-delivered letter to the Prime Minister by Sir David Omand, the Security and Intelligence Co-ordinator at the Cabinet Office.[15]

If there is a high-security alert, such as the threat in February 2003 when troops and tanks were despatched to Heathrow airport, MI5 is at the heart of assessing the seriousness of the situation. Usually, the intelligence comes from GCHQ which monitors and deciphers conversations taking place all over the world by e-mail, satellite and mobile phones. After consulting the National Security Agency, the head of GCHQ, Sir Francis Richards, takes the file to a meeting of the Joint Intelligence Commitee in the Cabinet Office under the chairmanship of former MI6 officer John Scarlett. Other members include Sir Richard Dearlove, chief of MI6, Air Marshal Joe French, head of defence intelligence and Eliza Manningham-Buller, the director-general of MI5, and an array of ministers, civil servants, generals and police chiefs. Recommendations are then made to the Prime Minister on how credible and real the danger to the country.[16]

These crucial decisions now make MI5's activities and performance vital and relevant to people's lives. In the past, its spying on the KGB could be dismissed as part of the relatively harmless intelligence game and mutually beneficial ideological Cold War. But now MI5's threat assessments have a real impact on our lives : do we take the London Underground or do we stay at home with plastic taped over the windows? Is it safe to fly? Should we be suspicious of all radical Muslims? Being able to weigh up an intelligence report – as filtered through the media – is now as vital a skill as applying for a job or sending an e-mail.

MI5 has finally come into our living rooms. For failure to pre-empt or at least supply accurate warnings about terrorist attacks can have appalling consequences. And so its methods need to be scrutinised now more than ever before.

In the recent past MI5 usually played the long game against the IRA, Libyans and Islamic operatives. Based on tip-offs from its agents, informants and GCHQ intercepts, MI5 would launch a long-term surveillance of the suspected terrorists. If there was a lorry packed with explosives travelling on the mainland, the response was to follow the vehicle in the knowledge that they were likely to meet IRA operatives planning an attack. But this was sometimes handled in a laborious, bungling and inept manner. As we reveal extensively in Chapter 5, MI5 failed to prevent several IRA bombings because it was far too slow in acting on the intelligence accumulated, even after conclusive evidence was obtained.

Known as 'risk management', MI5's instincts have been to monitor the movement of terrorist suspects to obtain as much intelligence as possible and then endlessly assess it. However, Special Branch sources have told us that MI5's rigid bureaucratic methods and obsession with self-indulgent analysis delayed crucial life-saving decisions and led to the loss of lives. They claim that the early arrest of suspects could have prevented the atrocities.

The threat of Al Qaeda is even more dangerous than the IRA. Apart from the suicide bombers, the new terrorist network is far more disparate and hence, far more difficult to detect. There is no discernible pattern to their operations, apart from killing as many people as possible, and they have penetrated deep into British society. The present head of MI5, Eliza Manningham-Buller, has told ministers that she cannot be sure that she knows the identities of more than 50 per cent of operatives in the UK who are linked to the Islamic terrorist network. 'She likens Al Qaeda to a piece of knitting,' an MI5 officer told the *Financial Times*. 'It is complex, interwoven and at times impenetrable. You think you've got a grip of one bit of it – then suddenly the whole thing unravels.'[17]

For MI5 to be effective, it needs to reject its ponderous bureaucratic methods and the long watching game. The police and Special Branch argue that it is better to act swiftly at the first sign of a plot rather than devote huge time and resources to chasing large groups over a long period of time. The priority should be to catch suspects involved in *any* criminal activity as a way of demobilising them and ideally put them in jail - if only for a short time. Known as the 'Al Capone option', it has been used all over the world whereby terrorists are convicted of tax fraud or arms smuggling when hard evidence for more serious charges is lacking.

MI5 also need to share more intelligence with the police, Special Branch and other agencies. This has been a long-term problem. Spies, by nature, tend to collect information, code it and hoard it, even from their own colleagues. It is the essence of their craft, but again, this is a luxury they cannot afford when dealing with fast-moving terrorist cells. Effective distribution is what Keith Veness, the Metropolitan police assistant commissioner, called 'the golden thread by which we can move intelligence into an operation and then ideally into a prosecution'. He told a parliamentary inquiry: 'There would be no forgiveness whatsoever in obscuring an item of intelligence which could lead to the saving of life or reduction of harm.' The assistant commissioner pointed out that the police were not warned that the Al Qaeda shoebomber, Richard Reid, was a potential security risk.[18]

MI5 has certainly increased its counter-terrorist activities in recent years. One priority has been to monitor the activities of young Muslims and students who have been targetted by extremist groups in the UK. 'We can identify people, but there is a problem of deporting them to countries with poor human rights records", an intelligence source told the *Guardian*. 'Many individuals are wanted by, for example, India, Egypt, Russia or Turkey and would face terrorist charges if they returned. MI5 and Special Branch are also aware of the sensitivity of appearing to be targetting people just because they are Muslims.'[19]

Nevertheless, in the late 1990s, a special MI5 unit was set up to investigate young British Muslims. Informants at universities were recruited and students who were suspected of gathering information useful for their nations' attempts to build weapons of mass destruction were placed under close scrutiny. The university authorities were asked to pay particular attention to students from the Middle East or 'rogue states' like Libya who were studying physics or chemistry.

One MI5 tactic to disrupt the extreme militant groups was to let them know they were being watched, according to the *Guardian*. MI5 sources would regularly visit these organisations and disclose they were being investigated in an attempt to deter and discourage their activities. However, many Muslim students resented such tactics and claimed that MI5 was fostering 'Islamaphobia' on campuses which resulted in innocent people being targetted unfairly.[20]

MI5's operation culminated in February 2001, when the Home Office banned 21 groups, the majority of them Islamic, from operating in the UK because of their association with terrorism. The list included Al Qaeda and PKK, the Kurdish Workers' Party which has a large following in the UK. Jack Straw, then Home Secretary, conceded that the large majority of groups had not attacked British targets, but he claimed that they were all 'concerned with terrorism' under the new, broader definition laid down in the Terrorism Act, which includes fundraising. 'Any perception that we are targeting the Muslim community is entirely wrong,' he added. But the Muslim Council of Britain expressed its 'grave concern' over the list and claimed that some proscribed groups were merely engaged in campaigning against the abuse of human rights.

After 11 September 2001, the pressure was understandably intensified. In an interview on BBC radio, the new Home Secretary, David Blunkett, authorised MI5 'to take whatever steps necessary, controversial or otherwise, without fear or favour, to take action to protect us.' Working very closely with the Metropolitan Police Special Branch, MI5 spread the net of surveillance over more foreign nationals and alleged terrorists.

However, it was not always effective or fair. In August 2002, Blunkett was forced to send an unprecedented apology to Muslims in Britain after MI5 was accused of engaging in indiscriminate 'fishing expeditions' to try and find evidence of links to Al Qaeda. The Home Secretary was forced to act after some 30 Muslims complained about 'harassment and intimidation'. In letters to the Home Office, they said that ordinary Muslims were regularly woken early in the morning and questioned about their 'links' to Afghanistan. One firm of solicitors, Arani and Co, were so concerned about these 'information

sweeps' that they produced a guide on how to deal with MI5 and
Special Branch and distributed it through the Islamic community.

Special Branch officers claimed that the names of those interviewed had been 'found in Afghanistan' or 'in the caves of Tora
Bora,' but no evidence was presented of any links and no arrests
were made. 'I am sorry that anyone interviewed was distressed by the
experience,' Blunkett wrote to one of the people interrogated.[21]

There is no doubt that MI5 has made a determined effort to
remove some of its pedantic, ponderous procedures since 11
September: it is working more closely with Special Branches
throughout the country and is quicker to pass on intelligence to
aid the detection of suspected terrorists. However, former officers
believe that a radical cultural revolution is required rather than
moderate reforms. David Shayler, who worked in most MI5
sections between 1991 and 1997 and investigated IRA and Libyan
terrorism, believes the agency's recent track record shows it is still
too wedded to the past and the bureaucracy is still too rigid and
cumbersome.

In 2000, his views were corroborated by another former MI5 officer, Jestyn Thirkell-White, who served for five years. He told the
authors that he backed Shayler's allegations of mismanagement
and bungled operations. He agreed that MI5 wasted valuable hours
in operations against terrorists, dithering about the wording of
warrants because of political turf wars with Special Branch. 'The
endless redrafting was nothing to do with protecting people's civil
liberties,' he told us. 'MI5 were desperate to keep their new role
(combatting terrorism) and ensure that Special Branch could not
regain it. They were desperate to ensure that Special Branch could
not point to any procedural mistake.'

Even Dame Stella Rimington, MI5's director-general from 1992
until 1996, is modestly critical of its track record on investigating Al
Qaeda. In September 2002 she wrote:

'The putting together of all the pieces of information, however
small, that come in from all sources, the following up of leads, all
the classic spy-catching techniques are also necessary against terrorist targets. It appears, looking at it from the outside, that this sort of
investigation may not have been done sufficiently thoroughly
before 11 September.

'The nature and extent of the Al Qaeda network seems to have
escaped observation. Perhaps there were no leads to investigate,

though there appear to have been indications of planned activity, however vague, which should have been followed up.'[22]

MI5's defence is that it is virtually impossible to eradicate all terrorism. They compare it to doctors treating a disease with no cure or to police solving all crimes. MI5 also argue that their performance cannot be truly evaluated as they cannot reveal their successful operations as it could endanger sources and the lives of agents. As President Eisenhower said in 1959: 'Success cannot be advertised and failure cannot be explained.'

However, MI5 has recently indulged in the selective and discreet art of news management and spin doctoring by private briefings of editors and planting of favourable stories. Soon after she was appointed, director-general, Eliza Manningham-Buller, went to the office of a prominent Sunday newspaper to disclose background information. MI5's joint operations with Special Branch against Al Qaeda activists in the UK are very openly advertised and publicised. MI5's anxiety to demonstrate its effectiveness is a measure of its political insecurity – a perennial historical characteristic.

The task of combatting terrorists who are prepared to sacrifice their own lives is MI5's greatest and gravest challenge. A Bali-style attack on a nightclub in a major British city centre is a real possibility, according to Lord Carlisle QC, the government's anti-terror watchdog. 'There are individuals and groups operating in this country who present a very great danger to ordinaty citizens . . . there are enemies in our midst,' he told the Commons Home Affairs Select Committee in March 2003, and added that it was naive to think that those most at risk were sitting in the Palace of Westminster or Windsor Castle. His assessment, based on access to Intelligence information, is that a bomb on a 'soft target' is the most likely method of attack.

Countering such a threat makes this era a pivotal moment in MI5's eventful and controversial history. As ever, it needs to balance the needs of security with civil liberties, but it will be judged by results. Nothing else.

The Security Service has always been embroiled in controversy. Traditionally, its role was to preserve the security of the state by combating both an internal, subversive, ideological threat and an external military one. Over the centuries monarchs and prime ministers realised that intelligence was their most potent weapon. If it was obtained by sinister acts of intrigue, deception and skulduggery, then so be it.

The true father of the British secret state was Sir Francis Walsingham, Queen Elizabeth I's chief Secretary of State from 1573 until his death in 1590. He understood that information was power, and set up a network of voluntary informants, many of whom needed no prompting to snoop and sneak on citizens they either disliked or suspected were up to no good.

Sir Francis was adept at making his agents feel their intelligence was valued and spread the word that he was insatiable for it. He also paid for information, initially out of his own purse because the Queen was too miserly. In fact, she paid him so poorly that Sir Francis was driven to the verge of bankruptcy.[23] However, for Sir Francis, 'knowledge is never too dear' in defence of the realm, and he successfully uncovered a number of plots against the Queen. In the 1580s, he recruited informants among dissenting Catholics. The most effective were 'priests, Jesuits and traitors' whom he 'corrupted with moneye', according to the later testimony of his brother-in-law. Some were sent as *agents provocateurs* into jails to secure the confidence of Catholic prisoners. Anthony Munday, a lay spy, infiltrated the English college in Rome and sent hair-raising accounts of treasonable talk among the inmates. One fervently expressed the view that the Queen – 'that proud usurping Jezebel' – should have her flesh torn apart by dogs.[24]

Sir Francis put such intelligence to good use. In 1585, the Queen's masterspy discovered treason when one of his agents, Gilbert Gifford, insinuated himself into the confidence of the imprisoned Mary Queen of Scots. Gifford persuaded her to smuggle letters out in secret watertight compartments in beer barrels. She readily agreed, not knowing that all her messages to her fellow plotters would be read by Sir Francis and that her plans would be scuppered.[25] There were some failures, notably one agent who was sent to spy on Lord Stafford, but then 'got merry' in his company and blurted out his secret mission!

While many became spies for patriotic reasons, others were blatant villains – thieves, confidence-tricksters, blackmailers, pimps and murderers. One, Roger Walton, was described as 'a swearer without measure and tearer of God, a notable whoremaster'.[26] For them espionage was merely an offshoot of their other exploits. This inevitably led to abuse, dirty tricks and corruption – framing suspects, planting evidence and provoking conspiracies. It really was the 'second oldest profession'.

Walsingham's death coincided more or less with the defeat of the Spanish Armada and for the time being both the ideological (i.e. religious) and foreign threats subsided. It was Oliver Cromwell who revived the spying game in the mid-17th century. He employed two 'intelligencers'. The most effective was John Thurloe, who later wrote a 'Discourse' on his activities. This described Cromwell's secret police, which employed 'a great number of subtil and sly fellowes'. Thurloe's 'Discourse' was a revealing testimony to his methods, notably how he intercepted 'suspicious mails'. According to Bernard Porter, author of *Plots and Paranoia – A History of Political Espionage in Britain*:

> He [Thurloe] advised that hostile factions should each be influenced by two spies, unknown to one another, so that 'they may be of checks to each other for the more sure discovery of the truth'. He also recommended that spies and informers did not report back to their spymasters' own offices or homes 'unless sometimes in a dark Winter night', because those places were likely to be 'constantly watched almost by all parties'.[27]

The Stuart period was notable for the establishment of the Secret Service grant. This was voted in 1660 by Parliament on the basis that it would not pry into how the money was spent. In fact, at that time only a small proportion was spent on espionage. The rest of the fund was secretly siphoned off by King Charles II to buy presents for his mistress, the actress Nell Gwynn.

The 'Glorious Revolution' of 1688 stimulated a new bout of spying and paranoia. This was due to the fear of counter-revolution from the Jacobites. Robert Walpole, Britain's first Prime Minister, took a particular interest in intelligence-gathering. He employed spies to infiltrate the Jacobite camp and intercept people's mail for his private political use. Agents were even sent to France to track the movements of potential plotters.

The secret service in the 18th century did not have a coherent or formal structure, but its defining characteristic was its allegiance to the monarch, not Parliament. What is striking about this period is how British parliaments of a much less democratic hue than the present body tried to make the service account for what it did. In

1742, a Treasury solicitor called John Scrope was told he would be sent to the Tower of London if he refused to answer a parliamentary committee's questions about the abuse of secret funds by the Walpole government. In 1782, the Civil List and Secret Service Money Act made it illegal for the Crown to spend more than £10,000 a year on the intelligence agencies.[28]

The government of the day immediately created a new and unlimited annual Secret Service Vote, which was retained for over two centuries. Parliament, however, continued to pressurise ministers to account for the uses to which this public money was put, largely because evidence suggested that prime ministers used the secret fund for their own election campaigns and for bribing MPs. The Tory premier Lord Bute set aside £80,000 to ensure that the Treaty of Paris passed through the Commons at the end of the Seven Years War in 1763. His Treasury solicitor, Ross Mackay, handed out cash to at least 120 MPs.[29]

There was a growing public contempt for espionage. As Porter states, in *Plots and Paranoia*: 'No one has ever had a good word for spies, except those who needed their service. When Shakespeare wanted a really offensive phrase to describe the sin of jealousy for "Venus and Adonis", he came up with "This sour informer, this bate-bearing spy . . ." A seventeenth-century alias for the Devil was "Black Spy".'[30]

The English viewed organised espionage as intrusive, dangerous, despotic and, due to its inherent secrecy, prone to political and financial corruption. This intensified after the 1789 French Revolution, with its bloody purges and inquisitions. But Prime Minister William Pitt argued that the threat of domestic subversion and foreign invasion warranted tough new laws. This was greeted with much scepticism, notably from playwright Richard Sheridan, who told the House of Commons: 'The present alarm has been created solely by ministers, for the corrupt purpose of libelling the country.' He claimed that violent threats against the King were invented and were at best gossip and rumour: 'When once a government encouraged spies and informers, it became a part of their business to commit such forgeries and create such terror.' He concluded that, unlike France with its autocratic excesses, revolutionary conditions did not exist in Britain where the monarch's powers were restricted and regulated. Consequently, there was no need for any domestic security service or draconian legislation.[31]

There were, of course, disenfranchised and impoverished people who demonstrated forcefully and often violently. But active dissent was not the same as overthrowing the state. The only part of the United Kingdom ripe for revolution in the 19th century was Ireland, where famine created huge resentment. Here, secret-service money was used for publishing black propaganda and intelligence-gathering on republicans. Irish informers were paid handsomely, mainly because of the greater risks. Some survived, but many were brutally murdered. Others 'sought refuge in self-destruction'.[32] But many starving Irishmen took cash and turned traitor. The nationalist leader Michael Collins believed in the early 1920s that this was a major reason for the failure of Irish nationalism before his time.

On the mainland, in 1817, a series of 'treason trials' were held after the Spa Fields riots. Revolutionary mountains were built out of political molehills and 12 men were executed. Even Earl Grey was incredulous at the verdict. 'These men,' he said, 'were without means, without influence, support or plan. Yet, it was said, they meant to barricade Oxford Road, block up the streets leading to the Bank, seize the shipping in the river and attack the Tower without cannon. Who could credit that?'[33]

However, the government's Committee of Secrecy maintained that the country was riddled with subversion. It claimed sedition was organised under the guise of 'Reform Societies' whose aim was to undermine the 'habit of subordination' among ordinary people. They said there was 'widespread talk of rebellion and overturning what they called the "privileged class"'. The committee said their evidence was convincing, but they could not reproduce it 'without hazarding the personal safety' of their secret informants.

Anger broke out when secret agents were caught deliberately fabricating unrest to justify their role. In 1840, a young boy was sentenced to three months in a house of correction for pinning up seditious handbills headlined 'Bread or Blood!'. As he was illiterate, it was unlikely he knew what the poster said, but the man who paid him knew full well: he was one Mr Franklin, a government agent. When a warrant was issued for his arrest, he had already fled the country.[34]

The government's network of spies in the mid-19th century was decentralised, unstructured and voluntary. They were not employed directly by the Home Office but by local policemen and magistrates.

The Home Secretary had little direct control over them, but this served a useful purpose: he could issue a plausible denial when the government was accused of employing spies. This also meant that the spies' calibre was dubious, both morally and professionally, and that information was often wrong or exaggerated.

There was an abhorrence in England of the sort of secret police force that was so insidious, notorious and ruthless in France under Joseph Fouché. 'They have an admirable police in Paris,' said Earl Dudley, 'but they pay for it dear enough. I had rather half a dozen people's throats should be cut in Radcliffe's Highway every three years than be subject to domiciliary visits by spies and all the rest of Fouché's contrivances.'[35]

From the end of the Napoleonic Wars, in 1815, until the launch of the first Fenian bombing campaign in England, in 1883, governments at best flirted with intelligence-gathering. Domestic political espionage virtually stopped. Far less money was spent by the Home Office under the Secret Service Vote, despite letters from volunteers offering information about plots and conspiracies. The Victorians despised spying. They viewed 'the gathering of knowledge by clandestine means' as unnecessary, invasive, oppressive and, above all, foreign. And they claimed they never suffered from the absence of covert intelligence.

In 1871, the French government, which was adept at surveillance of its own citizens, mistakenly presumed the same of the British. It asked the Home Office to help investigate the work of French Communist refugees in England. After some thought, a civil servant was instructed to write to Karl Marx, then living in London, who responded with an insightful letter explaining the philosophy of the Workingmen's International. Such was the naïve view of domestic intelligence before the Irish Republicans launched their violent campaign for independence.[36]

It was another story at Dublin Castle, the headquarters of the British government in Ireland. In the late 1850s, the Dublin Metropolitan Police mounted a sophisticated and successful surveillance operation against the Fenians. These counter-terrorism methods were adapted by Scotland Yard between 1881 and 1885 when the Fenians aggressively fought a dynamite war on English soil. A Special Irish Branch at Scotland Yard was hastily created with hundreds of policemen, detectives and informants. It was disbanded in 1885 when the bombings ceased, but was reconstituted as the

Metropolitan Police Special Branch (MPSB), which comprised 25 officers from the Irish campaign and the port police.[37]

Prior to the First World War, Britain was gripped by a hysteria that thousands of German spies were operating in British ports and dockyards. In 1909, the government's Committee of Imperial Defence recommended the establishment of the Secret Service Bureau, which marked the transformation from an open, liberal democracy to the modern security state that we live in today. The Bureau was staffed by Captain Vernon Kell, of the South Staffordshire Regiment, known as K, and Captain Mansfield Cumming of the Royal Navy, known as C. They quickly divided their work: Kell was responsible for defensive counter-espionage in Britain and Cumming took charge of secretly gathering intelligence abroad.

The Committee of Imperial Defence also called for the complete overhaul of the 1889 Official Secrets Act. This law had placed the burden of proof of espionage upon the accuser. The drastically revised Bill presented to Parliament in 1911 called for the exact opposite: those charged with spying must now prove their innocence. The new Official Secrets Act, said an outraged Liberal MP, 'upsets the Magna Carta altogether.'[38] The 1911 Act forbade anyone – without government approval – to obtain or communicate official information. The Secret Service agencies would now enjoy a virtually unchallenged omnipotence enhanced by the absence of any accountability to Parliament. In the heat of the hysteria about foreign spies a half-empty House of Commons passed the Act in just over an hour on a human August afternoon. Winston Churchill, as Home Secretary from 1910 to 1911, empowered the new counter-espionage agency with the authority to keep a top-secret list of aliens who might pose a threat to British security. He also authorised the opening of their correspondence.

The War Office believed that about 75,000 enemy aliens were living in the UK on the eve of the Great War, of whom 29,000 were listed in a secret registry kept by the Bureau. Yet only 37 proved to be genuine German spies. Vernon Kell, head of the agency, admitted the German spies were 'men of low morality or drunkards of a bad type, down-and-outs generally'.[39]

These misfits and others, who might be described euphemistically as romantics, did little to advance German intelligence about the British, but harsh sentences were handed out to the 37 spies: 12 were executed (most of them in the Tower of London), nine were imprisoned, one committed suicide, ten were interned (along with the 32,000 other aliens held in camps during the war) and five were deported, along with 20,000 others.

The government's punishment of the spies did not reflect the damage they had done to security, which was negligible. Instead, the Bureau's chief objective was to deter others from betraying any secrets entrusted to them.[40]

On 5 August 1914, the War Office's secret registry of aliens was formally set up by an Order in Council that required all aliens in the UK to register themselves with the police within 48 hours of their arrival. Soon the Bureau's growing staff began to compile files on 'odd-looking people' and British nationals who were considered to have 'alien blood'. Historian Professor Bernard Porter noted: 'Whether the royal family was on the list is not known.'[41]

Three days later Parliament passed the Defence of the Realm Act, limiting further the freedom of movement and speech that the Victorians had taken for granted. The overriding priority was to safeguard national security in the new climate of increasing paranoia about the country being overrun with enemy agents. In the interests of thwarting subversion, anti-war literature was seized and printing presses halted until they published material deemed more suitable by the Bureau.

The police could now arrest without explanation anyone they found near the coastline, military installations, railway lines and docks. Thus, architect and artist Charles Rennie Mackintosh found himself expelled from his own cottage on the Suffolk coast when the local officer failed to understand his Glaswegian accent, which he considered suspicious. The constable was also suspicious of Mackintosh's elaborate watercolours of flowers, which he thought just might be maps of local estuaries.[42]

In January 1916, the Secret Service Bureau, containing only ten officers, was relaunched as part of a new Directorate of Military Intelligence and renamed MI5. Hundreds of staff were hired, and operations were expanded to include censorship of the mail and telegrams, which kept busy nearly 5,000 clerks, most of them women. This scrutiny – unimaginable in Victorian times – proved the best source for MI5 to track enemy spies. Other unorthodox methods included burglary: Inspector William Melville, an MI5 officer during the First World War, instructed recruits on how to pick locks and break into houses. His course included practical training using the safe of an embassy of 'a so-called neutral power'. He told his trainees:

> The accent would no longer be on lifting the swag but on the identification of documents. When located they were likely to be photographed there and then afterwards replaced so that they appeared to have been undisturbed ... The guiding principle would not be the avoidance of conflict with the police but a clash with the vigorous security precautions made by the 'other side' ...

This would lead at best to a showdown and at worst to the embarrassment of the Cabinet. Nevertheless, a house-break was always a house-break and there must remain much that MI5 could learn from the crook.

But Inspector Melville also had a warning for his MI5 recruits:

> In case any of you should be tempted after the war to act up as a gentleman burglar, I think I should point out there is precious little in it for you. What you do for MI5 in wartime is strictly privileged. You may have to face risks because you are dealing with men [German agents] who are potentially desperate, but there are positively no legal penalties, even if very occasionally you shoot to kill.[43]

However, the Easter Rising in Dublin in 1916 – much like the Bishopsgate and Canary Wharf bombings almost 80 years later – was a huge failure of British intelligence. This was due to a lack of co-ordination and co-operation between MI5 and Special Branch. In particular, crucial first-hand information about the deadly plans of the Irish Citizens' Army was either ignored, dismissed or lost in the bureaucratic maze of the intelligence community.

As a result, the idea of a unified security service was mooted, but was rejected, and the separation of power between the two intensely competitive agencies was retained. MI5 was responsible for detecting espionage and domestic subversion, while Special Branch undertook the actual surveillance and, when necessary, arrested agents. This division of roles, according to Bernard Porter, made it 'more difficult to find out about covert counter-subversion ...

because MI5 has always been less accountable, and consequently more covert, than the Special Branch'.[44]

Although the Easter Rising of 1916 was crushed within a few days, its lasting legacy was to bring together many Irish people in unquali-fied support for the Republican cause. In the past, the British had found it relatively easy to recruit spies within Irish Republicanism. Now it was increasingly difficult. Michael Collins, the director of IRA intelligence, took full advantage and master-minded the successful undercover infiltration of Dublin Castle. This led to the single greatest British intelligence loss when 12 of their agents were gunned down in 1921.[45]

The advice of MI5's director, Vernon Kell, on how the guerrilla war might be suppressed had little effect.. He and most British intel-ligence officers failed to appreciate the threat posed by Republicanism. Instead, they distracted themselves during 1918 with the relatively insignificant danger posed by German spies in Ireland.

After the 1917 Bolshevik revolution, MI5's work expanded beyond the search for foreign spies and updating its infamous card index of 'persons potentially dangerous to National Defence'. The agency's greatest fear during the interwar years was the embracing of Communism, either by disillusioned members of the armed services or discharged service personnel, 20 per cent of whom were unemployed. MI5 thus began rigorous surveillance for subversion in the labour movement and the armed forces. But Special Branch held primacy and the inevitable turf war impeded operations.[46] The logical move was for MI5 to be absorbed into either MI6, responsi-ble for gathering intelligence abroad, or Special Branch, but this was resisted and the uneasy and unwieldy alliances continued.

January 1924 brought the election of Britain's first Labour Prime Minister, Ramsay MacDonald. MI5 was uncertain – as it would be in 1997 when Tony Blair entered 10 Downing Street – about a govern-ment 'whose leading members had at various times been under surveillance'. In both governments the left-wing members of the Party were excluded from the Cabinet and both leaders were at pains to appear 'statesmanlike' rather than radical.[47]

Unlike Blair, MacDonald faced an electoral challenge in less than a year. The fear that Labour was soft on Bolshevism appeared to be confirmed when the *Daily Mail* published the Zinoviev letter during the 1924 general election. The document, later revealed as a forgery, purported to show that the Communist International was instructing British Communists to promote and agitate for revolution by using their sympathisers in the Labour Party. Four days after its publication, the Conservatives won a landslide victory. Only later was it shown that the letter had been leaked to the *Daily Mail* by Conservative Central Office, acting in close concert with serving and former senior MI5 and MI6 officers. According to Professor Porter:

> It is the first major instance in modern British history of men associated with the official secret services acting independently of the government and in collusion with that government's political opponents with the object of undermining it ... The important aspect of the Zinoviev affair is that it may indicate a tendency on the part of the secret services to slide from being the secret agents of the state into something very different: a 'secret state' in its own right.[48]

MI5, meanwhile, was busy placing 'moles' or penetration agents in the Communist Party of Great Britain (CPGB) after its creation in 1920. The ultra-secret section for running agents was directed by one of MI5's most successful and eccentric officers, Maxwell Knight. Known as M, he worked under the alias 'Miss Coplestone' from a house in Dolphin Square, central London. His work, in part, led in 1925 to ten leaders of the CPGB being convicted and jailed for sedition after MI5 had become convinced that they would adversely influence the Labour movement. 'This was one of the few occasions in recent English history when men were punished for their opinions, not for acts of practical significance,' noted the historian A.J.P. Taylor.[49]

Although the 1926 General Strike involved hundreds of thousands of workers, the CPGB could claim just 6,000 members. Nevertheless, MI5 and Special Branch did their best to demonstrate that the dispute was ultimately a well-organised Soviet plot. 'Though MI5 scarcely underestimated the danger of Soviet subversion, they remained curiously traditional in their search for it, concentrating their attention on the Labour movement, the armed services and the CPGB apparatus,' noted Dr Christopher Andrew, in *Secret Service*, his first-rate history of the secret services.

MI5 and MI6 seemed oblivious to the possibility that subversion and treachery could be found within their own ranks and the upper classes.[50] This was largely because they recruited from people like themselves: upper middle-class, public school-educated men with the same political and social prejudices and narrow world view.

On 15 October 1931, formal responsibility for assessing threats to national security, apart from those posed by Irish terrorists and anarchists, was passed to MI5. It was now officially known as the Security Service, although the title MI5 remained in use.

The subversive threat posed by Sir Oswald Mosley was one of their primary targets and the Service looked for evidence of initially Mussolini's, and later Hitler's, support for his British Union of Fascists. One of its most controversial operations was intercepting diplomatic pouches with the help of the Royal Mail. Based on MI5's fears, Parliament passed the Public Order Act in 1936 prohibiting political uniforms and empowering the police to forbid political processions.

MI5 also investigated opponents of the Nazis. Sir Robert Vansittart, permanent secretary at the Foreign Office and later a chief diplomatic adviser, was the person most alert to the Nazi threat. But he was so critical of the government's policy of appeasement that Prime Minister Neville Chamberlain ordered MI5 to place him and officials at 10 Downing Street under surveillance.

During the late 1930s, MI5 was beset by bureaucratic chaos, which resulted in muddled assessments. 'The main problems of interpreting the raw intelligence supplied by Britain's underfunded intelligence services arose from the fragmented structure of the intelligence community and multiplicity of government departments with which it dealt,' noted Dr Christopher Andrew.[51]

During the Second World War, MI5 pulled off a major coup with its famous double-cross system of spies. In the First World War, German spies were either executed or incarcerated. Now the Service turned most captured Germans into double agents. Its approach was crude but effective: the prisoner was told he could either be shot as a spy or agree to work entirely for MI5.

MI5 intercepted most Nazi intelligence by code-breaking. This success is partly explained by a change in the Service character: more intellectuals were recruited and, similar to the highly productive atmosphere at Bletchley Park, the bureaucratic routine and restrictions were laid aside to encourage lateral thinking and problem solving. Based in temporary offices at Blenheim Palace, Oxfordshire, and 58 St James's Street, Mayfair, the new recruits were frustrated by the stodgy, ossified MI5 management. Young officers included Graham Greene, Malcolm Muggeridge and Hugh

Trevor-Roper, who described the senior MI5 hierarchy as 'of very limited intelligence' and 'by and large pretty stupid'.[52] Such disillusionment continued to undercut morale right through to David Shayler's tenure at MI5 in the 1990s.

This view was shared by Winston Churchill soon after he became Prime Minister in 1940. He promptly sacked Vernon Kell, MI5's 67-year-old director, and reintroduced a proposal he had made 20 years earlier that all branches of British intelligence should be combined in a single Secret Service. This was supported by the Foreign Office, who claimed that MI5 officers displayed 'a notable incapacity for weighing evidence and a tendency to conceal this incapacity by unnecessary recourse to secrecy'. Despite repeated efforts, Churchill failed to implement his vision and arguably MI5 has been handicapped ever since.[53]

The successful capture of hundreds of German agents meant that MI5 could genuinely argue that it had had a good war. But when peace returned, a deep suspicion of security agencies emerged, largely due to the public's wish to escape the suffocating security blanket that had existed during wartime.

The outbreak of the Cold War crystallised and enhanced MI5's role. As the Iron Curtain fell across Europe, Prime Minister Clement Attlee issued a directive that made the Service directly accountable to 10 Downing Street. Faced with the mighty force of the Soviet bloc, MI5 was given two key tasks: to prevent Communist subversion in the UK, and to counter the threat of foreign espionage by the KGB and its allied agencies.

Attlee was a fervent anti-Communist, and in May 1946 he secretly set up a cabinet committee on 'subversive activities'. This was prompted by the arrest of Dr Alan Nunn May, a British scientist who leaked secrets of the Allies' atomic programme to the Russians. The fear was that other scientists would do the same for ideological or financial reasons. Combined with the growing fear of the 'Red Peril' expanding through Eastern Europe, this resulted in new purge procedures for all civil servants: any official deemed to be associated with Communist or Fascist organisations would be summarily removed from a post related to national security. If no alternative posting could be found, they would be dismissed. Suspicion alone was grounds for transfer or sacking, and it was not necessary for the government to prove that any act of disloyalty had actually taken place. 'The general principle covers all those in service of the state where secrecy is involved,' stated Attlee, in 1948.[54]

These draconian vetting measures invested enormous power and influence in MI5. Using their secret files, the agency's recommendations changed the course of thousands of lives. Some victims were blacklisted and penalised unfairly, because certain MI5 officers could not differentiate between left-wing sympathisers and hardline supporters of the Soviet regime. Inevitably, some information was inaccurate and unverified.

Also, individuals were not allowed to see the evidence on which accusations against them were based, so a lot of this material remained on file. Between 1948 and 1955, 167 civil servants were removed from their posts; 25 were dismissed, 24 resigned, 88 were transferred to non-sensitive work and 33 were reinstated.

In 1950, security vetting was extended after the arrest of another scientist, Klaus Fuchs, who confessed to passing atomic secrets to the Russians. The Cabinet Secretary, Sir Norman Brook, recommended that new procedures would be 'achieved partly by a check of personal records, which will be kept in fuller form, and partly – in a minority of cases – by specific inquiries undertaken by the Security Service'. This meant that vetting investigators would also look out for 'serious character weaknesses of a kind which might make a person liable to blackmail'. These defects were later described as 'drunkenness, addiction to drugs, homosexuality or any loose living'.[55]

MI5's expanding role in vetting was also due to the embarrassing defection in 1951 of Donald Maclean, a highly placed Foreign Office diplomat, and Guy Burgess, a former MI5 officer, to Russia. The government immediately set up an inquiry into 'security procedures now applied in the public services'. MI5's job, after all, was to catch spies.

Burgess and Maclean were part of the 'Cambridge Apostles', many of whom became Communists and were recruited at university by the KGB in the 1930s. Their damaging espionage and subsequent escape made MI5 a laughing stock. Burgess, a drunken homosexual, was notoriously indiscreet about his Marxist views. 'Everyone knew that the Cambridge Apostles, an élite intellectual society to which he belonged, was a hotbed of Communist sympathies,' said the historian Professor Donald Cameron Watt. 'Everyone, that is, except MI5. Their stuffed-shirt officers, bedecked with old-school ties, never bothered to investigate persons who were so evidently "one of us".'[56]

The most important member of the Cambridge spies was Kim Philby, a senior MI6 officer who betrayed British agents and sensitive military secrets to Moscow for over 20 years. The fourth man was Anthony Blunt, an MI5 officer and later Keeper of the Queen's Pictures. He was eventually caught in 1964. Incredibly, in a secret deal, he was given immunity from prosecution in exchange for his confession and co-operation. Blunt, of course, told his MI5 debriefers very little of value, despite endless hours of interrogation. It was not until 1979 that he was publicly unmasked.

The humiliation for MI5 in allowing at least four traitors to slip through their clutches was not just the revelation of its mind-boggling incompetence. It was that social and class bias had overridden professional judgement and common sense. Along with the harm to the country, that was the real indictment.

Another damaging consequence was that MI5 became obsessed with other Soviet agents inside the Service and government departments. Encouraged by Soviet defectors of dubious credibility and the paranoid ramblings of CIA officer James Jesus Angleton, a massive mole hunt ensued. Roger Hollis, MI5's director-general, authorised the investigation, which was staffed by what were known as 'Young Turks'. These were hardline Cold Warriors who believed that the Soviet Union was evil with no redeeming features. They viewed the régime, according to the authoritative espionage author Phillip Knightley, 'as a grisly monster, capable of the most devilish conspiracies. They felt passionately that anyone who had at any stage so much as flirted with this monster, should be hunted down and destroyed.'[57]

The Young Turks, one of whose leading members was Peter Wright, an MI5 officer from 1955 to 1975, were important because they heavily influenced MI5 policy, attitudes and activity over the next 30 years. Like the Spanish Inquisition, their aim was to expose and prosecute any 'guilty man', no matter how flimsy the evidence or how long ago the 'offence' had occurred. They were assisted by Security Commissions, consisting of Privy Councillors, which often went beyond the concept of guilt by association, effectively stating that suspected officials were guilty until proved innocent.

One White Paper stated: 'In deciding these difficult and often borderline cases, it is right to continue the practice of tilting the balance in favour of offering greater protection to the security of the state rather than in the direction of safeguarding the rights of the individual.'[58]

MI5 was also assisted by a directive issued in 1952 by Sir David Maxwell Fyfe, then Home Secretary. This concerned MI5's relationship with government. One clause stated: 'You and your staff will maintain the well-established convention whereby ministers do not concern themselves with the detailed information which may be obtained by the Security Service in particular cases, but are furnished with such information only as may be necessary for the determination of any issue on which guidance is sought.' This left MI5 officers totally unaccountable for their actions because they were only required to report if they deemed it 'necessary'.

The beneficiaries of such latitude were the Young Turks, led by Peter Wright. They were obsessive and relentless in their pursuit and even claimed that Hollis was a KGB mole. But what they called 'circumstantial evidence' was derisory. It was only because they worked in such secrecy that their flawed methodology was never discovered. For example, they claimed that Hollis walked home from work to be in a better position to meet his KGB controller. It did not occur to them that he might need the exercise.

In this twilight world, events never have an innocent or alternative explanation. Never once do they take human error into consideration. Coincidence and conjecture become proof, and suspicion becomes guilt. In the real world, these 'investigators' would have been sacked.

The Hollis affair did enormous damage to MI5's reputation. When Oleg Gordievsky, a British double agent in the KGB, was asked whether the former director-general was really a traitor, he replied: 'Of course not. But when the KGB saw the chaos caused by the allegations against Hollis, their laughter made Red Square shake.'[59]

But the frightening feature of the spycatcher mentality was that it influenced MI5's security assessments of officials, trade unionists and politicians. Any connection, however tenuous, with the eastern bloc was used against them. One victim was Cyril Cooper, general secretary of the Society of Technical Civil Servants. In 1963, he was barred from negotiating with Whitehall departments. When he appealed to the Three Security Advisers, he told them he had left the Communist Party many years previously. But he was interrogated about his recent visits to the Bolshoi theatre and asked if he and his wife had artistic friends. He agreed that he had. 'Well, aren't all of those long-haired people of one political persuasion?' said a member of the board. Cooper replied that that was a dubious generalisation, but the questioner disagreed. The appeal was rejected.[60]

The paranoid delusions of Wright and the Young Turks remained unchecked throughout the 1960s and 1970s. Even the Prime Minister, Harold Wilson, was not safe. The Soviet defector Anatoli Golitsyn believed that the Labour Party leader was a Soviet agent, based on his trips to the Soviet Union while President of the Board of Trade in the late 1940s. As the KGB and the CIA later confirmed, there was not even circumstantial evidence against Wilson, but Wright and a few colleagues still conspired against him.

Fuelled by their own right-wing and class prejudices, some MI5 officers attempted to destabilise and undermine Wilson's 1974–76 Labour government by leaking false stories to the press: they claimed that Wilson was having an adulterous affair with his political secretary, was involved in corrupt land deals, and had links with the KGB. Edward Short, Labour's deputy leader and leader of the House of Commons, was also smeared: a Swiss bank statement in his name was forged and it was suggested, falsely, that he was involved in tax evasion and channelling secret funds to offshore locations.

Based on his own informants and some 20 burglaries of all his senior staff, Wilson believed that certain MI5 officers were plotting against his government. On 7 August 1975, he summoned Michael Hanley, then director-general of MI5, and confronted him about the plot. Hanley admitted that some of his officers were strongly anti-Labour, but denied that there was any organised conspiracy against Wilson and said that MI5 would remain under ministerial control.[61]

Wilson was not reassured and briefed journalists about his fears. Peter Wright later confessed that just before the 1974 general election he was asked by a small group of MI5 officers for information about Wilson. There was a secret file in MI5's safe on the Prime Minister codenamed 'Henry Worthington', and the plotters wanted Wright to show them the dossier so they could leak its contents. 'The plan was simple,' recalled Wright. 'MI5 would arrange for selective details of the intelligence about leading Labour Party figures, but especially Wilson, to be leaked to sympathetic pressmen.'[62]

In later years new revelations emerged about the MI5 conspirators, notably in books by David Leigh (*The Wilson Plot*) and Stephen Dorril and Robin Ramsay (*Smear!*) and documents released by former Army intelligence officer Colin Wallace: In 1994, Stella Rimington, then MI5's director-general, denied that anything had happened: 'No such plot existed – as ministers stated and as Peter Wright finally admitted,' she said, during her 1994 Richard Dimbleby lecture. This was untrue. In fact, Wright had merely substantially reduced the number of MI5 officers involved.

The most compelling new evidence was from Lord Hunt, Cabinet Secretary throughout the 1974–79 Labour government. As the accounting officer for the Secret Vote, which determined MI5's budget, he was intimately involved in monitoring its activities. As the principal official dealing with the Security Service, he also advised the Prime Minister. 'There is absolutely no doubt at all that a few malcontents in MI5,' he told Channel 4's *Secret History* programme, 'who were right-wing, malicious and had serious personal grudges, were giving vent to this and spreading damaging and malicious stories about some members of that Labour government.'[63]

The 1970s were turbulent and industrial unrest provoked MI5 into reviewing its targets. The Conservative government of 1970–74 had suddenly felt nervous about the growing power of the trade-union movement. This resulted in MI5 diverting some officers away from monitoring Soviet-bloc spies towards investigating left-wing trade unionists and non-Communist Party far-left groups. This was later confirmed by Lord Diplock, a law lord, who chaired a commission examining the state of security procedures. He reported that although the 'external threat from Soviet intelligence services' remained undiminished, the 'internal threat has altered considerably'. He continued:

> The fall in CPGB membership, however, has been accompanied by the proliferation of new subversive groups of the extreme left and extreme right (mainly the former) whose aim is to overthrow the democratic Parliamentary government in this country by violent or other unconstitutional means, not shrinking in the case of the most extreme groups from terrorism to achieve their aims.
>
> Membership of individual groups is small but, for the most part, active and conspiratorial. They might well seek to make public information injurious to the interests of this country, not at the behest or for the benefit of any foreign power, but simply to harm this country itself.[64]

That statement was the benchmark for MI5 from the mid-1970s onwards, but was MI5 capable of objective security assessments on such organisations and individuals? The late Lord Jenkins, Home Secretary from 1965 until 1967 and between 1974 and 1976, argued: 'I took the view that it was advisable that MI5 should be pulled out of its political surveillance role ... I am convinced now that an organisation of people who lived in the fevered world of espionage and counter-espionage is entirely unfitted to judge between what is subversive and what is legitimate dissent.'[65]

A revealing, and unpublicised, example of this concerned a young woman who was barred from joining the Civil Service purely because she read the *Morning Star* newspaper. In October 1974, she was refused security clearance by MI5 for a job at the Department of Industry. She was not given a reason except that she was 'not suitable'. Bewildered by the rejection, she appealed to her constituency MP, a Conservative, who took up her case. He wrote to the Secretary of State, Tony Benn, who made enquiries. Three months later, Benn received a copy of MI5's security report on the woman, which was sent to his department's security officer:

There is some evidence that Miss X may be a fairly regular reader of the *Morning Star*, the newspaper of the Communist Party. Reliable sources informed us of this on several occasions since 1967, when she is known to have been interested in holidays arranged by the Young Communist League and a sea trip to the Soviet Union. There was a reliable report in 1974 that her father also reads the *Morning Star*.

Though recent inquiries have provided no grounds for believing that she or her father are actively interested in, or supporting, the Communist Party, it has not been possible to discover her views on extreme political matters. She works alone as a chiropodist, and the most that can be said is that there have been no complaints about her attitude from either patients or staff at the various clinics where she has practised.

Reading a Communist newspaper does not in itself necessarily imply support for the Party. But we feel that to read it consistently over a long period (other than as an academic exercise or for research) may well indicate an attitude of mind, which on a security annotation, may cause some unease. We would therefore prefer to err on the side of caution in this case.

The Security Service advises that the above information should not necessarily debar the candidate from access to information classified 'Confidential' or above. But you may prefer to make other arrangements especially if access to particularly delicate material is involved.[66]

Two weeks later, MI5's recommendation was accepted and Benn was informed that the woman 'could not be employed' because of her 'interest in Communism'.

A major reason for such prejudiced adjudications was that the officers in F Branch, the anti-subversion section, were politically unsophisticated. Recruited mainly from the Army and the former colonies, they were ignorant and naïve about the nature of left-wing political activity. Lord Carver, former chief of the defence staff who dealt directly with MI5, thought its officers 'appeared to savour Sherlock Holmes, Richard Hannay, Bulldog Drummond or even James Bond' and 'lived in a completely closed world whereby what really went on and what people actually thought and did, they just did not understand'.[67]

In the 1980s, this led to MI5 compiling secret files, tapping the telephones and investigating innocent individuals and pressure groups. Files were compiled on people purely because they belonged to an organisation which *included* a subversive as a leading member. This practice was revealed by Cathy Massiter, a former MI5 officer from 1970 until 1984, who worked in F Branch for many years. She disclosed how the National Council for Civil Liberties (NCCL, now Liberty) was classified as subversive. Although its executive included only two Communist Party members, the other members were also targeted.

The chief culprit was Charles Elwell, an assistant director and head of F2 section, which was then responsible for investigating the Communist Party. He was irritated by NCCL's criticism of the police and he instructed his officers in a minute: 'These members of the NCCL executive may not be Communists, but we are going to classify them as Communist sympathisers because they are members of the executive committee.'

Massiter, who was directly involved in the operation, disclosed that MI5 opened files on, intercepted the mail and tapped the telephones of Patricia Hewitt, NCCL's general secretary, and Harriet

Harman, the legal officer. Neither was a supporter or member of any Communist or Trotskyist party. Both women were known for their moderate views: Hewitt later became press secretary to Labour leader Neil Kinnock, and Harman joined Tony Blair's cabinet as Social Services secretary. MI5 was later found guilty by the European Court of breaching their human rights.

The Campaign for Nuclear Disarmament (CND) was also targeted by MI5, even though it was not classified as a subversive group. In late 1983, MI5 planted a spy inside its headquarters and tapped the telephone of one of its leading officials, John Cox. Even Barbara Egglestone, the mild-mannered national organiser of Christian CND, was investigated. 'For several years the Security Service had been saying that CND was not a subversive organisation,' Massiter said, in an interview for *20/20 Vision*, 'That there were Communists and other groups active in it, but it was basically drawing support from a very wide range of political opinion . . . This was happening not because CND justified this kind of treatment, but simply because of political pressure.'[68]

David Shayler, a former member of F Branch, confirmed the secret surveillance of CND and the political coercion from the Thatcher government, but says MI5 backed off at the final request: 'Michael Heseltine [then Defence Secretary] demanded that MI5 hand over lists of CND activists and details of their activities gained from intelligence operations against Communists. Security Service chiefs, however, resisted – something which must be to their eternal credit.'[69]

What happened was that MI5 passed on reports to the government about CND, but they were restricted to assessments of the alleged Communist infiltration of the peace group – and excluded dossiers on CND activists. In MI5's eyes, this subversive 'penetration' amounted to the fact that members of the Communist Party also happened to be members of CND.

MI5 was secretly distorting the definition of subversion to justify its new choice of targets and the extra resources that were pouring in. Individual directors were deciding for themselves what constituted subversion. 'We were violating our own rules,' said Massiter. 'It seemed to be getting out of control.'[70]

By the mid-1980s, MI5 had moved from being an essentially counter-espionage organisation, aimed at hostile foreign powers, to a domestic surveillance agency. It was now politicised. Encouraged implicitly by Prime Minister Margaret Thatcher, with her strident talk of the 'enemy within', MI5 compiled files on radical trade unionists, students, feminists, black-power activists, pacifists, MPs and particularly teachers.

Suddenly Trotskyists, Maoists and anarchists were deemed worthy of investigation. More agents and informers were recruited. 'Subversion' was now whatever the state decided. 'The whole system was undemocratic,' said John Alderson, former chief constable of the Devon and Cornwall police force, who saw files compiled by Special Branch, MI5's foot-soldiers. 'When I looked at my records, I came to the conclusion that about 50 per cent of them should never have been in there.' This 50 per cent consisted largely of irrelevant political material and Alderson weeded the files.[71]

The Cold War was still being fought and MI5's middle-aged directors had no qualms about sacrificing a few innocent victims. These people (NCCL and CND) were in the line of fire and there are always casualties in war. They may not have been actual supporters of the enemy, but they were in the vicinity.

On a wider scale, MI5 and MI6 deliberately exaggerated the capability of the Soviet Union, according to former intelligence officer Michael Herman. This helped not only to justify its anti-subversion activities, but also intensified the arms race, costing the UK hundreds of millions in extra spending. Herman, a GCHQ official between 1952 and 1987 and former secretary of the Cabinet Office's Joint Intelligence Committee, stated that MI5 and other agencies often painted 'worst case' scenarios to bounce the government into taking action to meet what was described as the 'massive threat' to the West.[72]

These dire warnings of the relentless Soviet war and espionage machine also resulted in their failure to predict the end of the Cold War. Former senior defence staff, like Lieutenant General Derek Boorman, argue that the intelligence agencies were unable either to foresee or understand the changes in the Eastern bloc. Sir Charles Powell, Mrs Thatcher's foreign affairs advisor from 1984 until 1990, agreed:

> The biggest single failure of intelligence of that era was the failure of almost everybody to foresee the end of Communism. It caught us completely on the hop. All that intelligence about their war-fighting capabilities was all very well, but it didn't tell

us the one thing we needed to know, that it was all about to collapse. It was a colossal failure of the whole Western system of intelligence assessment and political judgement.[73]

What Sir Charles omitted to mention was whether MI5 and MI6 deliberately neglected to predict the decline of the Soviet Union because it was not in their interests to do so. If the enemy self-destructs, there is no threat to the security of the state. There was always a suspicion in Whitehall that MI5 saw the Soviet 'threat' and the KGB as an 'intelligence game' or a chess match that they did not want to end.

In the mid-1980s, MI5 directors were particularly unhappy when Soviet defectors told them that the KGB were hopelessly ineffective and idle. The most celebrated, Oleg Gordievsky, said that Soviet intelligence operations in the UK never recovered from the expulsion of 90 diplomats in 1971.[74]

According to Mark Urban, the BBC's diplomatic correspondent, another KGB defector, Vladimir Kuzichkin, revealed that his former comrades were renowned for 'drunkenness, corruption, loose living and more than enough operational failures'. This was not welcomed by his UK debriefers as it meant the 'game' would finish, and was downplayed by MI5 in its Whitehall reports. 'It was not in the institutional interests of British intelligence to tell ministers or officials what they knew about the inefficiency of the KGB,' said Urban.[75]

As the Berlin Wall crumbled, MI5 needed to reinvent and reform itself to a fundamental extent. If it was to survive in the post-Cold War world, it needed a revolution of its own. The scandals of the 1970s and 1980s had left its reputation bruised and battered. In 1989, it was forced to place itself on a proper legal footing because of a ruling by the European Court of Human Rights. This stated that an intelligence agency is allowed to invade a citizen's privacy for reasons of national security, but that there should be a system of redress for those who have been wrongly investigated. However, the subsequent Security Service Act was a largely cosmetic exercise to comply with the European Court. The real issue was whether the Service would adapt to new security threats: terrorism by Irish Republicans, Arabs, Libyans and Islamic fundamentalists.

This was a major new challenge. In a tense, fast-moving terrorism crisis, there is no time to analyse and peruse a file over several months, and no time to speculate about a potential security risk. Terrorists are not like the KGB. They do not play the long game. They bomb, kill and maim according to their own timetable, usually within hours.

For MI5 to be an effective force, the old methods, personnel, structures, management, culture, recruitment measures and priorities needed to be drastically reviewed and updated.

As the Cold War ended in November 1990, with the signing of the treaty of Paris by Western leaders, MI5 management agreed to one major initiative: they authorised a new recruitment drive designed to attract a wider cross-section of the population – away from the Oxbridge, upper middle-class intake of previous years. A recruitment consultancy was commissioned and a clandestine method of hiring new MI5 officers was devised. In 1991, a more representative younger group flooded into MI5's scattered offices in Mayfair, expecting a modernised, vibrant, flexible and reformed Security Service. They were in for a shock.

2

JOINING THE TWILIGHT ZONE

'Very little comes to he or she who waits.'

MI5 recruitment advertisement headlined
'Godot Isn't Coming', 12 May 1991

'I found that MI5 in the 1990s was a pale imitation of its old Stalinist enemies. Officers were only rewarded if they blindly followed the party line.'

David Shayler, MI5 officer, 1991–96

MI5 has always had recruitment problems. Traditionally, employees were found through an eccentric informal network of family connections, social acquaintances, the military, the colonies and universities. Candidates were tapped on the shoulder, taken aside and asked, in hushed tones, whether they would like to do some secret work for the government.

For decades there was no coherent policy or procedure. The criteria for employment were 'trust', 'loyalty' and 'reliability' to the services, rather than quality and ability. After the Second World War, the chief concern was staffing the Registry, where all the secret files from the branches were co-ordinated and indexed. There were also 'source books', which contained a regularly updated analysis of specific operations. It was a highly sensitive area and MI5's response was to hire young daughters of high-society and service families. Known as the 'Registry Queens', they were recruited either on the recommendation of girls who had worked there previously or were friends of members of the personnel department. Management believed this was the best way to keep out pro-Communist women who might destroy or weed out valuable records.[1]

Higher up the scale, former policemen and officials in the Colonial Service mixed with retired Army officers. Inevitably, this led to MI5 becoming an upper-class gentlemen's club with its own special tie and cufflinks. 'The people at the top,' recalled Peter Wright, 'all suffered from the extraordinary belief that the upper classes were trustworthy in matters of security and the lower classes were not . . . the received wisdom was that their own sort was loyal and that everybody else was potentially disloyal.'[2]

Discreet, if thinly disguised, advertisements in newspapers were a favourite means of recruitment. In the 1950s, MI5 successfully employed a woman to infiltrate the Communist Party of Great Britain (CPGB) via the secretarial pages of *The Times*. Other advertisements were tailored to attracting businessmen or former police officers for specific operations.[3]

However, most of the recruiting was accomplished by personal introductions through academic circles and at the Bar. Vice-chancellors of universities informed the Home Office of staff who could spot students of the 'necessary character' to be recruited for MI5. Candidates were then sounded out in whispered conversations after tutorials. 'The best way to recruit is through dons who have the interests of the services at heart,' said Lord Annan, former head of King's College, Cambridge, and vice-chancellor of the University of London. 'Sir John Masterman [Provost of Worcester College, Oxford, 1946–61] may have behaved exactly like a character out of John Buchan, but as a student of Christ Church he had a very keen nose for the kind of man whom the services needed. I believe Sir Dick White [later head of MI5 and MI6] was one of his protégés.'[4]

But handing the future security of the state to university tutors was not viewed elsewhere with great confidence. Lord Beloff, a Conservative academic and fellow at St Antony's College, Oxford, was asked to write references for students applying for MI5 posts. 'I gained the impression,' he said, 'that it was employing people whose degree of political sensitivity was rather low.'[5] Civil servants were harsher: 'MI5 is a way of finding employment for muscular under-achievers from the ancient universities,' said one official.[6]

This was vividly, if a touch too cynically, described by the spy novelist John le Carré, who served in MI5 during the 1960s. As he later described in a piece of non-fiction, the quality of recruits was not reassuring:

For a while you wondered whether the fools were pretending to be fools, as some kind of deception, or whether there was a real efficient Secret Service somewhere else. Later, in my fiction, I invented one. But, alas, the reality was the mediocrity. Ex-colonial policemen mingling with failed academics, failed lawyers, failed missionaries and failed débutantes gave our canteen the amorphous quality of an Old School outing on the Orient Express. Everyone seemed to smell of failure.[7]

Unlike MI6, the Home Civil Service and the Diplomatic Service, MI5 did not use the Civil Service Selection Board to find its senior staff. The Board operated a battery of tests, exercises and some psychological screening in an effort to evaluate the ability of candidates to make objective judgements. MI5 preferred its own bizarre 'talent-spotting' methodology. 'Recruitment was mainly through friends and contacts – the "tap-on-the-shoulder" style of recruiting,' recalled Dame Stella Rimington. 'This style had earlier resulted in the famous team of Burgess, Philby, Maclean and Blunt who were all friends and recruited each other with disastrous consequences . . . It remained a fairly mysterious process – young people were told not to tell their friends and some men never told their wives.'[8]

This approach exasperated customers of MI5, like the armed forces, who found the agency obsessively and unnecessarily secret-ive. Lord Carver, Chief of the Defence staff from 1973 until 1976, complained that recruitment and training of intelligence officers was still 'rather like that employed by the Army in the 18th century'. It might have produced generals like Wellington and Marlborough, but the armed forces had moved on from that era. 'The system operates on the basis that, provided the man or woman is a friend of a friend of a friend, then he or she must be all right,' said Lord Carver. 'The training consists of seeing that he or she learns on the job. Most organisations, especially the armed forces, would feel that was a totally inadequate system for a service as important as these services.'[9]

It was not until the mid-1970s that reform was introduced. As usual, a scandal was the catalyst. After Lord Trend, a former Cabinet Secretary, investigated the Sir Roger Hollis affair, Prime Minister James Callaghan realised that MI5 needed substantial reform. In 1977, he asked a senior civil servant to look into its past recruitment practices and assess its performance. Callaghan then summoned Sir

John Hunt, the Cabinet Secretary, Sir Michael Hanley, MI5's director-general, and Sir Maurice Oldfield, then head of MI6, for a meeting at 10 Downing Street. The Prime Minister reminded Hanley of MI5's pitiful past record of being penetrated by KGB-recruited traitors, most of whom were public-school and Oxbridge-educated.[10]

It was agreed that MI5's recruitment procedures needed a major overhaul. A central aim would be to hire people from a wider social background, who would have an understanding of the real world, particularly the new breed of subversive elements. The traditional civil-servant characteristics for a desk officer – painstaking attention to detail and bureaucratic procedures – were no longer sufficient. If a subversive group was to be infiltrated, the MI5 officer needed to be an imaginative thinker with the interpersonal skills to recruit a political activist from a completely different background.

Suddenly anonymous but more specific advertisements appeared in the newspapers and magazines like *New Scientist* and *The Economist*.[11] But the early 1980s was not a fruitful time for recruitment. Margaret Thatcher was attacking public servants as pampered and overpaid, and MI5 was not seen as exciting and rewarding by bright graduates. Compared with the bright lights of the City, it was viewed as a UK-based, bureaucratic desk job. Instead of academic high-flyers, it was still attracting intellectual mediocrity: those who had failed the Civil Service examinations, ex-military who could not find work elsewhere, former policemen and Special Branch officers.

The other major weakness was that MI5 was supposed to maintain domestic security and yet its own security record was appalling. This was vividly illustrated by the case of Michael Bettaney, an MI5 officer who was jailed for 23 years in 1984 for betraying secrets to the Soviet Union. A Security Commission inquiry later savaged the standards of management that had allowed the unbalanced Bettaney to develop a serious drink problem. MI5 directors were so negligent that they barely noticed when he had a nervous breakdown that led him eventually to throw files of secret documents over the gates of the Soviet Embassy in London.

By the late 1980s, MI5 realised it had a real problem and began recruiting from outside Oxbridge. Careers advisers from different universities were invited to discreet seminars at MI5 headquarters where they were told what the Service was looking for. But the sales pitch was not enticing, largely because it was so vague. 'They just talk about the fact that they need people to analyse information,' said

one. 'I am just left with a vision of people sitting in small rooms looking through piles of files. It all sounds even more bureaucratic than
other bureaucracies.'[12] According to the *Mail on Sunday*, Sandy (not
her real name), a graduate in Russian from Durham University, was
approached by her careers adviser:

> She asked me whether I would be 'interested in doing
> research work for a department that is not normally adver-
> tised. I can't tell you what the work is.' The intake was broader
> than the old days, when one simply 'knew a chap' . . . Now
> they are so short of suitable candidates because spying seems
> less glamorous, so they get you to join straight from university.
>
> In my intake, there were quite a few people from red-brick
> universities, but the overall tone was still right-wing. The
> people who I knew who were approached at Durham were all
> middle- class and public school. And they were all bright.
> What they are looking for is someone who is conservative, and
> probably Conservative, but they don't like people who are
> politically active, left or right.[13]

When asked about the personality of the people who join MI5,
Sandy, without a hint of irony, replied: 'Oddballs and social misfits.
The people I was working with had obscure degrees – they were
lacklustre pedants who wouldn't fit in anywhere else and could not
earn a living in competitive circumstances.'

By the time she joined, candidates underwent an examination
set by the Civil Service Commission, which included IQ tests. The
next day each applicant had to pretend to be a member of a
committee: they gave speeches and took part in question-and-
answer sessions. This was followed by a meeting with a psychologist.
'Nothing very searching went on,' said Sandy. 'He asked me lots of
questions about my childhood. His job is to check that you are
stable and that you won't suddenly fly off the handle and turn into
a traitor. But his questions were pretty banal.'[14]

Meanwhile, Sandy was positively vetted. Investigators checked
whether she had a criminal background, had been declared bank-
rupt, used drugs, joined a subversive or undesirable organisation or
indulged in any sexual activity that might expose her to blackmail.
'One friend showed me a photocopy of the incredibly lengthy form
she had to fill in about me,' said Sandy. 'One of the questions she

was asked was whether I was promiscuous. She told the man that I wasn't at all: that I only had two boyfriends in the preceding six months. "Hmmm," he replied. "Promiscuous."'[15] Despite her sexual 'decadence', Sandy joined MI5.

More recently, another applicant had a similar experience, but with a twist. After the same battery of tests and sessions, the candidate made it to the penultimate hurdle – an interview before a committee of six serving MI5 officers. The conversation flowed and the signs were positive until he asked the following question: 'Are MI5 officers ever involved in operations which trouble their conscience?' The response, about the complex requirements of Service life, took several minutes. But his interrogators left him with a clear impression: 'Don't worry too much about ethics, that's not your concern.' He was not invited back for the final interview.[16]

By 1989, the quality of applicants had not improved a great deal. University careers officers reported 'almost no interest at all' in the Security Service. Sir Patrick Walker, then MI5's director-general, was sufficiently concerned to call in a management consultancy to advise on future strategy. They were also faced with the legal implications of the new Security Service Act. This enabled citizens to take legal action against MI5 if they believed they were victims of illegal surveillance or blacklisting. MI5 responded by placing disguised advertisements in the national press via a head-hunting agency in an attempt to attract top-flight lawyers. The firm agreed to absolute secrecy and was told not to name the client in advertisements or initial interviews.

The job offered a starting salary of £30,000 to lawyers with an aptitude for 'logical and lateral thinking'. One applicant, aged 32, was interviewed. 'He told me the job would involve working for the Ministry of Defence, and would that make any difference to me,' said the candidate. 'It would involve work with new official secrets legislation, so I soon realised who my real employers would be. I really wasn't very interested in that kind of work.' He took an intelligence test, which he described as 'about 11-plus standard'. He did not get the job.[17]

In recent years MI5 has modernised and opened up its recruitment practices. In August 2000, an advertisement appeared in the *Times* Educational Supplement offering teachers the opportunity to join the Service and help screen new applicants. Seeking people from the worlds of healthcare and counselling, the advert stated: 'We are looking for people with experience of varied or ethnically diverse appointments to carry out pre-employment assessment of all jobs . . . Looking for something different. We are.' However, the cloak-and-dagger was not forgotten as applicants were advised: 'Please avoid telling your friends about your application because discretion is an essential part of working for the Security Service.'

Suddenly, recruitment advertisements were appearing in the most unlikely publications. Tucked away in the back of *She* magazine – almost lost among the adverts for liposuction, vitamins for children and breast enlargement – there was MI5 trying to entice readers to join the secret state. Looking like an ad for a temping agency, with a picture of an office chair and a bunch of balloons attached to it, the words in bold declared: 'Many happy returns. If you're looking to return to work after a break, or you'd simply like a change of career, why not let the Security Service provide the setting? With our flexi-time and generous holiday entitlement, you'll fit your working life around your other commitments with ease . . . Our office environment is relaxed and friendly, with a first-name culture throughout, and working towards a common and worthwhile aim which fosters an atmosphere of teamwork and mutual help.'

Combined with approaching ethnic minorities, there is no doubt that MI5 has tried to demystify, open up and embrace recruits from a range of socio-economic and ethnic backgrounds.

This drive to diversity started in 1991 when an obscure advertisement appeared in the press. It was to have significant and historic ramifications. On the afternoon of 12 May 1991, Anne Shayler was browsing through the Business section of the *Independent on Sunday* when her eye was caught by an interesting headline in the Appointments section. 'Godot Isn't Coming' read the caption. Illustrated with three modern-looking chairs, the text revealed little as to the real nature of the job advertised:

> Very little comes to he or she who waits. Much more comes to those who reach out and take new opportunities. If you have already achieved plenty but now find yourself marking time, stuck in a rut and unable to progress, then it's time to act. To use your strong interpersonal skills to move to a non-commercial organisation where an interest in current affairs is important. Where what also counts is your experience, your

good honours degree, your acute powers of analysis and your astute, practical common sense.

You'll benefit from excellent training. Promotion is merit-based. The roles reflect your experience. And the starting salaries vary between £16,500 and £20,500 but could be even more. No selling is involved. Any knowledge of European languages would be appreciated as there may be some opportunities for overseas travel, although your base will be in London.

Anne Shayler thought that her 25-year-old son David might be interested, so that evening she showed him the clipping. David, who had just spent a year running a newspaper for Scottish students, was intrigued.

The caption was derived from Samuel Beckett's famous play *Waiting for Godot,* which David had studied in English and French at Dundee University, in which two men sit around waiting for a man called Godot, who never arrives. The implication was that if one just hoped and waited for one's dreams to come true, one would always be disappointed. David Shayler took this as a sign that the prospective employer was a dynamic organisation and would not be caught 'waiting for Godot'.

It was the type of advertisement and job that appealed to someone like Shayler, with an arts degree, offbeat and slightly Bohemian, but with an interest in politics and current affairs. He sent a full CV to the advertising agency, T.G. Scott and Son Ltd, based in Southampton Street, central London. One night while he was sitting at home, the phone rang. 'Do you know anything about "Godot Isn't Coming"?' said a voice, without identifying itself.

After Shayler confirmed his interest, he went to a recruitment consultancy in Soho Square where they conducted psychometric tests and a short interview. That evening he received another telephone call while staying at a friend's house. 'The people are interested in talking to you,' said the contact.

'Can you tell me what the job is now?' asked Shayler.

'It's in the Ministry of Defence, but it's a secret position,' he was told.

A stunned Shayler put the phone down and gasped to his friends: 'This is really weird, I'm being lined up for a secret job.' He was so shocked that he stepped back and stood on a 100-year-old violin belonging to his friend.

That was the moment when he wondered if it might be MI5. 'I thought to myself, it can't be intelligence,' he recalled. 'What would MI5 want with someone like me, a journalist who printed extracts from *Spycatcher* at college and was involved with left-wing groups?'

For the second interview, on 5 June 1991, Shayler was directed to an unmarked building on Tottenham Court Road. The interview room was bleak and bare, with just a desk and two chairs. After a few seconds, a man walked in. Middle-aged, wearing a pinstriped suit and with swept-back silver hair, he had a distinctly patrician manner. He was a 'retread' – a retired MI5 officer hired as a consultant on specific projects.

Shayler decided to be open about his political views. He was asked about his childhood and his beliefs. He was probed about his view of a recent SAS ambush in which three IRA terrorists were killed. At the time there was speculation that it had been a shoot-to-kill operation. 'From what I have read,' Shayler told his interviewer, 'we would not expect everybody in an ambush to be killed outright. So I suspect the SAS may have been involved in murder. While I expect the SAS to defend themselves when attacked, I don't think they have the right to murder people. As we are not in a state of war with the IRA, the SAS should have arrested the terrorists and allowed them to be tried in a court of law.' The MI5 officer agreed, and said the Service was there to uphold the rule of law.

Shayler was then questioned about why he had printed illegal extracts from Peter Wright's book *Spycatcher* while editor of the student newspaper at Dundee University. 'I didn't think it was the business of the Security Service to go around destabilising democratically elected governments,' he replied.

'Well, Wright has retracted most of *Spycatcher*,' claimed the interviewer, who then asked, 'Why do you think you're here in an unmarked building?'

Shayler paused before replying. By now he was convinced that the job was with the Security Service, but he was unwilling to mention MI5 in case it was another agency. 'Perhaps you should tell me that,' he replied, only to be met with another question. Eventually, after some lengthy, embarrassed silences, Shayler asked, 'Is it intelligence?'

'Yes, it's the Security Service. We're better known as MI5.'

The consultant said he could not continue with the interview until Shayler signed the Official Secrets Act. After glancing at its contents Shayler quickly signed the document – fascination had

overridden caution. Then he became concerned about the implications. 'Oh, God, what the hell have I done?' he thought. 'I'm a
journ- alist and I've just signed the Official Secrets Act.'

The MI5 officer then explained, vaguely, what the work would
entail. 'Can I tell people about my job?' asked Shayler.

'Well, obviously you shouldn't tell too many people – only
trusted people,' replied his interviewer. 'Your cover story is "I am a
civil servant working for the Ministry of Defence".'

More interviews followed at the Civil Service Selection Board
office in Whitehall, and Shayler met other potential candidates.
During an intense two-day session, he was interviewed by a senior
MI5 officer, a civil servant and a psychologist. The latter accused
him of being an egomaniac. This was based on Shayler's rather
exuberant presentation of stories while he was editor of his university newspaper, notably an exposé of a medical students' initiation
ceremony, which made national headlines.

Then there were role-playing scenarios and management exercises, which involved reading a briefing document and chairing a
meeting at which contentious issues needed to be resolved. All
candidates were assessed on their input as chairman and as partici-
pants.

They were also given a two-inch-thick file containing conflicting
information from sources both inside and outside government.
They were to imagine they were required to write a brief for a
minister. They not only had to summarise the pertinent information but also make recommendations based on it with reference to
government policy. There was a two-and-a-half-hour time limit,
which made it impossible for them to read all the material in detail.
'That was the hardest test I've ever taken in my life,' recalled
Shayler. 'It was far more demanding than working for MI5.'

By this stage Shayler was so keen to join the Service that he
turned down other job offers. As a journalist he had always been
fascinated by MI5, but was also keen to do something useful for his
country: he had been told that the work would consist largely of
fighting terrorism.

However, he was still in a mild state of shock that the Service
wanted to hire someone of his political and journalistic background.
This resulted in a bout of premature paranoia. He became worried
that MI5 was trying to entrap or compromise him in some way. After
one telephone conversation during the recruitment process he

noticed an unmarked white van outside his house and for a time believed it was part of a surveillance team. On another occasion he was seduced by an older woman, who approached him in a pub and invited him back to her flat. Shayler feared that she had been tasked by MI5 to spy on him, particularly when she asked questions about his future career plans. All kinds of fears raced through his mind: 'Perhaps she was testing me to see if I would admit to being recruited by MI5.'

Meanwhile, the security vetting process was under way. An investigator came to Shayler's house in Beaconsfield and spent two hours asking about his life. On the day of the interview he bought a copy of the *Daily Mail*, which he placed prominently on the dining-room table during the interview. Just to make sure the vetting officer was convinced of his establishment credentials, he also served coffee in a Royal Wedding mug.

He was not prepared for the deeply personal nature of the inquiry. The questions came thick and fast: 'Have you ever had links, or known anyone who has had links, with the Communist Party?' The interviewer gave Shayler a list of about 15 countries, mainly from the Eastern bloc but which included Libya, Iran, Iraq and Cuba. 'Have you or your family ever been approached by an agent of any intelligence service from these countries?' he was asked. He replied no to all the questions.

Shayler was surprised by the next one: 'Are you or have you ever been promiscuous?'

'Chance would be a fine thing,' he replied flippantly.

There was a pause, during which Shayler thought he had blown it. Then the interviewer burst out laughing and said, apologetically, 'We don't employ homosexuals. If you discover you are a homosexual in later life, you are expected to resign. Are you a homosexual?' Shayler said no, and reflected that this was a bizarre way to ask the question: most people would lie, having already heard that they would not get the job if they admitted it.

Finally, he was asked about his family. He was obliged to disclose the names and addresses of all his relatives. The vetting officer was particularly interested in the fact that Shayler had an uncle who worked in Libya.

At the end of the session, he was asked to nominate four friends from different parts of his life for the agency to talk to. Still mystified as to why MI5 wanted to recruit him, he suggested one each from grammar school, Dundee University, Bordeaux (where he had worked as a teacher), and the *Sunday Times*. MI5 also took up references from his ex-headmaster, a university lecturer and his then employer. Even his neighbours in Beaconsfield were approached by Special Branch. After one final interview with six MI5 officers, Shayler was asked to join the Security Service. He had entered the twilight zone.

For anyone joining MI5 in the autumn of 1991, the first baffling experience was the most basic: their place of work. MI5 occupied five main separate buildings in central London, with different branches scattered and split around the city. It was a uniquely inefficient method of operating, with some officials spending much of their day shuttling from one office to another (one director needed to visit three locations just to see his staff).[18]

A major building was at 1 Curzon Street, off Berkeley Square, a drab, six-storey, BBC-style Orwellian Ministry of Truth office block built in the 1930s. In the basement was the infamous Registry, where secret files on security suspects were stored. It was in this vast area that the Royal Family sheltered during Second World War bombing raids. Legend has it that a secret tunnel connected MI5's HQ to Buckingham Palace, but that has never been confirmed. Curzon Street also contained the transcribers of tapped telephone conversations and the anti-terrorist units.

Around the corner in Grosvenor Street, Mayfair, next to a hairdresser's, was the training section. Across Berkeley Square was Bolton Street, the little-known but vast, black, Lubyanka-style office, which took up half of one side of the road. This was for counterterrorism, anti-subversion officers and technical support staff who were glamorised by the character Q in the James Bond films. The other important base was at 40 Gower Street, which looked like a 1960s tower block from an Eastern bloc state and contained counter-espionage officers, personnel and senior management.

It was a chaotic working environment. For years MI5 staff had been shunted into these offices as space became available. No thought had gone into the best use of people and resources, so the rooms were cramped, dirty and either too hot or too cold. The radiators clanked with monotonous regularity. The carpets were worn and the walls were painted standard government green, pale and almost sickly – the shade often seen in *Monty Python* sketches satirising Whitehall.

As these offices had housed MI5 since the Second World War, it was time to bring everyone under one roof. (Only the ultra-secret surveillance section, A4, would remain at Euston Tower.)

The site chosen was Thames House, an imposing neo-classical block designed by Sir Frank Baines in 1928, on Millbank, just north of Lambeth Bridge. Formerly used as their headquarters by the Department of Energy and ICI, it was converted and refurbished over three years in great secrecy and at huge expense – the final bill was £265 million. The modifications destroyed most of the listed building except the façade, which caused a minor outcry among conservationists. The only original feature remaining was a near full-size squash court in the sub-basement. Another court, a gym and aerobics facilities were added.

The new arrangement provided office space for 2,300 people and parking for 800 cars. When the renovation was completed in late 1994, it was a modern architectural fantasy park compared with what MI5 officers were used to. But there was a certain coldness to the precision of the design in Thames House: the desks were in a modern, icy grey, and the offices were divided from each other by frosted glass.

There were two glass-roofed courtyards for meetings: the North and South Atriums. Management tried to persuade people to use the South Atrium as an Italian-style piazza, but this failed because officers were scared of being seen in the 'wrong' company from the windows of the offices. The North Atrium was dominated by a futuristic, giant, Foucault-style rotating pendulum. The staff did not use the two bars – with specially insulated carpets – because of the no-smoking policy and the belief that their drinking would be inhibited by prying management eyes. The only areas in which the décor varied from the pristine whites and ice greys were the ward rooms and the director-general's office on the fifth floor opposite the library. The ward rooms were used to entertain high-profile guests, like the Home Secretary. Dominated by portraits of the Queen and former director-generals, including Sir Roger Hollis, they were heavy with atmosphere: the walls boasted the finest dark walnut panelling, every inch polished to shine like glass, there were large tables and deep claret or Prussian blue carpets.

All the files are in the basement, where a state-of-the-art mono-railway runs with mini-carriages to take files and papers from the Registry to the secretaries' offices on each of the eight floors.

No expense was spared at Thames House Palace. This was exposed by an enterprising *Daily Mirror* journalist, Ramsay Smith, and a photographer, who posed as workmen and strolled past security guards manning the gates. After borrowing a computerised swipe card, they inspected MI5's new premises for 40 minutes just before its completion. In itself this was embarrassing enough. After all, Smith might have been a terrorist. But equally so was the extravagance:

> The spies aren't stinting on themselves. There's nothing but the best gear in there. Even the carpet in the staff restaurant cost about 70 pounds a square metre. One of the squash-court floors had to be ripped up and put down again after it was laid at the wrong temperature and buckled with the heat.
>
> There are overnight suites as well, and they've been fitted with the best German kitchen units and microwaves. Everyone who has done a bit of work here is amazed by the amount of money that is being spent.[19]

A French artist was commissioned to design a six-foot sculpture of the Security Service crest for the entrance hall, at a cost of £25,000. There was also a piece of modern art in the lobby, which confused tourists, who would try to enter Thames House thinking it was the Tate Gallery. The new office even fooled Martin McGuinness, the Sinn Fein leader, who walked into the building thinking it was the Labour Party HQ. He went to Reception, identified himself and asked to see his contact. The shocked security guard asked him to take a seat and alerted staff. For a moment a wave of panic spread throughout the building until someone calmly pointed him in the right direction along Millbank.

The final cost of MI5's grandiose new headquarters generated irritation in Whitehall. It was equivalent to nearly double MI5's annual budget, and revenue from the sale of some of their old offices did not nearly cover the cost. One reason for this was that a builder was discovered to have IRA connections which were missed during the vetting investigation. This meant that, at immense cost, the walls had to be stripped after they had been decorated to search for bugs and bombs with long-delayed fuses.

An investigation in 1997 by the National Audit Office, the government's spending watchdog, found that millions of pounds had been spent over budget. But the report was kept secret from the public and Parliament, despite protests by Sir Robert Sheldon, chairman of the Commons Public Accounts Committee at the time. MI5 insisted that it should not be published and the new Labour government agreed to suppress the document.[20]

As the original estimate in 1990 for MI5's new base was £85 million, there was some suspicion among the mandarins about a secret long-term agenda: 'At the time they were planned, the new buildings [a new home was also built for MI6] may have seemed logical enough,' said a senior official, 'but by the time they were ready for use, the political and public expenditure was so very different.'[21]

Some civil servants told Mark Urban, the BBC's well-informed diplomatic correspondent and a former military intelligence officer, that MI5 deliberately expanded and spent more on its HQ when its role was most uncertain and under threat, between 1990 and 1994. They were reminded of Cyril Northcote Parkinson, whose study of the Royal Navy from its time of imperial greatness to its relative decline in the 1950s produced some apt observations on bureaucratic behaviour. His most famous, 'Parkinson's Law', stated: 'Work expands to fill the time available for its completion.' He had discovered that the Royal Navy's headquarters grew in size, splendour and expense as its role and relevance as a force declined: 'A perfection of planned layout is achieved only by organisations on the point of collapse,' he wrote. 'During a period of exciting discovery or progress, there is no time to plan the perfect headquarters.'[22]

Millions of pounds of taxpayers' money were also poured into the introduction of new information technology, although an undisclosed amount was absorbed by the building 'budget'. Computerisation in all government departments and agencies nearly always involves a costly learning process, but at least with health authorities and suchlike the cost is known by the public. The waste and overspending in MI5's case has been kept secret – until now.

MI5 first developed a computerised index of its 'suspect' files, known as R2, in late 1977. But a decade later, its database system was very much behind the times – a peculiar state of affairs for an organisation whose very existence depends on the processing of information. It was realised that MI5 needed an integrated information technology system, part of which would be an expanded database for new documents.

Codenamed Grant, the project was handicapped from the beginning by MI5's refusal to use outside software. Obsessed with secrecy, management wanted everything done in-house and devised from original concepts. Adopting the gentleman-amateur approach, inexperienced and untrained intelligence officers were assigned to the project.

In 1991, MI5 announced that Grant would be ready for use in two years' time. But the deadline came and went. Part of the problem was that it was a totally original system based on the most sophisticated new and complex techniques. But the main flaw was the refusal to employ qualified consultants from the private sector or to buy commercial software (MI5 was paranoid about hackers penetrating its files). The staff recruited to the MI5/MI6 Joint Computer Bureau were paid below the market rate and as a result the quality of their work was below standard. In the long term, this delayed its completion and increased the cost.

Eventually, in 1995, Stephen Lander, then head of H Branch, which was in charge of Grant for 18 months, scrapped it as an office management system. The estimated cost was £25 million. He took the decision without consulting his managers. The system was then downgraded to a database, and MI5 was forced to buy an off-the-shelf office management system based on Windows '95, which was customised for MI5 needs.

Grant was an immensely wasteful and inefficient exercise. The delay and cost was particularly damaging, especially in the light of how MI5 works. A desk officer writes a report in draft form, which often includes later amendments, and sends it to a secretary for typing. When it is returned, it might require further corrections before it is sent to management. The document, particularly if it is a warrant for telephone or mail interception, is then subject to endless dissemination and perusal. Aside from the bureaucratic procedures, each new draft has to be retyped and printed out which, of course, might have been avoided with an efficient information-technology network.

The ultimate aim was for MI5, MI6 and GCHQ to receive, create and file documents all in one integrated information-technology system, bridging the three wings of the intelligence services. But by early 1997 only 40 per cent of MI5 staff had access to the new system. Those without access had to fight for their own word-processor, but the models available were at least five years out of date. Due to a budget surplus, MI5 then bought a printer for each officer who had access to the new IT system, thereby defeating the principle of the paperless office.

The specific databases were also mismanaged. One system, known as Hawk, was dedicated to recording information on political subversives in F Branch, but it took so many years to develop that by the time it was ready for action and in use, the extremist threat had virtually disappeared. And as the database was specifically designed for political subversives, it could not be used to record other MI5 targets. By late 1995, the Security Service devoted only half a desk to subversives, so the system performs almost certainly at well below its capacity. Again, the delay and waste was due to the refusal to buy off-the-shelf software, which could have been adapted for F Branch requirements and other MI5 sections. The amount of financial waste is not known, but any analysis would need to take into account the cost of staff time in using the paper-card system during the development of Hawk.

Over in T Branch, the counter-terrorist section, there were similar problems with a database called Durbar. This system could not cope with the sheer amount and variety of intelligence. In 1992, it was an estimated five years out of date and was only recently upgraded. Once again, commercially available software could have fulfilled MI5's requirements. The financial cost is also unknown, but the poor quality control of Durbar has caused the most serious damage of all of the databases.

Informed sources have told the authors that intelligence on terrorist targets, probably the IRA, has been lost or missed because of Durbar's flaws. For example, in vetting cases, MI5 has been forced to state a 'nothing recorded against' assessment even though Durbar indicated that an applicant had 'terrorist traces'. This meant that the computer stated that the subject of vetting had key terrorist connections, but that it could not locate the original intelligence and evidence in the system. The implications for national security, needless to say, are enormous.

MI5's lack of professionalism and obsession with secrecy were also apparent when it invested in a new voicemail system in 1996. This was done not because of staff demand or for efficiency reasons but because the Service needed to absorb a large surplus in one of its budgets. As a highly sophisticated facility, it had many valuable features, but there was just one problem: MI5 would not allow officers to use it, for undisclosed 'security reasons'. In fact, staff were strictly forbidden even to indicate to an incoming caller whether he or she had reached the correct extension. It was difficult to see how 'Hello, this is John speaking' or 'You are through to H Branch' would breach national security, but all an incoming caller heard on the voicemail message was: 'The person you want to speak to is not here. Please leave a message, but do not leave any sensitive information on the machine.'

This, of course, defeated the whole purpose of voicemail, which is designed to save on the costs of employing support staff to take calls in the absence of officers. The standard message did not indicate whether the member of staff was away from his desk, in the lavatory or on a two-week holiday in Thailand, so virtually nobody used the system. It increased rather than diminished the workload for secretaries because they spent more time taking messages from people calling via the switchboard. It was a farcical misuse of resources.

As most of the bungling has been kept from the public and ministers, MI5 has been able to boast about their information-technology modernisation. In a 1993 public-information brochure, it claimed that: 'More sophisticated intelligence databases using the most modern technology are now being introduced.'

Civil servants also appear unaware of MI5's profligacy and incompetence. In 1994, the Cabinet Office agreed for the Service to advise government information-technology managers on nearly all computer-security issues. A spokeswoman told *Computer Weekly* that MI5 had more 'relevant experience' than the Central Computer Telecommunications Agency and had taken over its executive functions, notably on computer hacking and protective security. As MI5 is not registered under the Data Protection Act, this gave the agency complete freedom to browse through files on individuals throughout Whitehall.[23]

Apart from the £25 million wasted on Grant, it is difficult to assess the total cost of MI5's information-technology programme. One estimate is a minimum of £100 million,[24] a staggering amount by any standards, but, then, budgets inside MI5 are mysterious. Only those high up in the management chain have access to departmental budgets, which has led to another serious abuse: some MI5 officers have spent thousands of pounds travelling to the Middle East on the flimsiest of intelligence reasons and have combined the trip with a holiday for themselves or have sent for their families to join them. A few deliberately proposed to visit an MI6 station or foreign service with no relevance to their branch, just to see if their assistant director would authorise it. Israel and the Lebanon were popular destinations, and in many cases were officially approved. On many occasions officers did not write up a report for several months, if at all, so management was in no position to evaluate whether a trip had been value for money. Another even claimed a visit to a massage parlour in Czechoslovakia on his expenses, saying that this was the only way in which he could deal with the stress of his work. (The expenses claim was rejected.)

MI5's annual budget has always been shrouded in secrecy. From 1782 to 1994, the Secret Service Vote was processed and ministers did not have a clue as to how the money was spent. In 1919, Stanley Baldwin, then Financial Secretary to the Treasury, confessed: 'I have no knowledge of the way in which the money was spent.'[25] As recently as 1992, Home Secretary Kenneth Baker refused to publish the budget and payroll of MI5. Although he had sponsored a Freedom of Information Bill in 1979, he said that this information was 'closely associated with the Security Service's operations which must remain secret'.[26] It was not until 1994 that the government agreed for the aggregate expenditure of MI5, MI6 and GCHQ to be open to financial analysis by the National Audit Office, but there is still no real scrutiny as the agencies are not required to disclose any 'material items of expenditure'.[27] The Commons Public Accounts Committee has only investigated the issue twice in the past 60 years.

The new arrangement is called the Single Intelligence Vote. In 1993–94, the agencies' combined spending came to £961.3 million, and they were pressured subsequently to make cuts by Kenneth Clarke, then Chancellor of the Exchequer – whose response was 'Come off it' whenever he heard murmurs of protest.[28] Treasury officials had always suspected that the agencies were extravagant, notably when counter-espionage tasks at MI6 were also performed by MI5. They smiled ruefully when the intelligence agencies were able to find total reductions of £100 million. In 1994–95 the total budget was reduced to £855.1 million, and to £740.7 million in 1996–97, most of which was spent on GCHQ.

It was only when the Labour Party was elected in May 1997 that MI5, MI6 and GCHQ found new friends. They persuaded the new government to increase their aggregate budget to £743.2 million for 1999–2000, £745 million for 2000–01 and £746.9 million for

2001–02. The amount for MI5 alone has been estimated as £140 million a year, of which 25 per cent would be spent on countering terrorism relating to Ulster and 15 per cent on fighting international terrorism. Espionage now accounts for 12 per cent and subversion a mere one per cent.

In early 2002, faced with the new threat of international terrorism, MI5, MI6 and GCHQ submitted separate bids for extra funds that would bring their aggregate budget to several billion. This was on top of the extra £20 million emergency cash agreed by the government after 11 September 2001. The Treasury agreed to an annual budget of £1.1 billion for the three agencies for 2005–06 – up from £896 million in 2002–03. This represented an increase of 7.1 per cent in real terms from 2002–03 to 2005–06. This was less than the average increase of 8.1 per cent throughout Whitehall, but far more than the police received – 2.5 per cent in real terms.[29]

The budget for MI5 alone went up by seven per cent in the Treasury's spending review published in July 2002. Latest figures show that 56.9 per cent is spent on counter-terrorism, 14.4 per cent on counter-espionage, 11.5 per cent on serious crime and 11 per cent on guarding key government installations and secret documents. As of May 2003, the figure for terrorism is at least 60 per cent.

Most of the extra funds have been spent on recruiting extra officers for G Branch, which is responsible for counter-terrorism, new recruitment and training programmes and investment in surveillance and information technology. The main focus is hiring fast-track graduate trainees with a grounding in languages and understanding of suspect rogue states.

Remarkably, the actual amount for MI5 alone is still wrapped up in a blanket of secrecy (our estimate is about £200 million a year). 'No one except the director-general and her deputy knows MI5's budget,' said David Shayler. 'The Cabinet Office knows the aggregate budget – or "the vote" as it is mysteriously called – of the intelligence agencies. But it does not know the individual amount for each service. When MI5 ran out of money, they simply asked for more which they were always given. The real budget is hidden because responsibilities are spread across a number of organisations, notably about 50 different Special Branches across the country, Customs and Defence Intelligence.'[30]

So do our spies provide value-for-money? The Labour government certainly think so and intelligence agencies have not been so well-funded since the late 1970s and early 1980s at the peak of the Cold War. Treasury ministers treat the topic as if it is the nation's biggest secret, refusing even to give evidence in secret to the benign Intelligence and Security Committee. However, David Bickford, former legal director of MI5, argues it is a core issue. He describes MI5's expenditure as 'excessive' and believes the three services should be merged, saving 'tens of millions of pounds' of taxpayers' money.[31]

This, then, was the infrastructure that greeted the new intake of the early 1990s. After training by B Branch, officers are assigned to various sections. The most controversial is A Branch, which is responsible for telephone tapping, covert entry (i.e. burglary) and specialised secret photography. Known as 'Operational Support', this also runs mobile and static surveillance units, who cover long-term targets like embassies. Other parts of A Branch keep safe-houses and listening posts, and transcribe the tapes of tapped phone calls.

Many new recruits are sent to D Branch, known as 'Non-terrorist Investigations'. This deals with vetting of people outside MI5 – civil servants, the police, members of the armed forces and employees of private companies who work on classified contracts. Other areas of responsibility are counter-espionage against the Russians and Chinese, and organised crime. One of its special functions is to draw up contingency plans to cope with a state of emergency, such as a general strike or the occupation of a nuclear-power plant.

International terrorism is covered by G Branch, which includes counter-proliferation, co-ordinating threat assessments and countering terrorism from the Indian subcontinent, Libya, Palestinian groups, Kurds, Iraq, Iran and Islamic extremists.

Covert financial inquiries with financial institutions, government departments and hotels are dealt with by H Branch ('Corporate Affairs'). These officers interact with GCHQ, the police, customs, ports and immigration agencies. They are also responsible for liaising with the media and Whitehall, as well as managing information-technology policy.

At the heart of H Branch is the main Registry of secret permanent and temporary files, controlled by computer-automated storage and retrieval systems.

Countering Irish Republican and Loyalist terrorism on the mainland, in Europe and across the rest of the world is handled by T Branch, which also investigates arms trafficking.

All of these activities, particularly in T Branch, involve substantial liaison with local and Metropolitan Police Special Branch (MPSB) officers. Known as the eyes and ears of MI5, each constabulary has its own individual Special Branch. Working separately from ordinary policemen and women, their role is to supply raw intelligence gained from local informants. Trained by MI5, Special Branch officers liaise closely with the Service on ongoing operations and towards new priorities and targets. Armed with extra legal powers to arrest and search, Special Branch officers tap into regional networks of information. They are very much MI5's street operatives reporting back their findings. On specific operations, Special Branch officers will often do the fieldwork: they carry out time-consuming surveillance and assist with covert searches.

University-educated MI5 managers tend to look down on Special Branch officers as provincial, working-class informers. In fact, the Branch has important responsibilities: enforcing the Prevention of Terrorism Act and the Official Secrets Act, vetting and registering naturalisation applicants, watching ports and airports and protecting VIPs. For over 100 years, the MPSB, which has a national role, was in charge of countering IRA terrorism in Britain. The Branch's expansion has also resulted in independent police offshoots in diplomatic protection and anti-terrorism.

Despite MI5's lofty disdain, most local Special Branch officers are regarded as highly professional. Tension and friction exists between regional Branch and MI5 officers on one side and the MPSB. As the Met is a prestigious force in routine crime, its Special Branch officers tend to be arrogant and high-handed in their dealings with provincial Branch officers. In fact, MI5 view MSPB officers as inept at gathering and exploiting intelligence. It also sees them as poorly trained and managed.

One of the enduring myths about working for MI5 is that it is glamorous, exciting and romantic. The thrilling car chases and sexual adventures portrayed by Ian Fleming and the sinister, intricate conspiracies conjured up by John le Carré are far from reality. 'The last sort of person we want is someone who thinks he is going to be like James Bond,' said Dame Stella Rimington.[32] According to

David Shayler, the swashbuckling 007 image is more relevant to the Secret Intelligence Service (MI6):

> I would compare the two cultures as MI5 being the grammar-schoolboy culture and MI6 being the public-schoolboy culture. That was reflected in the way people worked. In MI5 you were always over-supervised, people trying to put their twopence-worth into what you were doing. Quite often these were people who had very little legitimate interest in what you were doing and knew very little about how you were working, whereas MI6 was perhaps too much the other way. People were very gung-ho. Certainly they saw themselves more in the James Bond–John le Carré sort of roles than people in MI5 did.[33]

In fact, working for MI5 is often mundane, as Miranda Ingram, an MI5 officer from 1981 until 1983, has testified:

> The obsessive secrecy surrounding the Security Service creates an aura of glamour – in the eyes of the public and among members of the service themselves – about those who belong to it. In fact, the day-to-day work of intelligence officers is not particularly glamorous. They spend a lot of time merely keeping files up to date and storing information.
>
> Only the secrecy of the information, and the elaborate procedures for locking away bits of paper, detract from the routineness of it all. However, the very nature of an intelligence officer's work, whereby he is acting as a judge on his fellow-citizens, does put him in a position above the ordinary man.
>
> Glamour and secrecy combined make for a very élite club. Some accept membership as a birthright. To those of a new, broader intake, who were not born to expect easy superiority, membership is a privilege. To both types, belonging to MI5 offers a private thrill. This can compensate for many social or personal inadequacies.
>
> The danger is that officers are tempted to enjoy the secrecy surrounding their work and to live the John le Carré legend. This hinders independent thinking and critical self-questioning. To retain, against all this, their sense of perspective and ability to question demands a strong character and an independence not encouraged by the Service.[34]

A more recent analysis comes from an unnamed former MI5 officer. Recruited from a university, she left because, she claimed, 'It
was like an upper-class club':

> The work is desperately dull, much more prosaic than all the
> fuss would suggest. Northern Ireland was dangerous, but it
> was real, an exciting posting which people wanted to do. The
> good thing about Northern Ireland was that it was perfectly
> clear what the job was. It was the same with the Middle East
> desk – the threat of terrorist bombs and so on.
> But much of the work was pure drudgery. They [MI5]
> wanted intelligent people, but the work is dull. It's bloody
> boring wading through people's phone taps. People talk
> about how the dog is getting on or that they bought some
> potatoes today.[35]

When David Shayler joined MI5 in October 1991, he was under no
romantic illusion about entering a world of cloak-and-dagger espionage and intrigue. But he also harboured certain expectations:

> Those who offered me the work told me it would be hard but
> rewarding and I took comfort from the idea of serving my
> country. I was one of the first of a new breed of operatives
> recruited following persistent media and political criticism.
> On the surface, at least, MI5 seemed to be changing with the
> times. The old-boy network, drawn from Oxbridge and the
> military, which had dominated the Security Service, appeared
> to be less powerful.
> But the reality was different. I soon discovered that MI5 was
> an inflexible bureaucracy, unable to shake off the outdated
> methods used for decades to investigate Communism and
> foreign agents. I realised that Stella Rimington's profile as a
> moderniser was an astute tactic to ensure MI5 retained its
> huge – and unpublished – budget of some £200 million a year.
> Behind the scenes, the organisation was dangerously intrans-
> igent.
> The MI5 leadership of the 1990s had all cut their teeth
> under the old regime . . . Even Rimington's successor, Stephen
> Lander, is a career bureaucrat of more than 20 years' standing,
> with little experience of running agents in the field or counter-

terrorist organisations. Long-serving officers, who in the real world would have been sacked years ago, are allowed to serve out their time on pointless exercises, lost in a past when MI5 happily spent thousands of pounds tapping the telephones of left-wing activists.[36]

Shayler discovered a quasi-military-style office culture. MI5 models itself on the 1970s Home Civil Service structure (since reformed in Whitehall), which is hierarchical, conformist and repressive. Individuality, initiative and drive are discouraged. If an officer acquires more responsibility than his or her grade designates, the line manager will seek out any trivial problem and use it against that officer. 'Ironically, I found that MI5 in the 1990s was a pale imitation of its old Stalinist enemies,' said Shayler. 'Officers were only rewarded if they blindly followed the "party line". I felt new ideas were unwelcome. Outmoded, status-protecting orthodoxy was preferred. Within a year of joining, one of my closest colleagues – also part of the new intake – had been told to "learn to curb his independent traits" and was accused of being "too enthusiastic". He has since left.'[37]

MI5 appears unable to shake off the worst elements of Whitehall – gradism and bureaucracy – despite not being part of the Civil Service. For example, it has created more, rather than less, management. In the early 1990s, within the sections (subdivisions of branches), eight extra managers were appointed – an increase of 20 per cent.[38]

Another feature of the old mandarin mentality is that junior ranks are still expected to follow orders unquestioningly. Arguing your case within MI5 is seen as wrong and line managers record this as a 'lack of judgement' on the part of the officer rather than an honest difference of opinion that needs to be debated and resolved. Staff have given up proposing new ideas or expressing an opinion, as they feared it would count against them. One line manager was bemused when an officer persistently questioned why he was performing a task in a particular way. The only justification he could muster was 'Because I say so', and 'We've always done it that way.'

Higher up the hierarchy, the chief characteristic among directors is arrogance. In 1996, Stephen Lander, the director-general, went on a walkabout to talk to his staff. He clearly hated the experience:

twitchy, rude, almost contemptuous in his manner, he barely said a word. He fidgeted like a troubled, nervous teenager – looking out of the window, biting his fingernails and tying and retying his shoelaces. He did everything except look at the officer, commented Annie Machon, who was trying to explain her work. She had spent several hours drafting and writing briefings for management on topics like MI5's relations with the French secret service. 'Oh, I never read briefs,' he snapped and moved on.[39]

Needless to say, this attitude demoralised and demotivated staff, and many have since left frustrated. MI5 may theoretically stand for 'Military Intelligence 5', but the new intake never believed they were joining the Army.

The oppressive regime and the pressures of secrecy led to an endemic and excessive drinking culture within MI5. Michael Bettaney was the most notorious case (he became an alcoholic and drank a bottle of whisky a night), but alcoholism is far more widespread than is realised and poses a real threat to security: it heightens the risk of disclosure of secrets and blackmail. For many years management has tried to discourage officers from frequenting pubs as other customers may overhear them talking about operations.

In an attempt to persuade them to drink in-house, the old Curzon Street office ran its own bar on the sixth floor, known as the Grapevine. However, this held only limited appeal and officers of all ranks preferred London pubs.

David Shayler experienced this only a few weeks after being recruited. During his first lunchtime after joining the vetting section based at the Bolton Street offices, a senior officer invited him out for a drink. He took Shayler to the Chesterfield, a regular MI5 haunt, in Shepherd Market, Mayfair. Shayler recalled:

> The pub in question was a standing joke. The ex-military types referred to our offices as 'Camp One'. Whenever they wanted to escape from the tedium of the office, they would slip out to 'Camp Two' to sink a few beers and loudly discuss security matters.
>
> This particular officer – suave, besuited and the epitome of the old guard – downed his first pint and quickly ordered another. I was slightly taken aback, but when he ordered another and then another I was surprised to say the least. After five pints he finally stopped and we staggered back to the

office. He then retired to his private office, closed the door and drifted off to sleep. My colleagues told me it was a daily occurrence.[40]

Such drinking habits could directly impede security operations. One serious case, in 1991, involved an MI5 operation against a Czech intelligence officer in London. The Czech had been under surveillance for weeks by a team from A4 section. 'MI5 knew he had been acting suspiciously and were desperate to find out what he was up to,' said Shayler. 'Unfortunately, the MI5 officer in charge was incompetent and unable to take his alcohol.'

One evening the officer met up with a group of friends for a drinking session. As the night progressed and the alcohol loosened his tongue, he began to boast to his curious companions – none of whom were in the Security Service – that he was engaged in top-secret surveillance of a Czech spy. His friends were slightly sceptical so the officer stood up. 'Come on,' he bragged, 'I'll bloody well show you!' And with that he led the motley crew of drunks out of the pub and directly to the Czech's house.

When they arrived the revellers bellowed through the letter-box, 'Wake up, you Commie bastard! We know you're a spy.' As the commotion mounted, the MI5 surveillance team sitting in a bedroom in a house directly across the street could hardly believe their ears and eyes. They were unsure what was happening and immediately called for support. In the confusion, the back-up team thought the loud drinkers were associates of the Czech spy.

The second A4 surveillance team was then directed to follow the revellers home. The next morning they told MI5 headquarters they had followed one member of the gang back to a house and, crucially, watched him put his key in the front door. As they believed he was somehow connected to the Czech spy, this was a breakthrough – 'housing the target', as it is known in intelligence jargon. It was, they thought, a major coup.

After the operation the A4 surveillance team reported their findings to the relevant desk officer. He checked the address against MI5 records, only to find that the house belonged to one of his colleagues. This was relayed to senior management and the officer admitted that the 'source' for the Czech spy was himself in the company of drunken friends. The surveillance team were shocked and dumbstruck, but they were even more amazed when they discovered that no disciplinary action was taken against the officer and he remained in his position.[41]

To Shayler, this was characteristic of MI5 in the early 1990s – complacent, old-fashioned and inefficient. The Service had fallen behind in its management practices, notably in information technology and personnel. Apart from recruitment, it indicated little interest in modernisation and professionalism. This became more serious when its annual budget was cut. It is no secret that management efficiency becomes more important when an agency has fewer resources, but branch and assistant directors appeared more concerned about protecting their bureaucratic empires. For example, MI5 has far too many middle managers, nearly all of them untrained, some promoted purely due to length of tenure, and many incompetent.

However, for decades it has resisted an external overview of its efficiency, citing 'security reasons'. It was not until late 1996 that management consultants were first commissioned, at a cost of tens of thousands of pounds, to review its working practices. Even so their advice was ignored. A few months later, the Service was subject to a management audit system imposed on all government departments, called 'Investors In People', designed to ensure that the objectives of each department were linked and matched with proper management structures, internal communications and training. Staff were not surprised that MI5 failed the official investigation.[42]

Until 1990–91, MI5's job as spycatcher was largely routine. The targets were the same: the Communist Party HQ in King Street, the Soviet embassy in Kensington Park Gardens and its trade delegation in Highgate. But the world was changing rapidly. The new threats were not only different – IRA and Arab terrorists – they used unfamiliar operational techniques. As the young intake of '91 settled into their desk jobs, the new world order provided MI5 with a stark challenge: was it willing and able to change? More importantly, was it equipped to do so?

3

THE SPYING GAME

'We do disagreeable things so that ordinary people here and elsewhere can sleep safely in their beds at night. Is that too romantic? Of
course, occasionally we do very wicked things . . .'

John le Carré, *The Spy Who Came In From The Cold*

The overnight flights arriving at Gatwick airport were packed with
the usual mix of businessmen and holiday-makers. As the bleary-
eyed passengers walked into the packed terminal, a tall, awkward-
looking man in his late 30s walked hesitantly among the waiting
crowds. Uncertain whom to approach, he tried to strike up casual
conversations. His mission was to gather enough information to
identify a complete stranger, simply by chatting to someone. He was
an MI5 officer and he was tasked to obtain the stranger's name, date
of birth and full address.

Alarmed by his inhibited, self-conscious manner and unconvinc-
ing cover story of being a journalist working on a story about
airports, few people would talk to him. Eventually someone became
so concerned that they approached airport staff. He had already
been spotted by security guards who were suspicious, so when the
awkward young man tried to interview officials they were wary. 'Do
you have any credentials?' asked one. Blushing, he groped in his
pockets and realised he did not have a press card or proof of identity. He was asked to leave the airport or be arrested.

Two hundred and fifty miles away, the same anxious-looking man
was well known to Merseyside Special Branch. A few years earlier, he
had been taken to a smoky working-class pub in Toxteth. When
asked what he would like to drink, he replied, in a Home Counties

cut-glass accent, 'I'll have a *crème de menthe*, please.' This immediately attracted suspicion to him and his police colleagues.

Across the Pennines, two experienced Special Branch officers in Sheffield, south Yorkshire, waited to meet their new MI5 liaison officer. They sighed and rolled their eyes when he walked into their office. Wearing an Old Harrovian tie and sports jacket, the trainee was a Classics graduate from Oxbridge. He was entirely unsuitable for his assigned role: advising hardened north-eastern Special Branch officers in the skills of agent-handling.

Sensing an opportunity to wind him up, the police told him they had bet the entire year's agent-handling budget on a horse. Pausing to let this sink in, they added, 'And it lost.' The officer panicked and was only calmed down with the news that the policemen were joking. 'In fact,' they confided, 'it won.' This, however, only alarmed him more as he knew he would have to explain to his bosses in MI5 that Special Branch had illegally acquired a larger agent-handling budget. Eventually, the police admitted they had fabricated the whole episode.

These uncomfortable MI5 officers were supposed to have the interpersonal skills to cope with such situations. They were sent out to learn the trade of one of MI5's most sensitive operations: how to be secret agents. Despite massive advances in modern technology, the human source, informer or spy is still the most effective method of gathering valuable intelligence. People are more likely to disclose important information if they trust the person. If the undercover MI5 officer is edgy, the source will realise this and be less inclined to supply information or be recruited. But MI5 has a curious policy of training agents: former public-school girls are sent to converse with tough northerners, and shy intellectuals are despatched to recruit agents in West Belfast. It is thought that this is a good way to groom versatile, all-round desk officers, and, in theory, it sounds like a constructive strategy, but it is based on the hope that recruits will somehow adopt new personality traits and gain skills that would otherwise be alien to them. Forcing introverted academics to recruit secret agents has not worked and has caused resentment and frustration. Instead of utilising their talents as specialist analysts and researchers, MI5 has sent them out because it was 'their turn' rather than because of their aptitude for the work. Inevitably, this has resulted in officers becoming disillusioned and many leaving the Security Service.

Although agents are the most important source of intelligence,

MI5 has been neglectful in this area. While MI6 and HM Customs view recruiting and running agents as a top priority, MI5 see it as just one of several different techniques. 'The great difference between MI5 and most of the intelligence services is that people are not routinely taught how to run agents,' said David Shayler. 'MI5, having this kind of bureaucratic history and having modelled itself on the Home Civil Service, is very bad at recruiting agents. It doesn't recruit enough of them.' Instead, the agency places more of a premium on paper skills.

Former MI5 director-general Dame Stella Rimington agrees with Shayler about the importance of agents. In her memoirs, she recalls the most effective method of agent-recruitment:

'You needed a fairly well-developed imagination and good amateur dramatics skills. But none of it was any good unless you could also make a convincing recruitment pitch to your target when the moment came to drop your cover and emerge as a member of British intelligence. The skill was to be able simultaneously to explain the deceit you had been practising on your target and to inspire his confidence in you, all in a very short time, before he panicked and left.

'Much imagination was expended in thinking of ways to get alongside the targets, who were mostly fairly well protected inside their embassies. Many a bizarre scheme was dreamed up to strike an acquaintance. Nothing you read in a spy story is more unlikely than some of the things that went on in those days. If I ever see a jogger in the park apparently spraining his ankle or a dog suddenly keel over and look sick, I look carefully at the scene to see if I can make out a likely target there and detect at work the successors of those agent-running officers of the 1970s.'[1]

Most agents are recruited from members of organisations and persuaded to work for the Service – as opposed to MI5 officers infiltrating an organisation from the outside. MI5 or Special Branch personnel might know a friend of a friend and approaches are discreet and careful. However, they are sometimes clumsy and backfire. In 1981, Adrian Chandler, a Conservative student at Aston University, Birmingham, was approached by two Special Branch officers. 'What we're interested in,' said one, 'is left-wing political subversives. The place is crawling with them.' Chandler resented the approach and refused to help. He complained to the chief constable of West Midlands police force, who refused to take any action against the two officers.[2]

People usually work for MI5 as agents because they are disillusioned for ideological reasons. They have lost the faith politically and regret their past actions. They have become patriots, notably in the case of former IRA operatives, and are thus highly motivated. Some turn because of personality clashes within the group and want to take revenge against former comrades, while others are motivated by cash payments. Then there are those who enjoy the thrill of doing important, glamorous-seeming secret work for MI5 and being taken into its confidence.

By far the most effective method of hiring an agent is to describe the proposition in terms of how it will help them. In running a check, MI5 may discover that he or she has committed a minor legal transgression, has financial problems or needs a job. The mention of such a factor subtly during a conversation is often beneficial, although some argue it is tantamount to blackmail. If the pressure is on, MI5 will also manufacture problems for the target. 'Sometimes,' a former officer told the *Guardian*, 'the position is created for a man so that MI5 can come along and help him – a bit like breaking a man's leg so you can offer him a crutch.'[3]

For foreign spies based in the UK, their immigration status is often used as a way to approach them. David Shayler recalled, 'I had to identify Libyan intelligence officers in Britain, get to know what they were doing, then interview them to assess whether we could turn them or not. Of course, I had intelligence on these people, so I was sitting there chatting with them about their immigration prospects, knowing they had blood on their hands. What I knew about them came from sensitive sources, and if I gave that away they'd know who was working with the Brits. It was quite a challenge.'[4]

Long-term agents and informants are run by specialist case officers in each branch or by Special Branch officers advised by MI5. This operation needs special care and attention. It is only these officers, known as 'handlers', who know the identity of their agents, and often build up a complex psychological and emotional relationship with them. Trust and reliability are of key importance, but this is undermined by MI5's posting policy. No sooner has a handler built up a special rapport with an agent than he is moved to another branch.

Once recruited, secret informants can supply priceless inside information and may influence the course of events. As David Shayler says:

'An agent is the bread and butter of information. The best way of getting information is by talking to somebody. MI5 has lots of technical capabilities, but if, for example, you are putting a listening device in a room and you walk next door, you have lost the product [source of intelligence]. But if you have an agent, they can follow that person around, you can task them to find a particular piece of intelligence and so on ... You know when they are going to meetings, you know when they are going to do something wrong and that is when you can put the surveillance on and pick up more intelligence.

'There are problems in running an agent because they are human beings: they get drunk and do stupid things. However, generally, the quality of intelligence that an agent produces is far better than any of the technical stuff and that includes GCHQ. And they are very cheap as well. When you are running an agent in, say, West Belfast and you recruit an IRA member, you'll be paying that guy about ten pounds a week. This is because if you pay him more than ten pounds a week, other people in West Belfast are unemployed and they're going to wonder where he got that extra money from. So it is a very cheap and effective way of gathering intelligence.'

Some organisations have been easier to penetrate than others. Operatives in terrorist groups are security-conscious and run their own vetting procedures against spies. But small political parties are easier to penetrate because they often need new members who are willing to undertake tedious paperwork. Agents tend to volunteer for roles that give best access to information and some become full-time officials.

Throughout the Cold War, the Communist Party of Great Britain (CPGB) was deeply penetrated by MI5. In the 1950s, a young woman called Betty Gordon was paid the princely sum of one pound a week by MI5 during a decade of political espionage. Her cover was twofold: she was an accounts clerk at the London office of *Soviet*

Weekly and she also spent a year as a live-in nanny at the house of Betty Reid, a senior CPGB member. Gordon had been recruited by MI5 after answering an advertisement in *The Times* for girls of good education with secretarial skills. She was instructed to memorise any information she discovered, including telephone numbers, and not write anything on paper. She was also asked to copy keys for Reid's house and office.[5]

The Trotskyist Socialist Workers Party (SWP) was also infiltrated, but only at grass-roots level. Despite its relatively small membership and minimal influence, MI5 recruited 25 agents to spy on SWP activists over a period of 30 years. They were motivated not only by cash inducements but also by ideological disaffection. Money was also the major reason why some 30 Militant Tendency (MT) members informed on their Trotskyist comrades for MI5. In the early 1990s, the number of agents inside the SWP and MT was reduced to a handful.

Based on their stated aim to undermine parliamentary democracy, the far right were also targeted. In the late 1970s, the National Front was seen as the major threat. Ronnie White, a Jew, was recruited by Special Branch after it was discovered that he had infiltrated the National Front on behalf of a Jewish organisation. Using a false name, he was given a rented flat in Leeds while secretly helping Special Branch to compile files on Fascist activists and photograph them. Unfortunately, in order to sustain his cover, White was also required to participate in violent attacks on black people. 'I did things while I was in the Front which I have got to live with for the rest of my life,' he recalled later, in an interview with 20/20 Television. 'We'd go in force, find a small group of coloureds and hit them with pickaxe handles.'[6]

More recently, as the National Front declined into a mere rump, the British National Party (BNP) has been seen as a more dangerous threat. By the early 1990s, MI5 had successfully recruited or turned several agents inside the BNP, although they also retained some full-time active agents inside the National Front.

More controversially, MI5 spies were placed inside trade unions, notably at least one inside the National Union of Mineworkers during the 1984–85 strike. 'These people were working within, sometimes actually employed by, legitimate organisations, working for the good of their members in the trade-union movement,' said Cathy Massiter, a senior MI5 officer from 1970 until 1983. 'And yet they have this dual role of reporting back to the Security Service certain aspects of what goes on within the union. It's a very ambivalent moral area.'[7] These industrial moles were asked to turn others, particularly in the local union structure.

While it is highly doubtful that small left-wing parties and trade unions ever threatened the security of the state, the same cannot be said of the IRA. In the 1980s and early 1990s the Metropolitan Police Special Branch did not have a single agent inside an IRA cell on the British mainland. Their main source of information was from telephone tapping. At one stage an informant walked in and provided valuable intelligence, but Special Branch lost control of him.

Money was rarely a motivating factor, but personal family problems were exploited as a way of turning comrades against each other. On many occasions IRA members were told by friends secretly working for MI5: 'Did you know that "Sean" is sleeping with your wife?' When they expressed outrage, the process of possible recruitment was set in motion.

Despite conventional wisdom, former MI5 and MI6 officers say they never used 'honey-trapping' – attractive female agents to ensnare vulnerable foreign intelligence officers. It was a technique employed mainly by the KGB in the Soviet Union to compromise visiting politicians and diplomats. New archive evidence shows that even Mata Hari, the Dutch erotic dancer who was executed by the French in 1917 for spying for Germany, did not provide any useful information to the enemy. In fact, she was probably a victim of a miscarriage of justice.

It has been established that agents are the most effective and cost-effective method of intelligence-gathering. While there is a danger that they may become a double-agent and work for both sides, it is extremely difficult for targeted organisations to know when they have been penetrated. The agents' real value is not only inside information – when and where a terrorist bomb is likely to explode – but as an enabling asset for other intelligence operations to take place.

An agent can supply the core data needed for some of MI5's most controversial techniques – breaking into premises and triggering static and mobile surveillance. Once an agent is in place, all these sensitive activities are more feasible. Known as 'Technical Operations', they are carried out by A Branch based at Euston Tower, near King's Cross. Physical surveillance teams – never referred to as 'watchers' in MI5 – are a small group of highly skilled specialist operatives who work in vehicles, on foot and from fixed observation posts. They only carry out surveillance and are not involved in intelligence assessments. They are highly regarded within the Service, while doing a job that is, according to Peter Wright, 'most of the time very dull, but which requires a lot of skill and intelligence, as well as patience and a phenomenal memory'.[8]

Known as A4, or the A-Team, these operatives are a curious mixture of people. 'We had a former RAF pilot who had flown Lysanders into France during the war and was confined to a wheel-chair,' one of the section's former officers told the BBC's Mark Urban. 'He would sit in flats overlooking Warsaw Pact embassies. We had another couple of chaps who had been supermarket managers and joined us in their 50s – don't ask me why we recruited them. Then, of course, there were quite a lot of ex-Army NCOs.'[9]

They are a highly effective crack unit. MI6 officers being trained for agent-running found themselves pitting their wits against the A4 in exercises on British streets. 'The truth is, it's impossible to spot them,' a former MI6 officer told Urban. 'They are very professional and they use an extraordinary variety of people: a black man driving a taxi or an old woman carrying her shopping.'[10]

The reality of physical surveillance is far from a Hollywood thriller starring Harrison Ford. 'It's not like someone walking down a street behind someone else,' said Shayler. 'It is done with teams of people. If you are following someone who is trained in losing or spotting surveillance, it can be very difficult to follow these kind of people around. I know of cases with IRA terrorists where you could not actually have them under what we call "eyeball" – where you can actually see the target. What you have is "target-controlled". You would have a number of cars in a number of streets all talking to each other through secure communications. They would have the car under control, but they wouldn't actually be able to see the target . . . If you put someone under surveillance for one day, just following them around, it can cost anything up to £10,000.'

Although MI5's cars are equipped with souped-up engines and special suspension, it remains difficult to follow moving targets. Vehicles have been modernised to meet this challenge. Based at a garage in Streatham High Street, south London – officially for use by the Department of Environment – MI5 mechanics go to work. The cars are equipped with VHF aerials, disguised as wing-mirrors, with UHF aerials fitted into a small fin on the rear shelf of the car. Radio messages are encrypted to prevent eavesdroppers intercepting communications. Servicing is undertaken in the strictest secrecy at a depot in Crawford Street, central London, guarded by uniformed government security officers.[11]

During the Cold War, the A Team's chief target was KGB officers and Eastern-bloc diplomats based in the UK, who used every evasive device to escape their shadows. It was a battle of wills and skills as cars packed with heavyweight Soviet security men would drive around London at high speed, creating false trails. Such is the technical aptitude of A4 that they have been redirected to chasing new targets such as terrorists.[12]

Another function of A4 is manning 'Stat OPs' (Static Observation Posts) in houses directly overlooking the entrances of hostile embassies. Faces are checked against a 'mug book' containing thousands of photographs of foreign intelligence officers. When Peter Wright left MI5 in 1975, 250 of his colleagues were operating out of a house in Regent's Park and later from Euston Tower. 'They spent their time sitting in drab rooms equipped with binoculars, telephoto camera, a log book and an overflowing ashtray,' recalled the former spycatcher.[13] Even more monotonous would be sitting in a car, waiting for something to happen. 'At one point I had to work with Special Branch,' recalled Shayler. 'I spent 12 hours watching this woman and she didn't go out once. Surveillance is duller than you thought possible.'[14]

Once the surveillance has been undertaken, officers are ready to implement MI5's most controversial operation: breaking into and entering private homes, offices and diplomatic properties. Every year a small batch of new recruits is sent out in pairs for the day, ordered to choose a house and draw up detailed plans of how to burgle the place. 'We had to note how busy the street was, whether the neighbours were there during the day,' said a former MI5 officer, 'whether there was a nosy cleaning lady or workman around and where the best escape routes were. Then we took the [operational] plans back and they were looked at by the A Team, who told us we were useless and then gave us their version of how to burgle the place.'[15]

Known as 'covert search', these officers are based in A1A section and assisted by specialist lock-pickers and carpenters in A1D. Breaking and entering by MI5 officers is known euphemistically as 'interfering with property', and requires a 'property warrant', approved and signed by the Home Secretary. Hundreds of warrants are issued every year, but only a small percentage lead to burglaries. The operatives tend to be ultra-cautious because of the high risk of being caught.

Before any operation begins, the target and his home are watched until the undercover officers have a clear idea of his routine. They wait for a time when all the residents are likely to be far away from base. When the break-in team moves forward, a second unit – usually staffed by Special Branch – is on watch outside, and other surveillance officers check for people in the vicinity. If the target appears to be on the verge of returning unexpectedly, they may try to divert him or her.[16]

Once inside the building the officers aim to leave everything precisely as it was when they broke in. They even take photographs of the scene so that they can leave the premises as they found them. If the odd document or computer disk is out of place, you can be sure it was not an MI5 operation but a 'normal' robbery. The A1A officers prefer to leave the rooms entirely untouched, but if they are rumbled by the occupant they trash them to make it look as though a routine burglary has taken place.

Until the 1989 Security Service Act such activity was illegal. Indeed, in 1963, Lord Denning said in his report on the Profumo scandal that MI5 had 'no special powers of search . . . they cannot enter premises without the consent of the householder, even though they may suspect a spy is there'. Most MI5 officers operated on the basis of what Peter Wright called the 11th Commandment: 'Thou shalt not get caught – and that in the event of apprehension there was little the office could do to protect its staff.' In the mid-1980s, a group of recruits attended a seminar run by Bernard Sheldon, MI5's legal officer, at their training centre in Grosvenor Street, Mayfair. When asked what would happen if one was caught red-handed during a break-in, Sheldon merely replied that the Service had always got away with it so far.[17]

Since the 1989 Act was passed, MI5 has legal immunity as long as it has a property warrant from the Home Secretary. A1A officers are instructed not to steal anything and only to photocopy or photograph documents and pictures. This is to ensure that no trace is left on the premises. They have the capacity to copy the entire contents of a computer hard drive.

Such clandestine entries were used extensively against the

Communist Party and other 'subversive' groups. As MI5 could not open a file on an individual without proof of the target's membership, a covert search would be implemented. During the Cold War, membership lists were seen as the most valuable source of intelligence. The most notorious burglary was of the Mayfair flat of a wealthy Communist Party member in 1955, while he was away for a weekend in the Lake District. In 'Operation Partypiece', MI5 officers copied all 55,000 membership files, including those of 'crypto' and 'covert' Communists. This ensured, claimed Peter Wright, that 'the Communist Party was never again in a position to seriously threaten the safety of the realm'.[18]

Another major reason for break-ins is to install bugging devices. Some are planted by drilling a tiny hole in an adjoining wall from a neighbouring property. A probe microphone is then installed to pick up conversations in the house or office next door. The most common method, though, is to plant them inside the room. Burglary is not always required. Sometimes MI5 will task British Telecom and other telephone companies to put a fault on a target's line. When the subscriber reports it, a special technician from the company is sent to the address, where he installs a listening device.

If an MI5 agent is resident at the premises, he can let officers in at an opportune moment, but covert entry is preferred for several reasons: there may be time pressures, the target may be getting suspicious or an agent may not be in place.

One documented case was the break-in to the house of Ken Gill, a member of the TUC General Council and from 1974 until 1988 the general secretary of TASS, the union that represented white-collar workers in the engineering industry. A long-standing Communist Party member and activist, his home telephone was tapped, but he underwent even closer scrutiny in the late 1970s, when TASS planned to merge with the manual engineering union, AUEW. Gill was at the heart of the negotiations and held important meetings about the proposal at his house in south London. According to a sworn statement by a former MI5 clerk given to 20/20 Television: 'His [Gill's] home was broken into and a bug placed inside a room to monitor talks between Mr Gill and other trade unionists prior to or during the merger. I found this a sinister intrusion into a person's civil rights and privacy.'[19]

Such operations have not always proved successful. In the 1970s, a bug was found on the leg of a wooden table inside the Communist Party head office in King Street. Unperturbed, MI5 decided to plant the device inside a piece of furniture where it was more difficult to detect. Through an intermediary, a sofa was sold to the Communist Party containing an MI5 microphone. The only problem was that a senior Party official did not like it and soon sold it on to a second-hand furniture dealer.

Covert searches and eavesdropping have been used more frequently in Northern Ireland, always with assistance from the RUC Special Branch. This back-up can be useful. If the agent is on the point of being discovered, techniques may be used to delay the person.

There have been some close calls in Ulster. In the early 1970s, Peter Wright broke into a house to install a tiny microphone. While walking in the loft he put his foot through a ceiling and the mission had to be aborted. Wright and his colleague ransacked the property to make it look like a 'normal' burglary and scuttled away into the night. In recent years, such operations have been of limited value – but senior MI5 directors continue to support and authorise them.

In February 1999, Dame Stella Rimington said that all intelligence agencies should have the legal power to break into people's homes to obtain information on international terrorists. She told a committee of legislators in New Zealand that their intelligence service needed these extra legal rights as the country contained targets for terrorism. Home break-ins are currently illegal in New Zealand. 'Terrorists often choose a country where they think that the security regime may be lax,' said Rimington. 'You've got the targets here. You've got US embassies, British and Israeli targets and you have international conferences to which important people from those countries and others at risk come.'

She cited terrorist attacks on US embassies in Dar es Salaam and Nairobi, American interests in South Africa and the 1998 attack on the Israeli embassy in Argentina. She said that since the Cold War there had been greater movement of terrorists internationally, often using false passports, as transport and access to countries has become easier. 'Without the power to enter, to eavesdrop and to search, you can't be an effective security service,' she concluded.[20]

However, other former MI5 officers argue that clandestine break-ins should only be used in exceptional circumstances – if at all. The modern international terrorist does not leave incriminating or sensitive material in their office, home or hotel room. Even their travel plans are deliberately made at the last minute and are subject to late change. An operation to plant a device can cost hundreds of thousands of pounds, which will be wasted if the target decides to use another room for a meeting. Unless he or she is an Inspector Clouseau-type amateur (which means they will be caught easily), then a search of their premises is highly unlikely to be beneficial.

Another outdated operation is the interception of mail. This is one of the oldest forms of intelligence-gathering, used extensively by Britain's first Prime Minister, Robert Walpole. A 'secret man' was installed with his own private room inside the Post Office where every night between 11 p.m. and 4 a.m. he opened, read and resealed any 'suspicious' letter. In 1711, Parliament insisted that no letter could be opened without a signed warrant from a Secretary of State, but the law was constantly flouted by secret agents who ignored the warrant system on the basis that 'secrecy made legality unimportant'. Many letters were intercepted based on warrants couched in the vaguest terms. And if concerns were raised in Parliament, the pretext of 'public safety' was used by ministers to avoid answering any awkward questions. In 1845, there was a Home Office inquiry, but it rejected calls for a law to prevent the Post Office opening people's mail on behalf of the Secret Service.[21]

Not a huge amount has changed in the past 150 years. In the pre-telephone, fax and motor-car era, letter-writing was the common form of communication and mail-tampering was the obvious means to keep track of a suspect's plans. During the Cold War, it was seen as a vital weapon as membership applications to subversive political parties were sent by post. It is still part of MI5's armoury today. A warrant signed by the Home Secretary is required, although there are loopholes. The mail of an organisation may be subject to a warrant, and may cover a range of people who happen to work for it or share its offices.

Mail-tampering is conducted by a special section called 'Post Office Bureau Services', a unit inside the 300-strong Post Office Investigation Division, which liaises directly with MI5. In London, targeted letters and packages are sent from local sorting offices to Union House in St Martin's-Le-Grand, near St Paul's Cathedral. There, the material is opened by specialists using equipment ranging from a hot needle to steam from a kettle. Extreme care is taken not to leave signs of tampering. In very rare cases, a letter might be withheld if it is deemed sufficiently important and suspicious. MI5 would never allow a letter that had been damaged in the process of interception to be passed on to the recipient. Any parcel or letter received torn was not subject to MI5 tampering. Most forms of written communication can now be intercepted using modern technology.

When opened, the material inside is photocopied. The copies are sent to MI5's office at Thames House for analysis and filing. Some people who suspect their mail is being intercepted place loose hairs or feathers under the envelope flaps in an attempt to catch out the tamperers. In the past, Post Office workers fell into this trap but now they are trained to replace such items. The priority is to ensure that the targeted mail arrives at its destination on time looking undisturbed. In 95 per cent of cases, if letters have been delayed or have not arrived at all, you can be sure that they have not been intercepted by MI5.

Mail-tampering is not a valuable, cost-effective method of intelligence-gathering. It consumes a huge amount of time and resources as all the post, even junk mail, is opened and photocopied. More significantly, no terrorist or any serious target is stupid enough to send incriminating or revealing documents through the post. It was useful for obtaining copies of membership cards, but the new security threats do not invite people to become members via the post.

If a target's mail is being intercepted, it is highly likely that their tele-phone is being tapped, too. For an intercept to be placed on the public-telephone network, a warrant is required from the Home Secretary. It can only be issued 'in the interests of national security, for the prevention or detection of serious crime or in order to safe-guard the economic well-being of the United Kingdom'.

Before MI5 proceeds with an application, the desk officer sends a minute consisting of the target's name, telephone number and a supporting justification to his line manager. A meeting is then held to discuss the case. Crucial issues are aired: 'Is there a case?'; 'What are the intelligence criteria?'; 'Can we obtain the information from other sources?'; 'Have other methods of investigation been tried and failed?'

If satisfied by the merits of the case, the desk officer will then draft the warrant. This is a summary of the intelligence 'justification' for the tap, and is passed to his line manager who checks it for accu-racy. After incorporating his amendments, the minute is passed back for further verification.

It is at this stage that MI5's bureaucratic procedures come into play. Several hours, even days, are spent on management tinkering with the precise wording of the warrant. 'I am absolutely full square behind all forms of protecting civil liberties,' David Shayler told BBC's *Newsnight*. 'But the way in which it was done was almost counter-productive to the investigation. You have to go through a deputy assistant director of the branch, then an assistant director, a director, over to H Branch [corporate affairs], back to the desk officer, back to H Branch and then the deputy director-general would see it. Finally [after his or her approval] you could probably go ahead.'[22]

As everything has to be done in writing, this is a laborious and time-consuming ordeal. The process has nothing to do with protecting people's civil rights or privacy – after all, MI5 has already decided to tap the target's telephone: it is about management justifying their positions and budgets and showing they are contributing in some way. If any word on the warrant is changed, then it is returned to the previous section for retyping and redistribution. MI5 directors spend hours over grammar and vocabulary with bizarre consequences worthy of a *Yes, Minister* script. For example, 'may' will be changed to 'might' and 'but' to 'however'. Even commas are deleted then reinstated. Quite often a director amends his own amendments. Sometimes, the wording of the warrant is changed back to its original form.

None of this linguistic indulgence has anything to do with checking a warrant's accuracy or whether it is justified. The officers are simply perusing and changing the draft's wording. An exercise that should take a desk officer a morning and his managers about half an hour each, occupies up to three days of their time. This, of course, gives MI5 officers less time to investigate targets and offers terrorists more time to escape detection. In Shayler's view, the pedantic method of warrant-processing seriously impedes and endangers intelligence operations.

Once the intercept warrant has been agreed it is forwarded to the Home Office. In the past, according to former MI5 officer Cathy Massiter, the application 'will be minuted with a one paragraph summary of two or three sentences, known as 'the short reason', which provides the justification for a warrant. This is usually all that the Secretary of State and the Permanent Secretary will see unless they request more.'[23] But, according to Shayler, the system is open to abuse: 'People can select and bump up information to make it look more important than it actually is,' he said. 'I wouldn't say they [MI5 officers] lied, but by taking information out of context to make it more important than it is, you can make a case sound quite strong.' Now MI5 sends the Home Office much more detail.

Within the Home Office the requests are scrutinised by the Permanent Secretary. After discussing the application with MI5 management, he consults the Home Secretary who makes the final decision. 'The process is not a straightforward one,' Leon Brittan, Home Secretary from 1983 until 1985, told Parliament. 'Unless there is urgency, there is much interchange between the agency [MI5] and those who advise the relevant Secretary of State.'[24] It is an uncomfortable moment for Labour home secretaries: they may be authorising MI5 surveillance on people with whom they have shared a public platform – trade unionists or even Party members.

By law, the Home Secretary can refuse to issue a warrant, but it is most unlikely that he or she will and they are nearly always authorised. 'The Home Secretary would be very loath to reject an MI5 warrant,' said Shayler, 'simply because he knows what would happen if something did go wrong. It would rebound on him politically, so he would be very loath to do it.'

The warrants run for six months and are regularly reviewed. 'Every three months the Permanent Secretary and Home Secretary go over the list and discuss whether or not to continue tapping individual members,' revealed Lord Callaghan, the former Prime Minister and Home Secretary.[25] But MI5 has the upper hand. 'It is very easy to review an intercept warrant once you have one,' said Shayler. 'Quite often some of the warrant renewals would say nothing has happened, but the case against the person remains good and the Home Secretary would sign that.'

There are loopholes: if the minister is away from the office, a civil servant of under-secretary status or above may sign the warrant, which is valid for two days. This may only be done if the Home Secretary has been informed of the reasons for the warrant.

In the past, there has also been collusion between officials and MI5 to backdate applications for taps that were already in place. This was done, without notifying the minister, by a benign official who brushed aside the red tape.[26] There is some nervousness within Whitehall about the effortless ease with which old warrants are renewed. Some of the information that justified the warrants was years old. That same data, however out of date, had been used to renew the warrants time and again. According to former Home Secretary Merlyn (now Lord) Rees: 'Some taps continue for a long time . . . They are blanket tappings. They are not on individuals.'[27] Another loophole is that in an emergency the deputy director-general of MI5 can sign a property warrant.

However, Jack Straw, who has been Home Secretary since 1997, is confident that the warrant system is not abused: 'One of the ways I know what they're [MI5] up to', said Straw, in an interview with the BBC's Michael Cockerell, 'is through my role authorising warrants for telephone tapping and other intrusive surveillance. That gives you a strong week-by-week sense of their major operations and gives you an authority to decide whether or not these operations should go ahead.'[28]

The experience of other Labour Home Secretaries does not support Straw's sanguine view. Lord Jenkins was highly sceptical of MI5's activities. During a House of Lords debate in 1993, he revealed that he had been forced to threaten MI5 and his officials before they allowed him to see all the warrants: 'It required some effort – indeed going on strike – in order to ensure that one saw the overall list,' recalled Lord Jenkins, 'which I thought was wholly desirable in the interests of ministerial supervision.' In a warning to ministers, he added, 'Never automatically sign anything coming up from the Security Service and be very cautious about signing it. It is increasingly my conviction that the Security Services cause more trouble than they are worth.'[29]

Jenkins's successor as Home Secretary, Merlyn Rees, took a close interest in MI5's eavesdropping operations. He visited the technical facilities, and since leaving government has spoken of his experiences. During his period in office (1976–79), he said, between 250 and 400 warrants were in force. But, more significantly, he disclosed that in fact 2–3,000 phone lines were tapped.[30] This is because, as with the mail-tampering, one warrant can cover a whole organisation, resulting in the bugging of perhaps thousands of members' or employees' work lines. Parliamentary questions to subsequent home secretaries on whether interception orders are cumulative in this way have remained unanswered.

The warrant system is full of anomalies. If MI5 wants to listen in on phone calls made by a British citizen living abroad, it does not need a warrant, it simply uses GCHQ. If a target is living in rented accommodation, MI5 needs only the permission of the landlord to enter the premises and place a bugging device without a warrant.

Some of these aberrations were disclosed by John McWilliam, a Labour MP and a former British Telecom engineer, who spent 20 years in the design, construction and maintenance of the telephone system. 'It is wrong to say that interception has not happened without warrants,' he said. 'Certain official tappings do not require warrants. That derives from an institutional relationship between the police, Special Branch and British Telecom. I do not believe the Home Secretary would recognise a bug if it jumped up and bit him.'[31] In reality, the Security Service is treated differently from the police and given far more latitude.

The actual tapping technology is operated by carefully selected and security-vetted telephone engineers. Paid out of a secret Home Office budget, these engineers belong to a special section of the companies. If the telephone about to be tapped is served by an old-fashioned exchange, the engineer has to visit the exchange in person and make a technical adjustment.

But there are other methods: 'A well-known secret service trick is that if a target is not actually using the phone much, MI5 asks BT to place a fault on the line,' said David Shayler. 'The unsuspecting punter then contacts BT who agree to send an engineer. Unbeknown to the target, the engineer works in a special section of BT called Operational Network Division. He then places a microphone in the phone junction box on the wall which records conversations in the room and sends them down the line back to the transcribers in Thames House (MI5's HQ).'[32]

With the more modern digital exchanges, telephones can be intercepted from BT premises at Euston Tower. As a result of these technical interventions, the entire traffic on the intercepted telephone is fed to MI5 transcribers at Thames House by a secure digital line. Since 1995, the transcribers have used a computer system known as Marshbrook, which has expanded the number of lines that may be intercepted. They are transcribed, analysed, logged and filed.

The transcribing process is then absorbed into MI5's unique bureaucracy. Once the conversations are typed into the computer, a printed copy is sent to a desk officer who marks up and analyses its contents. Occasionally the transcripts are inaccurate, as anyone who reads recorded transcripts will confirm: human dialogue is ungrammatical, ambiguous and open to misinterpretation. In calls involving

Irish terrorist suspects, English transcribers often have problems in understanding the heavy accents and the slang. This leads to misinterpretation of intelligence and creates serious problems.

An estimated 35,000 telephone lines are tapped every year for MI5, Special Branch, the police and Customs.[33] Contrary to popular legend, noises such as static, clicks or blips and crossed lines are not proof of bugging by MI5. This was confirmed in 1991 by the Commissioner for the Interception of Communications who stated: 'Neither the connection of the device itself, nor the interception of communications by such means, is audible in any way to the subscriber.'[33]

The relentless advance in modern technology has resulted in MI5 being able to tap most telephones, including mobiles. It has reached frightening proportions. BT's new System X now enables engineers to tap phones without interfering physically with individual lines or company switchboards. It is run from a new, high-security installation called the National Network Central Operations Unit, based at Oswestry, Shropshire.[35]

Information sent by computer is likely to be the next target and in 1999 MI5 lobbied the Home Office to make it easier to intercept e-mails. Under these plans, MI5 and MI6 would be given new powers to monitor paedophiles and terrorists operating on the Internet. MI5 would be able to hack into e-mails and access scrambled documents. In June 1999, then Home Secretary Jack Straw proposed that intercepting messages on the Internet should be incorporated into existing law – the Interception of Communications Act. This means that Internet providers will have to redesign their systems to allow easy tapping by MI5.

But Whitehall is concerned: the Department of Trade and Industry reflects the business community's fears that its commercial secrets will be available for government perusal. Commercial encryption systems, such as PGP, are already widespread and the issue now is the extent to which such enforcement agencies should be able to demand the 'keys' that unscramble such systems.[36]

Stimulated by new technology, BT's specialist team of tappers has increased in recent years. Between 1990 and 1992 it grew by 50 per cent. According to John McWilliam, the former BT engineer, 'The number of staff have increased from 50 to 75 . . . 75 do about 35,000 intercepts a year if they keep busy at it. Since the number of warrants issued is only about 500, and although some of these warrants will cover a number of lines, it still does not explain why that number of staff is needed. It's clear that a lot of unwarranted intercepts are going on.'[37] In recent years 1,000-plus warrants have been issued annually.

This expansion is reflected in the increasing number of warrants issued by the government. In 1981, 464 warrants were authorised by the Home Secretary, the Foreign Secretary and the Northern Ireland and Scottish Secretaries, serviced by 40 engineers. By 1992, the figure was up to 843 by 70 tappers, although that excludes the Foreign Office, which now refuses to disclose such data. In 1997, 1,657 new warrants were authorised. In 2001, the number of authorisations was down to 1,314, but there was a 15 per cent increase in applications and many warrants were modified with the agreement of civil servants. The Security Service Commissioner, Lord Justice Stuart-Smith, refuses to publish the number of warrants issued specifically to MI5 because 'it is not in the public interest',[38] but an informed estimate is that three out of four taps are security-related.

In some cases, basic errors resulted in innocent people being placed under surveillance. In 2001, MI5, MI6 and GCHQ repeatedly tapped the wrong phones, according to the annual report by Sir Swinton Thomas, the interception of communications commissioner. The agencies listened in on unsuspecting people after mistaking their phone numbers for those of suspects. The National Criminal Intelligence Service even monitored the phone calls of one of its own police investigators after his mobile number was mistaken for a 'known criminal' and included on an authorisation signed by an official. In 2001 alone, 43 errors involving mail interception and phone-tapping were reported to the commissioner.

The targets of MI5's secret eavesdropping have changed over the years. During the Cold War all embassies representing Eastern-bloc countries were permanently tapped as well as being staked out from across the street. Visiting dignitaries and Prime Ministers were also under surveillance. In February 1967, the room and telephone of Alexei Kosygin, the Soviet premier, were bugged by MI5 during his stay in Britain. One of his remarks about President Pompidou was picked up from the tape and included in a memorandum sent to Tony Benn, then Postmaster General. 'I didn't find it very useful as it happened,' recorded Benn in his diary, 'except that it indicated how very close Kosygin and Pompidou were.'[39]

According to Benn's diaries, even Britain's Western allies were not immune from Security Service scrutiny. In October 1968, the West German Secretary of State for Economic Affairs, Klaus von Dohnanyi, was targeted during his trip to London. He was due to have lunch with Tony Benn, then Minister of Technology, at Admiralty House. Just before the meeting, Benn received a note from MI5 that revealed the West German's private remarks on his government's attitude towards a multi-role combat aircraft. 'It shows the security people are always at work, even on our alleged allies,' said Benn at the time.[40]

Peter Wright and his colleagues clearly enjoyed themselves placing miniature microphones all over London. During his period of service (1955–75), all the rooms and telephones at Claridge's Hotel, Mayfair, were bugged on behalf of MI5. Top waiters at leading London restaurants were also on the Secret Service payroll. They would tip off MI5 on the identity of customers, then ensure that tiny listening devices were placed underneath or adjacent to certain tables.[41] As long as MI5 has the permission of the hotel or restaurant management, it can plant bugs or tap phones without the need for a warrant. This is normally done through the head of security, who is often a retired policeman.

Despite official denials, even Cabinet ministers believed they were under surveillance. Lord Gardiner, Lord Chancellor in the Labour government of 1964–70 and the highest legal officer in the land, considered that his line was tapped. 'I thought it more likely than not that MI5 was bugging the telephones in my office,' he said later. 'When I really had to speak to the Attorney General in confidence, I took him out in the car because I knew the driver and I knew that she would never have allowed the car to be bugged without my knowledge.'[42]

In the 1960s and 1970s trade unionists were certainly targeted for tapping. 'Whenever a major dispute came up – at Ford, in the mines or the Post Office – it would immediately become a major area for investigation,' said Cathy Massiter. 'The issue was "What were the Communists doing in respect of this particular industrial action?" Usually an application for a telephone check would be taken out on the leading comrade in the particular union concerned.'[43]

During the 1978 pay dispute at Ford, MI5 worked on behalf of the government to undermine the union's position. The telephone of Syd Harraway, a Communist Party member and the key shop steward convenor at the Ford plant at Dagenham, was permanently tapped. 'I was instructed by my superiors to listen out particularly for any reference to the Ford unions' bottom line in the pay negotiations,' recalled the MI5 clerk who transcribed the calls. 'It was considered of vital importance to obtain the union's private position. This seemed to be economic information from within a legally constituted trade union which the Security Service and the government had no right to know.'[44]

It was a blatant breach of the Home Office's directive then governing MI5 conduct, which stated, 'No inquiry is to be carried out on behalf of any government department unless you are satisfied that an important public interest, bearing on the defence of the realm . . . is at stake.'

The Prime Minister of the day was often aware of such activity. In the mid- and late 1960s when trade-union leaders Jack Jones and Hugh Scanlon caused trouble for the government, their phones were bugged. 'The government has big ears and we know what these two men are up to,' Harold Wilson disclosed at a private dinner.[45] Other trade unionists whose home telephones were tapped included Margaret Witham and Mick Duggan of the Civil and Public Services Association and Derek Robinson, a militant British Leyland shop steward.

MI5 was particularly paranoid about the National Union of Mineworkers (NUM) since its successful strikes in 1972 and 1974. Its deputy president, Mick McGahey, a prominent Communist and member of the Scottish TUC, was under constant surveillance. Apart from his home phone in Scotland, MI5 bugged his London hotel room and a café where he met other trade unionists. His close associate, later president of the NUM, Arthur Scargill, was also targeted, even though he was not a Communist Party member.[46] 'MI5 was obsessed with Scargill, who even had his own classification – "Unaffiliated Subversive",' said David Shayler. 'Operatives covertly followed him, tapped his home and office telephones and recruited an agent inside the NUM. When I saw his file it contained a massive 40 volumes.'[47]

In the early 1980s, MI5 continued surveillance operations on organisations and individuals who created problems for the government of the day. The bugging of CND activists, as disclosed by Cathy Massiter, was a case in point, but it also revealed the absence of any protection and compensation for the victims. Massiter described on Channel 4 how she had been specifically requested by her superiors to find a 'suitable candidate' within CND for a tapping operation. She chose Dr John Cox, a vice-president and Communist Party member, although MI5 already 'knew from our coverage of the Communist Party that he was not getting up to anything in CND'. The absence of any subversive threat from Cox was minuted in his file, but MI5 insisted that the surveillance proceed.

By targeting Cox's phone, the Service could eavesdrop on more senior officials like Bruce Kent and Joan Ruddock (later a minister in Tony Blair's government). In August 1983, at the height of CND's popularity, a warrant was issued by Leon Brittan, the Home Secretary, and Cox's home telephone was then tapped.[48] A year later Brittan said, 'There is no doubt that peaceful political campaigning to change the mind of the government and people generally about nuclear disarmament is an entirely legitimate activity.'[49]

After this was revealed publicly, the government was under intense pressure. Ministers refused to allow a debate or make any statement in Parliament. Instead, they asked Lord Bridge, chairman of the Security Commission, to investigate whether the Home Secretary had improperly issued phone taps. The scope of the inquiry was deliberately restricted, avoiding the possibility that MI5 had undertaken their own unauthorised taps. In just three days, Lord Bridge studied 6,129 telephone-tapping applications between 1970 and 1984. He concluded that every warrant had been correctly authorised. This almost-unbelievable conclusion was much derided, notably by Lord Jenkins, who said that Bridge had 'made himself appear a poodle of the executive'.[50]

Backed by a detailed sworn affidavit from Cathy Massiter, CND went to court to challenge the legality of the bugging of Cox. The Crown's lawyers chose not to cross-examine Massiter. Instead they argued that the court should not adjudicate because it was 'contrary to national security' to hear evidence on whether a warrant had been issued. After three days of legal debate, the case was adjourned. On 2 September 1986, Lord Justice Taylor rejected CND's claim that the Home Secretary had acted unlawfully in approving the warrant. However, he also rejected the government's case that the court had no jurisdiction in matters of national security. This was an important ruling, because the government was anxious to avoid court cases involving MI5 where evidence could be produced and witnesses cross-examined. In 1985, as part of the Interception of Communications Act, they had banned appeals by people who wanted to pursue their case. Decisions of the Interception of Communications tribunal 'shall not be subject to appeal or liable to be questioned in court'.

MI5 could not – or would not – differentiate between government critics and genuine security risks. One dissident was Lieutenant Robert Lawrence, a hero and casualty of the Falklands War, whose story was told in the controversial television film *Tumbledown*. Lawrence and his father, Wing-Commander John Lawrence, a retired RAF officer, were not the normal, ultra-loyal military veterans: they complained about the soldier's treatment and demanded compensation from the Ministry of Defence, which created political embarrassment.

According to Granada Television's *World in Action*, MI5 responded by tapping both their phones. 'He [Robert] always said that wounded heroes were a great embarrassment,' John Lawrence told *World in Action*. 'Dead ones were absolutely fine. You could glorify them, but one [soldier] who was wounded but still sufficiently articulate to shout about things that went wrong or about his feelings was an embarrassment, I think.'[51]

This distinction between security subversives and political activists was never more unclear than in the surveillance of the far left-wing groups. The telephones of Communist Party officials were always tapped, notably those of Bill Dunn, Gerry Cohen and Mick Costello, a *Morning Star* journalist, in the 1970s,[52] because of their avowed allegiance to the Soviet Union Communist Party. But their power and influence dwindled rapidly in the 1980s.

MI5 then focused its attention on the various Trotskyist groups. Every week, officers in F2, the anti-subversion section, produced a list of lines that should be bugged. The SWP was seen as the main threat and the home phones of John Deason, its industrial organiser, and Tony Cliff, the Party's founder and leading light, were tapped – the latter from 1951 until 1991. In the SWP's head office all 12 lines were under surveillance. Other targets for tapping were the 15 phone lines in the Merseyside HQ of the Militant Tendency (MT) and members of the Revolutionary Communist Party (RCP).

After reading the transcripts many MI5 officers began to realise that the exercise was futile. These tiny organisations posed no threat to the security of the state: their lack of political and industrial influence in undermining parliamentary democracy was almost comical. Yet this expensive and time-consuming operation continued. In early 1993, over three years after the end of the Cold War, MI5 was still tapping the phones of the head offices of MT and the SWP. The operation was only stopped because the organisations had so many lines in their offices that MI5 did not have enough staff to transcribe the tapes. Eventually, in late 1993, a vast backlog of untranscribed tapes was destroyed – in itself an admission that they posed no security threat. 'It was a complete waste of time,' said a former MI5 officer. 'Everyone agreed it was a joke and there was no intelligence case for tapping these people's phones.'

The problem was that MI5 management in the 1990s had been trained to run operations in the 1970s. Then a tap on a Communist target was easy to manage, as it was static and the subject was not always security-conscious. But in the post-Cold War world terrorists are mobile and security-conscious: by the time MI5 and the Home Office have processed a warrant – which takes up to two weeks – the target may have moved on. Terrorists are fully aware that their phones are bugged, so never disclose sensitive information on the line. They use public call-boxes rarely and at random. They deliberately spread disinformation and even call sex lines so that MI5 transcribers waste their time.

The reality is that telephone intercepts produce only low-grade intelligence and are resource-intensive. The only people who are indiscreet on the phone are those who either don't care or have nothing to hide. They are, therefore, of little national-security interest. Yet even today MI5s first reaction to a new security target is to tap their phone, rather than think of alternative sources of intelligence. 'You can spend hundreds of thousands by the end of it [the phone-tapping operation] and come up with nothing,' reflected Shayler, 'because three days later the targets run off and put the bomb down . . . The telephone-intercept operation is very expensive – getting it up and running for the first three months costs £200,000 – whereas some agents will cost you absolutely nothing at all.'

In Northern Ireland, the RUC has virtually stopped this form of surveillance and has achieved notable success against the IRA. Like many of MI5's traditional operational methods – mail-tampering and burglary – telephone tapping has become overused and is ineptly directed. The most valuable and comprehensive intelligence is derived from agent sources. They are 'taskable', to use an MI5 term, and even if they are paid £100,000 a year – as some are in sensitive areas – they are still cheaper and more effective than planting an eavesdropping device on a telephone.

4

SUBVERSION AND THE X FILES

'If files were kept on them [Peter Mandelson and Jack Straw] . . . they would have been kept because they were either associated or were linked with some organisation which was wishing to overthrow our democratic system.'

Dame Stella Rimington, director-general of MI5, 1992–96,
Woman's Hour, BBC Radio 4, 27 April 1999

'I've seen so many of these [MI5] reports and alleged happenings from people who were so obviously biased and bigoted.'

Sir Edward Heath, Prime Minister, 1970–74, quoted in
Muddling Through, Peter Hennessy

A week before the 1992 general election campaign was launched, David Shayler was summoned by his manager on the second floor of MI5's office in Bolton Street. He was working in F2 section, respons-ible for monitoring the Communist Party, and did not expect a huge workload – the Cold War was over and the Marxist left was hopelessly and comi-cally split. He was surprised when his manager handed him a list of ten Labour parliamentary candidates. Some were well known, like Bruce Kent, former general secretary of CND, and Peter Mandelson, the powerful adviser to Labour leader Neil Kinnock. Others were relatively obscure political and trade-union activists and officials.

Shayler's task was to summarise the intelligence in the files and assess whether any of the candidates posed a security threat if appointed to government. He filled in a slip with their personal-file numbers and sent it over to the Registry in the basement of Curzon Street. Over the course of the following week, the manila files were delivered to his office.

As Shayler read through the reports and accompanying documents, he was shocked at the extent and volume of the surveillance and resources devoted to political activists over the previous 20 years. Some of the material was in the public domain – photographs of people on demonstrations and published articles – but there was also substantial covert intelligence: edited transcripts of tapped telephone conversations, minutes of private meetings and source reports from agents attending political gatherings. The latter had often been organised by pressure groups, which included Communist or Trotskyist members. Very little of what had been said was included in the source documents. Instead there were notes on who had attended, the prominent speakers, any decisions taken and an impression of the mood and broad sympathies of those present.

As part of Shayler's routine work in F Branch over the next six months, he received a number of other personal files for review. His task was to decide whether they should be kept open or destroyed. If they were to be retained, he was required to recommend the level of access and how the file should be categorised.

He felt that MI5's definition of subversion was undermining parliamentary democracy and was shocked by the lack of hard evidence against targets. Files were compiled on people often more because of their associations than their subversive activities. If they had attended trade-union or CND meetings that Communists had also attended, personal files would be opened on them. For MI5 that was the criterion for categorising someone as a potential security risk. For example, if an individual attended six public meetings organised by the Socialist Workers Party (SWP) to oppose NHS spending cuts, then they would be recorded as an SWP member and activist.

During his stint in F Branch, files on schoolchildren came across Shayler's desk for review. He was dumbstruck: MI5 had compiled secret security dossiers on children who had written to the Communist Party head office in the 1960s and 1970s asking for information on Eastern-bloc countries and Communism. The request had clearly been for a harmless school project, yet the letters had been intercepted and photocopied. After noting their names and addresses, MI5 had carried out routine inquiries by checking with NHS, Department of Health and Social Security records. When the children were officially identified, MI5 opened a file on each one as a 'suspected Communist sympathiser'.[1]

Shayler was stunned, not only that such dossiers had ever been compiled, but also becauseMI5 had kept the material open for use in the summer of 1992. It should have been destroyed long ago. The danger was that if one of the former schoolchildren applied for a job in the defence industry, the civil service or the police, he or she would require security vetting, which meant that MI5 would check the file and report back to the prospective employer: 'A secret and reliable source has reported that X [the job applicant] was in contact with the Communist Party in 1972.' The assessment might have concluded that they now posed no security threat, but it would still have sown seeds of doubt and concern in the minds of the employer's personnel department. If interviewed for a job where security clearance was required, the candidate, to test their honesty, might be asked if they had ever had any contact with the Communist Party. Naturally, they would have forgotten writing a letter for a school project 25 years earlier and would deny any Communist association. Vetting officers, unaware of the context of the 'contact', might view their response as evidence of dishonesty and refuse them employment.

Despite such negligence, the system for supervising files is supposed to be strictly controlled. MI5's huge reservoir of secret archives is stored in the basement of Thames House. The files are held on open shelves behind glass partitions. The only way to access them is by a remote-controlled mini-robot, which takes the dossiers off the shelves and delivers them to the other side of the glass partition. The research index is held on a vast database called Star, which may be accessed from computer terminals anywhere in Thames House.

During investigations, an MI5 desk officer will inevitably encounter a new name. His first task is to check with the research index as to whether that person is known to the Service. If the individual flashes up on the terminal screen, the entry will include their name, date of birth and 'recording category' – for example, a member of a subversive or terrorist group or 'agent of a hostile intelligence service'. Most important of all, their personal file number will be displayed.

An 'action slip' is completed and passed to the 'Registry Queens', who are mainly middle-aged women known for their almost theatrical devotion to the rules and ensuring that the forms are filled in correctly. They too have instant access to Star and can research the potential target via the computerised index.

If the individual is not known to MI5, then a temporary file is opened. This is called a GEN. A temporary investigation is then conducted and a decision taken on whether a GEN should be converted to a permanent file. If not, it is 'destroyed', which means it is kept in a separate system in case the target complains to the Security Service Commissioner.

A file cannot be compiled unless the subject is fully identified and falls into a 'recording category'. The Home Office and MI5 have been vague about what justifies opening a security file on an individual. The 1989 Security Service Act came closest to defining it. It stated that MI5's role was to safeguard the state against 'threats from espionage, terrorism and sabotage, from the activities of agents of foreign powers and from actions intended to overthrow or undermine parliamentary democracy by political, industrial or violent means'. If MI5 believes that a person's activities meet one or more of these criteria, a file is opened. It is then subject to a regime called 'traffic lighting'. All permanent dossiers are initially given a 'green' coding and while it retains this category further inquiries can be made about the individual. After five years it is reviewed and MI5 may decide that active investigations should be prohibited, but that any incoming material may be added to the dossier. That signals a change to 'amber'.

At the end of the designated amber period, the file is coded 'red'. After that officers cannot conduct further probing or include extra intelligence, but the file may be used for research purposes: the contents are microfilmed, the hard copy is destroyed and its entry in MI5's central index is transferred from the live section to the research index.[2] For members of subversive groups the file is kept open for five years. For IRA operatives it remains open for 75 years or until their death.[3]

There are also 'green' files, which include documents for active investigation pending a decision on whether or not to open a permanent dossier. After three years, these must be converted into a permanent file or 'destroyed', which means that the name is deleted from the research index – although the actual file is kept in a separate registry.

The most confidential are categorised as 'Y-boxed', which are marked with a yellow card inside the front cover known as 'the Yellow Peril'. They are particularly sensitive and separated from general access. All MI5 agents and informants are Y-boxed, and so are suspected spies, defectors, MPs and ministers. Officers may only gain access to this material with the permission of the agent-handler.

Another top-secret document is a list of about 15,000 subversives, compiled for the 'War Book', who might be considered for internment under Defence Regulation 18b in time of war or state of emergency.

Computerised indices are compiled for recording basic details about individuals or organisations, on the basis that insufficient information is known before a decision can be made on whether to open a file. Then there are blue-covered Subject Files, intelligence on political parties and subversive groups. In the recent past this included the Communist Party, the Socialist Workers Party, the Militant Tendency, the Revolutionary Communist Party, Class War, the British National Party and the National Front. Now it is more likely to include Islamic extremists and Irish Republican groups operating worldwide.

MI5's secret files have been a source of controversy ever since their foundation in 1909, when Britain was gripped by a pre-war hysteria that thousands of German spies were operating in the mainland. Then known as the Secret Service Bureau, the agency set up a card index of 30,000 aliens who were classified using codes. This ranged from 'AA' ('Absolutely Anglicised' or 'Absolutely Allied') to 'BB' ('Bad Boche').[4] The first three personal files compiled were on Vladimir Lenin (PF1), the Irish nationalist leader Eamon de Valera (PF2), branded a 'violent Irish Republican extremist', and Leon Trotsky (PF3).

During the interwar years the Service's files grew at a phenomenal rate. This was because of the fear that the 1917 Russian revolution would lead to Marxist insurrection in Britain and political and industrial unrest. As mass unemployment and poverty spread across the country in the 1930s, support for Communism and Fascism grew. MI5 responded by stepping up its political surveillance and since 1931 counter-subversion has been at the heart of its remit. In 1940, Sir Eric Holt-Wilson, deputy director-general of MI5, told the US State Department that its central index of 'suspected persons' contained 4.5 million names, although this would have included Nazi sympathisers.[5]

After the Second World War, MI5 reviewed its records and began to destroy personal files. In 1970, however, it was decided that weeding files was hampering the investigations of espionage cases, so many survived and were microfilmed. With the rise of trade-union and far-left militancy in the early 1970s, the number of personal files increased again substantially. That meant a huge number of citizens were, in effect, under political surveillance. By the early 1980s, the Service had compiled a total of one million personal files, but this included 'destroyed' files (placed on microfilm), personnel records of MI5 employees and possibly other intelligence agencies. The vast majority were permanent files on subversives.

One of the most prominent 'New Left' groups that emerged in the 1970s was the Trotskyite Workers Revolutionary Party (WRP). Backed and financed by the actress Vanessa Redgrave and her brother Corin, the WRP attracted a small but devoted and active national following. MI5 immediately targeted the WRP and, according to David Shayler, cultivated 'a well-placed informant who kept them briefed' on the Party's activities.[6] This source discovered that one of the WRP's secret benefactors was John Lennon, who donated thousands of pounds to its cause.

Lennon was already well known as a radical and vocal supporter of environmental causes and was an icon of the peace movement. When he spent a weekend in a Totonto hotel bedroom with his Japanese lover Yoko Ono as an anti-war protest, the whole world watched and young people were captivated. Paradoxically, he was also a vociferous backer of the IRA. The WRP connection enabled MI5 to open a file on the superstar, which contained some fascinating items, including a copy of the handwritten lyrics of one of Lennon's biggest hits, 'Working Class Hero', which were intercepted after they were sent by mail to the WRP.

In 1971, Lennon announced he was planning to settle in New York City with Yoko Ono. This caused uproar among Beatles fans who, already upset by the group's split, blamed Ono for the decision. In fact, the move was motivated more by political than personal reasons. According to declassified FBI files, obtained by Professor Jon Wiener, Lennon wanted to become a more active force in the campaign against the Vietnam war.

Following his visa application to live in the USA, the FBI began a routine investigation into Lennon and sent a request to MI5 for detailed intelligence on all his activities. They were particularly interested in his use of drugs, notably heroin. This placed the Service in an awkward position. 'The information on Lennon's donations to the WRP would have been enough to destroy his hopes of living in the USA,' recalled Shayler, but MI5's mole was inside the WRP and they were wary of compromising him. 'It was this source who alerted the Service to Lennon's donations,' Shayler went on. 'MI5 feared that telling the FBI about the money would put the source at risk of exposure and so the decision was taken to withhold much of this incriminating evidence from the Americans.'[7]

However, MI5 was also investigating Lennon for his opposition to British troops occupying Ulster. This was no secret: after the introduction of internment without trial in Northern Ireland, the former Beatle had attended a rally at which he held aloft a sign that stated 'Victory for the IRA Against British Imperialism'. A year later, he joined outraged protesters after the killing of 13 civil-rights marchers by British paratroopers on 'Bloody Sunday'. 'If it's a choice between the IRA and the British Army, I'm with the IRA,' he said. 'But if it's a choice between violence and non-violence, I'm with non-violence. So it's a very delicate line.'[8]

The FBI files reveal little substantial support by Lennon for the IRA, but it appears that MI5 sent a report on the singer's pro-Nationalist activities to its US counterpart. Despite the release of hundreds of previously censored papers from Lennon's FBI file in 1997, ten pages have been withheld from public scrutiny. The agency refused to release them on the basis that they are 'national security documents which originated from a foreign government' – almost certainly MI5. It is a convention of intelligence work that information supplied to a foreign government remains the property of the originating agency.

By the mid-1980s, few objective analysts believed that the factional splinter groups of the Communist Party or the tiny Trotskyist sects of the WRP, SWP and Militant Tendency were capable of organised insurrection. The notion that such outfits could undermine or overthrow Parliament was laughable and their only value was in providing material for BBC television comedy series like *Citizen Smith* and *The Young Ones*.

However, displaying a rare talent for empire-protection and institutional inertia, MI5 continued to target its traditional enemies as a threat to the security of the state. This was done, as former director-general Sir Antony Duff later admitted, for no other reason than that they had been operating for many years and still existed.[9]

Until the late 1980s, an estimated 70 MI5 officers worked full-time on investigating the Communist Party. That did not include agent-handlers. Another 40 officers targeted other 'subversive' groups. There was even a section – the Universities Research Group – whose sole function was to collect information on people who had been active in left-wing politics at Cambridge University in the 1920s, 1930s and 1940s. Known as F2/URG, it was a belated attempt to discover Communist fellow-travellers who might still be alive. It was disbanded in the mid-1980s.

In its 70 years of extensive coverage of the Communist Party, MI5 never once collected a piece of intelligence indicating that the Party sought to infiltrate the civil service, thereby undermining or attempting to overthrow the state.

Oblivious to the outside world and changes in political reality, MI5 management continued to monitor demonstrations and strikes as potentially subversive rather than legitimate protest. Their view was that because Communists and Trotskyists were involved, the industrial action was an act of subversion rather than an exercising of the democratic right to strike. Until 1994, when F2 was closed down, MI5 sent dossiers, known as Box 500 reports, to ministers about demonstrations attended by members of subversive groups.

Even the tiny chaotic rabble of an anarchist group was the subject of these reports. The Service accepted an offer from an alcoholic, unstable, self-proclaimed anarchist to report on his fellow conspirators. He was paid cash-in-hand, although MI5 knew he had a drink and drugs problem. 'They had a big thing about crusties with dogs who sit around talking about throwing Molotov cocktails,' said Shayler. 'They're no threat.'[10]

This lack of understanding of left-wing politics was identified by Lord Jenkins, who had first-hand dealings with MI5 during two periods as Home Secretary. He believed that living in a secluded spy-bound environment gave officers a distorted view of the world. Addressing what he called their 'political surveillance role', Lord Jenkins said: 'That involves above all a fine judgement between what is subversion and what is legitimate dissent, which in my experience is unlikely to be found in those who live in the distorting and Alice-through-the-looking-glass world in which falsehood becomes truth, fact becomes fiction and fantasy becomes reality.'[11]

From the Conservative vantage point, Sir Edward Heath, Prime Minister from 1970–74, confirmed that MI5 officers often operated from a highly subjective partial view of the world. 'I've seen so many of these [Box 500] reports and alleged happenings from people who were so obviously biased and bigoted,' recalled the former Prime Minister.[12] 'I met people in the Security Service who talked the most ridiculous nonsense and whose philosophy was ridiculous nonsense,' he told the Commons. 'If some of them were on the tube and saw someone reading the *Daily Mirror*, they would say, "Get after him, that is dangerous. We must find out where he bought it."'[13]

Even Sir Antony Duff, MI5's director-general between 1985 and 1987, acknowledged that the agency was living in the past, and that the internal threat to the state was dead. In an interview with the BBC's Mark Urban, Duff 'questioned the value of much intelligence work. He was appalled by the traditional methods, which seemed cumbersome and frequently unjustified'. He also discovered from Soviet defectors like Oleg Gordievsky that the KGB was second-rate and relatively harmless. 'The vast amount of material gathered by the KGB was really pretty unimportant,' recalled Duff. 'They were not working to politically undermine the state, but were trying to learn what is confidential and secret.'[14]

In this context, Duff ordered a major reduction in counter-subversion activities in F Branch. However, according to former MI5 officers, this process was not accelerated after Sir Patrick Walker became director-general in early 1988. Walker had been a director of F Branch and showed little apparent enthusiasm for diverting substantial resources from subversion and destroying files. However, political events forced MI5 to reduce its monitoring of the Communist Party. In 1990, the Party split and one section became the Democratic Left. MI5 studied the group for six months until it was satisfied that the new incarnation did not have subversive aims.

Despite the collapse of the Communist regimes in the Eastern bloc in 1989, MI5 retained its counter-subversion operations for at least another five years. By late 1991, F Branch still had six officers, five agent-handlers and three managers plus 20 support staff. Their targets were the Communist Party of Britain (an offshoot of the original CPGB), the SWP, the Militant Tendency, the Revolutionary Communist Party, the National Front, the British National Party and assorted anarchists like Class War.

Only the director of F Branch supported the surveillance. 'It was a ridiculous waste of time and money,' recalled Annie Machon, a former F Branch operative. 'We were basically trying to track down old Communists, Trotskyists and Fascists, but the Berlin Wall had come don several years before. We were horrified that during the 1992 general election we were summarising files on anybody who stood for Parliament. We were also horrified by the scale of the investigations. We argued most vociferously that we should not be doing this.'[15] As other officers read the transcripts of tapped phone calls and reports from agents, it became obvious that these groups posed no security threat. The officers found it difficult to take their work seriously and the 'subversives' became the subject of black humour rather than earnest scrutiny.

The Communist Party was hopelessly splintered into tiny warring segments. The SWP had always openly advocated a people's uprising through popular direct action rather than the Communist tactic of overthrowing the state through its connections to the Soviet Union. There was not a shred of evidence that the Trotskyists were ever close to succeeding. In fact, they were incapable even of organising their own largely middle-class members, let alone persuading the proletariat.

Yet MI5's surveillance of their activities was maintained and reached farcical proportions. Every February thousands of pounds were spent on surveillance of the SWP's weekend jamboree at the rainy coastal resort of Skegness. Undercover MI5 and Special Branch officers groaned as they surveyed the scene from inside a grotty caravan. It was hardly a den of revolutionary iniquity. Unfortunately for MI5, the members were stimulated more by liquor and libido than Leon Trotsky and armed insurrection.

However, according to former F Branch officers, there was a secret agenda behind such surveillance. 'MI5 management exaggerated and distorted the political importance of this Trotskyist rump [SWP] as a threat to the state, to ensure work for idle hands,' said Annie Machon.[16]

The other major Trotskyist party, Militant Tendency [MT], were of more significance as they had engaged in secret long-term entryism of the Labour Party. This was more of a security case because of their covert methods. In 1992, the MT renounced entryism and F Branch officers believed that the expensive surveillance should stop. However, MI5 continued to tap their phones and intercept their mail and faxes at considerable expense.

In early 1993, the Home Office warrant for this surveillance needed to be renewed. The F Branch officer in charge researched the case and concluded there was no security justification: the MT were a marginalised sect and no longer a security threat. 'There is no intelligence case for renewing the warrant,' the officer told the branch director.

'I don't care,' he replied. 'Go and find a case.' Shocked by this response, the officer was forced to conjure up some spurious criteria and the Home Secretary, Kenneth Clarke, renewed the warrant for another six months.

This abuse of state power was not about political bias. It was motivated by MI5 management protecting its bureaucratic fiefdoms. If the targeting of the MT was cancelled, the director knew that his quota of staff would be reduced and therefore his influence within MI5 in general would decline. That might signal the end of targeting other subversives and F Branch would be disbanded. That was the secret agenda for maintaining surveillance on political activists.

By the early 1990s, most objective observers would agree that trade-union power was also greatly diminished and certainly posed no security threat. The days of 1974, when miners' strikes were perceived to have brought down the Conservative government – itself a contentious proposition – were a distant memory. But MI5 continued to target and devote serious resources to industrial disputes and demonstrations. Working closely with Special Branch, MI5 placed strikers and marchers under intense surveillance. This happened in October 1992, during a mass protest in London against pit closures, and in the spring of 1993, during the Timex dispute in Dundee. Their 'justification' was that the demonstrations included Trotskyist activists.

Using undercover agents, F Branch obtained a mass of detail about the demonstrators, picket lines, number of coaches, their travel plans and the leaders – all public-order information and nothing to do with national security. Data on the Timex strike in Dundee, for example, allowed police to scale down the number of officers required at the demonstrations. Yet MI5 management decided to pass on the material to the government. It was summarised in Box 500 reports and sent to 10 Downing Street, the Joint Intelligence Committee in the Cabinet Office and the police. 'It was an abuse of MI5's powers,' said a former F Branch officer. 'It had nothing to do with subversion and everything to do with preserving their status.'

This was the atmosphere that greeted David Shayler on joining F

Branch in January 1992. To borrow John le Carré's phrase, MI5 marched on its files and Shayler became one of the infantry. But the barracks was far from exciting. Based on the second floor at Bolton Street, Shayler and seven others shared a large, open-plan room. The job of the support staff was clipping and filing obscure far-left- and right-wing periodicals. They also entered routine information on the database or the paper-carding system contained in vast carousels.

Shayler's responsibility was to analyse and assess information from agent sources and Special Branches across the country. Where necessary, he compiled reports either for MI5 management or for government departments. He also carried out extensive research into the Communist Party of Britain and Class War.

In early March, Shayler was given his special assignment. The general election was looming and all parliamentary candidates for the three main political parties were checked against MI5's records. Where a record existed, Shayler assessed whether any of his ten candidates would pose a security risk if they became ministers. If there was any relevant information that affected national security, this was summarised and sent to the director-general with a recommendation. After appraisal, the director-general would decide whether to pass on the intelligence to the incoming Prime Minister and (since 1992) the Leader of the Opposition.

The head of MI5 is the third person to see the new Premier in 10 Downing Street after the election. Before any ministerial appointment can be made, the candidate must wait for the security assessments. This makes the Service the most powerful agency in Whitehall, with the gift of destroying political careers in one short paragraph.

MI5 has officially stated that up to nine leading politicians were singled out as potential security risks during the 1992 and 1997 elections and their names given to John Major, Neil Kinnock and Tony Blair.[17] Normally such sensitive files would have been assessed only by senior management, but for the 1992 election, F Branch officers like Shayler were granted access to MP's files because of a staff shortage. The irony was that Neil Kinnock, then Leader of the Opposition, was himself the subject of an MI5 personal file. Based on a specific piece of intelligence from his youth, it had been opened in the early 1970s when he was a left-wing firebrand Labour MP.[18] The file was still active in 1988 and was almost certainly open during the 1992 general election campaign.

As Shayler examined the files during his eight-month stint in F

Branch, he was shocked to discover who had been targeted. 'MI5 was still riddled with "reds-under-the-beds" paranoia,' he recalled, 'and showed little inclination to get to grips with the threats posed to the UK in the post-Cold War world . . . There was still a study of people involved in subversion. That meant there were people tasked to find out information about these people and their organisations' phones were tapped. There was a budget of hundreds of thousands of pounds – if not a million. Essentially, they were people who were just political activists, nothing more dangerous than that.'[19]

Shayler found it incredible that Monsignor Bruce Kent, general secretary of CND from 1980 until 1985, had been branded as 'a Communist sympathiser'. MI5 had reached this conclusion purely because CND contained Communist Party members. More seriously, Kent was categorised as a 'contact of a hostile intelligence service': he had unwittingly met a KGB officer at a social function at the Soviet embassy in London. After reading the file, Shayler stated that there was no indication that Kent was a Communist sympathiser, although he was obliged to send it to the counter-espionage branch for further assessment.

Two names on the secret list of potential 'security risks' submitted to Kinnock in 1992 and Blair in 1997 were Harriet Harman and Joan Ruddock. Harman was legal officer of the National Council for Civil Liberties (NCCL) from 1978 until 1982 when the organisation was considered subversive. She later became a Labour MP and Social Security Secretary in Tony Blair's Cabinet.

Ruddock was targeted because she was chairperson of CND and an active supporter of the Greenham Common women's peace camp. Greenham Common had been a major target for MI5. As some of the women were SWP members, MI5 placed the protesters under surveillance. Ten thick volumes of material were collected on the peace camp and its supporters. Ruddock's file included Special Branch references to her movements, products of mail and telephone intercepts and police reports recording her appearances at CND demonstrations and public meetings.[20] Despite MI5's objections, Ruddock became a Labour MP and joined the Blair government as Minister for Women.

A third name on the list handed to Blair was Ken Livingstone, the Labour MP and aspiring Mayor of London. MI5's concerns about the popular former GLC leader focused on his contacts with members of Sinn Fein over a period of 30 years. A summary of his file was passed to 10 Downing Street by director-general Stephen Lander. Livingstone believes he was targeted because of his uncompromising criticism of MI5. 'I would be amazed if I was not on it, given how appalling, right-wing and paranoid MI5 is,' he told the *Sunday Times*. 'They are a pretty derisory bunch and a complete waste of money. I conducted a very vigorous campaign against them. I was arguing that there were disloyal MI5 officers around Peter Wright who were planning cross-border assassinations [in Northern Ireland].'[21]

Other Labour MPs subject to MI5 investigation were Eric Heffer, Ron Brown and Tony Benn, a former Cabinet minister in three Labour governments.[22] A file was compiled on Labour MP Tam Dalyell for his outspoken comments on the Lockerbie bomb. 'Dalyell was trying to put around the line that the Libyans were not responsible for the Lockerbie attack,' said Shayler, 'and I put in an assessment saying that I thought that Dalyell was honestly duped. He had been misled by the Libyans, but he was not a paid agent of influence to the Libyans.'[23] This was accepted by MI5.

By far the most ironic file concerned Jack Straw, the Home Secretary since May 1997. 'He was deemed to be a "Communist sympathiser",' said Shayler, 'merely because he was president of the National Union of Students [NUS] between 1969 and 1971 and an activist at the radical Leeds University at a time when the Communist Party was a powerful force within student politics ... The NUS was full of people who were paid-up Communist Party members, as were many at student executive levels at universities around the country.'[24]

Although he was not a Party member, Straw was tarred with the Communist brush and MI5 opened a file on him anyway. A church-going, well-behaved Christian Socialist, he immersed himself in student politics at Leeds University where he took a 2:2 in law. Throughout the 1950s and early 1960s, the NUS was controlled by the Labour right. But the Vietnam war radicalised the young and Straw was swept up in the changing ideological tide and swam with it. His election as NUS president in 1969 was a historic shift to the radical left.

It was the high summer of student rebellion and Straw became a national media figure. But what MI5 failed to grasp was that Straw was as hostile to the Marxist left as he was to the Tory right. He sailed with the political wind. The only Communist influence on the NUS president was their strict discipline and professionalism. He was a machine politician and loved to quote Stalin: 'Once the political line has been settled, organisation counts for all.'[25]

In February 1974, after he had practised as a barrister for two years, Straw was asked by Barbara Castle, the Social Services Secretary, to become her political adviser. As all government aides required security vetting, an investigating officer interviewed Straw. Almost as soon as the officer sat down, he placed a manila dossier on the table: 'This is your file,' said the officer. 'He had to tell me about it,' recalled Straw, 'because there was an issue where the questions he was asking me could only have made sense if he said, "We have this information from your file and we have this information from what you have said. Can you explain the difference?"'[26]

The ambitious young politician did not ask to see the contents of his file. Two decades later, after Shayler revealed its existence publicly, Straw remarked, 'I'm pretty clear that I know what it contains because I knew what I was doing.' This was said during a press conference to launch an MI5 booklet called 'Myths and Misunderstandings'. It was a strikingly naïve statement and characterised much of Jack Straw's dealings with MI5.

The implication of what Straw said about a discrepancy between the contents of his MI5 file and his own responses to the vetting officer is highly significant: it meant that there might have been mistakes in his MI5 dossier. But Straw still refuses to inspect his file. 'I've positively said that I don't want to see it,' he said. 'I don't think I should have any more rights over that file than any other citizen in the same position. It's an accident for which the Security Service were themselves responsible 25 years ago.'

The idea that MI5 compiled and kept open an official dossier on him for so many years by 'accident' again shows staggering naïvety. When it was suggested by the BBC's Michael Cockerell that by reading his own file he could verify the efficiency of MI5 and correct any mistakes, Straw replied, 'Well, that's one argument. The other side of that is that it would be abusing my position as Home Secretary . . . I should not have any more rights in respect of that file than any other citizen. It would be an outrageous abuse of my position and I'm not going to do it.'[27]

So what was in Jack Straw's file? One document has emerged that indicates its contents. It was a briefing paper about Communism written by an MI5 officer in 1974. A copy was sent to Colin Wallace, then an Army intelligence officer running a secret black propaganda operation against the Labour government. Based at Army headquarters in Lisburn, Northern Ireland, Wallace showed these reports to journalists on a non-attributable basis. The memo was entitled 'Communist Front Organisations in Ulster Unrest'. In the section on students, the MI5 officer had written: 'Jack Straw is a hardline revolutionary socialist. As a member of the National Union of Students, he publicly supported motions in favour of British withdrawal from Northern Ireland and the end of American involvement in Vietnam.'[28]

Privately, Jack Straw made excuses for MI5, saying that he had been targeted at the height of the Cold War. He told colleagues that perhaps it was because students had been recruited by the KGB in the past and there had been concern that he might be a Communist fellow-traveller. In fact, what it revealed was MI5's lack of political understanding and sophistication. Even Lord Carr, the Conservative Home Secretary in 1972 when MI5 was compiling the file, laughed when asked why young Straw had been categorised as a Marxist revolutionary. 'Don't always get it right, do we?' he giggled.[29]

For David Shayler, the real concern was not the contents of Straw's file, but that such outdated and irrelevant material was still retained by MI5. But as he cross-checked other parliamentary candidates with MI5 records prior to the 1992 election, he was in for a bigger shock. There, in two thick volumes, was a personal file on Peter Mandelson, then Labour's candidate for Hartlepool and a close adviser to Neil Kinnock. Mandelson was a key strategist for the forthcoming campaign: if Labour won the election, he was destined for at least a junior ministerial post. Shayler's task was to summarise both volumes and send a report to the director-general. Opened in 1972, Mandelson's recording category was 'Member: Communist'. Attached to the file was a Home Office warrant that authorised the direct tapping of his telephone. Inside were a number of supplementary notes about his political activities and contacts, transcripts of intimate phone conversations, source reports, newspaper articles and photographs. According to the file, Mandelson's phone had been tapped for nearly two years between late 1978 and mid-1980. In 1983, his security status was reduced to 'amber', which meant that further active investigations were prohibited. But the file remained open and continued to receive intelligence material. It was not until March 1992, after

Shayler had reviewed the two volumes, that the future Cabinet minister warranted a 'red' category – for research purposes only. But it was still an open file and could be called up on the computer at any time.

MI5's investigation into Mandelson can be traced back to late 1971 when he joined the Young Communist League [YCL] as a 17-year-old sixth-former at Hendon County Grammar School. That he had signed up at such a tender age was not surprising as the future spin-doctor had been born into a political family: he was the grandson of Herbert Morrison, Labour's Deputy Prime Minister during the 1945–51 government, but he refused to join the Labour Party because of Harold Wilson's implicit backing of the Vietnam war.

Instead, consumed by politics, Mandelson immersed himself in YCL activity. He sold *Challenge*, the YCL newspaper, on the school grounds and encouraged other recruits. Former comrades recall his 'fantastic energy'. Although Mandelson would later play down his involvement, in 1972 he was appointed a steward at the YCL conference in Scarborough – a job that would only have been given to a 'trusty'.[30]

After turning 18, it was routine for YCL members to graduate to the Communist Party of Great Britain and Mandelson was no exception. The future Cabinet minister later denied joining the Party. 'I was never a member of the Communist Party,' he said. 'That is a pure smear.'[31] But Shayler, who assessed his file, is adamant: 'When I reviewed it there was a membership card which Mandelson filled out and a photograph which was fairly conclusive proof,' he said.[32]

According to the file, Mandelson came under low-grade surveillance while he was at St Catherine's College, Oxford University, from 1973 until 1976. He was photographed while attending demonstrations, and articles he wrote for left-wing journals were clipped and filed. 'He wasn't a really vociferous Communist,' recalled Shayler. 'Most of the material was the people he was associating with. He was very active in student politics and labour relations. It was straight left-wing politics basically.'[33]

However, MI5 stepped up their surveillance in May 1977 after Mandelson became chairman of the publicly funded British Youth Council (BYC). This was a co-ordinating body, which covered a wide diversity of groups from the Boy Scouts to the YCL. Open to all, its aim was to campaign for young people on issues like youth unemployment and to sponsor cultural events. Mandelson showed real organisational flair and was particularly adept at coaxing potential warring factions into agreement.

The BYC was harmless, but MI5 targeted its vibrant new chairman for two reasons. First, he had just joined the TUC as a fulltime researcher in the economics department. This was suspect, in MI5's eyes, as the late 1970s was a time of industrial strife and Mandelson, a Communist Party member, was in a key position to foment class warfare. Second, and more significantly, he was intimately involved in organising the BYC's delegation to the World Festival of Youth and Students, held in Havana, Cuba, and sent others to Poland, Hungary, Romania and the Soviet Union. However, he also established relations with the youth councils of Israel and the USA.[34]

According to Shayler, MI5 viewed the forthcoming festival as 'a Communist front' and targeted it as a vehicle for subversion. 'These occasions used to preoccupy the Foreign Office [funders of the BYC], which was obsessed with the idea that they were used by the Soviet Union to recruit fifth-columnists to infiltrate British life,' he said.[35]

But it was Mandelson's growing reputation as an organiser, negotiator and political moderate that really attracted MI5. In the bizarre, arcane and conspiratorial world of espionage, the earnest young activist was suspected not just of being a Communist but also a possible 'sleeper' – a covert sympathiser.

According to Shayler, 'As is well known from KGB files opened in Moscow, the Soviets deeply distrusted any officials of the Communist Party of Great Britain because they knew it had been penetrated by MI5 and Special Branch. But the Soviets did need their own agents and targeted lesser lights in the Party. If that was successful, these agents were instructed by Moscow to publicly distance themselves from the Communist regime, as had happened with the master spy, Kim Philby.

'And Peter Mandelson seemed to fit this profile because he soon began, as most idealists do, to become active in more mainstream politics, in the student and trade-union movements. He only mixed with Communists as part of his day-to-day legitimate political activities. But to the suspicious minds of those in the Security Service and Foreign Office, he seemed to be taking the role of a "sleeper".

'And the more moderate he became in reality, the more the

suspicions mounted. It was within this atmosphere that, in 1978, MI5 applied to the Home Office, when Merlyn Rees was Home Secretary, for the warrant to tap his telephone.'[36]

In July 1978, Mandelson led the BYC's 180-strong delegation to the World Festival of Youth and Students, a 12-day jamboree of political debate, dancing, pop music, sport and socialising. The British section was submerged within 23,000 young people from 140 countries, but they were vociferous and active. Although they criticised Soviet-bloc countries for human-rights violations and blocked attempts to praise Eastern European Communism, all their names were sent to MI5 for analysis.[37]

When Mandelson returned from Havana, he joined the Vauxhall Labour Party in south London and aligned himself with the right-wing Solidarity Group, led by Roy Hattersley. Yet MI5 continued to tap his home telephone at huge expense to the taxpayer. Shayler argued: 'It was an act of pure paranoia . . . There was no indication that his activities were anything other than legitimate political protest.' He added, 'What the intercept transcripts showed, in fact, was that Mandelson was a devoted politician who spent most of his life as a moderate left-winger who put considerable effort into trying to bring the extreme left round to his viewpoint. This counted against him among his watchers because they interpreted it as cover for covert Communist activities. But most important of all, MI5 had absolutely no indication from the phone tap that he did any of the things inherent in spying. There was no indication that he ever met a Soviet handler or any suggestion that he was trying to communicate with the Soviets. He did meet Soviet agents at public functions, but there was no evidence at all to show that he knew they were agents.'[38]

Despite the absence of any case against Mandelson, MI5 maintained its surveillance for two years and kept the file open for 15 years – long after he had deserted the Communists. The reason, says Shayler, was 'bureaucratic'. 'MI5 ran into one of its long-running problems,' he said in August 1997. 'No one dared to make a decision one way or the other. There was, and I believe still is, such a lack of leadership within MI5 that even senior officers would not say, "This is a complete waste of public money directed at an innocent target and we should stop it."'[39]

When Shayler reviewed the dossier in March 1992, he was amazed that such material was *still* used as a reference point. 'There was no intelligence case against him and it should have been closed years ago,' he said. 'Within a short time of my perusal of the file, it was simple for me to decide that Mandelson did not pose any possible and realistic threat to national security.'[40]

When the authors of this book disclosed the MI5 investigation of Mandelson in the *Mail on Sunday* on 24 August 1997, he was on holiday in the United States. By then he was Minister without Portfolio in the Cabinet Office and Tony Blair's most influential adviser. As he was abroad, Mandelson was in no real position to respond to the story in detail. Irritated by the revelations, he telephoned his private office and spoke to the Prime Minister, who wanted the issue cleared up quickly.

Two days later Mandelson attacked MI5. 'Of course I do not like being bugged,' he said. 'But it is the muddle and incompetence that is amazing.' He denied being a full Party member, but confirmed being in the YCL for 'between three and six months'.[41]

The minister was not as angry about the disclosure as it appeared from his press comments. Perversely, the story helped his bid to be elected to Labour's National Executive six weeks later as it highlighted his past left-wing credentials and origins. Constituency delegates now viewed him less suspiciously.

Mandelson was curious rather than outraged by the revelations. An avid fan of James Bond films, he was fascinated by the secret world of espionage. In 1994, he urged for more accountability and sponsored an amendment to the Intelligence Services Act, which aimed to prevent MI5 officers from promoting their own party political interests. 'It is because they [MI5] have extraordinary means available to them to pursue their political views, that it is important that this special safeguard is introduced,' he said. 'The Bill should be . . . sending a clear message to all Service personnel that what might have happened in the past is totally unacceptable to Parliament in the future.'[42]

Initially, an irate Mandelson wanted to see his MI5 file and verify whether his phone was tapped. He demanded a meeting with Stephen Lander, MI5's director-general, which took place on 17 September 1997 at the Home Office, arranged and attended by Jack Straw, the Home Secretary. An embarrassed Lander began by explaining the workings of MI5. He then confirmed to Mandelson that MI5 had opened a file on him in the early 1970s, and apologised for the leaking of its details. Lander indicated that Mandelson's name was on a Communist Party list seen by the

Service. But he said he could not reveal the file's contents because that meant granting him 'privileged access'.

Lander denied that Mandelson's phone had been tapped, but admitted that his file included transcripts of his calls made to other MI5 targets, notably to targeted premises like the East German embassy. The minister reluctantly accepted these reassurances and informed Blair of the outcome. 'The important thing for me is not so much their apology,' he said, after the meeting, 'but their categorical statement that I was not bugged – because it would have been wrong and totally unjustified to have bugged me. I was not a subversive or a threat to national security. I was a teenager holding ordinary left-wing views. For a time I was a member of an organisation regarded as too left-wing for the government, but that did not mean that I posed any threat.'[43]

However, Shayler was not impressed by Lander's denial. On 28 September 1997, in a detailed open letter to the Prime Minister from 'somewhere in Europe', the former MI5 officer was categoric.

I know Mr Lander is not telling the truth [he wrote, in the *Mail on Sunday*]. 'I clearly remember that Mr Mandelson was the direct target of an intercept because I reviewed his MI5 file. Attached to this file was the Home Office warrant which authorised the direct tapping of his phone and therefore his conversations.

Mr Lander knows that he only has to have the confidence of government ministers rather than be more widely accountable. For this reason I believe Mr Lander has decided to deny the revelations concerning Mr Mandelson.

Shayler then issued a challenge to Lander: 'There is, of course, one way to settle this dispute: show the file in its entirety to Mr Straw, Mr Mandelson, the entire parliamentary Intelligence and Security Committee and even Parliament.'[44]

After reading this article Mandelson reconsidered Lander's denials. He was disturbed and impressed by the sheer detail in Shayler's open letter. 'It was a very closely argued piece,' a minister told the *Financial Times* the next day. 'It is really rather worrying.'[45] Mandelson asked MI5 for an immediate explanation, but Lander refused to allow anyone to see the file and kept to his original version of events.

Access to the full dossier on Mandelson will, of course, resolve the dispute over the electronic surveillance, but it would also provide an insight into how MI5 distinguished between subversion and political dissent in assessing security risks. Like Straw, Mandelson was a hard-working political junkie. Apart from the Vietnam war, perhaps, the two ministers were not motivated by issues or ideology. They were driven by the pursuit of power. Both men were and are fascinated by the machinery, organisation and presentation of politics. They are, above all, pragmatists. The 'moral dimension', to quote *Yes Minister*, is irrelevant and Mandelson has long sneered at 'the romanticism of the class struggle'.[46] Policies are only important if sufficient people vote for them. To brand these two men as even potential revolutionaries for 20 years shows a fundamental misunderstanding of political reality.

The targeting of Straw and Mandelson was defended by Dame Stella Rimington, former director-general of MI5: 'If files were kept on them – and I'm not saying whether they were or not – they would have been kept because they were either associated or linked with some organisation which was wishing to overthrow our democratic system.' But when pressed by her interviewer on *Woman's Hour* whether such people 'were really planning to overthrow the democratic system', Rimington conceded, 'I think it highly unlikely.'[47]

It was not just Labour politicians who were investigated by MI5: security assessments of certain Conservative MPs have also been dispatched to 10 Downing Street and the Cabinet Office for analysis by the Joint Intelligence Committee. The most notable was Sir Edward Heath. 'Ted Heath, I was informed, had an MI5 file because he was very keen on rapprochement with the Eastern bloc,' recalled Shayler. 'He had a lot of contacts with people from those embassies and that would have made him recordable as a suspected Soviet sympathiser ... They would have certainly wanted to gather information on him to check whether he was suspect or not.'[48]

The vetting process of ministers was based on the fear that some were vulnerable to potential blackmail. Compromising connections with Communist or hostile countries and agents were viewed as dangerous and so were sexual indiscretions. One Conservative MP and former minister targeted by MI5 was Alan Clark, the military historian, *bon viveur* and celebrated philanderer.

On 24 June 1983, Clark was summoned for a meeting by Robert

(now Lord) Armstrong, the Cabinet Secretary, to discuss his appointment as a Junior Employment Minister. In the Cabinet Office anteroom Armstrong produced two files – one red, the other orange. 'There are certain matters that the Prime Minister has asked me to raise with you,' said the Cabinet Secretary. He opened the red file. 'You have been spoken of with approval by the National Front.'

'Not at my solicitation,' replied Clark sharply.

'If any of them should at any time try to make contact with you,' said Armstrong sternly, 'I must ask that you inform my office immediately.'

The Cabinet Secretary then opened the orange dossier. 'There are also certain matters of personal conduct which could leave you open to blackmail,' he said, with a faint smile.

'No, no. Perfectly all right,' replied Clark, with a trace of panic in his voice. 'They've all married into grand Scottish families by now.'

Later that evening the Tory MP recorded the episode in his diaries and reflected, 'I thought about it for a little while. They [the Security Service] *must* have been bugging my phone. There was no other explanation. And for ages.'[49]

The fact that Labour politicians were investigated by MI5 in the 1970s at the height of Cold War paranoia is not, in itself, a great surprise. The real revelation is that MI5 kept their files open so long after the individuals ceased to be even a remote security risk. At least three – Jack Straw, Peter Mandelson and Harriet Harman – have been Cabinet ministers since Labour formed a government in 1997.

Informed sources have told us that MI5 has 'almost definitely' had a dossier on John Prescott, the Deputy Prime Minister, since his militant role during the 1966 seamen's dispute. He was targeted after MI5 briefed Harold Wilson, then Prime Minister, about his trade-union activities. Wilson attacked the strike as being manipulated by a 'tightly knit group of politically motivated men'.[50] The headquarters of the seamen's union was being bugged by MI5. It has since been established that Prescott was targeted by Special Branch as one of the 'politically motivated men'.[51] The same sources argue that Robin Cook, the former Foreign Secretary, would also have been investigated by MI5 because of his active membership and support for CND in the early 1980s. He, too, is a former sharp critic of MI5.[52]

As Maurice Frankel, director of the Campaign for Freedom of

Information, has pointed out, these files were not sealed in some inaccessible top-secret archive and restricted to a select few senior directors. They were available to and used by ordinary MI5 officers. The danger is that their retention for decades, despite the absence of justification, creates the potential for abuse. The dossiers include personal information, from which smear campaigns could emanate.[53]

This is not an argument for the destruction and pulping of MI5's archives. However, it is worth pointing out that inadequate supervision and management of the files might lead to individuals being subject to unwarranted investigation.

The most direct use of MI5 files is when they are consulted during security vetting of people applying for certain jobs in the public and private sectors. This affects an estimated 800,000 people.

Vetting was originally set up in 1948 by Labour Prime Minister Clement Attlee in the wake of the onset of the Cold War. Ministers and MI5 were concerned about the leaking of nuclear and other defence secrets to the Soviet Union and Communist-bloc countries, and purge procedures were established. For decades there were two forms of vetting: open and secret. Both involved trawling through MI5 and Special Branch files. In positive vetting, candidates were aware of the process because they filled in a vetting form and provided details of family members. These relatives were also checked against MI5 records.

Civil servants in sensitive posts (notably in the Ministry of Defence and Home Office), middle and higher ranks of the armed forces, some in the nuclear industry, British Telecom employees and all MI5 and Special Branch applicants were subject to positive vetting. This was done with their knowledge, but if they failed the security clearance, they were not informed why.

The secret system was known as 'normal vetting'. This covered hundreds of thousands of individuals applying for jobs in the BBC, defence companies, junior posts in Whitehall, nuclear plants and on government building sites. None of these people knew they were being checked out by MI5 and Ministry of Defence vetting officers. The secrecy led to widespread abuse as applicants were refused employment even though they would have little access to classified or sensitive information. On the recommendation of MI5, management took advantage of the covert procedure to blacklist people. Under the pretext of security, many were barred from jobs because they were political or trade-union activists. It was a convenient device for employers to marginalise people of whom they disapproved.

The worst abuse was at the BBC where graduate trainees, film editors, journalists, arts producers and drama directors were vetted. The operation was run from Room 105, a secluded office on the first floor of Broadcasting House. There the BBC employed a security liaison officer, known euphemistically as 'Special Assistant to the Director of Personnel', who received the names of all successful job applicants from interviewing boards.

The list was then sent to C Branch of MI5, who checked the names against the records. Where a record existed, C Branch made a preliminary assessment and sent it to F Branch for verification. It was usually returned with the assessment confirmed. Then C Branch would write to the BBC's security officer with a recommendation. Quite often if they said a person was a 'security risk', that was sufficient to blacklist him or her. No reasons were provided and no questions were asked. It was only when a BBC executive or editor put pressure on the personnel department that MI5's decision was overruled.[54]

Security vetting of BBC staff was deliberately kept secret from the Home Secretary by MI5 and its officials. When the operation was exposed by the *Observer* in 1985, Lord Rees was shocked and wrote to the permanent secretary, who confirmed that Rees had never been informed. The official line was that such vetting was part of the BBC's responsibility to co-ordinate their contingency plans for a wartime or emergency broadcasting servic, but at least 80 per cent of those investigated were not remotely involved in sensitive areas or had access to classified information. The practice was abolished soon after its public disclosure. Today, only the director-general and two senior executives are vetted by MI5 as they are considered key personnel in the event of a national emergency.

In 1990, the government was forced to abolish all 'normal' (i.e. secret) vetting. The European Commission on Human Rights had ruled that covert security checks violated European law. They found that individuals should have the right to know if they have been investigated and the reasons for rejecting their security clearance. As MI5 had just been placed on a statutory basis by an Act of Parliament, the Service was now vulnerable to legal actions by people who believed they had been secretly blacklisted. Anxious to avoid such probing litigation, MI5 and the government changed the rules: all job applicants subject to vetting would now be aware that their background, interests and activities were being checked out.

The current security procedures were installed in January 1995, and there are now two levels of vetting. One is called a 'Security Check'. This applies to those taking up posts that would place them close to public figures at risk of attack by terrorist groups: individuals with unrestricted access to likely terrorist targets. They are assessed for whether they are connected, or may be vulnerable, to pressure from terrorist organisations. Those subject to this form of vetting are police constables, privates in the army, employees of defence contractors, cleaners and manual workers in government buildings.[55]

Applicants are required to complete a security questionnaire, which is sent to MI5 where it is checked against their files and the police national computer for any criminal record. The checks are not always operated efficiently: in 1993, a builder worked inside MI5's headquarters at Thames House despite his terrorist record. MI5's security check had missed the trace and only later discovered it. The construction worker was swiftly sacked.

The second level of security assessment is called 'Developed Vetting'. This covers individuals who seek material classified as 'secret' and 'top secret' (middle-ranking and senior civil servants and Special Branch officers) and 'beyond top secret' documents (MI5, MI6, GCHQ, permanent secretaries and the highest-ranking military officers). This investigation is more rigorous. A detailed financial report is also compiled: credit checks are made and bank statements inspected to see if the subject is susceptible to bribery. Apart from the standard checks, the applicant will be interviewed and officers will talk to his or her past and present employers and relatives, including grandparents.[56]

The criteria for refusing an individual security clearance were announced in December 1994 by Prime Minister John Major. 'No one should be employed in connection with work which is vital to the interests of the state,' he told Parliament, 'who is or has been involved in or associated with any of the following activities: espionage, terrorism, sabotage, actions intended to overthrow or undermine parliamentary democracy by political, industrial or violent means. Or is, or has recently been, a member of any organisation which has advocated such activities.' An individual will also fail security vetting if they are 'associated with any organisation or any of its members in such a way as to raise reasonable doubts about his or her reliability. Or is susceptible to pressure or improper influence, for example, because of current or past activities', or if he or she 'has shown dishonesty or lack of integrity which throws doubt upon their reliability, or has demonstrated behaviour, or is subject to circumstances which may otherwise indicate unreliability'.[57]

MI5 has overall authority in making the recommendation, but the final decision is made by the security officer in the relevant department. In the defence industry, the Service is particularly powerful where it is responsible for all security and personnel vetting. Prior to the acceptance of a government contract, a firm receives a 'secret aspects' letter from MI5, listing all its security requirements. If the firm wants to retain the lucrative business, it has no choice but to accede to these demands. MI5-trained security officers then supply a list of prospective employees to Thames House for analysis.[58] These names are collated by D1 section of the Service. It is a daunting task with no little burden of responsibility, as David Cornwell (a.k.a. John le Carré) later reflected:

> I toiled from morning and often till late into the evening at the dossiers of people I would never meet. Should we trust him? Or her? Should their employers trust them? Might be a traitor, spy, lonely decider, a suitable case for blackmail by the unscrupulous opposition? Thus I, who seemed to have no understanding of myself, was being made to sit in judgement on the lives and loves of others.[59]

When a vetting application arrives in D1, a clerical worker checks the name with police, MI5 and RUC computer records. If there is no file or trace, the form is stamped 'NRA', which stands for 'Nothing Recorded Against', and returned to the state agency or employer. If there is a minor reference on a computer database, the form will be stamped 'No Security Objection'.

If there is something of interest, the vetting section will send a recommendation to the relevant intelligence desk who will normally confirm it. This is a delicate decision. The vetting section then writes a letter to the security manager of the Whitehall department, state agency or government contractor. Essentially, the letter states that MI5 has recorded information that should be taken into consideration. It concludes by recommending whether or not the applicant should be employed and provides the security director with four options:

1. Based on the fact that the intelligence is insufficiently serious, you should still hire the applicant.
2. Interview the person concerned before making a final decision.
3. Employ him or her, but do not grant access to certain information and documents.
4. Do not employ him or her.

If there are any doubts, the applicant will be refused security clearance. MI5 is always informed of the outcome because it needs to record the verdict on the subject's personal file.

Many MI5 officers dislike vetting because of the implications to each subject of their decision. However, although MI5 has enormous influence, the security manager delivers the final verdict. A fair proportion of people in such posts are former Army officers and policemen, who are instinctively suspicious of the left wing. MI5 fears that some security managers will ignore their recommendation and blacklist an individual, based on their own prejudices.

However, some MI5 managers have their own long-running bias, which they find difficult to eradicate. As late as 1993, Cold War mentality dominated security assessments of ordinary people. That year a young man applied for a job at the Inland Revenue. In the early 1980s he had been a member of the Militant Tendency, and MI5 had opened a file on him and his political connections. When the dossier was passed to a desk officer, it was found to contain only old material and it was clear that the man was no longer politically active. But one item of intelligence in the file intrigued the officers involved in assessing the case. It was an edited transcript of a tapped telephone conversation that had taken place within the previous five years between the applicant and an activist at Militant's head office in Liverpool. During the discussion the man was called 'Comrade' by the Trotskyist. After rereading the transcript, the desk officer felt it had been said in a jocular, almost casual, manner. Committed Militant members often used the term as an expression in social situations without thinking. It did not necessarily mean that they were addressing a fellow Trotskyist: they might use it with a former activist, a drinking friend or even a political opponent.

The officer assessing the case was inclined to clear the man as it was too trivial and opaque. However, she was obliged to refer the file to a senior manage and was shocked by his response. The manager said that the Militant Tendency reserved the term 'Comrade' only for its members, so the man might still be an active Trotskyist and subversive. He concluded that the applicant should be refused employment. Other MI5 officers were stunned, and most disagreed. The file was passed around for review. The final verdict was negative, and a letter was sent to the Inland Revenue recommending that the young man should not be offered the job.

Such arbitrary rulings have a profound impact on people's lives. Some sections of MI5's management, trained in a different era, have not adapted to new attitudes and conditions. Until recently, ever since vetting procedures were introduced, homosexuality was an absolute bar to security clearance. The irony was that British intelligence contained several prominent homosexuals. 'The secret world I went into', recalled John le Carré, 'was a man's world and infused with that was homosexuality, which is peculiarly English and regimental.'[60] In the closet were Sir Maurice Oldfield, head of MI6 from 1973 until 1980, and Alex Kellar, head of MI5's F Branch in the 1960s.[61] Former MI5 officer and traitor Guy Burgess flaunted his homosexuality and the Service was fully aware that Anthony Blunt was gay yet continued to employ him.

MI5 argued that it was not the sexual preference that mattered but the vulnerability to blackmail. 'The crucial element is the desire to conceal,' said an MoD vetting officer in 1983. 'That is what makes a man blackmailable.' This was reinforced in 1987 by Robert Armstrong, then head of the Civil Service, who stated that homosexual officials should not be barred from access to sensitive information. Openness was the key issue.[62]

A year later, a 22-year-old data processor at GCHQ, Andrew Hodges, decided to test the new policy of tolerance. He openly and publicly stated that he was gay. He was promptly suspended from his job. A series of senior civil servants then declared their homosexuality. They also lost their security clearance and were barred from promotion.

Eventually, the government conceded defeat and, in 1991, announced that, 'in the light of changing social attitudes,' admission of homosexuality was no longer a bar to access to classified material. Gay men and women were encouraged to come out for the sake of honesty. 'There are an increasing number of men and women who have declared themselves to be homosexual,' said David Pepper, GCHQ's deputy director of administration. 'The fact of homosexuality is not of itself a security worry.'[63]

However, homosexuality was still viewed as a potential security risk until 1994. Inside MI5 being gay was one of seven 'character defects' taken into consideration by the Service during vetting. The others are profligacy with money, alcoholism, drug-taking, unreliability, dishonesty and promiscuity. The Service kept a 'Pink List' of individuals where MI5 had made a decision against an individual because they were suspected homosexuals and lesbians. This was confirmed by Duncan Lustig-Prean, a former commander in the Royal Navy who runs Rank Outsiders, which represents gays in the armed forces. On 5 September 1997, he wrote to the *Guardian*:

> Among my members and clients are former intelligence staff and senior officers who regularly worked with MI5, MI6 and Special Branch. Some of us have had first-hand experience of the files these agencies hold.
>
> The 'Pink List' does indeed exist ... The private sexual preferences of ordinary citizens are listed, cross-referenced to any partners or gay contacts known to the agencies. The list is updated by MI5 and the police who regularly pass across information. This list was routinely accessed by members of military intelligence and has, to my certain knowledge, frequently been used in the gay witch hunts which continue in the military. I know that at least two of our members involved in security matters have, within the past month, been required to use the Pink List as part of their work.[64]

Within days of Lustig-Prean's disclosure, a gay author, Alisdare Hickson, was targeted by Special Branch. He was researching a book on gays in the military, commissioned by Duckworth. After a day's work at the library he returned to his south London flat to find a note from Detective Constable Nigel Robson: 'I would like to arrange a brief appointment to discuss your current research.'

Intrigued, and anxious to ensure he had not broken the law, Hickson met Robson at a café opposite New Scotland Yard for coffee. 'He asked me questions about where I was born, my parents, education, travel plans, what languages I speak, sources of income, who I live with,' he said. 'He even wanted to know if I read spy novels. The whole thing lasted two hours. I feel it was a disturbing business.'[65]

Despite such incidents, MI5 and the MoD continue to insist that homosexuality is no longer a bar to security clearance, as long as the candidate declares it on the vetting form. In 1997, MI5 let it be known that gay men and women would be welcome to apply for advertised jobs in the Service. The MoD's Defence Vetting Agency has also officially lifted its ban on homosexuals, but there is a qualification, linked to the 'character defects' issue. 'People can still find themselves with financial, drink, drug and other personal problems which make them vulnerable,' said Michael Wilson, the agency's chief executive. 'There is still a bar on military personnel having gay liaisons and adulterous relations if it threatens operational efficiency'.[66]

What emerges from MI5's vetting procedures is that outdated and outmoded attitudes have not been fully expunged. Security assessments are largely a matter of judgement and interpretation. While the Service retains accessible files of fading old material for potential use, the opportunity for mischief remains. MI5's often bizarre criteria for compiling and keeping dossiers were disclosed by David Shayler. In 1997 he told the *Mail on Sunday how a* file called 'Subversion in Contemporary Music' was still open for inspection by staff. It included microfilm material on reggae band UB40 (whose songs protested against unemployment) and the anarchist group Crass. MI5 also targeted the notorious Sex Pistols. Their number-one hit 'God Save The Queen', with the lyric 'It's a fascist regime/God made you a moron', would not have endeared them to MI5 management, who keep photographs of the Queen on the office walls.

There was marginally more political substance to targeting former rock journalist Garry Bushell, who championed many skinhead bands. He originally came to MI5's attention in the early 1970s as a supporter of the Socialist Workers Party, but when he joined *Sounds* magazine he was known for his vociferous support of 'Oi!' music – a brand of racist punk rock. 'In the 1980s an informant had reported that Bushell had close links with far-right parties,' said Shayler.[67]

Bushell, now television critic of the *Sun*, branded such intelligence 'a joke':

> It's no secret that as a teenager I was very left-wing. I even did my journalistic training on *Socialist Worker* – a fact that embarrasses the comrades far more than it does me. But the most militant thing I ever did was to headbutt a brick during the Lewisham riots of 1977.
>
> Anyone who remembers *Sounds* knows I covered every sort of music happening at street level, from 2-Tone to the New Wave of British Heavy Metal. The Oi! Bands I wrote about were into football – not invading Poland!
>
> It is laughably alleged that I had links with the far right. Presumably that's the same far right who attacked me in the 100 Club in 1981. And then they published my home address in their hate rags, denouncing me as 'a race traitor'.
>
> It's all very bizarre . . . It certainly makes you wonder if MI5 didn't have anything better to do. They obviously fell for the myth that rock 'n' roll can change the world.[68]

On reflection, Shayler agreed with the bemused Bushell. 'It was another exercise in making work for idle hands,' he recalled. 'The file ["Subversion in Contemporary Music"] consisted of cuttings from the music press. Why MI5 thought this was of any relevance to the security of the nation is beyond me.'[69]

Former cabinet minister Peter Mandelson was so concerned that his dossier was still open that, in September 1997, he called on MI5 to 'weed out and destroy' such files compiled during the Cold War 'which are now entirely redundant'.[70]

Opposition to the burning of Service archives has come from both ends of the political spectrum. 'I do not want my file destroyed,' said Marjorie Thompson, former chair of CND. 'It could be important material in the history of CND and I would, some day, like to know what they had down on me. It's shocking to think that we can find out now what the Stasi [East German Security Service] were up to, but not our own people.'[71]

CND's arch enemy, Dr Julian Lewis, the Tory MP and former deputy director of the Party's research department, is equally horrified by the proposal – but for a very different reason. He compared the idea to George Orwell's formula for *1984*: 'Who controls the past controls the future. Who controls the past?' He claimed that 'those who call most loudly for files to be destroyed are obviously prime suspects as characters who know they have something to hide'.[72] Lewis called on MI5 to 'resist partisan and self-serving political pressure' from Labour ministers and refrain from shredding files. On 28 October 1997, Jack Straw replied on behalf of MI5: 'The policy of the Security Service is to retain only those records which it needs to carry out its statutory functions or which are of historical importance. Files held by the Service are therefore reviewed against those criteria periodically as resources permit.

'There is no question of consigning whole categories of files for destruction without proper review. On the other hand, given the need to ensure that files are not retained unnecessarily, the Service will not retain files which do not seem to merit retention on any of the grounds I have mentioned.'

The key issue is: who does the weeding and what is 'of historical importance'? As Alan Clark, a former defence procurement minister, said, 'The problem is that, almost invariably, judgement is made by civil servants – although, laughably, ministers may occasionally try to get something taken out to protect their political reputation. For a historian, the really obstructive thing is when civil servants, to defend their reputation as administrators or having made colossal errors of judgement, weed out or repress things that will reflect badly on them.'[73]

The former Home Secretary Jack Straw addressed this issue – but only up to a point. He agreed for security-cleared officials from the Public Records Office (PRO) to read MI5 files that have been earmarked for destruction to check their historical value. Straw added that he had increased the number of categories of files that should be preserved. These will include dossiers on organisations and individuals on which security action was required but which were not considered of great significance at the time. About one in a thousand files on people investigated – but not pursued – will be saved.[74]

However, the PRO involvement still leaves MI5 in overall control of the files without any independent oversight. Officially, the Service applies the following criteria for deciding whether its records are of 'historical interest':

Major investigations; important subversive figures, terrorists and spies; individuals involved in important historical events; *causes célèbres* in a security context; files which contain original papers of historical interest; major changes of Service policy, organisation or procedures; files which are in some way 'period pieces', e.g. they illustrate clearly Security Service attitudes and techniques of the time; milestones in the Service's history.[75]

Ever since its foundation, the Service has jealously guarded its files and refused to disclose any information about their number, structure or contents. Successive Home Secretaries have been compliant, claiming either that to do so was not 'in the interests of national security' or would 'jeopardise operational capability'.[76] In 1995, the parliamentary ombudsman taxed the Home Office on the number of MI5 records on people, then estimated at about half a million. At first officials said they did not know the exact figure, then that the information was available but it was not going to be released, even to Parliament. The Labour government continued this policy, based on the recommendation of Stephen Lander, MI5's director-general. As head of the Registry in the late 1980s, Lander was resistant to review and kept open many contentious files.[77]

Eventually, in July 1998, after a series of embarrassing revelations by David Shayler, the official figures were announced in the Commons by Jack Straw. They showed that in 1972 MI5 had an estimated 535,000 files on individuals and organisations, although unofficial sources claim that the figure was far higher. From mid-1992 until mid-1998, 'more than 110,000' files were 'marked for destruction', which, in reality, means that their subjects' names were removed from the main research index.

That leaves 425,000. Of those, there are still 330,000 dossiers on individuals and groups who have been investigated, by MI5 as 'security risks'. They remain open but with varying degrees of accessibility and importance. The remaining 95,000 files relate to people and organisations who have never been investigated but have received 'protective security advice'. This includes those people against whom MI5 has made a recommendation based on its criteria of character defects.[78]

What Jack Straw did not mention was that these figures referred only to current files recorded on the main research index. On top of these official figures, MI5 has hundreds of thousands of other closed files on microfilm. They can only be accessed in exceptional circumstances.

By June 2001, very few have been actually destroyed. 'There are

400,000 paper files, a great many of these are multi-volume,' said Sir Stephen Lander, then MI5's director-general, at a private conference at the Public Record Office. 'Many of these are still living entities that record the lengthy interest the Service had over decades in a single subject, organisation or individual. Much of our work has long antecedents, knowledge of which is important to our success today.' He added that secret files would eventually be made available on emminent public figures who were involved in major historic events. A tiny number of personal files on individuals who turned out 'not to be suspicious' were also being witheld until a time when they could not embarrass the people concerned.

The latest figures, released on 12 March 2002, show that of 210,000 personal files held by MI5, about 20,000 are 'green' which means they are open and active. Of the rest, 70,000 are 'amber' (further investigation is prohibited, but extra information can be inserted) and 120,000 are 'red' (closed although they can be accessed in exceptional circumstances).

The government's blanket ban preventing anyone from knowing if MI5 holds a file on them has come under increasing legal and public pressure. In October 2001, the Information Tribunal ruled that the claim in 1998 by Jack Straw, then Home Secretary, that MI5 should never admit to retaining a file on an individual even when it did not damage nationl security was unlawful. This was based on a case brought by Norman Baker, Liberal Democrat MP for Lewes, who received an anonymous letter from an MI5 officer calling himself 'The Mechanic' which disclosed details of his file. The MP was told that it was opened because he was a radical activist on environmental issues in the 1980s. 'Intelligence' from Sussex Special Branch was included, based on an informant in the South Downs Earth First Group of which Baker was a member. He was also listed as a Greenpeace supporter. The file was closed in 1989 when Baker started work in the Liberal Democrats' whips office.

After the tip-off, Baker then wrote to MI5 asking to see details of his file. This caused a mild panic inside the Service because to confirm its existence would show that files were held on political activists not just subversives. MI5 refused, falling back on its official policy: 'No member of the public is permitted to see any Security Service files, except for historical records which have been declassified and released by the public record office. Confidentiality is essential to protect details of investigational and operational techniques and to maintain the effectiveness of the service. The dangers that would be posed, for example, by members of terrorist groups or foreign intelligence services embarking on "fishing expeditions" in the Service's records are obvious.'

However, the Baker case and the fact that the Data Protection Act provided powers to prevent terrorists from seeing their files made the Home Office blanket ban unsustainable. On 10 December 2001, the day that parliament broke up for the Christmas recess, the Home Secretary David Blunkett placed a document in the House of Commons library that in part reversed the ban. He issued a certificate that enabled individuals to gain access to their files under the Data Protection Act – as long as MI5 deemed that the release of the information 'is not required for the purpose of safe-guarding national security'.

At first glance this appeared to be real progress. But in practice this exemption enables MI5 to stonewall applications which could end up in long-running court cases before any files are made available. The omens for real accountabiity are not promising. In 2002, Peter Hitchens, the right-wing columnist for the *Mail on Sunday*, applied under the Act to see his file. In the early 1970s, he was an active member of the Trotskyist International Socialists (later renamed the Socialist Workers Party). Now an iconaclastic right-winger, Hitchens says he deserved to be spied on, but was curious to see the contents of his file. 'I am not seeking my file because I object to it, or because I want to complain or sue,' he wrote.

Former officers have told us that there is absolutely no doubt that MI5 retained a file on such a senior member of the SWP, but its contents could not conceivably harm national security or betray tradecraft, particularly as it relates mostly to industrial disputes from over 30 years ago. As Hitchens remarked wrily: 'In 1970 there were no mobile phones and no personal computers. I have a feeling that MI5's technology may have moved forward a bit since then.'

After formally applying, Hitchens received a polite refusal, on MI5-headed notepaper, which neither confirmed or denied the existence of the file. The columnist is appealing against the decision. Usually a staunch defendant of such agencies, Hitchens dismisses the notion that releasing a file that would have ended in 1974 could compromise MI5's current operational procedures. 'It no longer has any bearing on me,' he said. 'I long ago grew up and changed my mind. It no longer has any bearing on the safety of the country, if it ever did . . . the Cold War, which linked some of the left with our enemies in the USSR, is over. The USSR has ceased to exist. The MI5 case is painfully thin.'

In many Western democracies, notably Sweden, Canada and the United States, individuals have the right to inspect their file – under the appropriate security and privacy supervision. Genuine national security material (rather than historical files) is exempt, and references to informants are blacked out, but the current Labour administration steadfastly refuses to grant such access. 'In everything we have said about freedom of information,' said Straw, in September 1997, 'we have always made an exception for national security. If you accept the need for security and intelligence agencies within a democracy – which is that there are some threats which require secret investigation and monitoring – then you have to accept there must be secrecy about much of that information.'[79]

A more direct insight into government thinking was provided by David Aaronovitch, a columnist on the *Independent on Sunday* and presenter of BBC's *Newsnight*. A former president of the National Union of Students and former Communist Party member in the late 1970s, Aaronovitch is well connected in New Labour. He spoke to a Cabinet minister – who is 'as high up as you can get in this government and not play flamenco guitar' – and asked when he and others of his background could see their MI5 files.

'Never,' replied the minister, but added that in the early 1990s he had been shown (under exceptional circumstances) part of his own file. It dealt with his family's connection with the Communist Party in the large, depressed city where he grew up, and some of it had been compiled by an informer. 'The Communist Party was not big in that area,' recalled the minister, 'and I soon realised that this chap could only be one of three people. Some of them were friends of the family . . . But you see, these informers, no matter how you feel about them, were recruited on the basis that they were doing a job for their country. As far as they were concerned, they were patriots not sneaks. And the condition of their employment was that no one would ever be told about them . . . Therefore, it would be better to destroy the files.'[80]

In fact, most files were not 'destroyed' – in the conventional meaning of the word. They were simply moved to another part of the building, recategorised and access was reduced. As recently as 1994, marginalised Trotskyist groups were still under surveillance and F Branch's management even blocked some resources being transferred to counter-terrorist sections.

It was not until after Shayler's disclosures in 1997 that the issue was fully addressed and MI5 stopped investigating political activists. 'I had argued this while I was still serving within the organisation,' said Shayler, 'but my complaints fell on deaf ears.'[81] His line managers in F Branch agreed in principle with what he said, but in practice realised they had little to gain from raising their concerns with the branch director.

Today the old F Branch is staffed by just one part-time desk officer and has been absorbed into the new D Branch, which covers counter-espionage. But many old files remain and so do the old structures, techniques and management that compiled that archive. MI5 has been looking for new targets and as IRA bombs exploded in the busy streets of mainland Britain they found one. Whether the Service was equipped to handle such an important operation provided the Security Service with its toughest ever challenge.

5

THE SECRET WAR AGAINST
THE IRA

'MI5's agenda is built around counter-espionage: a slow process, keeping information for themselves long after it has squeezed things dry.'

RUC officer, quoted in *The Times*, 9 May 1992

'It was farcical. There I was with a fast-moving target – the IRA were planting bombs down the street and our Security Service remained obsessed with pedantic redrafting of documents.'

David Shayler, MI5 officer (1991–96) and member of
T Branch (1992–94)

On 15 December 1991, the Home Office announced the appointment of Stella Rimington as the new director-general of the Security Service. It was a historic promotion. She was the first woman head of any intelligence agency in the world and it was the first time a new director-general had been named publicly in Britain. But there was a more profound significance to her elevation. It marked the painfully slow transition of MI5 from a counter-subversion and espionage one that combating terrorism. This process had been started six years previously by Sir Antony Duff, then director-general, but was never fully implemented.

MI5 was like a sleeping giant and Duff's successor, Sir Patrick Walker, was too cautious to wake it. He agreed in principle with switching targets, but was far too gradualist in his approach. Rimington, a steely, astute operator, realised that if MI5 was to survive in the post-Cold War world, it needed a more prominent role in countering terrorism. The most immediate and concentrated threat was from the IRA. The day after her appointment, on 16 December 1991, the Irish Republicans sent the new director-general a warning message. That afternoon they set off explosive devices in London shops, at the National Gallery and at Victoria railway station.

A lateral thinker, Rimington knew that catching terrorists was risky and expensive, which meant persuading ministers to authorise more resources. It was a tough political task as other agencies, notably the Metropolitan Police Special Branch and the Anti-Terrorist Squad, were in no mood to concede primacy. The new director-general, however, had the IRA in her sights. It would prove to be MI5's greatest challenge and a test to see if their personnel and internal methods were equipped for the war with terrorism.

Rimington's past reveals few clues that she would become Britain's first female MI5 director-general. Born in 1935 in Croydon, Stella was the only daughter of David Whitehouse, a skilled engineer. Her family moved around and when she was 12 they settled in Nottingham, where she attended the Nottingham High School for Girls. She graduated from Edinburgh University with a second-class degree in English.

Little is known about her education, as MI5's weeders have been hard at work removing photographs and documents from her records.[1] But she is remembered as academically bright (though not exceptional), independent, headstrong and outspoken. 'I was nominated to be head girl,' she recalled. 'The process of choosing the head girl at the time was that the children had a vote. I suspect that I was the children's candidate, I certainly wasn't the teacher's choice. Although I think I got more votes, the teachers thought I was not sound and so I didn't become head girl.'[2]

In 1959, aged 24, Stella moved to Liverpool where she trained as a historical archivist at the university, which provided a type of apprenticeship for a future in intelligence. But joining the secret world was as remote a prospect as the Communist Party winning a general election. 'If anyone at the time had told me I would end up as director-general of MI5, I would have thought they had taken leave of their senses,' she reflected.[3]

In her first assignment in Worcester, Stella spent her time driving around in a little van trying to persuade vicars and stately-home owners to deposit their archives in the county records office. 'I had the job of persuading some of them to do something they didn't want to do,' she said.[4]

Settled in her career, in 1963 she married John Rimington, a civil servant in the Board of Trade and later chief executive of the Health and Safety Executive. Two years later, he was posted to the British High Commission in New Delhi as a first secretary. Stella found life as a diplomatic wife and hostess tedious and looked for distractions. The couple took up amateur dramatics, with Stella playing Lady Julia Merton in Oscar Wilde's *Lord Arthur Savile's Crime* and a more vulgar role as Maria Helliwell in J. B. Priestley's *When We Are Married*. 'On stage she could do the grand dame all right, but she was rather better at the northern fishwife,' said a friend who knew her in India. 'She was a remarkable lady, very funny in a rather astringent way. There was never any doubt about her intelligence, but she was a bit low in personal charm. She is a nice woman, though, very no-nonsense, very unpretentious. Not a prude, not a boozer. Not strongly right-wing, certainly not looking for reds-under-the-beds, but not painfully left either. And too much of a realist to have truck with the middle ground.'[5]

Bored with the diplomatic cocktail circuit, she looked for more substantial outside interests. After meeting MI5's full-time officer in New Delhi, she realised that her archivist training might enable her to be effective in such an occupation. She worked for him as a temporary clerk and typist and when her husband returned to Britain in 1969, she applied for and was offered a full-time job at MI5.

Rimington joined the Service as a secretary. 'It was male-dominated, white and middle-class,' she recalled. 'Women were second-class citizens who typed and dealt with papers, but had no "sharp end" work.'[6] She began her career in F Branch, analysing and sifting intelligence material on political subversives. Industrious and efficient, she gained a reputation for bluntness and boundless ambition.

In 1983, Rimington was promoted to assistant director and head of F2, responsible for monitoring trade unions and political activists. It was the most controversial period of her career. She was party to some of MI5's most dubious operations, notably the bugging of trade unionists, passing on public-order information from strikes to the government and the surveillance of CND activists. She played a central role during the 1984–85 miners' strike, co-ordinating and authorising MI5's operations.

According to GCHQ and police sources, a co-ordinated campaign was run by MI5 to discredit the National Union of Mineworkers (NUM) and its president Arthur Scargill. The home and office telephones of Scargill and Communist Party Member Mick McGahey, his vice-president, were tapped. At least one MI5 agent was infiltrated into the union and there is some evidence that he deliberately destabilised the NUM at critical moments. Other agents provocateurs were deployed to provoke violence on the picket lines, notably in the Scottish coalfields. This caused enormous tension and was deeply resented by the local police force.[7]

Rimington accumulated and collated a lot of detailed information about the miners' activities, largely from agents and mass surveillance, but most of it was not intelligence material about the security of the state: it was basic public-order data about the strategy and movement of the strikers. This was handed over to the police and some of it was included in MI5's daily Box 500 reports, which were circulated to 10 Downing Street, key ministers and the Cabinet Office. These are intelligence digests on targets, written in vague language. It was difficult for ministers to judge the exact source of the material and therefore its accuracy because it was attributed to 'secret and reliable sources'. But Margaret Thatcher, then Prime Minister, lapped it up: she was convinced that the year-long dispute had been orchestrated by a secret Communist cell led by Arthur Scargill.

Rimington was responsible for the Box 500 reports and was deemed to have had 'a good strike'. In 1986, she was promoted to the influential post of director of K Branch, responsible for counter-espionage, but it was the growing threat of IRA and international terrorism that made her reputation while she was head of G Branch between 1988 and 1990. She had never been a field operative, but she became an expert at managing the collating and assessment of data acquired by agents. A former colleague recalls that she 'had a dramatic ability to read the terrorists' intentions and second-guess them'.[8]

In 1990, Rimington became senior deputy director-general and was very much the protégée of her boss Patrick Walker. In Whitehall, officials who dealt with her were reminded of Margaret Thatcher: she lacked charm but had a formidable grasp of her brief. An extremely effective administrator and organiser, she was attuned to the nuances and shifts in mood of senior Home Office civil servants.

But she was also domineering and robust. Like Thatcher, she was intent on getting her own way, and if that meant being unpleasant it was a small price to pay. 'If you are too laid-back,' said Rimington in 1996, 'I don't think you perform as well as when you are a bit tense. The adrenaline flows and it makes you focus that bit more on what you're doing . . . I think I have always been a bit bossy and I probably still am.'[9]

Inside MI5, the comparisons with the former Prime Minister were thought apt. A former officer said she had 'an incredibly clear brain, very broad and imaginative, very incisive in argument and extremely quick to pick up the weak point in anybody else's argument – extremely good in committee'.[10] It was these qualities that impressed Home Office civil servants and ministers and elevated her to the top job.

From her first day as director-general, 3 February 1992, Rimington was resolute in her aim to preserve MI5's budget and power base. She was more open than her predecessors, but this was restricted to MI5's external image and role. Crucially, she did not address the internal problems that concerned many staff, such as MI5's inability to adapt its methods to new targets. She was also prone to be sidetracked by trivial office issues.

On one occasion, she threw a temper tantrum when she found pigeon droppings on her window-sill. She demanded a bird of prey to deter the invaders and MI5 hired a specialist handler to operate a pigeon-killing falcon, which was nicknamed 'Golden Eye'. The handler would come to Thames House with the falcon perched on his forearm and take the lift to the roof. On one occasion, an officer was in the lift at the same time and stared warily at the bird. At first he thought it was a stuffed specimen to decorate the director-general's office. It was only when the falcon moved that he realised that it was alive. Once on the roof the handler would release the falcon, which killed the encroaching pigeons. But the falcon flew away and had to be replaced. Eventually the operation was successful, much to the amusement and bemusement of staff.

Rimington saw MI5 as part of the Crown Service rather than Whitehall, and a photograph of the Queen was prominently displayed on her office wall.[11] The prospect of a visit by Her Majesty to the six-storey building at 40 Gower Street in 1993 created considerable excitement. Not only was the office spring-cleaned; so was the whole of the underground car park.

For the new 56-six-year-old director-general, expanding MI5's role in combating terrorism was the number one priority. The IRA and UDA were the primary threats. In 1991, 94 people were killed in Northern Ireland and more than 900 were injured. That year there were more terrorist incidents on mainland Britain than at any time since 1975. The IRA's strategy was to spread a climate of fear and chaos that would force the British people and the politicians to confront the issue. By late 1991, shops and public transport in the UK were being fire-bombed.

Rimington set out to transfer resources from F Branch (subversion) and K Branch (counter-espionage) to the newly formed T Branch, responsible for investigating terrorism. At first there was some resistance. The director of F Branch prevented the transfer of some officers to T Branch. Other hardliners were sceptical about the change, arguing that it was not MI5's role to investigate terrorists. They were encouraged by Charles Elwell, who had been Rimington's boss in F Branch in the 1970s and retired in 1980. 'The intrusion [into counter-terrorism] of MI5 which is specifically a counter-espionage organisation', he said, 'is absolutely wrong. MI5 has nothing to do with terrorism, which is a crime. It should be dealt with by the police.'[12]

Historically, the Security Service has had limited involvement and experience in Northern Ireland. The province was regarded, in effect, like a colony with just one security liaison officer based in Belfast. Most of the intelligence work was done by the Royal Ulster Constabulary (RUC), military intelligence and Special Branch, who by the early 1960s had over 200 officers in place. MI5 was preoccupied by the Cold War and did not consider it a matter for them.

However, the chiefs of the Defence Staff were anxious that the right agency be assigned to handle 'up-to-date information on the IRA threat'. As far back as 17 March 1966, Air Marshal Harold Maguire, deputy chief of the Defence Staff (Intelligence), raised the issue at a Joint Intelligence Committee meeting in the Cabinet Office. But Martin Furnival Jones, then director-general of MI5, replied that IRA activities constituted a 'law and order' problem, not a security one. He said that terrorist crimes should be dealt with by the normal processes of law, and any intelligence assistance could be channelled through Special Branch. Instead, it was suggested that a special unit called the Defence Operations Centre was best equipped for this task.[13]

MI5 preferred to play a semi-detached role and provide training and technical security advice to the RUC, but as the crisis in Northern Ireland worsened, pressure grew for better intelligence. In 1973, MI5 was tasked to support the security operation in Ulster, but it was not their finest hour. Young female MI5 officers with barely a year's experience were dispatched to Belfast. They spent most of their time in offices in Stormont Castle, shuffling paper.

MI5 was capable of acting as the bureaucratic and communications interface beween the RUC, Special Branch and the police forces. It also provided useful technical expertise and intelligence from its files on suspected terrorists. But it was not equipped or experienced to run operations in Ulster. Until the late 1970s, the Army Intelligence Corps had primacy against the IRA in Northern Ireland, backed up by MI5 and RUC. Then the RUC took charge of all intelligence operations in Northern Ireland. Both the RUC and the British Army ran their own agents for surveillance and intelligence-gathering on weapons supplies.

In late 1979, the new Prime Minister, Margaret Thatcher, was dissatisfied and sent Sir Maurice Oldfield, then head of MI6, to Belfast to co-ordinate intelligence. MI5 was furious that an MI6 chief should be sent to oversee their senior officers in Northern Ireland. It was tantamount to a public criticism of their work. Suddenly, journalists in Belfast were receiving calls from RUC Special Branch alleging that Oldfield was a closet homosexual who combed the towns of Ulster looking to seduce young men. These malicious stories were traced back to MI5.[14]

The problem was that a bewildering intelligence bureaucracy was emerging, with the result that security operations became cumbersome, time-consuming and resource-intensive. Oldfield retired for 'health reasons' in 1980 before he could unravel the labyrinth.

Outside the UK, MI5 was responsible for collecting and investigating intelligence on the IRA in conjunction with the security services of various countries.

However, MI5's long-running rivalry with MI6 impeded success. In 1980, MI6 launched Operation Scream, whose aim was the 'offensive penetration' of Irish expatriate communities in Europe. Although MI5 had a security liaison officer in Germany, it was not informed of this recruitment drive. A year later, the more co-ordinated Operation Ward – controlled by Army Intelligence, MI5 and MI6 – was initiated. With 16 Irish informants, it was another attempt to penetrate the

IRA, but secret MI5 documents leaked to the IRA revealed that it was a failure. 'Only two can be said to be active in the sense of reporting anything at all,' stated one paper in 1984. 'Operation Ward has not so far produced any worthwhile intelligence at all,' said another.[15]

MI5 urgently needed a successful hit to justify its power base, and the political pressure was on after an IRA bomb killed 11 people at a Remembrance Day service in November 1987, at Enniskillen in Northern Ireland. The opportunity came three months later in February 1988, when three suspected IRA terrorists were under surveillance by MI5 and the Spanish police as they crossed Europe to Gibraltar. Hard intelligence showed that they were planning a major attack on the local British Army base.

Due to the inexperience of the local police in terrorism matters, a crack SAS unit was sent in. When they arrived in Gibraltar, they were briefed by the MI5 officers. Convinced that the IRA members were in possession of a bomb primed for detonation by remote control, the SAS gunned them down without warning in multiple bursts. They died instantly.

In the bloody aftermath, the reality was compared with MI5's intelligence. The victims were unarmed, as no weapons were found by the Spanish police. They did not have the bomb with them and it was not remote-control activated. Accusations followed that the SAS conducted a shoot-to-kill policy. 'When we heard the SAS were being brought in, we knew how it would end,' said a former MI5 officer. 'It felt very doomy.'[16]

What was said during that midnight briefing before the shooting is highly contentious. The SAS are adamant that MI5 told them the IRA members were definitely armed. 'We were told it was 100 per cent certain to be a [remote-control] button job,' said one of the SAS operatives at the inquest. This was denied by the Security Service, who said they were misinterpreted. The more likely truth is that MI5 said to the SAS, 'We have intelligence to indicate that the IRA ASU [Active Service Unit] is in possession of a remotely controlled, improvised, explosive device.' The SAS were not familiar with understanding the nuances and subtleties of such a briefing, but they gained the clear impression that they were all that stood between the terrorists and a horrific loss of life when, in fact, the intelligence had not been confirmed.

The Gibraltar shooting was heralded as a triumph for MI5 by its senior management. In the ensuing controversy it was claimed that

MI5 directors leaked operational information to the media. Stephen Lander denied the accusation.

On the British mainland the Metropolitan Police Special Branch (MPSB) was in charge of all intelligence operations against the IRA. A crucial task was to co-ordinate the activities of local Special Branch officers and gather intelligence about IRA cells in Britain to prevent imminent attacks. If the IRA exploded a bomb, the Anti-terrorist Squad took over responsibility for gathering evidence about the blast and the surrounding circumstances. Recruited from CID, its officers specialise in searching bomb sites and arms dumps for evidence that could put terrorists in jail.

In the late 1980s, the MPSB operation was relatively successful as a number of high explosives were discovered and arrests were made. But 1990 was the worst year for terrorist atrocities in Britain since 1975 and the police were struggling to cope. Part of the problem was structural: if an IRA cell went north, it could affect several different police forces, each with autonomous powers. It was a recipe for confusion and procrastination.[17]

As the IRA ran riot, media and political pressure for action intensified. The catalyst came in early 1990 when the IRA attacked 10 Downing Street during a Cabinet meeting with a home-made mortar. Hard intelligence was vital to prevent terrorism, so Margaret Thatcher asked Christopher Curwen, former chief of MI6 and intelligence co-ordinator at the Cabinet Office, to review the situation. By the autumn of 1991, Curwen had written three reports. Two concluded that MI5 should continue to have a limited and subordinate role. The other strengthened the hand of George Churchill Coleman, commander of the Anti-terrorist Unit.

However, Stella Rimington was determined to refocus and relaunch MI5 as the primary anti-terrorist intelligence agency. She lobbied ministers and the new intelligence co-ordinator in the Cabinet Office, Gerry Warner, a former senior MI6 director. She correctly assessed that penetrating the terrorist groups at every level was the crucial operational method. If that could be accomplished, bombing atrocities could be anticipated and avoided. By this stage MI5 was receiving copies of all intelligence relating to IRA operations on the mainland.

MI5's pitch for primacy was that Special Branch only understood how to run 'informers' whereas what was needed were 'agents'. An informer was paid for occasional intelligence while an agent was asked to penetrate terrorist groups and actively discover new information on the instructions of case officers. It was a much more aggressive, proactive approach. An effective agent could produce higher grade and regular intelligence, whereas an informant produced sporadic, fragmentary material.

MI5's lobbying was deeply resented by the MPSB, which argued that the Service had neither the expertise nor the experience to deal with the IRA on the mainland. A bitter turf war broke out. Each side accused the other of incompetence and failure to share information. A former MPSB officer, interviewed by the author Martin Dillon, explained the hostility between the two agencies: 'We were across this issue when Five [MI5] was too busy watching Soviet diplomats and engaging in a lot of its other curious activities. We didn't need interference from people in Five who did not have the expertise we had on the ground ... Of course there was a lack of co-ordination because they constantly refused to share information with us. They had their people in Ireland and it would have been valuable to us to have had constant access to intelligence which had a bearing on the IRA's activities over here. That was denied us time and time again.

'There was a feeling at the Yard that after the Cold War there was a lot of spare capacity in Five and they wanted to take up the slack by snatching control of the whole security apparatus which was targeted at the IRA. They were pointing the finger at us as though we were at fault for not stopping the IRA campaign in Britain.'[18]

In their submission to the Cabinet Office for retaining primacy, the MPSB stated that MI5 had been responsible for the death of WPC Yvonne Fletcher outside the Libyan embassy in 1984. It claimed that the agency had failed to pass on vital intelligence, which was a telegram sent from Libya to their embassy in London. In fact, the telegram had been intercepted by GCHQ and not passed on at all, because it arrived outside their then office hours of 9 a.m. to 5 p.m.

When MI5 furiously demonstrated this as a false allegation, the MPSB retracted and apologised. However, the episode turned the Home Office against the MPSB, as did their leaks to the press about their rival's alleged inefficiency. Intelligence co-operation between MI5 and MPSB was now at an all-time low and the IRA benefited considerably from the friction.

The final nails in the MPSB's coffin were hammered in during April 1992, when an IRA bomb exploded in London's Soho. It was pure luck that there were no casualties, but what emerged was that the IRA bomber, James Canning, had been under police surveillance until moments before the blast. Although he was later sentenced to 30 years in jail, he was acquitted for the Soho bombing. This was because the police admitted that they had lost 'eyeball' (sight of the target) on him for the crucial few minutes before and after he placed the bomb.

Four days after the 1992 general election, a huge IRA device exploded in the City of London. Loaded into a van, it killed three people, injured 91 and caused damage worth hundreds of millions of pounds. The next day another large bomb exploded in London, ruining several shops and damaging a strategic motorway bridge. It was an astonishing successful blow against the infrastructure of the capital, designed to make people's lives as difficult as possible.

The MPSB was on the defensive and this was exposed ten days later on 21 April, when highly sensitive minutes of a Metropolitan Police Policy Committee meeting were leaked to the *Irish Times*. According to the document, William Taylor, the Met's assistant commissioner for Special Operations, acknowledged that the vital weapon against terrorism was intelligence, 'of which there was little at this stage.' It was an embarrassing disclosure. Although Taylor strongly denied that the document was leaked by MI5, senior MPSB officers were convinced that it was part of a black propaganda campaign by the Security Service to secure primacy.

These incidents erased any final doubts in the government's mind. On 8 May 1992, Kenneth Clarke, the Home Secretary, announced that MI5 would have 'lead responsibility' for gathering intelligence on the IRA in Britain. 'The purpose of this change', he said, 'is to enable the Security Service to use to the full the expertise and skills which it has developed over the years on counter-terrorism. Operations on a wider basis, including the collection of evidence, the arrest and prosecution of those suspected of terrorist offences, are plainly essential in dealing with terrorism. Those wider responsibilities must rest with the police.'[19]

For Stella Rimington, who had been director-general for just over three months, it was a triumph for her Whitehall networking and lobbying, but now she was required to deliver the promises she had made to the Home Secretary.

The arrangement came into effect on 1 October 1992. MI5 immediately set up a special section of T Branch with 75 staff. Its role was to manage and co-ordinate intelligence operations against Nationalist terror in Britain. The new target required a new approach: IRA cells behaved differently from KGB spies and subversive targets. Terrorists were constantly mobile, they acted quickly and at short notice. There were no rules or certainties. Above all, the IRA's policy was never to be predictable.

For MI5 to be effective against such tactics, their internal procedures needed to be dramatically reformed. The new threat required lateral thinking, flexibility, faster action under pressure as events unfolded, less bureaucracy and closer co-operation between all the intelligence agencies. Rimington appeared to accept this reality: 'The Security Service tries to gather advance intelligence about threats to the country. But it also has to assess it and work out with others what action should be taken to prevent the harm that's intended . . . You must have people who are able to think on their feet, who can cope in a situation where they're out on the street, where they can't ring up the boss and say, "What shall I do next?" and whose judgement in those circumstances you are going to be able to rely on. You're looking for that element of individualism, of ability to take responsibility.'[20]

MI5's managers did not adapt sufficiently to their new responsibilities in this way. Trained during the Cold War, they remained faithful to familiar methods. This culture, imposed by the old guard, was to place a greater premium on analysing intelligence on paper rather than driving forward investigations and pursuing imaginative solutions to catch terrorists.

Over the years, this deficiency has been rectified to some extent, particularly on the technical and agent-running side. But working for MI5 remains a UK-based, advisory desk job. Officers spend much of their time writing, redrafting and distributing briefings for civil servants and ministers on issues and individuals. They copy out reports – disguising anonymous agent intelligence and product from telephone taps – and send them to other agencies. Vast amounts of paper are produced and consumed and the overriding ethos is bureaucratic not operational. That is a major reason why MI5 has not been staffed by the best and the brightest who can 'think on their feet'.

Despite MI5's new powers against the IRA on the mainland, it remained an introverted organisation. One of its most important new tasks was to pool its intelligence with other agencies, but an inherent obsession with secrecy and fear of compromising sources often prevented it from handing over its most powerful asset. Insecure and suspicious, MI5 adopted a lofty disdain for the MPSB. In early 1993, it rejected several requests for updated information on terrorist suspects.

Inevitably, relations between MI5 and the MPSB became tense and strained as data tended to be hoarded rather than shared. This, of course, seriously impeded security operations against Irish terrorism, but MI5 appeared unperturbed. This infuriated the RUC Special Branch, who had retained primacy in Northern Ireland and felt that the Security Service was unsuited to such operations. 'MI5's agenda is built around counter-espionage, a slow process, keeping information for themselves long after it has squeezed things dry,' said a senior RUC Branch officer.[21]

MI5 was equally wary of the MPSB, and with good reason. When the IRA files were delivered to MI5's T2 section, desk officers were horrified. The intelligence was insufficient, ancient and inadequate. Yet MI5 did not incorporate MPSB records into its database and neglected to follow up any leads. Instead, it concentrated on irrelevant and outdated targets. Bizarrely, this was because MI5 did not want to embarrass the MPSB over the intercept warrants it inherited, which were out of date and inaccurate.

Apart from sending them copies of correspondence and reports, MI5 began to exclude the MPSB from certain covert operations. During the height of the IRA's mainland campaign in mid-1993, a group of MI5 and regional Special Branch officers met for a drink in a pub. 'By working closely together, we will beat the common enemy,' said one.

'Yeah, the Met,' quipped another, much to the merriment of all those present.

For MI5 to be effective against the IRA, agent-recruitment and handling were the vital techniques. Here the Service has had a mixed record. Its success rate was helped by IRA operatives who felt genuine remorse for the atrocities and the victims. MI5 officers used the 'let's stop this senseless killing' approach to good effect. But their inexperience was displayed in dealing with 'supergrasses' based in Northern Ireland. These were informers whose lives were in danger and who needed a new life and identity. Some demanded a home in an obscure country where the IRA would not be able to find them.

The RUC asked MI5 to use their influence with their counterparts overseas. That proved impossible as Western intelligence agencies refused to relocate people with a criminal record (most supergrasses had committed terrorist acts to maintain their cover). After this approach failed, the RUC agreed to provide special protection, but said that it was MI5's responsibility to find them new identities. Then, when a supergrass was released or granted immunity, the RUC would ensure his safe passage to a house in Britain where he remained under guard until he received details of his new life.

However, MI5 replied that there were still serious obstacles to resettling supergrasses overseas: it could not necessarily trust the foreign agency and most countries would be loath to accept responsibility – financial and moral – for such an obvious terrorist target. This was greeted with some scepticism by the RUC. 'It was ludicrous that MI5, which everyone believes is the *crème de la crème* of the intelligence world,' an RUC source told author Martin Dillon, 'doesn't know how to hide agents. Surely they did it with the KGB when they turned them.'[22]

MI5 poured resources into agent-recruitment and running. Although this produced some positive results, it also created legal and ethical problems. There are no strictures on how far these agents can go to defeat terrorism. To preserve their cover inside the IRA, some have shot British soldiers and planted bombs that have killed or injured civilians. For MI5, who have been ruthless in running agents, this is the high price of fighting terrorism.

In 1992, a former MI5 undercover officer broke the Official Secrets Act and went public about his activities. He acknowledged in a *Daily Telegraph* interview that it was difficult to 'maintain the line between what is lawful and what is not'. He admitted that he was 'guilty of conspiring to commit some minor offences. If murder or bombs had been mentioned, I could have made an excuse and left. But where the targets are involved in day-to-day killing such nicety is impossible. Any lack of enthusiasm would be an instant pointer for men already alert for infiltration. The agent must, if discovery is to be avoided, join enthusiastically in the activities of the organisation even if they are seriously criminal.'[23]

MI5 has always lobbied the Home Office to give immunity from prosecution for agents or informers who may be involved in criminal activity. 'A deep-cover agent has one link to the sane world – his controller,' said the anonymous former officer. 'There has to be complete trust between the two . . . But that trust extends to believing that behind the controller is the support of the state.'

The activities of one agent, Patrick Daly, highlighted not only the improving performance of MI5's involvement but also the doubts about its techniques. Daly was a long-term asset who had infiltrated the Irish Nationalist Liberation Army (INLA) in the Irish Republic. He later testified that he had been asked by the INLA to find explosives for a campaign in Britain. After tipping off his MI5 controller, T Branch officers supplied fake explosives to their agent. When Daly told two INLA members that the devices were ready to be picked up in a quarry in the West Country, several armed police were ready to arrest them. The two INLA operatives were later convicted and jailed for 25 years.

For MI5 it was a major coup: two dangerous terrorists had been captured and a bombing operation was averted. The INLA members' lawyer argued that Daly was an agent provocateur who had conspired to entrap his clients, but MI5 could justifiably argue that the INLA were clearly intent on serious criminal activity and many lives had been saved. In MI5's view, paying Daly a total of nearly £400,000 for his resettlement was good value. 'I was risking my life,' he said later.

The trial also revived the simmering tensions and rivalry between intelligence agencies. As the case progressed, an MPSB officer could barely suppress his joy when it looked as if the two INLA terrorists would be acquitted as a result of legal arguments about entrapment. The day the men were convicted, MPSB officers were stunned and despondent. Such is the consequence of a multi-agency intelligence community.

In the invisible war against the IRA, where the volunteers wear no uniform, using agents is the internal method of penetration. The external route is deploying bugging and surveillance equipment. According to SAS and MI5 sources spoken to by author Tony Geraghty for his book *The Irish War*, the Security Service goes to extraordinary lengths to plant listening devices:

One in particular, used in Britain as well as Ireland, was to entice a target away from his house through the offer of a lavish holiday in the sun, all expenses paid. The target was persuaded that he or she had won the holiday by chance in a competition to promote a breakfast food. MI5 took care to confirm that a real competition existed and that a real prize was on offer. The agency's lookalike holiday was also real and paid for from MI5's secret budget. While the target was away, the Security Service would plant a host of listening devices. In time, it was even possible to install a miniaturised video camera inside a domestic light switch.

A former Security Service officer confirmed that the decoy holiday (known as the 'dodgy holiday') was a standard part of his repertoire: 'We only had trouble once in persuading a Republican family to go away. The father was an IRA quarter-master in Luton. He was happy to take the bait. It was his wife who was really suspicious.'[24]

This technique was also used to persuade IRA members to leave Northern Ireland, because they could not be approached for agent-recruitment purposes on their home patch. When the target arrived at his holiday destination abroad, he would be met by an MI5 officer with a suitcase full of money. The officer would show the target the suitcase crammed with used notes and say, 'This could be all yours if you come and work for us.' If he expressed interest, the IRA opera-tive would be given contact details. If he refused, MI5 might try to approach him again during the holiday.

MI5 prefers the close-up form of surveillance in Northern Ireland: breaking and entering to install secret devices in houses or cars – always with a plausible cover story if their officers get caught. In Ireland wiring a terrorist suspect's home with concealed cameras and microphones is a joint MI5–Army activity. 'There are homes in this Blessed Isle where the occupant sits to watch his television, which we have rigged so that the television is watching him,' said one Security Service operative.[25]

Mobile surveillance of terrorists is run by A4 Branch. Field offi-cers on foot are trained using a drill called the 'ABC' system. According to Geraghty, who served as a military liaison officer with the US forces during the Gulf war:

At least three teams are used to follow the target: A (for Adjacent, also known as 'The Eyeball') is the nearest. B (Back-up) is further back, preferably concealed from the quarry. Both usually stick to the same side of the road. C (Control) has a wide field of vision on the opposite side of the road, guiding the other two with concealed throat microphone and/or discreet hand signals.

A guide for novice trackers suggests: 'Behave naturally, have a purpose for being there, be prepared with a cover story (ensure that it fits the situation) and remember you are most vulnerable when coming from cover.' The guidelines deal with distance from the target, anticipation, body language, local knowledge, concentration and teamwork.[26]

The means by which the target is kept off-guard include 'boxing' and 'paralleling'. According to official guidelines:

The subject is allowed to proceed on a route where there are a minimal number of surveillance officers. The idea is to let the subject 'run' from point to point to be checked at various places by surveillance officers on parallel routes or ahead . . . The most important factor about surveillance is the need to be honest about exposure. It is better to have a controlled loss rather than to hang on to the subject too long.[27]

For pursuing an IRA target on the streets, MI5 uses a convoy of four cars plus a motorcycle outrider. This 'heel clipping' operation is particularly difficult across country where pursuing vehicles are more easily detected. On one occasion, MI5 officers chasing an IRA car overnight from Cricklewood, in north London, to Stranraer, Scotland, knew that the target was carrying weapons. They lost him briefly at a motorway halt and several hours later the suspected terrorist was clean when arrested. For similar operations a small aircraft, like an Islander, might be hired from a civilian contractor.[28]

By late 1992, these A4 surveillance teams were put to good use by MI5. Backed up by police units, IRA operatives were being hunted all over Britain by hundreds of people in T Branch, A4, Special Branch and the Anti-terrorist Squad.

However, MI5 had not succeeded in penetrating any of the IRA Active Service Units (ASUs) in Britain with agents. To be fair, this was an extremely difficult exercise. The IRA avoided using sympathisers in the Irish community, knowing that this was the first place MI5 would look to recruit agents, and were on full-scale alert. They have also rotated their ASUs on the mainland so that none spend too long in the country. This makes them less vulnerable to surveillance.

Instead MI5 concentrated on sources in Ireland for intelligence on the arrival of a terrorist or arms shipment to the UK. Then their surveillance units took over and kept suspects and explosives under observation to monitor their movements. Once the terrorists' intentions were clear, they could be arrested and the bombs defused.

For this strategy to work, it required quick, decisive action and creative thinking by MI5 management. In theory Stella Rimington appeared to accept this point: 'If your job is to gather intelligence on terrorism, and then use that information in order to prevent, in the most effective way, something unpleasant happening, you've got to be able to assess the risk of taking or not taking action at any given moment and balance that risk. If you merely want to follow the rules, intent on not causing any ructions, you are not going to be very good at the job. It's a job where individuals are given responsibility and they have got to be able to balance the risk and take the responsibility for what they do.'[29]

The reality, however, was that the Security Service never changed its internal culture to implement those words. According to David Shayler, who worked in T Branch from August 1992 until October 1994, MI5 managers demonstrated an unthinking adherence to ancient procedures that seriously hindered the fight against terrorism. The 'rules' were followed blindly precisely because they were 'intent on not causing any ructions'. MI5 behaved like a Civil Service department rather than an anti-terrorist force.

Shayler claimed that some IRA terrorists escaped capture because of time-wasting bureaucratic procedures and management ineptitude. 'It was farcical. There I was with a fast-moving target – the IRA were planting bombs down the street and our Security Service remained obsessed with pedantic drafting and redrafting of documents,' he recalled. 'I questioned whether time would be better spent investigating these IRA terrorist targets ... I could see no point in spending days poring over the wording of routine documents.'[30]

The documents in question were telephone-intercept warrants, which were increasingly used but with limited value. In 1988, the Home Secretary approved 412 warrants and by 1992 the figure had reached 756. Shayler argued vital time was wasted discussing the precise wording of documents rather than their substance. And later when the crucial moment arrived MI5 managers would not commit themselves to an executive decision and the IRA operatives escaped.

In 1997, Shayler compiled a detailed document that focused on what he called 'operational inefficiency in MI5' and described three 'spectacular' cases. 'It details, for example, how an IRA member was able to carry out large-scale attacks which threatened public safety,' said the former T Branch officer, 'because an intelligence agency had not passed on relevant information quickly enough. It also details how the attack at Bishopsgate in the City in April 1993 should not have happened.'[31]

The memorandum was offered to John Alpass, former deputy director-general of MI5, who was conducting a Cabinet Office review of all three intelligence agencies. As Shayler's document contained sensitive operational material, he suggested sending it by a secure method. But Alpass refused to accept his submission. He cited a High Court injunction that banned Shayler from disclosing any information gathered while he was an MI5 officer.

However, we have pieced together and corroborated Shayler's allegations about how MI5 could have prevented the IRA bombing at Bishopsgate. This is the story of the events of that day:

At 9 a.m., on Saturday 24 April 1993, two members of an IRA cell drove a dark blue Ford Iveco tipper truck through the peaceful streets of the City of London. Inside the 30-tonne vehicle is a massive 500kg bomb cleverly conceived from home-made fertiliser and fuel oil. Undetected, the truck grinds to a halt on the north side of Bishopsgate outside the Bank of Dubai. It is a tranquil, if cloudy, Saturday and there is little traffic.

Across the street is the glass labyrinth of the Hong Kong and Shanghai Bank and nearby is the 52-storey NatWest Tower. The IRA operatives park the truck, leaving the hazard-warning lights flashing, and walk to a car driven by an accomplice before departing the area. Ten minutes later two policemen notice the lorry with its lights flashing and no driver. They walk into the Hong Kong and Shanghai Bank and ask at reception if anyone knows who is respons-ible for the huge vehicle. Nobody does.

The warning call to the police comes at 9.20 a.m. Using a recognised code word, a man with an Irish accent says the bomb will explode in about 40 minutes. The bomb squad at Cannon Row police station is immediately alerted. Usually they would be on the scene within ten minutes, searching for the detonator to defuse the bomb. As this is one of the IRA's typically huge devices, there is a real chance of success because it is almost impossible to conceal the detonators and timers – and a Semtex high-explosive booster. For the brave disposal officers the crucial factor is time.

As the deadline grows closer, the odds are stacked against the bomb squad. That Saturday morning, one officer is in a remote area of north London, inspecting some Second World War hand grenades. The duty officer is off work with flu and his superior is at home near Heathrow, in Middlesex, which, on a good day, is an hour's drive to the City. As soon as he gets the call the senior officer races to his car and begins the drive.[32]

Meanwhile, City of London police begin sealing off Bishopsgate and Leadenhall Street. Security guards at the Hong Kong and Shanghai Bank are told to evacuate their positions. Instead they shepherd about 50 technical workers to safety down in the basement car park. At 10.10 a.m. other office employees are told not to leave their buildings as an explosion is imminent.

The bomb squad officer is still driving through central London when the blast erupts at 10.27 a.m. in a cacophony of noise – breaking glass, snapping metal and collapsing concrete. The sheer force of the explosion sends debris hurtling in every direction. Glass flies through the air, ceilings collapse and the large diesel engine from the truck is thrown at least 50 metres up the road.

Seconds later, Bishopsgate is shrouded in smoke and flames leap from a vast 15-foot crater where the lorry had stood. It is a scene reminiscent of Beirut during its worst war years. The area is a sea of rubble, twisted metal and broken glass. Thousands of windows have been smashed. Churches, banks and offices in the line of fire have suffered devastating damage. For hours afterwards the streets are still dominated by the sound of alarms.

Unusually, the IRA had delivered eight telephone warnings to police and television stations, but, as many people were still being led to safety when the bomb exploded, that only reduced rather than prevented human suffering. None of the warnings saved Edward Henty, a 34-year-old photographer for the *News of the World*. He was standing just 25 metres from the truck when the blast erupted. He was killed instantly and his mangled body was later found under rubble near the Hong Kong and Shanghai Bank. He left a wife, Yasmina, 33, and two young sons.

Good fortune rather than vigilance prevented further casualties. Many of the injured were alerted to the danger only a minute before detonation. One man, in his mid-40s, lost several fingers when his hand was hit by flying debris. Another, aged 35, suffered a collapsed lung when he was flung against the wall of his flat. A third was afflicted with deep abdominal shrapnel wounds. Among the injured was Raymond Fayers, a 44-year-old security guard who guided people to safety after the blast brought a ceiling down on top of him. 'It all went black and then the next thing I was looking up and seeing the ceiling come down on me,' Fayers said later from his hospital bed. 'The doctors have told me I have got glass embedded in my head but I am not too bad.'[33]

For those trapped in the basement of the Hong Kong and Shanghai Bank, it was a horrific experience. 'Everyone around was thrown or dived to the ground for cover,' said Tina Hornsey. 'Office girls began screaming hysterically. Some panicked and tried to get through the exits. It was terrifying. The basement was pumped full of thick black smoke. I felt trapped and I didn't know whether we would get out or not. We couldn't see in front of our faces and groped through the smoke.'[34]

One young man, working on a scaffold near the Stock Exchange, saw the flash when the bomb went off. He was blown backwards. He was so traumatised that he sat trembling with his head in his hands on a traffic island near Bank underground station, refusing to talk to either police or reporters.[35]

The final toll was one dead and 44 injured. It was one of the biggest IRA terrorist bombs ever detonated in mainland Britain and caused destruction estimated at £350 million. Insurance companies collectively paid out 10 per cent, but that left the taxpayer with a bill of £315 million.

For the IRA, the bombing was a stunning propaganda and military coup as they were switching away from civic to City and financial targets. The previous month the terrorists were concerned by the intensity of protest against them after their bombing of Warrington shopping centre killed two children. The Bishopsgate attack created less public outrage, but achieved two of the IRA's key objectives: first, it struck at the heart of the financial nerve-centre of the UK, damaging the British economy; second, it generated paranoia and fear among the security and intelligence forces about whether they were capable of combating IRA terrorism.[36]

Among those shattered by the news of the Bishopsgate outrage that Saturday afternoon was David Shayler. He was one of the founding members of a special unit within the Security Service's T Branch whose purpose was to investigate IRA terrorism on the mainland.

For eight months Shayler had been compiling intelligence on IRA operatives and tracking their movements. But as he assessed reports from MI5 and Special Branch surveillance units and liaised with agents, he was increasingly frustrated.

MI5 was in overall charge of countering the IRA threat and yet Shayler felt that potentially life-saving decisions were not being taken. The Service was not geared up for its expanded role and officers were handicapped by what he considered over-bureaucratic and inflexible management. Meanwhile, the IRA were running rampant through the mainland, and between October 1992 and April 1993 planted more bombs than at any other time during the 20 years of hostilities.

When he heard the blast Shayler was in his flat in Clapham, south London, preparing to host a party for some friends. Despite being five miles away, the windows of his home shook. 'That's probably a bomb and I'll have to spend all day Monday drafting and redrafting the brief for the DG [director-general],' he remarked, half jokingly. At 5 p.m. that afternoon Shayler watched the news on television and was stunned at the extent of the injuries and damage. He wondered if it had been caused by the IRA Active Service Unit (ASU) that MI5 had been following around that past week.

For months his section had been investigating the activities of certain IRA members in Britain. It had been handed specific intelligence, which had not been followed up by the Metropolitan Police Special Branch (MPSB), but MI5 was slow to pursue these leads because, bizarrely, it was reluctant to embarrass the MPSB over warrants for telephone tapping it inherited, which were out of date and inaccurate.

It was a catalytic moment for Shayler, whose job was to write briefings on the IRA's activities on the mainland. Over the following weeks he was briefed on the progress of separate investigations by MI5 and the Anti-terrorist Squad. He discovered that in fact the culprits could have been arrested six months beforehand: a breakdown in communications between MI5 and Government Communications Headquarters (GCHQ) prevented the Service from reacting to prior intelligence about the attack. He was angry as well as sorrowful. 'The attack on Bishopsgate should never have happened,' he said.[37]

Shayler later described, in breathtaking detail, the evidence for this allegation in a secret report on 'Operational Inefficiency' in MI5.

The authors of this book are prevented by a High Court injunction from publishing that report, but City police officers shared his view of MI5's culpability. As proof, they point to several written warnings prepared by MI5 assessing the latest intelligence on IRA activity on the mainland. One of these reports, a Box 500 document that was distributed to the police and Whitehall, predicted that the IRA was planning a major attack at least a week before the tragedy. The document, later leaked to the press, stated:

> You will already be aware that the current threat from the Provisional IRA to the mainland is high. In addition to this high threat, it is currently assessed that some form of attack on the mainland in the immediate future is a distinct probability. Therefore, whilst the high state of alertness of patrolling officers is recognised, it is recommended that a degree of heightened vigilance will be necessary, at least for the next seven days.[38]

Despite this warning, no co-ordinated action was taken. This was confirmed three years later when an official Anti-Terrorist Squad inquiry suggested that MI5 blundered over the bombing. Their confidential report claimed that an MI5 surveillance team walked past the bomb lorry just minutes after the IRA unit parked it and set the timer. The terrorists were missed completely.[39]

Nobody has been arrested for the Bishopsgate blast. The police say they know the identity of the culprits – from south Armagh and County Monaghan in Ulster – but lack sufficient evidence to bring them to justice.

For Shayler, this débâcle crystallised his view that MI5 was unsuited and unable to act as an anti-terrorist agency. Its obsession with bureaucracy and procedure combined with inertia and lack of initiative by senior officers prevented vital decision-making that might have saved lives and millions of pounds of public money.

MI5's management countered that it does not possess any executive power of arrest, but, as Dame Stella Rimington, its director-general at the time of Bishopsgate, has acknowledged: 'We pass information on to others and discuss with them what action they can take – to the police, for example, so that arrests can be made, or to the Home Office or Foreign Office, so that terrorists or intelligence officers can be deported or expelled.'[40] MI5 holds extensive authority to recommend and encourage action by the police and courts, and provide them with the required evidence. After all, it is the senior and controlling partner in the intelligence war against the IRA on the mainland.

Bishopsgate was just one graphic – if tragic – example of a growing belief by Shayler and many colleagues that MI5 was fundamentally flawed. Its structure, methods, priorities and management required urgent major surgery. The bureaucracy was too inflexible, resources were wrongly distributed and operations were based on outdated techniques. If reform was not imminent and substantial, he believed, 'MI5's effectiveness against terrorist organisations will be undermined'.[41]

One of the most important was how MI5 incompetence allowed IRA operatives to explode bombs on the British mainland. The best documented case concerns MI5's investigation into Sean McNulty, an IRA supporter from North Shields, Tyneside.

Ostensibly a construction worker, he was in fact a key member of an IRA active service unit operating in the UK. In early 1992, MI5 targeted McNulty as a prime suspect for terrorist activities and he was placed under surveillance. For a year there was little hard evidence to link him to any atrocities. MI5 assessed that he played a support role for the IRA, which included locating sites for his accomplices to bomb or looking after weapons hides. Transcripts from his parents' tapped telephone showed that McNulty was extremely secretive. But all the evidence was circumstantial.

That all changed in the early hours of 10 June 1993, when a gas plant in the North Shields area exploded. The next morning the IRA let off another bomb at a nearby Esso plant in Wallsend, Tyneside. The explosions caused huge damage to the fuel stations and it was only by good fortune that a nearby row of houses was not destroyed and the sleeping occupants killed or maimed. They only survived because the perpetrator had placed the explosive device next to pipes that did not contain highly inflammable fuel.

At the time, David Shayler was a member of T2, one of MI5's counter-IRA sections, and responsible for the north-east area. That morning, 10 June 1993, was a busy one for him as he was tasked to compile a report on the bombings. He telephoned the Metropolitan Police Special Branch (MPSB) for details of the attacks, but this was not particularly productive as MPSB often resented supplying any information to MI5. Bizarrely, he obtained more accurate and updated data from Ceefax on television than from MPSB.

Then came the laborious task of writing a briefing for Stella Rimington, then MI5's director-general, on how this affected MI5's assessment of the IRA's mainland campaign. Although this was supposed to be a concise and simple record of events and its implications, Shayler's section manager insisted on the document being redrafted several times.

McNulty was a suspect, but MI5 had no decisive proof. Then there was a dramatic development. That afternoon Shayler was walking past his section leader's office when he noticed a pile of photographs on her desk. He immediately identified them as coming from closed-circuit television (CCTV) coverage of people entering the house of Hugh Jack. Jack was running an IRA active-service unit from his home in Sauchie, a tiny village near Alloa, central Scotland. At the time it was the nerve-centre of the IRA's mainland terrorism.

As Shayler looked closely at the photographs, he noticed one that showed a burly figure walking down the garden path. The camera was above ground but it had captured his face almost full-on and his distinctive, thick-pointed eyebrows. There was no doubt at all that it was Sean McNulty. His presence in Jack's house clearly indicated that he was receiving orders from IRA's northern command.

'Where were these photos taken?' Shayler asked his manager.

'At Hugh Jack's house in Sauchie,' she replied grudgingly, implying that he had no business to ask such questions.

'Do you realise this is Sean McNulty?' asked Shayler.

'I thought he looked familiar,' said his boss, almost casually.

'How long have you had these?'

'They arrived on my desk this morning.'

Shayler then peered at the white digits in the bottom right-hand corner of the scratchy, slightly blurred black-and-white CCTV pictures. They stated '29 May 1993' with time codes.

Shayler was stunned. For the photograph of McNulty arriving at the IRA safe house had been taken 12 days before. 'At this point we did not know if McNulty was involved in the attacks,' recalled the former MI5 officer. 'But if we had received that picture beforehand –

even a day or two earlier – McNulty would have been placed under round-the-clock surveillance on his way to Tyneside. We could then have prevented him from carrying out the explosions. We later discovered that during his visit to Jack's house, McNulty was told the location of the explosives and bomb-making equipment. If MI5 had had him under surveillance, we could have followed him to where the weapons were hidden and he would have been caught red-handed.'

It transpired that the vital surveillance photographs had arrived at MI5's HQ in Curzon Street, London, two days before the bombings. They were moved from Scotland by the antiquated method of a transport van rather than over the wires. 'It was typical of the outdated and bureaucratic rubbish that we had to deal with,' Shayler told the authors. 'A van was driven around Scotland to collect all the intelligence and pictures of suspects. The van would also stop off at various points in England before heading to London. But because McNulty's picture missed the first bag, we did not receive the photos until ten days later.'

When the pictures eventually arrived at headquarters, MI5's bureaucratic procedures ensured that T2 section did not receive them until 10 June – *after* the atrocities had occurred. Even then they languished on the section leader's desk. It was only by accident that Shayler spotted them. 'I was amazed,' he recalled. 'It would be laughable if it wasn't so serious. These people were professional killers and because of incidents like this we were allowing them to remain on the streets.'

Two weeks later, on 24 June 1993, McNulty was arrested in a dawn raid. A year later, he was convicted at the Old Bailey for conspiring to cause explosions and is currently serving a 25-year jail sentence at the Maze Prison in Belfast. He was the first IRA member to be found guilty on the mainland following an MI5-led investigation. But his conviction was not easily secured. A key piece of forensic evidence was lost by the police and the judge was obliged to accept a 10–2 split jury verdict.

Despite his eventual capture, MI5's failure to act decisively and quickly and pass on the photographic evidence had damaging consequences. Apart from preventing the explosions, arresting McNulty earlier would have saved the cost of the two-week surveillance operation and the long court case as a conviction would have been much easier to secure. More significantly, it would also have enabled the capture of IRA explosives and weapons. This would have prevented other IRA members from using them and a forensic investigation of the arms might have produced leads to capture other IRA operatives or at least provide new evidence against those already under criminal investigation.

Instead of conducting an internal inquiry into the bungled operation, MI5 management organised a major cover-up. In September 1993, after the McNulty conviction, Shayler wrote a short summary of the investigation as a contribution to MI5's annual 'Operational Reports'. Copies were distributed to his managers, notably Stephen Lander, then head of T section and now director-general. The reports were then sent to the Queen, the Prime Minister, John Major, and the Home Secretary, Michael Howard.

But when Shayler received his copy, he was horrified to discover that the chronology of the McNulty case had been deliberately falsified and ten key pages were missing. The report gave the clear impression that the CCTV stills of McNulty arriving at Jack's house were taken the day before they arrived at MI5's head office on 10 June. In fact, as the original CCTV photographs clearly state, they were taken on 29 May – 12 days earlier.

At first Shayler thought he had misled his manager so he checked the original version of his summary, which did indeed refer to the 12-day delay. Shayler was outraged because MI5 had lied to the Queen, the Prime Minister and the Home Secretary over an operation against the IRA, which directly affected the defence of the realm. He approached the senior manager in question and pointed out the falsehood in the official 'Operational Report'. The manager merely raised his finger to his lips, clearly indicating that Shayler should keep quiet about the matter.

There was a very human postscript to this inept investigation. MI5 had also arrested McNulty's parents under a section of the Prevention of Terrorism Act, which makes it a crime not to inform on close relatives if you suspect they are involved in terrorism. This was designed to pressurise McNulty.

It was true that McNulty's parents knew of their son's IRA activities. but MI5 was fully aware – because they were tapping their phone – that they were also trying to persuade their son to stop working for the IRA. The parents were both opposed to the armed struggle. McNulty's mother, Dorothy, was a Geordie who had no sympathy with men of violence. His Irish father, Bernard, had left Northern Ireland 30 years earlier, purely to escape the Troubles. And yet both were interviewed by Northumberland Special Branch under caution as suspects.

Probably believing they were only witnesses and wanting to be helpful, McNulty's parents gave the police a detailed statement about their son's activities. This included how he had obtained a gun and his preparation for a terrorist attack. To their shock, they were then charged with withholding information about terrorists and were held on remand awaiting trial.

McNulty's father was not in good health, and he died in custody of a heart attack. Clearly, his death was at least partly induced by the stress of prison and the prospect of a criminal conviction. The day before her trial the Crown Prosecution Service dropped the charges against his mother. She was then released after spending nearly a year in jail.

Shayler felt the operation against McNulty's parents was unnecessary and unjust because it had no effect on capturing McNulty or preventing terrorism. 'When I announced the sad news [his father's death] to the T2A long room in MI5, pointing out the injustice and comparing it to *In the Name of the Father*, the film about the Guildford Four, my boss burst out laughing,' recalled Shayler. 'That would have been bad enough if Sean McNulty's father had been a terrorist, but for a man who had the misfortune to be in the wrong place at the wrong time, it was inexcusable.'[42]

As for Sean McNulty, he is considering an appeal based on the role of MI5 in securing his conviction. 'We had some evidence that incompetence on the part of the Security Service may have extended beyond that indicated by Mr Shayler,' his solicitor told the authors.

Shayler accepts that there were some successes – mainly from 1994 onwards – but this was too late, as many of the worst atrocities had already occurred. 'I think there was a real chance in 1993 that MI5 really could have finished off the IRA bombing campaign if they had taken advantage when they had it,' he said. 'There were a lot of arrests in a sequence in mid-1993 and the IRA really were on the ropes on the mainland. Everything they seemed to do appeared to end in disaster. If MI5 had really gone for it and clued themselves up, they could have finished off the IRA.'[43]

MI5's counter-argument is that its officers operate on a long-term basis and are not pressured in the same way as the police to produce instant results. Rimington claimed that their strategy would take time to become effective. She was adamant that the IRA would be ultimately defeated by comprehensive intelligence.

However, Shayler and RUC sources argue that MI5 should not have had the luxury of time for painstaking analysis while the bombs exploded and people were killed. The slow pace and delay while intelligence is analysed can have disastrous consequences. For example, RUC Special Branch officers in Belfast have a close working relationship with the Anti-terrorist Squad in London.

In the past, as soon as the RUC – which has excellent sources in the IRA – received important information, they immediately communicated it to their mainland counterparts. Since October 1992, however, MI5 has insisted that all intelligence is relayed first to them for scrutiny and appraisal. Officers are assigned to work on a layered principle: assessing terrorists groups from the outside, learning how they function and about the social, political and cultural environment in which they flourish. Only then will they focus on individual terrorist suspects and decide what action, if any, to recommend.

RUC Special Branch officers regard this laborious technique as 'an academic exercise rather than operational policing'.[44] It not only weakened their link with the Anti-terrorist Squad, but the delays could have led to catastrophic consequences. While reports were dissected and discussed, bombs may have exploded. RUC sources also claim that some vital intelligence had not been passed on by imperious MI5 officers.

MI5 maintains that it is not a law-enforcement agency with powers of arrest and prosecution so it cannot be held directly responsible for terrorist blunders, but its leading role is designed to save lives and convict terrorists, and the agency has not been slow to take credit for any success. In fact, MI5 is intrinsically involved in law enforcement. It has occasionally provided several officers as witnesses during terrorism trials and Rimington herself has stated that MI5 is 'fully committed to supporting the police in detecting and preventing crime'.[45]

Far from it being a detached monitoring agency, the former director-general viewed the Service as directly participating in evidence-gathering procedures. 'We will, where appropriate, use our intelligence resources to collect evidence in support of a prosecution,' she said in 1994. 'We pass information on to others and discuss with them what action they can take – to the police, for example, so that arrests can be made.'[46] At the bare minimum, MI5 should be a more aggressive enabling force in the war against terrorism and integrate intelligence into the judicial process.

The disasters of 1993 jolted MI5 into action and success. In early 1994, Feilim O'Haidmaill, a senior commander of the IRA in Britain and effectively in charge of their ASUs, was captured. Sources in Ireland informed MI5 about O'Haidmaill's movements in England and he was arrested after collecting a car containing 17 kilos of Semtex. 'I deeply regret being captured and I suppose congratulations are due to the security forces,' said the softly spoken IRA man, who was also a Ph.D.[47]

In the two years after MI5 acquired primacy, arrests of IRA operatives produced 14 convictions. Of these, six were due to improved surveillance and intelligence by the Security Service. Boosted by better use of GCHQ intelligence and improved intelligence from agents on the mainland, MI5 became more effective. By the mid-1990s, the IRA was feeling the heat in their mainland campaign. Intense MI5 observation made communications for the invisible Republican army a major problem. According to Tony Geraghty,

> For the Republicans, there was a limit to the number of contacts that could be made in person, though this was the only certain way to avoid the pervasive, baleful presence of Box 500 [MI5]. Coded signals in newspaper small-ads lacked the flexibility of a two-way conversation. The terrorists learned not to write letters, even in code. The agency would stake out the likely letterbox as well as the target's home, then follow a well-rehearsed drill to intercept the target's mail.
>
> As one field officer explained: 'One of us would address a letter to himself and stamp it. As soon as the target had posted his letter, we would do the same. We would have authority to order the postman or sorter to hand over all the mail. The letter we wanted was immediately beneath our dummy letter, or very close to it.' As an alternative the IRA tried pagers, but British cryptologists broke the codes being used.[48]

However, during the IRA's 16-month ceasefire from August 1994, MI5 again became complacent about the terrorist threat. This was surprising, as it was adept at monitoring the terrorists' funding and the trafficking and stockpiling of arms. Once again bureaucracy prevailed over common sense: MI5 always suspected that the ceasefire would end, but it never had any reliable intelligence to confirm this view.

Despite these worries, the agency stuck rigidly to its policy of posting desk officers to a section for a maximum of two years. As a result, all the experienced T2 officers who had been responsible for the successes against the IRA in 1993–94 had been moved to other sections by the time the ceasefire ended. When the bombing campaign was renewed, they were working in different areas and the IRA was handed a significant advantage.

This was graphically, if morbidly, illustrated on 9 February 1996, when MI5 confirmed further cutbacks in military agents. Later that evening, shortly after 7 p.m., the ceasefire was shattered by the explosion of a huge bomb on South Quay in Canary Wharf, which killed two people and injured almost a hundred.

According to police sources, there was 'an intelligence failure'. MI5 had sent a warning to the government a month earlier, but it was vague and did not specify any date for a possible renewed bombing campaign. In fact, there had been specific prior intelligence, but it was not vigorously followed up. Three separate coded warnings were received about the Canary Wharf blast, but MI5 discounted the threat. It regarded the calls as 'a hoax' and gave a 'negative assessment' to Special Branch. As a result the police sent only one sergeant and three constables to clear the streets. Just over an hour later a 500kg lorry bomb exploded, causing terrible human suffering and damage estimated at £100 million. It sent a shudder through the City of London.[49]

The Service should have been on its guard regardless of the warnings. Just before Canary Wharf there had been a hostile reaction from the Irish nationalist community to British proposals for elections prior to talks with Sinn Fein. It was no secret that this might derail the peace process and endanger the ceasefire. It was also known that weapons and explosives were being stockpiled for a possible resumption of hostilities. That alone should have set off alarm bells inside MI5. Instead, the agency spent much of its time exploring gradual cutbacks, redistributing anti-terrorist officers, returning seconded agents and examining new roles for itself. A permanent peace would leave about a thousand of its 1,850 staff redundant.

This miscalculation was not made by front-field MI5 operatives working in high-risk locations or by desk officers: it was a policy decision taken by those at the highest level of MI5 who either had been misled by IRA misinformation or had misread the state of play. 'You could say,' said a security source, 'that, like some second marriages, it was a triumph of optimism over experience.'[50]

After Canary Wharf, the Security Service continued to achieve a mixed record in preventing Irish terrorism on the mainland. In January 1999, an ASU of the Continuity IRA group eluded an MI5 unit in London. The terrorists' car had been tagged so that their movements could be monitored from a safe distance, but then the car was sold at an auction. When the MI5 surveillance team discovered this and returned to the unit's base in north London, the terrorists had vanished.[51]

On the other hand, in July 1996, MI5 provided crucial intelligence that led to the prevention of an IRA attack. In a co-ordinated investigation, two London premises were raided, foiling a plan to explode a bomb within hours. Seven men were arrested and 36 of the latest timer-power units for detonating bombs were seized. Maps and other documents, indicating potential targets, were also recovered. The inside intelligence about the plot came from an MI5 informant inside the IRA.[52]

The following year, six IRA terrorists were jailed for 35 years for conspiring to blow up six major electricity-supply stations feeding London. In a ten-day surveillance operation, involving more than 300 undercover MI5 officers, A4 operatives broke into and bugged IRA safe-houses. They also placed tracking devices on cars. During the Old Bailey trial, it emerged that the terrorists had been hand-picked by the IRA's Army Council. And yet they had had no idea that they were being followed.[53]

These achievements are due to several factors. There was a huge increase in manpower and funding – 44 per cent of the Service's £150 million budget was consumed in countering Irish terrorism during 1994. The technical skills of its surveillance teams were a major contribution, and there was the diligent handling of agents and informants by desk officers.

Even MI5's most hostile critics would be hard-pressed to ignore its victories against the IRA, but a failure to share intelligence and an excessive bureaucratic structure has impeded the efforts of the security forces to save more lives. There are currently at least ten agencies responsible for different aspects of intelligence-gathering against Irish terrorism. Clearly, the more organisations the greater the opportunity for confusion, delay and error, which allow terrorists to escape or detonate their bombs. Then there are the traditional rivalries between the agencies and their different methods of working, which are exploited by the IRA.[54]

This weakness was identified by Sir Edward Heath who, as Prime Minister between 1970 and 1974, was involved in countering the early IRA threat. In an article in *The Times*, published nine weeks after the Bishopsgate bombing, he accused the Home Office of 'arrogant smugness' for claiming that 'effective [security] arrangements' were already in place. He advocated a more unified centralised organisation. 'I welcomed the decision to give MI5 the leading role in intelligence gathering,' he stated, 'but the task of combating terrorism remains far too fragmented. There is not one European Community country that has succeeded in defeating terrorism without first establishing a proper, national central agency.'[55]

There is also substantial evidence that some bombings might have been avoided if it had not been for MI5's negligence and incompetence. 'There is no doubt that the agency has proved more effective than the Metropolitan Police in intelligence-gathering against the IRA,' reflected David Shayler. 'However, there was always a feeling among the new intake [of officers] that these successes were in spite of, rather than because of, our inflexible management.'[56]

Dame Stella Rimington, director-general during the worst of the atrocities, would speak sensitively of 'a corporate sense of failure when a bomb goes off'.[57] But her successor, Stephen Lander, was petulant and predictable in his response: he blamed the MPSB. 'He told his masters in government that the Met had left policing the IRA in such a state that MI5 was trying to make up lost ground,' said a source formerly close to Lander. 'It was a feeble excuse, designed to hide the excessive bureaucracy which hampered MI5's efforts against the IRA. Lander had little to do with turning the situation around – this was largely the work of committed officers who often worked long hours for little extra reward.'[58]

MI5's senior directors appeared unwilling or unable to adapt to the new pressures and demands of counter-terrorism. Rimington often spoke publicly about 'the need for rapid action and reacting to events as they unfolded',[59] but her carefully chosen words were never applied by an intransigent middle management who preferred a bureaucratic approach to complex and dangerous problems.

Although MI5 openly advertised for new recruits capable of 'lateral thinking', experienced officers were never allowed to put this theory into practice. Instead, 'analysis' and bureaucracy were considered paramount and decisive action based on flexible thinking and initiative was frowned upon. What delayed and impeded potentially life-saving decisions during operations against the IRA was not the quality of the intelligence, but the use of it.

6

TERRORISM IN THE UK:
HOW MI5 FAILED TO COUNTER THE
AL QAEDA THREAT

> 'The biggest surprise in all of this for me has not been the
> terrorist act itself but the reaction . . . It was as if the fact of an attack
> had come as a total surprise to the governments and counter-terror-
> ist authorities.'

> Dame Stella Rimington, *Guardian*, 4 September 2002

A combination of Britain's long imperial history, traditions of
asylum and lax anti-terrorist laws meant that during the 1980s and
1990s the UK became a centre for the growing Islamist movement. Soon people were dubbing the capital 'Londonistan' in
recognition of the growing numbers of exiles from Islamic countries who had chosen to settle there. There was little public sign
of the intense ferment of debate taking place in Britain amongst
the radical elements. The Arabic-language press that has flour-
ished in Britain is not widely read and there was little political
violence. Terrorism, as most British people knew it, stemmed
from the Republican movement in Ireland and MI5 was largely
occupied with tracking IRA and dissident Republicans intent on
bombing missions on the mainland.

But as Britain's intelligence agencies looked the other way, a well-
funded and well-organised network was being built across the country. New mosques sprang up to cater for the growing Muslim
community, the vast majority of which were respectable and whose
congregations rejected the new militant form of Islam being
preached by followers of Osama bin Laden.

Others had a different outlook. After 1996, when bin Laden moved his operations to Afghanistan, small groups were set up and were heavily influenced by radical preachers. Some of them had spent time in the training camps along Afghanistan's borders with Pakistan. Others had taken part in the fighting against the Soviets in the 1980s. Hundreds, possibly several thousand, young British Muslims travelled to Afghanistan to gain experience – and probably in many cases just to take part in what seemed like an adventure – of guerrilla fighting.

In addition, refugees from Middle East regimes arrived in Britain claiming asylum after fleeing persecution in their own countries. Amongst them were a handful of radical Islamists, supporters of bin Laden, who continued to campaign and organise for their vision of an Islamic future.

The full significance of what was happening was never fully appreciated by MI5. Geared up for a long-term struggle against the Provisional IRA and its offshoots, it kept only the most rudimentary watch over the growing presence of the Islamist diaspora gathering in London. Noisy clerics and ideologues were figures of fun, who needed an occasional word of caution from their Special Branch contacts to ensure they did not disturb the peace. Their supporters, meanwhile, were left in peace to plan and organise.

When Osama bin Laden launched the International Islamic Front for Jihad against Jews and Crusaders in February 1998, the announcement was first made public in the London-based Arabic newspaper *Al-Quds al Arabi*. Britain's press laws protected a statement that was banned in much of the Arab world itself.

Abroad, Britons were often exposed to danger and several lost their lives to Islamic terrorists operating on their own soil. The notorious former British public schoolboy, Omar Sheikh, kidnapped three Britons in India in 1994, holding them for two months in an attempt to win the freedom of an imprisoned Islamic cleric.

Two British backpackers, Keith Mangan and Paul Wells, were amongst six people kidnapped in Kashmir in July 1995 and held as bartering chips for the same cleric and Omar Sheikh himself, who had by that time been incarcerated in an Indian prison. When the Indian authorities refused to consider a ransom, the hostages were brutally murdered and their bodies buried in secret.

Later, in October 1998, three Britons and a New Zealander working for Surrey-based Granger Telecom and BT were kidnapped in

Grozny, the capital of Chechnya, and held for ransom. Their kidnappers were Chechen terrorists held by Arbi Barayev, a notorious warlord with close contacts to Al Qaeda.

Barayev initially agreed to accept a ransom payment for the men of $10 million, but suddenly broke off negotiations. According to one report, Barayev agreed to accept a $30 million payment from Osama bin Laden to murder the men. Two months after their kidnap, the men were murdered. Their heads were found in a sack by the side of the road. Barayev's closest ally in Chechnya was a Jordanian-born fighter known as Omar ibn al-Khattab, who was, until his death in March 2002, regarded as bin Laden's representative in country.

According to a BBC investigation, Foreign Office advice about travel to Chechnya was not passed on to Granger Telecom and security on the ground for the men was woeful. The number of bodyguards was gradually reduced during 1998 and the house they stayed in had no special protection. However, it appears that the Granger employees had been approached by the Foreign Office to ask if they would collect information on the country. A letter of 13 August 1998 to the company asked if they could provide 'a read-out of your contacts with Chechen authorities . . . who are the movers and shakers?'[1]

Back in Britain the radicals were also gaining in strength. One organisation that grew quickly amongst young Muslims was al-Muhajiroun, led by a dissident Syrian sheikh (religious preacher) called Omar Bakri Mohammed. A statement from the organisation in March 2000 in response to a Special Branch raid on the Maktabah al Ansar bookshop in Birmingham, spelled out the growing reach of radical Islam:

'The rapid rise of Islam in the West, with many embracing Islam on a daily basis and with more and more Muslims going back to the unwavering implementation of Islam in their lives, has meant that the support for the mujahideen, an obligation upon every Muslim, wherever it be verbal financial or physical, has increased rapidly, putting the government on the back foot. Indeed it would be difficult to find a mosque in Britain which does not have a collection tin every Friday for either Kashmir, Chechnya, Palestine, etc. Despite the reported confiscation of cash, documentation and electronic equipment in the recent raid, Muslims all over Britain will never stop supporting Jihad to liberate these Muslim lands under occupation for they do not do it because the law of the land allows it, but rather as a response to the divine command of the legislator Allah (swt).'[2]

Bin Laden's connections with Britain go at least as far back to 1994 when Khaled al Fawaz founded the Advice and Reformation Committee in July of that year. In 1999 he was arrested on a US extradition warrant on the grounds that he was connected with the Al Qaeda bombings of the US embassies in Kenya and Tanzania the previous year. According to the FBI, he was also suspected of publishing religious fatwas calling for a jihad against American civilians.

Another close link is the Azzam publishing house, which has operated with little restraint for several years. Named after bin Laden's mentor, Sheikh Abdullah Azzam, it describes itself as 'an independent media organisation providing authentic news and information about jihad and the foreign mujahideen everywhere'.[3] Azzam operates from a London postal box and runs a well-informed website.

Much of the Islamic militancy movement in Britain congregated around three men: Abu Hamza al-Masri, Abu Qatada and Sheikh Omar Bakri Mohammed. Abu Hamza (whose real name is Mustafa Kamel) based himself at the Finsbury Park mosque in north London, from where he ran the 'Supporters of Sharia' organisation. Originally from Egypt, he came to Britain in the mid-1980s, graduated in civil engineering and married a British woman. In 1989, he travelled to Afghanistan where he lost an eye and both hands in an explosion. On his return to Britain in 1993, he began preaching and encouraging young Muslims to travel to fight jihad in Bosnia, Chechnya and Kashmir.

He also had very close connections to a group of eight young men who travelled to Yemen in December 1998, allegedly on a holiday trip. The police in Yemen thought differently, however, and raided their hotel rooms, finding weapons, explosives and videos from the Supporters of Sharia organisation. They were planning attacks on the British Consulate in Aden, the Anglican church and a hotel and were linked to an organisation called the Islamic Abyan Army of Aden, run by Abu Hassan. The eight men included Hamza's son, Mohammed Mustafa Kamel, and his godson.

In revenge for the arrests, Abu Hassan ordered his men to capture 16 Western tourists and hold them as hostages, threatening to kill them unless his demands were met. It was later proved that Abu

Hamza received phone calls from Abu Hassan. The kidnap gang was eventually tracked down and the Yemeni government launched an attack on their hideout, resulting in the death of four of the hostages. Abu Hassan himself was captured and sentenced to death. Abu Hamza's son, Mohammed, and several of the other Britons received a three-year prison sentence. When he returned to the UK in January 2002, his solicitor complained that the British government had failed to act robustly on his behalf. Despite numerous requests from the Yemeni government, the British authorities refused to extradite Abu Hamza himself.

Abu Hamza appears to enjoy the notoriety he has attracted, declaring after the attacks on Washington and New York that 'there are many exultant people now. America is a crazy country and whatever we perpetrate against it, is done in self-defence. If the perpetrators of the attack were Muslims, justice is on their side.' He said the attacks 'made more worshippers to come to the mosque, not only from London but from dozens of other towns'.[4]

The Finsbury Park mosque became a meeting point for many of the most radical figures passing through Britain. Several credible reports stated that weapons training took place in the basement. Zacarias Moussaoui, the so-called 20th hijacker, arrested in America weeks before the attacks, worshipped there, as did Richard Reid, the 'shoe-bomber', sentenced to life imprisonment in America for his attempts to blow up an American airliner over the Atlantic in December 2001. So, too, for a while, did Ahmed Ressam, who came to public attention in December 1999 when he was intercepted as he attempted to smuggle bomb-making equipment across the Canadian border into America as part of a plot to blow up Los Angeles airport during the Millenium celebrations.

Another worshipper and close confidante of Abu Hamza was a young America convert to Islam called James Ujamaa. Ujamaa (born James Earnest Thompson) spent several years in London where he helped to design and maintain the Supporters of Sharia website for Hamza. In the autumn of 1999, Ujamaa attempted to set up a training camp for Muslims at a remote farmhouse in Bly, Oregon. According to his indictment, the object was to offer and provide training in firearms and guerrilla tactics for people interested in 'violent jihad' and to provide safehouses for Al Qaeda members.[5]

The indictment says that Ujamaa pledged 'bayaat' (i.e. loyalty) to an unindicted co-conspirator, now widely known to have been Abu

Hamza. It says that Ujamaa and Abu Hamza planned, along with others, to arrange and conduct firearms training for volunteers, who could then move on to camps run by Al Qaeda in Afghanistan. Abu Hamza, says the indictment, would have provided the requisite letters of introduction or sponsorship to ease the passage of trainees into these camps.

Ujamaa's plans were discovered when he faxed a proposal to Abu Hamza in London that compared the terrain in Oregon to that in Afghanistan, stating that the property could store and conceals guns, bunkers and ammunition and invited the cleric to come and see it for himself. As the indictment followed soon after a visit by Special Branch officers to Seattle in the summer of 2002, it seems likely that the fax was intercepted by GCHQ and passed on to MI5, who made it available as evidence to the FBI.

The plan to set up a training camp came to nothing when two men selected as trainers, who described themselves as bodyguards for Abu Hamza, arrived at the camp and found that conditions were not as they had been led to believe. In the two months they spent at the camp, no one was trained and they left in disgust in January 2000. Abu Hamza himself subsequently became the subject of a grand jury investigation, which, at the time of writing, has yet to announce any indictment.

Ujamaa had another connection to jihad training camps. Officials in the US confirmed he had helped to design an Internet site for Sakina Security Services which advertised a military training course called the 'Ultimate Jihad Challenge'. The owner of the company, former chef Sulayman Bilal Zainulabidin (known, until his conversion from Catholicism in 1979, as Frank Etim), 44, was later charged under the Terrorism Act 2000 with seeking to 'assist or prepare' for terrorism. He was arrested in October 2001 after more information came to light about a training camp he had hoped to establish in Marion, Alabama.

Zainulabidin's trial at the Old Bailey in August 2002 was the first since the 11 September attacks to be tried under new anti-terrorism laws. He was charged after complaining to police that he felt vulnerable because a newspaper had published an article by the Labour MP Andrew Dismore about his website. He told the court he had been running a legitimate security company and that he had been charged because '11 September happened and they have got to show the public they are fighting Islamic terrorism'.[6]

The prosecution argued that the Sakina Security Services website offered courses in 'bonecrushing' and 'the Islamic art of war'. A fortnight-long course in firearms training in the United States called the 'Ultimate Jihad Challenge' cost £3,000. They said police found a copy of bin Laden's 1998 fatwa against the West at Zainulabidin's house in Greenwich, south-east London and described the security firm as 'a front or veil' for 'the pursuit of jihad, a holy war, against the perceived enemies of Islam'.

In response, Zainulabidin described his business as 'Britain's first Islamic threat assessment unit', saying he was a trophy scapegoat for the 11 September attacks. Only one person, a security guard at a Sainsbury's supermarket, had applied to attend the course using the website.

Zainulabidin claimed he was being victimised. 'At the magistrates court, the prosecutor said they had got 40 anti-terrorism officers on this case working 24 hours a day, seven days a week in 55 countries,' he told the court. 'Now I have appeared before the highest court in the land and what evidence have they produced? What was in my house all the time? I'm their trophy, I'm their prize.'

He added that he had worked at the Royal College of Obstetricians and Gynaecologists for four years up to his arrest and that his aim was to teach Muslims to survive if they needed to flee Britain. In the end, after four days of deliberation, the jury believed him and he walked free of the charges.

Two other cases collapsed in 2002 for lack of evidence. Lotfi Raissi, an Algerian pilot, was said by US prosecutors to have been the 'lead trainer' of the 11 September hijackers, but in February 2002 his extradition case collapsed when no evidence was submitted. Raissi, an Algerian pilot living in the UK, was released after being detained at Belmarsh high-security prison for five months. He was arrested on the basis of an unsubstantiated FBI allegation that he had helped in organising the attack on the World Trade Center. On 21 April 2002 the judge in his case ruled that there was no evidence at all linking him to terrorism.

A second case involved Yassir al-Sirri who ran the Islamic Observation Centre in London. He provided press accreditation to the two men who killed Afghan Northern Alliance leader Ahmed Shah Massoud two days before the 11 September attacks. Al-Sirri had also been accused by the Egyptian government of involvement in a plot to kill the Prime Minister of Egypt in 1993, a charge that he strongly denied. He was arrested in October 2001 and charged with involvement in the Massoud killing. The case collapsed in May 2002 and al-Sirri was freed. A subsequent attempt to extradite him to the United States on charges of disseminating terrorist messages also failed in July 2002.

A Home Office spokesman said: 'Mr al-Sirri's extradition had been sought by the US government. The Secretary of State had to decide by today whether to issue an order to proceed on the information and legal advice available to him. He was not satisfied that the prima facie evidence test was met. He therefore concluded that it would not be right on this occasion to issue an order to proceed.'[7]

The activities of Abu Hamza also surfaced as a result of the activities of an Algerian journalist called Reda Hassaine who had been recruited by both the French and British intelligence services to infiltrate the Islamist movement. Hassaine, 41, was an official in the Islamic Salvation Front, but quit over his opposition to the party's decision to take up terrorism. In 1994, he and his family fled to London after agreeing to work for the Algerian security service as an informer. In 1998, he was recruited by a French security officer to inform about any potential attacks on the World Cup then being hosted by France. Let down by the French who promised him citizenship but failed to deliver, he offered his services to MI5 and in 1999 he was asked by his Special Branch handler to infiltrate the Finsbury Park mosque.

Throughout the period when Abu Hamza's son was being held in prison in Yemen, Hassaine provided detailed reports to Special Branch about what he was hearing at the mosque. He compiled detailed diagrams of the layout of the mosque, marking all the escape routes. In March 1999, Abu Hamza was arrested, along with four other men at the mosque, but was released after four days. Hassaine was frustrated. 'I was shocked,' he told one newspaper. 'There is a big problem in the law here in London. Islamists can claim assassinations, they can do propaganda. And all these things are "freedom of expression" – even if you call for killing people. The law is very, very weak. In France, these people would have been in jail a long time ago.'[8]

Hassaine's career as an MI5 informant suddenly came to an end in April 2000 when he was sent to check information on someone who had been to Afghanistan to meet bin Laden. He says that he was confronted by a group at the Finsbury Park mosque and chased, caught and beaten, losing two teeth in the process. His handler told him he had been compromised and should now retreat into the background. His request for asylum, over which he had received assurances while working for the Security Services, was eventually rejected.

Abu Hamza, though, remained a target. In January 2003, his Finsbury Park mosque was raided by police. Hundreds of officers took part in the early morning operation and seven people were arrested. The raid followed an earlier operation in Manchester, in which a Special Branch officer was killed while attempting to arrest a suspect.

The second cleric who came to the attention of MI5 was Abu Qatada. Originally from Jordan, he was granted asylum in Britain in 1993, but continued to keep in contact with terrorist groups across Europe, using such names al al-Taqfiri and Omar Mahmoud Uthman. Even after he was convicted of terrorist offences in Jordan in 1999, the British authorities refused Jordanian requests for his extradition. He was responsible for recruiting a wide range of contacts across Europe, including the professional footballer Nizar Trabelsi, Djamel Beghal and Kamel Daoudi, all of whom were involved in a plot to blow up the US embassy in Paris.

Another close contact was Abu Dahdah, who Spanish investigators believe was bin Laden's main contact in the country. Spanish judge, Baltasar Garzon, is on record stating that he believes Abu Qatada helped in the planning for the 11 September attacks.[9] Casettes of his speeches were found in the Hamburg flat used by hijack leader Mohammed Atta and he has spoken many times in support of bin Laden. Despite claiming benefits in Britain for his family, when US authorities froze his accounts in the aftermath of the 11 September attacks, they found £180,000 in deposits.

According to Hassaine, Abu Qatada recruited the petty criminal Richard Reid and Zacarias Moussaoui into Al Qaeda. Both men worshipped at a small mosque in Brixton, made up mainly of black British converts, but were kicked out for their radical views. Mosque chairman Abdul Haqq Baker told police about the two men and how Abu Hamza and Abu Qatada were targeting young men in the mosques, but his warnings were ignored. Another worshipper at the mosque was the Algerian Djamel Beghal, a senior Al Qaeda recruiter and contact of Abu Qatada.

Abu Qatada disappeared in December 2001. He was tracked down a year later, when surveillance of his family home in south

London revealed that he was due to make a visit. Questions remain about how such an important figure was able to 'disappear' in London for such a long period of time.

The third member of the triumvirate of clerics is Sheikh Omar Bakri Mohammed who came to Britain from Syria. While living in Saudi Arabia he founded the al-Muhajiroun organisation and after being deported in 1985, he brought it with him to Britain. The organisation's well-organised website is full of items supporting the jihadis. Like many other Islamists, he refused to accept that bin Laden was behind the attacks on America. He instead praised bin Laden, supporting the formation of the International Islamic Front for Jihad against Jews and Crusaders in 1998, while his organisation described British Prime Minister Tony Blair as a 'legitimate target' in the wake of the attacks on America. He believes in the concept of a world caliphate, run by religious scholars and based on the teachings of the Koran and condemns what he calls 'man-made laws'. He regularly issues fatwas, or religious opinions, on many subjects. For example, he has issued a ruling saying that it is against Islam for any Muslim to co-operate with the intelligence services.

Al-Muhajiroun has been a vocal organisation, building its network at street level and via a series of stunts and publicity events, such as inviting bin Laden in 2000 to speak via a satellite link to a meeting due to be held in London's Albert Hall. When the management found out what was being planned, the meeting was cancelled. Bakri claims to have sent 700 young men to train for jihad in Pakistan, Bosnia and Chechnya.

One person with close connections to Bakri's al-Muhajiroun organisation was Zacarias Soubra. Lebanese-born Soubra became the subject of much interest to FBI agent Kenneth Williams who wrote the now-notorious 'Phoenix Memo' to his colleagues about him and his close associates at the Embry riddle Aeronautical University in Prescott Arizona in July 2001.

Soubra had lived in London and Manchester before leaving for America and flight engineering training. He had been interviewed by the FBI after only three months in Arizona after visiting a shooting range with a friend. Soubra was very active as an organiser for al-Muhajiroun and admitted being a member of what he called their Arizona 'chapter'. Williams' interest had been stimulated by the fact that he was organising anti-US and anti-Israel demonstrations in the early summer of 2001. He decided to write a memo to FBI headquarters recommending that they should draw up a list of American flying schools and start monitoring the students who were attending classes. The memo contained no warning of an impending attack, but was a vital part in the intelligence jigsaw. Unfortunately, Williams' colleagues in the FBI did not see it that way and sent his memo off to Oregon, from where it only surfaced *after* the 11 September attacks. Soubra has not been charged with any offence. Later it emerged that another person mentioned in Williams's memo had been linked to Al Qaeda's operations chief, Abu Zubaydah, who was later captured in Pakistan.

Numerous other important figures with close connections to bin Laden were able to settle in Britain during the 1990s. One of them, Dr Saad al-Fagih, helped bin Laden purchase a satellite phone, which was later used by the terror chief to direct his worldwide operations. Fagih headed the London-based Movement for Islamic Reform in Arabia, that is dedicated to the overthrow of the Saudi regime. According to US court documents, al-Fagih helped to pay for the phone that was bought in the United States and shipped to his house in north-west London.

The phone was later passed on to Khaled al-Fawwaz, a key bin Laden contact in London as head of the Advice and Reformation Committee, and then sent on to Afghanistan. Fawwaz is currently in prison in Britain as he attempts to fight extradition to the United States on charges relating to the bombing of the East African embassies in 1998. Al-Fagih claimed that he was doing his friend a favour in helping with the purchase of the satphone.

Documents recovered by the Anti-Terrorist Squad from al-Fawwaz's house show that the satphone was a direct contact to bin Laden and to his close associate Mohammed Atef, who was killed by US airstrikes in October 2001. Over the two years in which it was in use, over 143 calls were made from Afghanistan to al-Fawwaz's London numbers. More than 200 calls were made to Yemen and more than 100 calls each were placed to Sudan and to Iran. Around 60 calls each were placed to Saudi Arabia, Pakistan and Baku.[10]

Other calls were traced to the Nairobi, Kenya home of Wadih el Hage, who was found guilty in America for his role in the US embassy bombings. Despite his role in helping to purchase the phone, Dr al-Fagih has not been arrested or charged with any offence and has been granted asylum by the British authorities.

However, it should be noted that when al-Fawwaz was arrested, in 1999, on a US extradition warrant for his alleged role in the bombing of the US embassies in East Africa, he revealed that he was in regular contact with MI5, both before and after the attacks. His lawyer, Edward Fitzgerald, told the court that his contacts with MI5 were hardly behaviour typical of a terrorist. He said that MI5 had warned the Saudi dissident about a plot to assassinate him by 'agents of a foreign government . . . possibly the United States'. He added: 'It is hardly likely that they (MI5) would be advising someone they thought was a terrorist that he's a target, and that there are precautions he should take.' He asked the judge to subpoena Paul Banner, an MI5 officer who allegedly had several meetings with al-Fawwaz.[11]

The evidence is that prior to the attacks on America some Islamist radicals in Britain were watched closely by MI5, although only limited resources were devoted to this issue. In the case of Omar Sheikh, for example, despite the fact that he had kidnapped three Britons and an American in India and later freed in 1999 in exchange for hundreds of hostages held on an airliner hijacked to Afghanistan, he was allowed to return to the UK and visit his family in east London. No effort was made to track him down and British anti-terrorism laws at the time meant he could not be tried for offences committed against British subjects abroad.

In diaries written in prison, Omar Sheikh recounts how he was radicalised while studying at the London School of Economics, later travelling to Bosnia and then Afghanistan to take part in guerrilla training before being captured in India in 1994.

Sheikh, it is now known, never stopped his jihadi activities after his release by India and lived openly in Pakistan, playing a major part in planning the kidnap of Daniel Pearl. He is now facing a death sentence in Pakistan for his role in that affair.

More evidence that illustrates the lax attitude to security prior to 11 September came to light after an internal Foreign Office memo was leaked in November 2002. The document, dated 20 September 2000, showed that the Foreign Office's computer system known as FORTRESS, designed to give quick access to intelligence and secure links with other agencies, was causing problems. 'The system is less reliable and often slower than paper distribution,' said the memo. 'There have been a number of occasions when immediate threat intelligence arrived too late in CTPD or did not arrive at all, because of technical hitches . . . Vital threat telegrams to our missions overseas have been delayed as a result, causing Ambassadorial consternation (as with the pre-summer UBL threat to Brussels).'[12]

As 'UBL' stands for Usama Bin Laden, the threat referred to was probably linked to an Al Qaeda cell in Belgium which had plans to attack American targets in France. Its members, including the Tunisian Nizar Trabelsi, were arrested two days after the attacks on America. In Trabelsi's Brussels apartment police discovered documents containing chemical formulae for bomb-making. He had lived in London in 1997, where he had come under the influence of Abu Qatada, who urged him to travel to Afghanistan for training, before returning to Belgium.

Despite the generally complacent attitude towards Islamists living in Britain, MI5 was able to claim a number of successes. In December 2000, they intercepted calls to the London home of Abu Doha, an Algerian who trained in Afghanistan and who was suspected of being a leading figure within Al Qaeda's London network. The phone call talked of an imminent attack on the Christmas market in the French town of Strasbourg. As a result, four men were arrested and, in March 2003, were sentenced to long prison sentences of between ten and 12 years. Three of the men had lived in London and vital evidence for the trial was found in the Sheffield flat where one of them had lived under an assumed name.[13]

Abu Doha was also connected to the US Millenium bomber Ahmed Ressam and other Al Qaeda cells in France, Italy, Germany and Spain. He was arrested in February 2002 at Heathrow airport while attempting to leave the country and is now in prison on a US extradition warrant.

The attacks on America have had a profound impact on Britain's security establishment. The 67 Britons who died in the attacks constituted the largest number of British civilians ever killed in a terrorist incident. In its first report after the attacks, the Intelligence and Security Committee admitted that only around 23 per cent of MI5's activities were concerned with countering international terrorism. That figure was quickly doubled and now stands at more than 60 per cent, according to informed sources. More than 250 extra staff have been taken on since 11 September 2001, particularly linguists, of whom there is still a great shortage.

Despite this, MI5, MI6 and GCHQ admitted that they had no intelligence warnings of the attacks. A summit was held with the CIA in June 2001 where 'considerable anxieties' were expressed about the lack of specific intelligence on bin Laden and events in Afghanistan.[14]

An assessment by the Joint Intelligence Committee in July 2001 suggested that bin Laden was in the final stages of preparing an attack, but had little further information.

The Home Secretary at the time, Jack Straw, told the Committee: 'There is nothing as visionary as hindsight and I don't pretend for a minute that I would have been able to foresee what was going to happen, so while I think that they (the Agencies) were "on the ball" in terms of recognising that there was a network, that it was operating effectively, that it did take years to put a plan into operation, I don't think that had been translated in quite the way we can now see.'[15] In other words, as the Committee itself spelled out, the scale of the threat and vulnerability of Western nations was not understood.

In the immediate aftermath of the attacks, the director of GCHQ, the chief of MI6 and the deputy director of MI5 flew to Washington to co-ordinate with their US counterparts. MI6 sent some of its staff to work in the London-based counter-terrorism team and the focus of much of the organisation's work was redirected. GCHQ also doubled the size of its counter-terrorism team and was soon directing 30–40 per cent of its total effort to this work. The Treasury immediately agreed an additional £54 million in each of the following financial years. In October 2001, Chancellor Gordon Brown announced the creation of a multi-agency terrorist finance unit within the National Criminal Intelligence Service to examine the banking system and bureaux de change for signs of terrorist activity. The unit has been able to pass onto US authorities evidence from British financial institutions about the activities of the 11 September hijackers, many of whom passed through London on their way to America.

Better links were established with European intelligence agencies, although much suspicion remained, particularly between MI5 and its Spanish counterparts, who continued to believe that Britain was not taking the threat seriously enough.

MI5's laid-back approach emerged in the wake of the Al Qaeda attack on the Indonesian resort of Bali on 12 October 2002. The Intelligence and Security Committee conducted an inquiry into the attack to establish whether or not intelligence was overlooked. Their report, published in December 2002, noted that the security agencies received 150 threat reports each day in more than 20 different countries in the period leading up to the attack. This raw intelligence was then used by MI5 to compile threat assessments.

The ISC found that sufficient priority had been given to collecting intelligence and that no information had been received indicating an attack would take place. However, it stated that the threat assessment should have been raised to HIGH, calling this a 'serious misjudgement', while conceding that this would not have prevented the attack. It recommended that the threat level system and the FCO Travel Advice be examined as a matter of urgency.[16]

Within Whitehall three Cabinet committees were set up to oversee anti-terrorism work: DOP (IT), chaired by the Prime Minister; DOP (IT) (T), chaired by the Home Secretary to co-ordinate policy on protective and preventative security; and the Civil Contingencies Committee (CCC), also chaired by the Home Secretary to ensure essential supplies and services during an emergency. Sir David Omand was appointed to the new post of Security and Intelligence Co-ordinator and Permanent Secretary to the Cabinet Office.

In addition to the establishment of the National Counter Terrorism and Security Office, the Police International Counter Terrorist Unit was also established, made up of Special Branch, Anti-Terrorist Branch and MI5 officers. More than 300 arrests of suspected Islamist militants have taken place since 11 September.

According to the Institute of Race Relations, British police made 304 arrests under anti-terrorist legislation between September 2001 and February 2003. Only 40 of those arrests led to charges being brought and only three resulted in convictions, none of which were for involvement in Islamic terror groups.[17] The three successful convictions were related to membership of banned organisations. Two of those found guilty were sentenced for membership of the International Sikh Youth Federation. They were arrested in Dover and were carrying membership cards of the organisation. Police said they were on a fundraising trip.

According to the IRR, out of the 154 most significant arrests, six of the 40 people charged were acquitted or had charges dropped. A further 31 were awaiting trial. However, many of those arrested under suspicion of terrorism offences were charged with other offences, mostly immigration offences.

MI5 officers have also been given access to the Guantanamo Bay detention camp set up by the Americans in Cuba, which now holds more than 600 Al Qaeda and Taliban suspects. At least eight Britons are being held at Guantanamo Bay, including four from the small east Midlands town of Tipton.

However, the actions of the police and security services has also been strongly criticised by civil liberties groups. Special Branch was accused of going on 'fishing expeditions' when conducting raids on the houses of suspects. In August 2002, Home Secretary David Blunkett issued an unprecedented apology to Muslims living in Britain after several wrote to him about MI5 officers engaging in 'information sweeps' throughout their communities.

Amnesty International issued a detailed report in September 2002, stating that there had been serious human rights violations in Britain following the 11 September attacks. They included the detention of suspects without charge under the Anti-Terrorism, Crime and Security Act (ATCSA) 2001 and the failure of the British government to ensure the human rights of British nationals held without charge, trial or judicial review in Guantanamo Bay.[18]

Amnesty was particularly concerned about the fate of those arrested and detained without charge under the ATCSA legislation. Around a dozen people are being detained under the law, although the names are covered by a UK contempt of court order and cannot be published. Most are either asylum seekers or have been previously recognised as refugees in the UK. Under the law, detainees can be held for an unspecified and unlimited period of time once the Home Secretary has certified they are 'suspected international terrorists'. They can leave the country 'voluntarily', but in many cases this is impossible. All are held in high security prisons including HMP Belmarsh in London and HMP Woodhill in Buckinghamshire. One, the Palestinian Mahmoud Abu Rideh, is being held in Broadmoor Psychiatric Hospital.

In its report into the detentions, Amnesty says 'detention without charge or trial, for an unspecified and potentially unlimited period of time, under the ATCSA is tantamount to charging a person with a criminal offence, convicting the person concerned without a trial and imposing on him/her an open-ended sentence.' It added that some of the provision of ATCSA are 'inconsistent with a number of international human rights and refugee law standards, including treaty provisions by which the UK is bound'.

The British government refused to change the regime under which detainees are held without trial and now faces a number of legal challenges through the courts to the procedures.

Britain's close identification with US foreign policy in the Middle East and continuing presence in Afghanistan will ensure that Britain remains a potential target for Al Qaeda and its offshoots. The high security alert around Heathrow airport in February 2003 was based on information that an Al Qaeda team in Britain had received a surface-to-air missile and were intent on shooting down a passenger aircraft. Other plots linked to the production of the deadly chemical poison ricin and to the use of poisonous gases on London's underground system have been disrupted, but many intelligence analysts are working on the assumption that terrorists will eventually find a way of carrying out an atrocity.

After a period during which MI5 and the security establishment paid scant attention to the dangers posed by followers of bin Laden, procedures have been tightened up significantly, albeit at the cost of the human rights for some of those detained. Even so, large gaps in Britain's intelligence-gathering operations remain, particularly in the field of linguists. The War on Terror is unlikely to go away and vigilance will have to be maintained for years to come.

The intelligence elite, meanwhile, still finds it hard to come to terms with its own inability to piece together the scope and ambition of Al Qaeda prior to 11 September.

In his first-ever speech on the record, at the Law Society in London, retiring MI5 director-general Sir Stephen Lander stressed that the 11 September attacks were not due to a failure in intelligence but possibly in security. 'Intelligence is about security information that others wish to keep secret,' he told the gathering of lawyers. 'If you were so minded, you could say an event like 11 September might show some failure of security – that's a different question. If you expect to predict every attack, you haven't been paying attention.'[19]. The public record, not least in America, suggests he was wrong.

7

BOMBINGS, ASSASSINATION
AND THE BUGGING
OF A JOURNALIST

'When I first heard this story I thought this was James Bond SIS [MI6] stuff . . . Then suddenly it was very real. We were talking about tens of thousands of taxpayers' money being used for an attempt to assassinate a foreign head of state.'

David Shayler, *Panorama*, BBC1, 8 September 1998

'This is the most exciting thing to happen here [at MI5] in the last ten years.'

MI5 branch director, 1994, on the prospect of placing Victoria Brittain, deputy foreign editor of the *Guardian*, under surveillance.

In the tense, bloody and heated atmosphere of the War on Terror in the early 1990s, one man loomed large as Public Enemy One. He was Colonel Muammar Gaddafi, the controversial, charismatic non-aligned ruler of Libya. Dubbed 'the mad dog of the Middle East' by President Reagan, he was responsible, according to MI6 and the CIA, for orchestrating the period's most deadliest terrorist attacks like the Lockerbie bombing. and financing guerrilla groups across the globe.

As the UK became increasingly vulnerable to terrorism, MI5 targetted Gadaffi and Libya as its most dangerous exponent. Its origins lie in the shooting of WPC Yvonne Fletcher outside the Libyan embassy by a diplomat firing a sub-machine gun from within the building. The incident, on 17 April 1984, caused outrage. All Libyan diplomats were expelled and Gaddafi's regime was fiercely condemned (although it was not until 1999 that Libya admitted responsibility for the shooting). As a result, all Libyans entering Britain became subject to increased surveillance by Special Branch and MI5.

The prospect of more terror increased in March 1986, when the USA bombed Tripoli and killed Gadaffi's 15-month-old adopted daughter. Libyans in the UK were outraged and a few days later, one of them, a trainee pilot at the Oxford Air Training school, telephoned Tripoli radio: 'The aggression perpetrated by America against the heroic Libyan Arab people, who do not fear imperialist fleets and aircraft, will be destroyed...We will hit with an iron fist anyone, like dirty Reagan, contemplating aggression . . We, the revolutionary force, are prepared to become suicide squads against America.'

The radio message said it was from 'The Revolutionary Force at Oxford Aerodrome, Britain'. It was picked up by the BBC's monitoring service in Caversham and Thames Valley police were alerted. MI5 were then brought in to investigate and a month later sent their report and recommendations to the Home Office. After police raids, 21 Libyan students were expelled because 'their deportation was conducive to the public good and in the interests of national security'. And over 300 Libyan trainee engineers and pilots were also, in effect, expelled because they were told their six-month educational visas would not be renewed.

The government confirmed it was a 'security decision', although the instructors at the flying schools were not convinced. 'As far as my own students are concerned, I am quite sure they present no threat at all,' said Colin Beckwith, principal of the Oxford Air Training School. 'I would not have thought it necessary here, where students are under instructor-control.'[1]

However, in the light of the suicide bombers who trained at flying schools in Florida before crashing into the twin towers on 11 September, it provokes an eerie resonance and contrast.

The bombing of Tripoli and the expulsions provoked an inevitable backlash from Gaddafi and his intelligence agency. Two years later, in December 1988, their revenge was the bombing of PanAm 103 over Lockerbie in which 269 people died. Forensic evidence, based on material provided by a defector, blamed two Libyan intelligence officials who were later extradited and found guilty at a trial in Holland. Their indictments identified them as operatives of the Jamahirya Security Organisation which 'conducted acts of terrorism against other nations'.[2]

Britain and other Western countries had good reason to be concerned about Gaddafi. In 1990, the USA, Britain and others staged a joint intelligence effort that succeeded in shutting down a chemical-weapons plant that the Libyans were operating in Rabta. By the end of 1992, drawing on satellite photos and reports from spies to MI6, the CIA had constructed a computer model of a second nerve-gas plant Gaddafi was building near Tarhunah, about 40 miles south-east of the Libyan capital, Tripoli. This time it was carved into the side of a mountain and included a huge underground chamber, almost three storeys high.

A secret conference was called at CIA headquarters in Langley, Virginia, attended by MI6 officers. It was decided to wage a covert war to prevent Gaddafi finishing the new factory, which was planned to enter production in 1995. The plant was well defended, based on designs used in Russia to build a large network of underground bomb shelters during the Cold War. It was likely to be impervious to air attack or sabotage. Instead, it was decided to slow down construction by preventing the delivery of machinery needed for building and drilling into the mountain. Some of the drill bits came from Germany, and Chancellor Helmut Kohl was persuaded to ban further exports. Skilled engineers from Europe and the Far East were also 'discouraged' from taking up job offers. The measures were successful and construction came to a near halt.

A report by the US Congress Task Force on Terrorism[3] says that by 1995 Iraq was sending its top scientists to Libya to assist in efforts to produce chemical weapons. According to US Congressional sources, in 1995 and again in 1996 the CIA provided classified briefings on Libya which stated that Gaddafi was vulnerable on the home front. There was religious unrest within the country and it was spreading into the armed forces. The CIA itself was financing at least one tribal group to encourage it to revolt. Britain had long been cultivating various opposition groups in Libya, including the London-based Libyan National Movement and the National Salvation Front. MI6 had often co-operated with the CIA on anti-Gaddafi operations, knowing that Libya had been a major supplier of weapons and explosives to the IRA. The Americans were good at electronic eavesdropping, but it was MI6 who had the contacts on the ground.

MI5 BLUNDER. The horrific bombing in Bali which killed over 200 people. The government later admitted that MI5 made "serious misjudgements" in assessing the terrorist threat facing British people in Indonesia.

MURDANI USMAN/CORBIS

CATASTROPHE. The devastating attack on the twin towers of the World Trade Centre is widely regarded as a failure of intelligence. With so many Al Qaeda operatives and supporters active in the UK, MI5's role in attempting to counter international terrorism has been crucial.

EVAN BROWNE/CORBIS

Public school-educated Omar Sheikh kidnapped three Britons in India and helped organise the kidnapping of Wall Street Journal reporter Daniel Pearl.

Abu Qatada was granted asylum in Britain in 1993. Jordanian requests to extradite him to face terrorism charges have been refused and he is now held in prison under new anti-terror laws.

SPY MISTRESS. Dame Stella Rimington, director-general of MI5 from 1992 to 1996. A tough astute, negotiator with Whitehall, she attempted to transform the Service into a counter-terrorist agency. She had some success against the IRA, but failed to reform MI5 internally.

(News International Syndication)

THE DESK MAN. Dr Stephen Lander, MI5's director-general from 1996-2002. Despite a sharp intellect, he lacks Rimington's dynamic personality and leadership qualities. Critics argue that his bureaucratic, almost academic, approach has hindered the Service's counter-terrorist opportunities.

(Press Association)

NEW BOSS, OLD GUARD. The Hon. Eliza Manningham-Buller, MI5's director-general since October 2002. She has a lot more operational experience than her predecessors but is viewed as part of the old-guard axis and Cold War generation.

AFP PHOTO

DEVASTATION. Bishopsgate shortly after the IRA exploded a 1000lb bomb killing one person, injuring 44 and causing an estimated £350 million of damage. MI5 was heavily criticized for its lack of vigilance and failing to react to prior intelligence about the attack.

(*DAILY MAIL*/SOLO SYNDICATION)

SHATTERED. MI5 again failed to act despite warnings about an IRA bomb in South Quay, Canary Wharf. Two people died, 100 were injured and damage worth £100 million was caused in the explosion.

(*DAILY MAIL*/SOLO SYNDICATION)

THE DAMAGE caused to the Israeli Embassy in London after a massive car bomb exploded directly across the street injuring 13 people. An MI5 officer received specific prior warnings about the attack, but failed to act on it. The information was later found 'buried' in a cupboard by a colleague. *(Above and right)*
(MIRROR SYNDICATION / SOLO SYNDICATION)

JAWAD BOTMEH and SAMAR ALAMI, two Palestinians who were convicted of conspiring to bomb the Israeli Embassy. Both serving 20-year jail sentences, there is strong evidence that they are innocent. The government refuses to release documents that could prove their innocence. *(Below)*
(PRESS ASSOCIATION)

JACK STRAW, whilst President of the National Union of Students in 1970. At the time MI5 targeted him as 'subversive' and kept a file on him until the early 1990s. Since May 1997 he has been Home Secretary, responsible for overseeing ... MI5.

(PRESS ASSOCIATION)

PETER MANDELSON (second from right), introducing the British Youth Council (BYC) report on youth unemployment on 28 March 1977. Later that year MI5 began tapping his home telephone because of BYC trips to the Communist bloc and Mandelson's Party membership. His MI5 file was kept open until 1992.

(MARX MEMORIAL LIBRARY)

ASSASSINATION. Taken from video footage, these unique images show a failed attempt to assassinate Colonel Gaddafi in 1996. They show a hand grenade being thrown from the crowd by a man (top, circled). According to Shayler, the plot was organized and financed by MI6.
(ASSOCIATED PRESS AND ARAB NEWS NETWORK)

SMILES BEFORE THE STORM. Machon and Shayler in Paris on 31 July 1998 after nearly a year in exile. The next day Shayler was arrested and thrown in jail by the French Security Service at the request of Special Branch. (ALASTAIR MILLER)

THE GREAT ESCAPE. On 18 November 1998, after three-and-a-half months in jail, Shayler was released. A French appeals court rejected a British request to extradite him on the grounds that the MI5 whistleblower was motivated by political and public interest factors. *(Above)*
(JACQUES BRINON / ASSOCIATED PRESS)

JAILBIRD. Shayler's official identity photograph from La Sante jail in Paris *(Right)*, where he was refused any visitors for seven weeks. His fellow inmates were mostly former government employees, but also included Carlos the Jackal.
(PRIVATE COLLECTION)

D'IDENTITE

0 NOM   SHAYLE
1 Prénoms   DAVID
2 Surnom
3 Né le   14.12.65   à
4 Nationalité
EMPREINTE AU VERSO

O.M.A.P. 77/12

269151

One of MI6's main objectives in its dealings with Libya was to bring to justice the perpetrators of the Lockerbie bombing, which meant somehow delivering the two chief suspects, Abdelbasset Megrahi and Lamin Fhimah, for trial in Scotland. In late 1994, MI6 had embarrassed itself in front of MI5 when it had assured officers that the two suspects were in an office in Tripoli awaiting a flight to Scotland. Nothing came of this.

In addition, MI6 had tried to recruit Khalifa Bazelya, the most senior Libyan intelligence officer in Britain, who could have been an invaluable source of inside information on Gaddafi's foreign policy and operations. This was despite the threat he posed to national security as a senior member of the Libyan External Security Organisation and as a former gun-runner in Africa. But Bazelya spent most of his time in Britain leading MI6 a merry dance and gathering information on Libyan dissidents and chemical and biological warfare from British universities. By 1995, MI6 had begun to accept that he was unlikely to be recruited. Embarrassed by its lack of progress on the Lockerbie issue, it was looking for a quick-fix solution. When a Libyan code-named 'Tunworth' walked into their hands, needing finance for a plot to kill Gaddafi, it was ready to accept any proposal. Using a shadowy group of Islamic militants to carry out its plan was the perfect solution. At the time, David Shayler was a member of G9, MI5's section responsible for Libya. His job consisted of analysing intelligence reports based on transcripts of tapped phone calls and from spies working for the British. As such he attended regular meetings with his counterparts in MI6. At one of these meetings he had learned of the existence of the Arab agent Tunworth, a secret member of a group of Islamic militants.

The BBC correspondent Mark Urban later ascertained that two or three officers from both MI5 and MI6 knew about Tunworth and met to discuss him. They included Shayler (G9A/1) and two other MI5 officers, both using the MI5 internal acronym G9A/15. Shayler later said: 'I briefed my boss in MI5 during the course of the operation on planning and funding. One other officer in MI5 was fully briefed on the operation.' The three MI6 officers were called PT16, PT16 OpsB, and the man meeting and running Tunworth, PT16B. As Shayler told Urban, 'PT16B, who was my opposite number in SIS [MI6], started to talk about how this guy was involved in trying to plan an assassination attempt on Gaddafi, using a Libyan Islamic extremist group.'[4]

Shayler said that a four-page special report, known as a CX report, was sent through the usual channels to Whitehall – the Joint Intelligence Committee, the Foreign Office and GCHQ. It contained details of what was effectively a plan to kill Gaddafi – athough it was not explicit on this point – and requests for equipment and weaponry. 'When I first heard the story I thought this was James Bond SIS stuff – we'll probably hear about this for a month and then we'll never hear about it again,' said Shayler.[5]

But the plan was very much alive. PT16B continued to meet Tunworth and eventually paid him over £100,000 in three or four instalments. Shayler says Tunworth became MI6's link with the Militant (or Fighting) Islamic Group, a hardline, anti-Western organisation headed by Abdallah al-Sadeq. Members of his group, which was fiercely anti-Gaddafi and at the same time close to Islamic groups in Egypt and Algeria, had been known to visit the UK, although most of their supporters were based outside Britain. Sadeq himself was resident in Britain at the time of the Lockerbie attack.

In February 1996, the Militant Islamic Group received information that Gaddafi was to pass a certain road near the northern Libyan city of Sirte and planned a bomb attack. The bomb exploded as the Libyan leader's cavalcade passed, killing several bodyguards but leaving Gaddafi shaken though otherwise unharmed. In the ensuing gun battle, three members of the Militant Islamic Group were reportedly killed. Shayler told Urban that shortly after the failed attack he received details of the incident. 'Gaddafi was travelling in the cavalcade, but in a different car. So the explosion had gone off and there'd been various casualties, fatalities, but in fact they'd got the wrong people. Even then I was still thinking this could be a result of the Islamic extremist activity going on in Libya in general . . . It was only when I met PT16B, discussing other matters with him, that he mentioned this thing in a kind of note of triumph saying that "Yes, you know, we've done it! We are the kind of intelligence service that people think we are," almost, you know.

'I was absolutely astounded when I heard this was the case because my thinking up to then about SIS was that they were involved in a kind of *Boys' Own* comic and suddenly this was very real. We were talking about tens of thousands of pounds of taxpayers' money being used for an attempt to assassinate a foreign head of state.'[6]

Urban confirmed Shayler's story by speaking to someone who had confirmed many of its key facts. There had been contemporaneous press accounts of an attack. It was true that a series of meetings had taken place between Shayler and PT16B. Britain did know about an attempt to kill Gaddafi before it happened and was using Tunworth as a cut-out for contacts with Libyan militant groups. Shayler added that PT16B had told him that the operation had gone 'all the way to the top' for approval, which it had received. Urban says he was told categorically that the Foreign Secretary at the time, Malcolm Rifkind, was not informed of the assassination attempt and that the plan was approved solely within MI6.

Gaddafi compared the Lockerbie bomb with the attempt on his life: 'How can we talk about Lockerbie and forget the assassination attempt that British intelligence organised?' he said.[7] Early in September 1998, Libya showed television footage of what it said had been an assassination attempt in 1996 on Gaddafi. The images were broadcast by the London-based Arab satellite TV channel ANN during a live interview with Gaddafi from Tripoli.

The footage shows Gaddafi being greeted by large crowds at a rally in Wadi Achatt, in the central province of Fezzan, about 200 miles south of Sirte. First he is shown being driven along in a jeep. Later he gets down and walks amongst the crowd. Suddenly an object can be seen flying through the air and landing at his feet. Gaddafi and his entourage bend over to examine it then walk away. According to the Libyan authorities, this was a grenade, thrown by a man in the crowd. As Gaddafi walks away, closely surrounded by bodyguards, other guards move in to arrest the man. According to the commentary with the film, the man was 'an agent of British intelligence'. He had confessed his role. No further details of the detained man or his fate were provided. The story differed from Shayler's account in that there appeared to have been no explosion. According to one source, the Libyan cameras showed a firefight, which broke out immediately after the incident as the bomber's accomplices tried to make a getaway. According to this account, several innocent people died in the crossfire.

Gaddafi repeated his claims to the BBC's *Nine o'Clock News*: 'Britain was behind this campaign. There is evidence, and when the time comes we will bring this evidence forward,' he said.

Colonel Gaddafi did not have long to wait. On 13 February 2000, a highly classified four-page MI6 document dated 4 December 1995 was distributed to the most senior civil servants, notably Sir John Coles, permanent secretary at the Foreign and Commonwealth

Office, the defence intelligence staff and key sectors of MI5 and MI6. The report outlined in astonishing detail how MI6 officers liaised with Libyan dissidents, who were intent on blowing up Gaddafi's car cavalcade as the precursor to mounting a *coup d'état*. Headlined 'Libya: Plans to Overthrow Gaddafi in Early 1996 are Well Advanced', it stated that the plotters passed detailed information to their MI6 handler in anticipation of assistance from Britain. MI6 was told in detail who, how, where and when Gaddafi would be assassinated:

> One group of military personnel were being trained in the desert area near Kufra for the role of attacking Gaddafi and his entourage. The aim was to attack Gaddafi after the General People's Congress, but before he returned to Sirte. One officer and 20 men were being trained for this attack.
>
> The source said that the plotters would have cars similar to those in Gaddafi's security entourage with fake security number plates. They would infiltrate themselves into the entourage in order to kill or arrest Gaddafi. The plotters had already distributed 250 Webley pistols and 500 heavy machine guns amongst the groups.[8]

It was a devastating disclosure because it showed that British intelligence knew of the murder plot at least two months in advance. And it made clear that the conspirators wanted money and equipment, including military supplies, from MI6. The arms requirements were believed to be set out in a separate document. The report's publication was particularly embarrassing for then Foreign Secretary Robin Cook, who had told BBC TV's *Breakfast with Frost* in August 1998: 'I am perfectly satisfied that MI6 never put forward any such proposal for an assassination attempt, nor have I seen anything in the 15 months that I have been in the job which would suggest that MI6 has had any interest, any role or any experience over the recent decades of any such escapades.'

The leaked document did not prove conclusively that MI6 orchestrated the assassination, but it certainly lent substantial credibility to Shayler's claim that MI6 paid at least £100,000 to their Libyan agent to fund the operation.

Despite the unprecedented contents of the CX Report, the government's response was to issue a D-Notice requesting British newspapers not to reproduce it. It is still, however, available on the Internet and has been republished in *Punch* magazine. What's more, the Portuguese newspaper, *Tal&Qual*, published the names of the two MI6 officers – David Watson and Richard Bartlett – who were the chief points of contact with the Libyan dissidents. Their names also remain on several Internet sites, despite efforts by law officers to close them down.

The Home Office's response was to order a criminal investigation under the Official Secrets Act into the leaking of the CX Report. It was strongly suspected that Shayler himself was the source of the leaked document and the police were tasked with finding the evidence. Special Branch officers visited the offices of the *Sunday Times*, who first published the story after it appeared on a California website (subsequently shut down). They served notices on the newspaper to hand over tapes and documents relating to its article.

Then when the *Observer* ran a story claiming that Shayler had privately named the two MI6 officers involved in the Gaddafi plot, the journalist Martin Bright was investigated under the Official Secrets Act. And the *Guardian* was ordered to hand over the full text of a published letter by Shayler, even though at a court hearing the Old Bailey judge admitted that it did not contain any new information.

The government's attempt to prosecute and censor the press was even criticised by two of its most loyal ministers – Robin Cook and Peter Hain, Minister of State at the Foreign and Commonwealth Office. Cook made protests at the 'highest level', and Hain was said to be 'horrified' over the Home Office's attempts to force the *Observer* to hand over material. 'The Home Office has gone manic over this,' a senior civil servant told the *Observer*. 'It's bloody crazy. The government should not be picking a war with the press.'[9] In Vienna, the director of the International Press Institute, Johann Fritz, described the moves against the *Guardian* and the *Observer* as 'chilling'. He said that any decision taken against the papers in a British court would be challenged under the European Convention on Human Rights. The judiciary appears to have agreed with Hain and Cook's private doubts. On 21 July 2000, the appeal court dismissed the disclosure orders against the *Observer* and the *Guardian*. In a remarkable defence of press freedom, Lord Justice Judge overturned the application and told the court: 'Inconvenient or embarrassing revelations, whether for the Security Services or for public authorities, should not be suppressed.' He added that such orders should be made only when there was 'compelling evidence' in the public interest. It is not known if the Crown Prosecution Service will appeal to the House of Lords.

Despite their legal setbacks, the state authorities continued to pursue Shayler's allies. On 6 March 2000, a mature student at Kingston University, Julie-Ann Davies, was arrested by Special Branch officers and questioned over the leaking of the CX report. Her computer was confiscated and police later returned to the university with a warrant to obtain access to the computers on campus.

At the very moment that MI6 was informed of the planned assassination, the agency was implementing another dirty tricks ploy against Gaddafi. At the heart of the clandestine operation was a smear story, planted in the *Sunday Telegraph* by MI6, which linked Gaddafi's son to an attempted currency fraud. The article represented a high-water mark for a shadowy MI6 programme called I/Ops – 'Information Operations' – whose activities have never been fully explained or exposed.

But the planted story backfired. Gaddafi's eldest son, Saif al-Islam, sued the *Sunday Telegraph* for libel. 'The allegations are completely untrue and he is determined to set the record straight,' said his solicitor, Norman Chapman of Evershed's.

At the time, Gaddafi's lawyers were unaware that beneath the legal surface lurked the hidden hand of MI6 and a conspiracy to destabilise and overthrow the Libyan regime.

The importance of this revelation is the timing and the identity of the operatives involved. The *Sunday Telegraph* article was published in late November 1995 – the exact period when MI6's agent in Libya, Tunworth, was briefing its officers about the assassination plot. Even more significant is that the MI6 officer who leaked the story to the newspaper was the very same officer, codenamed PT16B, who authorised the assassination attempt by funding the conspirators.

MI6's black propoganda scheme can be traced to early 1995 when the son of Major Jalloud, Gaddafi's deputy and most influential adviser, slipped into London virtually unnoticed. This caused consternation inside MI6 – even though Jalloud Junior did nothing more sinister than frequent the city's nightclubs.

So when MI6 learned about a plan by Gaddafi's son to visit the UK in July 1995, they scuppered it. Saif Gaddafi, then a 22-year-old architectural university graduate, was refused entry because it was 'not conducive to the public good'. From that moment, MI6 looked for opportunities to discredit Gaddafi.

The opportunity came after a discreet lunch on 19 October 1995, attended by Malcolm Rifkind, then Foreign Secretary, two senior diplomats and several *Sunday Telegraph* journalists, notably Charles Moore, then the paper's editor. Rifkind briefed the reporters about the danger of 'certain Arab countries' obtaining nuclear and chemical weapons. He said the arms proliferation was funded by covert schemes to obtain hard currency, usually US dollars. The Foreign Secretary told Con Coughlin, chief foreign correspondent of the Sunday Telegraph, that this was in breach of UN economic sanctions and encouraged him to investigate.

Over the next ten days, Coughlin attended two lengthy meetings – on 25 October and 31 October 1995 – with a senior MI6 officer, whom he had known for several years. The intelligence officer claimed that a company was raising hard currency for Iran to fund its weapons programme by selling surplus oil on the black market.

Meanwhile, at that very moment, MI6 had also received a dramatic approach from an agent in Libya. Details were telexed to London of an assassination attempt on Gaddafi, planned for the following February by dissidents in Libya. The conspirators wanted British backing. MI6 replied by debriefing its informant.

Within a few days of that debriefing, on 21 November, Coughlin had another private lunch with the MI6 officer. The journalist was introduced to a different MI6 operative, who was described as having expertise in 'Middle East banking and finance'. This new source said there was a 'Gaddafi connection' to the currency swindling and a failed money-laundering plan to obtain US dollars for Libyan dinars. He added that he would only disclose details if he was guaranteed 'complete confidentiality'.

The next day the two spies briefed the foreign correspondent over four hours. According to legal documents, they spun a complex but intriguing tale. MI6 claimed that Colonel Gaddafi's son, Saif al-Islam, was authorised by his father to enter into a money-laundering deal with Iranian middlemen.

The alleged scam involved the drawing of 'clean' $8 billion from banks in Egypt. In return, the Libyans agreed to pay the Egyptians the same sum in Libyan dinars for a massive commission. At first the Egyptians were tempted as they stood to make a handsome profit. But, according to the MI6 officers, their bankers rejected the scheme when they 'discovered' that Gaddafi's son was behind it.

As his sources were two senior MI6 officers, Coughlin regarded the story as credible. But he was concerned about the lack of any hard evidence and so met the two intelligence officers the next day, 23 November 1995. At the meeting Coughlin was shown photocopies of what purported to be banking records proving Saif Gaddafi's business links with one of the Iranian middlemen. But the MI6 officers refused to allow him to make copies.

Three days later, the *Sunday Telegraph* published the story. Headlined 'Gaddafi's Son Linked to Sting on Iran', the article alleged that Saif Gaddafi was 'an untrustworthy maverick' who was linked to 'an outrageous plan to flood Iran with fake currency'. The story was entirely unsourced, except for an anonymous quote from 'a British banking official'. That was untrue. In reality, he was a senior MI6 officer.

Gaddafi's son promptly issued a writ for libel. In March 2000, his lawyers, Evershed's, filed papers at the High Court asking for directions for future action. The *Sunday Telegraph* defended the action. 'We stand by the story which appeared in the *Sunday Telegraph*,' Dominic Lawson, editor of the paper, told the authors. 'We are not in the habit of discussing our journalistic sources.'[10]

The case was been delayed because of legal disputes over the *Sunday Telegraph*'s complex and wide-ranging defence. But the case was eventually heard in the High Court in April 2002.

Apart from new revelations into MI6's secret war against Libya, this episode provided a unique insight into 'Information Operations'. Known as I/Ops, it specialises in black propoganda and leaks to the media. 'I/Ops,' said a former MI6 officer, 'is dedicated to manipulating media opinion. The existence and operations of I/Ops are kept secret, even within MI6 itself, such is its obvious sensitivity.'[11]

A primary function of I/Ops is to influence events in another country or organisation in a direction favourable to Britain. It tends to focus on trouble-spots like the Balkans and non-aligned regimes like Libya. As such operations do not require ministerial approval, I/Ops is free to play the information and dirty-tricks game. This occurred in the run-up to the 1992 elections for UN secretary-general. MI6, according to a former officer, 'planted stories in the

American press about Boutros-Ghali [the leading candidate] because they regarded him as dangerously Francophile.'[12]

The *Sunday Telegraph*'s story about Gaddafi's son clearly fell into this category. As the case reached the High Court, MI6 was in a state of high anxiety as two of its senior officers were to be summoned as witnesses because they were the only sources of the article. Even worse, they were to be questioned in depth about the dubious activities of I/Ops and its operations. And Shayler was lined up as a crucial witness, because he was MI5's desk officer for Libya at that time and liaised directly with the MI6 officer who was plotting against Gaddafi and his children.

Three days into the libel hearing, just as the MI6 connection was raised in court, *The Sunday Telegraph* agreed to settle the case and conceded defeat. The paper paid a portion of Saif Gaddafi's legal costs and published an apology. Reading from an agreed statement in open court, James Price QC, counsel for Gaddafi, said: '*The Sunday Telegraph* has accepted that not only is there no truth in these allegations, but that there is no evidence to suggest that there is any truth in them, and they have agreed to apologise to the claimant (Gaddafi) in this court and in the newspaper.'

Both the MI6 officers and *The Sunday Telegraph* journalists breathed a sigh of relief as they were both due to face an uncomfortable few days in the witness box and interrogated about the source of the article. But the case had more profound implications. As the MI6 officer who authorised the press smear against Gaddafi was also directly involved in the plot to assassinate his father, it would have opened up the whole controversy once again. Robin Cook's original statement that Shayler's allegation was 'pure fantasy' is looking increasingly discredited.

The conspiracy against Gaddafi showed just how far the security agencies were prepared to go to counter the Libyan menace. By the mid-1990s, MI5 was on red alert for any intelligence activity in the UK and this led to one of its most controversial operations: the secret surveillance and investigation into Victoria Brittain, deputy foreign editor of the *Guardian*.

In the late 1980s and early 1990s, Victoria Brittain was known to have visited a foreign embassy often, where she had close contact with an intelligence officer, although there was never a suggestion that she was working for him.

Brittain had once again come to the attention of MI5 in September 1993, after it was alerted by a bank in the City that more than £100,000 had been paid into her building society account. Over the next 14 months that sum grew to over £300,000. Incredibly, MI5's initial assessment was that Brittain was involved in laundering money on behalf of the Libyan intelligence service.

When the large amounts of money started coming into her account, MI5 could have tasked a Special Branch officer to question her under the guise of a routine police inquiry. It is highly likely that this would have cleared the matter up, but because she was a *Guardian* journalist they did not.

According to Shayler, MI5 quickly discovered that much of the cash had come from Libyan sources, including Khalifa Ahmed Bazelya, head of the Libyan-interest section at the Saudi Arabian embassy in London. Bazelya was already under close observation by MI5 and was suspected of threatening the Libyan dissident community in Britain. There was intelligence that he had been involved in intimidation and surveillance of people opposed to Colonel Gaddafi's regime. Other money paid into Victoria Brittain's account had come via the Libyan Arab Foreign Bank.

It is not surprising that these substantial transactions were brought to the attention of the Security Service: since 1990, banks have been required to report any transactions over £10,000 to the police as part of a growing campaign against drugs-money laundering. No sooner had information about the transfers been received by MI5 than the Libyan desk decided it required detailed investigation. The investigation was codenamed Shadower. The first action was to place a tap on Brittain's home phone, which stayed in place for at least a year.

Shayler was initially briefed on the case, but did not take over its day-to-day running until February 1995. From that moment, he argued that an inquiry into public sources should be launched to find out if there was any known reason for the money transfers. He said he was overruled in favour of applying for a telephone-tapping warrant under the 1985 Interception of Communications Act, then later for a 'property warrant' under the 1989 Security Service Act, which allowed a bug to be placed in Brittain's house. In both cases, the warrant had to be approved by the then Home Secretary, Michael Howard.

The telephone tap quickly revealed that Brittain was in contact with Kojo Tsikata, former head of the Ghanaian Security Service – and someone who must have been well known to MI5's colleagues in MI6.

MI5 was now closely monitoring movements of cash through Brittain's bank accounts. Their analysis, in which Shayler was closely involved, showed that some of the money was being transferred to the law firm Bindman & Partners. On the surface it looked like a classic money-laundering operation, but Victoria Brittain was a highly respected senior journalist: she had been editor of the *Guardian*'s 'Third World Review' for several years and had written substantial sympathetic pieces covering the national liberation movements in Angola, South Africa, Namibia, Uganda, Ethiopia, Iran, Grenada and Nicaragua. The former wife of the then executive chairman of News International, Andrew Knight, she had not previously been considered a security risk.

As a journalist, Victoria Brittain had had a long association with Africa. Her first national newspaper job had been as a stringer for the *Guardian* in Nairobi in 1976. At the time she was married to Peter Sharrock, the Reuters correspondent in Nairobi. After her marriage broke down, she returned to London in 1979 where she continued to write on African issues. Before she joined the staff of the *Guardian* she worked for *The Times* in Washington, and was ITN's first woman reporter. She has written several books on Africa. By 1994, she was deputy foreign editor of the *Guardian*.

Shayler says that several of the 'old guard' within MI5 became highly excited at the prospect of investigating a *Guardian* journalist, particularly one with such a pedigree. According to Shayler, the director of the branch within MI5 called it 'the most exciting thing to happen here in the last ten years'. The *Guardian* has long been MI5's most vociferous critic. It was just like the old days, as described by Peter Wright, when MI5 operatives freewheeled their way round London, investigating whom they pleased with legal immunity.[13]

As excitement grew, the resources devoted to the case were increased. Operatives from MI5's A Branch were tasked to follow Brittain and discover whom she was meeting. There was even pressure to tap the lawyer Geoffrey Bindman's home phone, but that idea was rejected by MI5's legal advisers.

After nearly a year of surveillance and still no clear picture of what was happening, the decision was taken in 1995 to try to plant a listening device in Brittain's Islington home, which Shayler says horrified him. The plan was for the bug to be installed while she and her daughter were on holiday in the United States. It called for the FBI to arrest Brittain's 19-year-old daughter and detain her on a trumped-up charge while the break-in was under way. In official burglaries the risk of being disturbed must be reduced to an absolute minimum, and even Brittain's son Casimir, a Foreign Office diplomat then based in Prague in the Czech Republic, was to be entertained for the evening by the MI6 station there.

The break-in was to be handled by a specialist MI5 recce team, which surveyed the house and brought in a team of lockpickers to assess how easy it would be to get in. The plan was abandoned when it became clear that the chance of being caught was too high: the house was in a square, which made it difficult for MI5's burglars to make a covert entry.

Shayler said that he argued throughout the whole operation that there was bound to be a straightforward explanation for the movement of the funds. In fact, it took MI5 more than a year to work out the reason behind the money transfers. And yet MI5 could have discovered what was happening from public sources at an early stage and saved the estimated £750,000 that was spent on surveillance.

The money was being used to fund Bindman's work in fighting a libel action against the *Independent* by Kojo Tsikata, who was a long-standing friend of Ms Brittain. She had first met him in April 1982 at a press conference in the House of Commons arranged by Lord Gifford. He was then adviser to the Provisional National Defence Council (PNDC) which had ruled Ghana since a *coup d'état* in late 1981, and she was a contract journalist, looking for a permanent position on the *Guardian*. She interviewed Tsikata and subsequently wrote an article for the *Guardian*'s 'Third World Review'.

The press painted a somewhat sympathetic picture of Ghana in the months after Flight Lieutenant Jerry Rawlings seized power, without touching on any of the more controversial aspects of his rule.

In November that year Brittain visited Ghana and over the next couple of years got to know many of the young officials working with Rawlings. His regime was not popular with the US State Department, and during this time there were a number of attempted coups against him. By then Tsikata had risen to head of security under Rawlings, and his briefings to Brittain enabled her to write several exclusive reports on American involvement in the coups.

Brittain's friendship with Tsikata did not fully develop until after she had stopped writing regularly about Ghana. She told the *Guardian* ombudsman, who investigated the affair for the paper, that their friendship began to grow in 1988 because they had mutual friends in Angola. Tsikata was the first foreigner to fight with the MPLA in Angola, and Brittain frequently reported from there. Eventually she wrote a book on the country's devastating civil war.

Tsikata's libel action against the *Independent* went back to Brittain's first meeting with him in 1982. Six months after the coup that brought Rawlings to power, three High Court judges and a former Ghanaian Army officer were abducted and murdered. A subsequent Ghanaian official inquiry named ten people, including Tsikata, as responsible.

Tsikata, it said, was the likely mastermind behind the murder of the judges. However, there was also substantial evidence that he had not been involved. The only evidence against him came from Amartey Kwei, another of the other ten accused of responsibility for the murders. Kwei cited Lance Corporal Amedeka, also among the ten, saying that Amedeka had brought him a coded note from Tsikata authorising the killings. However, at his trial Amedeka denied the existence of the note. Tsikata also had two alibis which contradicted Kwei's allegations. In the end, Ghana's Attorney General found inconsistencies in the evidence and Tsikata was never prosecuted. According to reports, Kwei recanted his confession twice before he was executed.

According to Stephen Glover, a former editor of the *Independent on Sunday* who wrote articles strongly critical of Victoria Brittain in the wake of the *Mail on Sunday* revelation about her involvement with Tsikata, the circumstances of Kwei's recanting were extraordinary. In a *Spectator* article he wrote,

Imagine the scene. The place is Ghana. It is August 1983. Amartey Kwei, convicted of the murder of three judges, is about to be executed by a firing squad. As he awaits his death, the Ghanaian head of state, Flight Lieutenant Jerry Rawlings, arrives at the execution ground with a tape recorder.

In these appalling circumstances Kwei retracts his previous evidence that a certain Kojo Tsikata was the mastermind behind the murders. If he hopes that his confession will help him, he is about to be disappointed. Amartey Kwei is shot.[14]

None of this would have resurfaced had it not been for freelance journalist Karl Maier writing an article in 1992 for the *Independent* about the upcoming general election in Ghana. His main purpose was to examine the likelihood of Jerry Rawlings retaining power. As evidence of Rawlings's alleged unreliability on human rights, Maier cited the continuing presence in his government of Captain Kojo Tsikata.

He mentioned the recommended prosecution of ten people, including Tsikata, for the judges' deaths ten years previously, and said that he had been named as a mastermind of the plot. However, he did not say that Ghana's Attorney General had ruled that there was insufficient evidence to mount a prosecution against Tsikata.

Tsikata decided to sue the *Independent* for libel, and on the recommendation of Victoria Brittain, he asked Geoffrey Bindman to act for him. Brittain had known Bindman for 15 years and thought he would be the right lawyer for Tsikata. She told the *Guardian* ombudsman, John Willis, who produced a detailed report on Brittain's involvement, that she did not discuss the case with Bindman. 'I have not been involved in the conduct of this case at all, nor have I been involved in any meeting, briefing or discussion concerning Kojo Tsikata's litigation against the *Independent*.'[15]

It was an important point. To be seen to be aiding a libel action against another journalist – albeit on another newspaper – would be poor form and contrary to the code of conduct of the National Union of Journalists.

Bindman told Willis that he initially saw Tsikata and his cousin Tsatsu Tsikata, his Ghanaian lawyer. A cheque for £5,000 covered initial costs. What followed in terms of payments was what excited the MI5 officers. On 17 September 1993 the first sum of £100,000 was received into Victoria Brittain's account. It was followed by another payment of £60,000 on 6 June 1994. Both payments came from Credit Lyonnais UK, the first made by the Libyan interest section at the Saudi embassy, the second by order of Khalifa Bazelya. Three further payments, each of £34,980, were made in December 1994, January 1995 and February 1995 from UBAF Bank in London. A one-off payment was also made in November 1994 from Midland Bank International in the name of Ambassador Kojo Amoo-Gottfried, then Ghanaian ambassador to Peking. A final payment of £62,502.34 was made to Ms Brittain's Abbey National account in October 1996 from an unknown source via Citibank in New York.

The combined total of all the payments was £327,442.

Victoria Brittain told the Willis inquiry that she had no idea where any of the money had come from. She had agreed to help Tsikata by allowing him to use her bank account to channel money from his friends to Bindman to pay for the libel hearing. Brittain told Willis she had subsequently allowed her bank account to be used in a similar way to pay Tsikata's son's school fees. 'I had no reason to ask Kojo Tsikata who his friends were who wished to help him,' she said.[16]

Tsikata corroborated this in his letter to Willis's inquiry: 'She did not know who was helping me. It was not an issue and I do not believe that over the years she has known me I have given her cause to doubt my good faith and therefore be suspicious about the sources of funds being paid into her account for the case.'[17]

Bindman told Willis that he had subsequently made inquiries at the Bank of England and the Foreign Office to ascertain whether or not the payments from Libyan sources contravened the United Nations embargo on that country. He was told that 'no funds subject to any embargo were involved and this is consistent with what the Bank of England led me to believe was probable'.

In examining the allegations raised by Glover, John Willis stated that Brittain's reports of affairs in Ghana 'probably reflect fairly common journalistic values of the time, which you would expect to find in the *Guardian*'.[18] She had written twelve articles specifically on Ghana and reported from the country twice – in December 1988 and July 1992.[19]

He accepted that, as head of security in Ghana, Tsikata was a legitimate subject of interest for MI5, but that even if the initial interest was justified, 'it was completely indefensible to continue the monitoring for over a year at a reported cost to the taxpayer of £750,000. A competent MI5 should have discovered that the money was being transferred to Bindman and Partners to fund a libel action.'[20] He added that it was equally indefensible that MI5 was willing to involve Ms Brittain's teenage daughter in the affair.

As for Victoria Brittain's involvement in the case, and Glover's charge that she was more than a 'mere postbox', actively managing the funds coming into her account, Willis accepted that this was true.

When money arrived she faxed Mr Tsikata's office in Ghana to notify him and he would ring back. He was busy as the main negotiator for ECOWAS countries, trying to find a solution to the crisis in Liberia at the time. She says she was not informed in advance, but knew that a payment had been made when she made her weekly trip to take out cash from the cashpoint.

Unlike several of the clearing banks, every withdrawal from an Abbey Link cashpoint is accompanied by a slip giving customers their current balance. So Ms Brittain would know if a large payment had been made, but not the source of the payment.[21]

Willis confirmed that on the account statements he was shown there was no indication of the source of the incoming funds. The statement merely said 'account adjustment'.

That leaves the question of whether or not Ms Brittain should have known the source of the huge sums of money pouring through her account. She was dealing, after all, with the head of security for a foreign state, no matter what her personal connections, and the case was controversial in Ghana. J. H. Mensa, head of the Ghanaian New Patriotic Party, later launched an astonishing attack on Brittain. Mensa, a well-known economist, revealed that he had known the *Guardian*'s deputy foreign editor for 15 years and had always been astonished by what he called her 'dogmatic, left-wing politics'.[22] He said he was not surprised that she had allowed her account to be used by Tsikata and found it odd that she had no idea that the money being channelled through her account had come from Libya. He called on the *Guardian*'s editor, Alan Rusbridger, to take disciplinary action against her. 'Shocking Revelations About Tsikata Cash Deals With Libya' was how the *Ghanaian Chronicle* headlined their piece on the affair.

Willis argued that although technically Brittain had done nothing wrong, it was curious that she showed no obvious concern about the transactions: 'Given her position as a journalist with its accompanying potential conflicts of interest, in my opinion she might have expected a sophisticated international figure like Mr Tsikata to have protected her from any potential embarrassment or at least to have kept her informed.'[23]

The one question that Ms Brittain does not seem to have answered adequately is why the money went through her account at all. Why was it not paid directly into a client account at Bindmans? Could it not have been paid via Tsikata's lawyer cousin to Bindmans? Willis's conclusion is clear:

> To allow your bank account to be used in this way without thinking that you could be compromised and not to encourage your friend, a significant Ghanaian political figure, to run the finances of his libel action by the obvious, more direct route, is surprisingly naïve.
>
> The fact – however unpleasantly revealed – that the money came from Libya and that Ms Brittain was, in my view, let down by her friendship, reveals poor judgement. Given the potential sensitivity of Mr Tsikata's money, why did she not think it was appropriate to tell her Editor?[24]

Willis said that the saga would make it difficult for Ms Brittain to write about Ghana again without being accused of bias by one side or another.

Yet Brittain had cause for serious complaint. Her personal privacy had been grossly invaded and it was clear that she had never been a threat to national security. After the publication of the *Mail on Sunday* article, she lodged a formal complaint with the Security Service Tribunal, which is presided over by a senior judge. Her editor, Alan Rusbridger, demanded an official explanation from Stephen Lander. He said she should have access to her personal file, given the amount of misleading information in it and that its contents appeared to have been leaked selectively to other newspapers. Neither Victoria Brittain nor Alan Rusbridger ever received a satisfactory outcome to their requests.

A major reason for MI5's investigation into Brittain was the involvement of Khalifa Bazelya, Libya's most senior diplomat in Britain and an active intelligence officer. Bazelya was a major target for the Security Service, An internal MI5 report, written by Shayler, set out its suspicions that Bazelya might have been involved in the murder of a Libyan dissident in London. The report called for the diplomat to be expelled from the UK: 'We recommend that Bazelya, head of Libya Interests Section in London, be declared "Persona Non Grata" for engaging in activity incompatible with his diplomatic status which we believe poses a direct threat to the national security of the United Kingdom.'

This document revealed that Bazelya had been allowed to enter Britain despite MI5 knowing that he had been a highly controversial Libyan intelligence agent. This was because MI5 and MI6 thought that he could be recruited as a British spy. MI5 was prepared to over-look an informant's report that he had a revolver in the glove compartment of Bazelya's car, and his reported links with Sinn Fein in the Republic of Ireland. While stationed in Ethiopia in the 1980s, Bazelya was also suspected of importing weapons, using the Libyan diplomatic bag. He was expelled from that country in 1991.

Attempts to recruit Bazelya came to nothing, according to the MI5 document: 'Although his cultivation [by British intelligence] has continued, he has not provided intelligence of value and has continued to work against UK interests.' In fact, Bazelya was running at least four Libyan agents in Britain and threatened several people who refused to work for him. He was also trying to set up a network of informants who would supply him with important scientific and technical material. Not surprisingly, Bazelya was eventually expelled from the UK in December 1995 for his intimidation of dissidents.

The move angered the Tripoli regime and shortly afterwards several Libyan intelligence officers, posing as students, were sent to Britain. MI5 strongly suspected they were on a terrorist mission.

Immediately on arrival, one of them enrolled as a language student. He soon became the subject of a classic MI5 sting. An undercover officer struck up a friendship with him and moved into the same house. He won the Libyan's trust and before long took him to visit a brothel, where he was secretly filmed enjoying various sexual services and smoking marijuana. It was an old-fashioned honey-trap. The student was later confronted by a Special Branch officer and told that he had transgressed his host country's hos-pitality. The officer said he had a police contact who could help smooth out things – in exchange for a little information about Libyans in Britain involved in political activity. The student went straight to his Libyan handlers, who got him out of the country quickly. The honey-trap had failed.

Despite this setback, MI5 continued to receive information about Libyan activity in Britain. Shayler said he really began to lose his faith in MI5 over an attempt to intercept communications between Libyan agents and Tripoli. 'In an attempt to mislead us they started sending documents back to Libya via overt commercial channels, thinking this method would never be spotted,' he said. The problem for MI5 was what to do now. In normal circumstances I could simply write out a warrant and use the usual methods of intercepting the mail.'[25]

Shayler said that it was the subsequent extraordinary bureaucratic wrangle over intercepting these commercial communications that caused him to lose faith in the organisation. 'When I approached an MI5 lawyer, the first response was to say they were unsure if there was any legal way of intercepting the documents. Not surprisingly, I told them we were not dealing with a Sunday school, but hardened Libyan terrorists. This had little effect. Then I was told that each individual dispatch needed a separate warrant, each one of which took almost a day to write . . . It became farcical. I had to refer every warrant up the hierarchy. They would be handed backwards and forwards between lawyers, group leaders, assistant directors, right up to the highest level within the organisation. When I complained about this paper-shuffling exercise, they had the audacity to accuse me of failing to respect civil liberties.'[26]

However, Shayler had had enough. He decided there was no future for him in MI5 and that he would make a break in the most dramatic way.

8

THE WHISTLEBLOWER

'I would like you to tell me [what the *Mail on Sunday* was planning to publish about MI5], otherwise the heavies will move in.'

Alastair Campbell, press secretary to Tony Blair,
speaking to Jonathan Holborow, editor of the
Mail on Sunday, 28 August 1997

Even before he had resigned from MI5, Shayler had decided to speak out about his employers. He knew he might be sent to prison, but it was a risk he was prepared to take. Originally he had planned to give journalists an off-the-record briefing in July 1996 while he was still working there. However, although he was less likely to go to prison, Shayler believed that this would provoke a witch hunt rather than lead to reform and better oversight.

In late 1996, Shayler met with Nick Fielding, one of the journalists he had initially intended to brief during that summer. The first meeting took place in the Three Greyhounds pub in Soho. Shayler introduced himself as 'Mike' and Fielding was not to know his full identity for another six months. It was a strange meeting and both sides were unsure what to make of each other. Fielding wondered if this was a semi-official approach from the Security Service, that perhaps they were trying to recruit him to publish particular kinds of stories, while Shayler constantly feared being turned in to his employers.

The two continued to meet over the following months, usually in a pub near the *Mail on Sunday* offices in Kensington, and agreed a secure method of contacting each other. Initial discussions were about publishing an article in the paper, but the idea developed of a book on the Security Service. At this point, in early

1997, Fielding introduced Shayler to Mark Hollingsworth, a fellow journalist with a number of books to his credit. Once the book was published, it would be serialised in the *Mail on Sunday*. Ironically, on his first day in C3, then MI5's vetting section, Shayler's mentor in MI5 had given him a copy of Hollingsworth's book *Blacklist* about vetting.[1]

A meeting with a literary agent followed. Shayler was working out his last six months in MI5 and was officially on contract. Strict security arrangements were followed. The literary agent spent several weeks trying to spark some interest in the book, provisionally entitled *MI Farce: Five Years at the Heart of British Intelligence*. Publishers showed some initial enthusiasm, but rejected the idea on the grounds that MI5 would take out an injunction preventing publication.

In May 1997, Shayler asked the authors of this book for legal advice on the possibility of publishing *MI Farce*. Mark Hollingsworth approached Geoffrey Bindman, a solicitor and senior partner at the north London legal firm of Bindman & Partners who was well known for his stance on civil rights matters. He asked him to comment on how the Official Secrets Act affected the prospect of a former intelligence officer speaking about his work. Hollingsworth prepared a detailed brief for Bindman, including the meagre details he knew at that time about the *Guardian* journalist. Shayler had told them that the surveillance operation against the journalist was code-named Operation Shadower, but otherwise there was little to go on. Bindman's reply was cautious:

> You have asked me to advise on the risks which would be entailed by publication of the book 'MI Farce', based on the proposal which you have handed me. I understand that the author [Shayler] was employed in MI5 from 1991 until 1997.
>
> The first crucial point to make is that Section 1 of the Official Secrets Act 1989 makes it a criminal offence for such a person to disclose without lawful authority any information relating to security or intelligence which is or has been in his possession by virtue of his position as a member of MI5. He would have no defence to a prosecution unless he could prove that at the time of the alleged offence he did not know and had no reasonable cause to believe that the information in question related to security or intelligence.[2]

Bindman went on to suggest that a defence could be mounted by analysing the material in the book and seeking to establish that some or all of it did not relate to security or intelligence. However, he thought there would be difficulties with this approach. 'My unequivocal view, therefore, is that the book cannot be published in the form proposed without the commission of criminal offences by the author.'

But what about the writers? It appeared that they would be affected by Section 5 of the Official Secrets Act 1989 because they would be in possession of information protected against disclosure that had come into their possession through a person to whom it had been entrusted as a Crown servant. Bindman's advice here was more optimistic: he said that a co-author or publisher would be guilty of an offence under Section 5 only if the prosecution could show that the disclosure of the information was damaging to national security and that the person disclosing it knew or had reasonable cause to believe it would be so. He felt that the Government would be unlikely to prosecute in a case in which the disclosure was not thought to be damaging to national security. It could not be relied upon, said Bindman, but 'it may be that the author would be prepared to take the risk of a prosecution if the publishers at least could mount a satisfactory defence on the basis that the disclosures were not damaging'.

Bindman went on to consider the matters set out in the proposed chapters of the book and to offer a personal opinion. 'That opinion will necessarily be based simply on the summary in the prospectus and could be affected when the full text comes to be written,' he added.

His general assessment was that the themes listed for inclusion in any potential book did not seem to endanger national security. 'On the contrary, it seems to me that informed criticism of the short-comings of MI5 should be beneficial in encouraging improvement which would enhance the protection of national security. Thus I would not consider that details of past investigations of subversive groups or the investigation into a *Guardian* journalist as a "suspected supporter" of Libyan terrorism would be damaging to national security.' On the 'Shadower' story, he said there might be problems if details were revealed of the techniques used by MI5 in carrying out surveillance: 'Care would need to be taken to make clear that this was historical and did not relate to current practices.' He reiterated that the precedent of the *Spycatcher* case indicated that there was now a government policy of refraining from prosecution in cases where any possible damage had already been done or where no damage seemed likely.

In the end Bindman's advice came to nothing because we decided to proceed with a series of articles in the *Mail on Sunday* rather than a book. However, Bindman's words must have come to haunt him. It was not until two days before publication of the articles in August 1997 that Bindman realised that he was himself intimately involved in the whole Shadower saga, although he could have had no clue that Shayler's revelations would engulf him. He could scarcely have envisaged that the *Guardian* journalist in question was Victoria Brittain, a long-standing friend and someone with whom he had been involved in a series of unusual financial transactions involving a Ghanaian security chief and Libyan money, which had become the centre of a sustained MI5 operation.

Based on Bindman's advice, a decision was taken to approach the newspaper, which would run a substantial story and hopefully stimulate demand for a book. Even at this stage it was decided that anything published would cover only the areas of Shayler's work in which there was a strong public-interest issue. Also, any article would be dropped if there was a risk to national security. No one wanted to court danger and there was no logic in producing stories that would compromise Security Service operations.

In early August 1997, *Mail on Sunday* editor Jonathan Holborow was given a detailed memo setting out the bones of what Shayler wanted to say. He acted on it immediately and a special room and production facility was set up at the *Mail on Sunday* to allow work to proceed in total secrecy. At the same time, Shayler continued to meet with his old MI5 colleagues for drinks and the many leaving parties that were taking place. Shayler told anyone who wanted to know that he was writing a spy novel and actively looking for a publisher – which was partly true: at the time he was working on a rough draft for an off-the-wall thriller called *The Organisation*.

It was just as well. From the last week in June to the middle of July a series of strange incidents occurred. The first was at a farewell party for a capable officer at the Old Father Thames, a pub across the river from the Thames House headquarters of MI5.

Like Shayler, 'Tom Kane' had entered the Service as a former journalist and had tried to maintain his motivation and enthusiasm, despite seeing incompetent time-servers rise through the ranks. Disillusioned, he had decided to leave.

Word had got round about Shayler's novel and G9/0, Shayler's last boss, quizzed him about it at some length. He was one of the old school, with a face the colour and complexion of a cork freshly pulled from a bottle of claret. 'I remember thinking at the time that it was ironic that he took far more interest in me that evening than he ever had when I was working under him,' said Shayler. 'I then wondered whether top management in MI5 had tasked him to check out whether the novel proposal was genuine. I obviously took him in as it was reported that I was writing a novel in the injunction which was served upon me after the articles in the *Mail on Sunday* finally appeared.'[3]

About ten days later, Shayler tried to send a copy of his nascent novel through the post to a long-time trusted friend. Two days later the friend phoned to say that he had still not received it and the following day Shayler returned to the flat he shared with Annie Machon in Pimlico to find a message on his answering-machine from B2/0, the head of personnel. Shayler did not return the call immediately, and the following day set off for a wedding in Guernsey. At the airport he and Machon were stopped for no obvious reason by Special Branch. The copy of the novel, on a floppy disk, was never seen again.

The following week, on his return from Guernsey, Shayler returned the call to B2/0. The officer was a Geordie, who spent much of his time trying to play down his north-eastern background to get on in MI5. He asked if Shayler was aware that he had to submit his book to the Service before publication. 'You mean my novel,' Shayler corrected him. He said he was happy to submit it when it was ready.

None of these events made sense to Shayler. MI5 would not normally alert a target to its interest in such an obvious way. It was clear that they were interested, but the cover story and the intercepted novel had reassured them.

By Saturday 16 August 1997 everything was in place. Shayler returned from a meeting with Hollingsworth at which he had been informed that the articles would go ahead, to tell Annie Machon, his partner of four-and-a-half years, that he was about to go public. When he had first started talking to Fielding he had not told Annie what he was doing. When eventually he broke the news she had said she wanted little to do with it and certainly not to know the details.

That night the couple went out to a local restaurant in Pimlico called Grumbles. It was a tense evening. 'At one point I dropped the whole project because Annie was too stressed by it, but I was determined. During the previous few months it had nearly cost me my relationship with Annie, until she realised that I was driven to follow my decision through to its conclusion. Over the meal we avoided talking about "the novel" – as we had begun to refer to the whole project – and talked instead about the many nights we've enjoyed at this place with our friends.'[4]

The following day Shayler met Fielding and Hollingsworth at Café Rouge in Kensington. Everyone was tense. When Shayler could not find the building he wondered if he was being set up. By this time he was working as a consultant to the Ministry of Defence on, of all things, stationery contracts. He had taken the morning off and was amazed to hear that the paper intended to publish his story that weekend. He knew that he must be out of the country when the story broke. His fear was that if he was arrested, no matter what the strength of his defence, he was likely to spend many months on remand as a Category A prisoner. That night he told Machon. 'I remember she was sitting bolt upright in her chair all night, looking into space and distracted to the point of making me paranoid. She was chain smoking and the tension would come out in occasional niggling arguments about the arrangements we were making to leave the country: were Special Branch officers at the airport likely to note any flight bookings? Shouldn't we go by ferry to avoid this? We had quick conferences on the flat balcony, just in case MI5 had placed a listening device in the flat while they knew we were away in Guernsey.'[5]

They sat and watched *The Oasis Story* on TV. Liam Gallagher told of how he had spent 22 years as a nobody, then suddenly he was famous. Shayler's thoughts wandered to the media reaction at what he was about to do. He knew that his life would never be the same again. He hoped that the press would not offer him up as a sacrificial lamb or wade through the dustbin of his life. He imagined long-forgotten girlfriends appearing in the *News of the World* describing in lurid tabloidese about his performance in bed and how he was a rat for dumping them.

The following day, Wednesday 20 August, Shayler returned to the *Mail on Sunday* offices. For the first time he revealed the identity of the *Guardian* journalist who had been put under surveillance after it was suspected she was laundering money for the Libyans. He also disclosed that 'the left-wing lawyer' involved was Geoffrey Bindman. Both Fielding and Hollingsworth were astonished. Hollingsworth recalled how when he had asked Geoffrey Bindman for advice on whether or not Shayler's story could be published Bindman, had not known that the *Guardian* journalist was Victoria Brittain. If he had he would have realised his own part in the story and things might have been different. 'I wonder who the left-wing lawyer could be,' asked Hollingsworth. In one of those immortal moments of dramatic irony he replied: 'Wouldn't it be funny if it turned out to be me?'

That day, Shayler also met Jonathan Holborow. He told him a few Service jokes, how MI5's motto, '*Regnum Defendere*' (Defence of the Realm) has irreverently been transmuted into '*Rectum Defendere*' (defending your backside!). And how the pubs in Shepherd's Market in Mayfair were alcoholic refuges from the tedium of the office.

Later Shayler was photographed in front of the old MI5 offices in Bolton Street, Grosvenor Street and the building in Tottenham Court Road where he had been recruited. He had a panic attack. What if the cabby was curious about someone being photographed at these locations? Perhaps he knew they were ex-MI5 buildings? The final shots were taken on the south bank of the Thames, close to MI5's new headquarters at Millbank, and were the only ones of Shayler that appeared in the press.

Returning home in the evening, Shayler found Machon desperately anxious. He reassured her that he would not be sent to prison, but they decided to leave for Holland before the weekend. The country had a liberal constitution and English was widely spoken.

Work on the series of articles was proceeding apace in the offices of the *Mail on Sunday*. The following evening Shayler returned to check the copy. The pressure he was undergoing was now almost intolerable. That evening he and Machon shared a bottle of wine as they tried to come to terms with what he was about to do. Friends were told that they were going on holiday for a few days, and Shayler's employers granted him a week off work.

Annie had booked Saturday-morning flights to Amsterdam and a hotel near Heathrow for Friday evening. On their last night in the Pimlico flat where they had lived for almost exactly four years, Shayler's brother Jeremy (Jem) arrived to borrow their car. Shayler longed to tell him what he intended to do, but Machon had ruled that out and he left none the wiser, asking when he should return the car. 'Whenever,' replied Shayler.

That night neither of them slept much. The following day there were a few chores still to complete. They moved their money from their bank accounts to those of friends in a vain attempt to prevent MI5 from seizing it. It was frozen anyway, a few weeks later. Machon called back at the flat during the day, pale and drawn, while Shayler made a final visit to the *Mail on Sunday* offices to correct the page proofs of the articles: 'After we cleared the articles with the lawyer and everyone else who needed to be consulted – a process of hours rather than days, as it would have been in MI5 – I looked at the proofs as they appeared on the page and checked them one last time. I looked at the photo of me and reflected how fat I became working in MI5. I must have put on three or four stone while there, largely as a result of the wholly unnecessary stress. I resolved to put the anger behind me and embrace a new, healthy future.'[6]

That evening Shayler took a taxi to the Heathrow Ramada Hotel. The die had been cast and there could be no going back. He reflected uneasily on what he had done. At 8.45 p.m., he met Machon, who was slightly happier. They went to their room and ordered up club sandwiches, chips, Coke and white wine. They set several alarm clocks for 5.30 a.m., but there was little need: Shayler hardly slept at all.

The next morning at Heathrow's Terminal One a 50-foot-long queue snaked its way back from the check-in desk. As they reached it the couple noticed that checking in next to them was television personality Janet Street-Porter. The whole process was painfully slow, and Machon began to panic. What if they missed the flight? Shayler walked off to post a letter to his friend Graham Dunbar, telling him what he was doing. In case of interception he put the name Kevin Keelan on the envelope. Keelan was the Norwich goalkeeper in the 1970s, principally famous for having a name that was nearly the same as that of the much more famous Kevin Keegan. He knew Graham would get the joke.

They boarded Flight BA 426 to Amsterdam, which took off on time at 7.50 a.m. Shayler remembered Donald Woods in *Cry Freedom*, leaving South Africa by road and private plane. Less than an hour later they were clearing Dutch customs before catching a train to Amsterdam. At the central booking office a woman told them there were no hotel rooms in Amsterdam because they were all full of bank holiday Brits. As they wandered along Damrak, the main drag,

Machon suddenly hugged Shayler and told him how proud she was of him for standing up to MI5.

Each hour, as instructed, they called in to the *Mail on Sunday* from phone boxes, never using the same one twice. During the afternoon Shayler bought a hat and a pair of sunglasses as a makeshift disguise before they caught a train to Utrecht, which pulled out past the new 50,000 all-seater Ajax Stadium. In Utrecht they booked into the penthouse suite of the Hotel Smitt, which sounded expensive but was not.

In Utrecht, Shayler woke up on Sunday morning and flicked on Ceefax on the hotel television only to find there was no coverage about the *Mail on Sunday* article. Once again, as he and Machon sat by the canal for breakfast, paranoia set in: no one was interested, the story had flopped, he thought. Later he walked to the main railway station, wearing his newly acquired hat and sunglasses to buy an English newspaper. He scanned the front of the broadsheets, only to be disappointed, then realised that they were the first editions and would have been printed before the story broke.

Then he caught a glimpse of the *Mail on Sunday* and saw his face on the front. He folded over a copy before the man behind the counter recognised him, and paid for it. As he walked through the station he read the headline on the front page – 'MI5 Bugged Mandelson – Intelligence Officer Reveals Three-year Phone Tap'. Inside was a four-page special supplement entitled 'The Truth That Must Not Be Hidden About MI5', and the revelations about Jack Straw, Mandelson, Victoria Brittain, the secret files and a catalogue of MI5 blunders. All the anger and frustration he had felt while he was in MI5 evaporated. He smiled with satisfaction.

In the meantime Machon phoned her mother, Michele, and stepfather Steven to hear their reaction to the story. Michele told her that she was sure Shayler would spend the next ten years in prison. Her stepfather was impressed by the clarity and readability of the article. Apparently he had picked up the paper as usual without glancing at the front cover and left it on the kitchen table. It was only when Michele was walking through the kitchen that she spotted Shayler's face on the front page.

The couple spent the next few hours in their hotel room. Shayler called his brothers and parents but no one was in. His parents were actually in Rotterdam for the weekend. He left a message on Jem's answering machine: 'Tell Big Ron and Mavis not to worry. I know what I'm doing. I'm not going to prison.' He called other friends, but everyone was out. He spoke briefly to Steve Boggan of the *Independent*, who had been put in touch with them by Nick Fielding.

The following day, Monday 25 August, the whole of the British press was trying to follow the story, but they were hampered by the fact that MI5 refused to put out any statement.

That evening the couple saw John Wadham, director of Liberty, being interviewed on the BBC *Nine o'clock News*. He offered to represent them and they made a mental note to contact him.

The following morning the *Independent* led with the interview Boggan had done with Shayler. On a flight home from Rotterdam, this article was the first Shayler's mother saw about the exploits of her son. Later, Shayler told Nick Fielding he would meet pressmen in Amsterdam that evening. *Newsnight* had told Fielding they wanted to interview Shayler. Machon was reluctant to go – she had not even met Fielding, let alone any other journalist – but in the end she agreed to lend moral support to Shayler for his first television interview.

Before they set off for Amsterdam, Shayler spoke to Matt Guarente, his oldest friend, and Jem. Guarente told him he had only found out that Tuesday morning about what Shayler had done when his flatmate picked up the *Independent*. Jem was at the Reading rock festival for the weekend and also discovered what had happened when he got to work on Tuesday. Both were supportive, but wondered if they would ever see Shayler again.

Machon and Shayler got on the 17.16 train to Amsterdam and took a cab from the station to the Amstel, a fve-star hotel near the Leidesplein and the Rijksmuseum. As they stood in the lobby waiting for Fielding, they spotted Michael Crick of *Newsnight* and a *Newsnight* producer. They were whisked up to a room that had been prepared as a makeshift studio. Two minutes later Fielding arrived, worried at first by the presence of Machon, who was in the process of considering whether or not she would talk to the paper. No one from *Newsnight* realised that she, too, was a former MI5 officer who had left the organisation for reasons similar to Shayler's. He had merely introduced her as his girlfriend.

The interview went well and was previewed in the *Nine o'clock News*, which led on the story that Edward Heath had been the subject of MI5 interest. Shayler was not relaxed for the interview, in which Michael Crick gave him a good grilling, but in the circumstances this wasn't surprising.

Next morning, Wednesday 27 August, Margaret Thatcher's former press secretary Bernard Ingham was interviewed and ranted against Shayler with the usual 'secrets should remain secrets' argument.

Later that day, Mark Hollingsworth arrived in Amsterdam, with *Mail on Sunday* photographer Phil Ide. The priority was for Shayler and Machon to get away from the Amstel in case they were recognised from the television coverage. (In fact, two days later the *Daily Mail* published the location of the interview.) Two taxis arrived at 11 a.m. to take the group of five back to Utrecht. Machon was so worried about security that she insisted on being dropped off several blocks from their hotel. Unfortunately, once she and Shayler were out of the car they realised they didn't know their way and spent 45 minutes trying to find the hotel.

Shayler spent that afternoon with photographer Phil Ide. Machon had agreed that for the next issue of the *Mail on Sunday,* although she would not give details of her work with MI5, she would write a piece explaining why she supported Shayler. She was reluctant to be photographed, but agreed in the end to a profile picture in which she wore unfamiliar clothing. A phone call to London elicited the information that Special Branch had been called in to investigate a possible breach of the Official Secrets Act. Shayler also heard that selected journalists had been called to a briefing by MI5, presumably to be given 'background' on him designed to smear his character and downplay his allegations.

By this time, with meetings in hotels, unscheduled cab rides, photo sessions and disguises, the saga had taken on the air of a 1960's spy movie. 'If only it was really as exciting as this,' Shayler commented at one point. That evening, as he sat reading at the Hotel Smitt, he heard on the television in the background that David Shayler, an ex-MI5 officer, had claimed that MI5 had failed to finish off the IRA on the British mainland. 'It is a strange feeling, I can tell you,' Shayler wrote at the time. 'As if this other person is some impostor or *doppelgänger*.'[7]

During Thursday morning Nick Fielding returned to London, and assistant editor Peter Dobbie flew to Holland. By this time the first background article on Shayler had appeared in the *Daily Telegraph,* notable for its closeness to the intelligence service. It quoted Shayler's former headmaster, who said that he was 'a born rebel who likes to sail close to the wind'.

Once again it was decided to move on. Every paper in Fleet Street would now be looking for Shayler to snatch a picture or get a few words from him. They drove to Leiden, a small town about 50 miles west of Utrecht. When Dobbie arrived late in the evening, the party transferred to yet another hotel, the four-star Tulip, where they arrived early on Friday morning.

In London, as the media grasped the full significance of what Shayler had said in the *Mail on Sunday*, Tony Blair's government began to organise. They had seen the strapline on the articles promising 'Next Week: More Extraordinary Revelations about MI5', and were determined to prevent this happening.

Scotland Yard Special Branch officers had already started the investigation into possible breaches of the Official Secrets Act. That same day, 27 August, then Home Secretary Jack Straw received a visit from MI5's director-general, Stephen Lander, who presented him with a paper on Shayler's allegations. The meeting was 'amicable', press reports said.

On Thursday 28 August, *Mail on Sunday* editor Jonathan Holborow received a telephone call from Tony Blair's chief press officer Alastair Campbell, who told him that due to considerable government concern he wanted to know what the paper was going to publish the following weekend under broad headings. He added, 'I would like you to tell me, Jonathan. Otherwise the heavies will move in.'[8]

Holborow explained that in the first set of articles he had been careful not to compromise national security. He also explained that although the articles had covered the IRA and Libya, there had been no intention to impede or jeopardise the peace talks taking place. Campbell accepted the point, but insisted on knowing next weekend's headings and how many words were to be published. Holborow, bristling at the implications of what Campbell was saying, told him that the policy adopted the week before would still apply. Campbell replied that MI5 was claiming that damage had already been done, but he refused to give any details. 'That's what they said,' he reiterated.

Campbell asked Holborow to ring him back to let him know whether or not he would allow the government to vet any new material in advance. Late in the afternoon Holborow told him there would be no change in position. The *Mail on Sunday* would do nothing to jeopardise MI5 operations, but it would go ahead with a second series of articles, most of which had already been prepared and were ready for publication.

By Thursday night, preparations were made for production of the follow-up articles. On Friday, Holborow contacted advertising agency Bartle Bogle Hegarty (BBH) to finalise a press campaign to publicise the articles. They had drawn up a script for a radio advert in the form of a 60-second taped message from Shayler to Tony Blair, to be broadcast on Saturday. BBH asked for, and received, a legal indemnity to cover them against any claim or costs arising from broadcasting the advert. The script, which was never transmitted because of subsequent developments, read:

> This is a message for Tony Blair from myself, David Shayler, a former MI5 officer. My recent disclosures concerning MI5 mean it's necessary for me to speak from a hidden location. I know I risk prosecution under the Official Secrets Act, but I feel it's important for you to be made fully aware of MI5's inappropriate activities. Tapping the phones of your Cabinet ministers is just the tip of the iceberg, Mr Blair. I will answer my critics in this weekend's *Mail on Sunday* and reveal fresh details of how Britain's largest counter-intelligence agency has repeatedly jeopardised major operations and wasted taxpayers' money spying on the innocent. I was shocked by what I discovered working for MI5. You will be too. Who guards the guards, Mr Blair? I urge you to read and then act on my full account of an outdated, ineffective and wasteful MI5. This will only be published in the *Mail on Sunday* tomorrow.

At 9.50 a.m. on Friday morning Campbell rang Holborow again. 'Jonathan, look, there was a meeting late last night at which concerns were still expressed about what the *Mail on Sunday* was going to publish,' he said.

Holborow replied, 'Alastair, I am still in consultation with my lawyers and I cannot give an answer straight away.'

'I would be grateful if you could let me know straight away because action is being considered against you,' Campbell replied.

Later in the morning, Holborow spoke to him once again. By this time Campbell was in the Prime Minister's constituency of Sedgefield. 'I think you know my decision now,' Holborow began. 'I have decided for journalistic reasons to protect my reporters. My duty is to my story and I cannot reveal what will be in the *Mail on Sunday* this coming weekend. I should tell you that our lawyers are Kingsley Napley.'

Campbell said, 'Jonathan, as one journalist to another, can you tell me what you are going to use?'

'Alastair, it would not be fair to you to do that,' came back the response.

There was a click as the phone was hung up in Sedgefield.

At just past 3 p.m. that afternoon a fax arrived from Roland Phillips, at the Treasury Solicitor's office. 'I act for the Crown,' said Phillips, in his carefully worded letter. He went on to explain that Shayler was in breach of undertakings he had given before joining the Security Service that he would not, either during his service or after, publish any information about MI5 without prior approval in writing. He added that the Crown had no desire to prevent 'legitimate debate' about the Security Service, but that ministers had an 'overriding responsibility to protect the safety of sources and lives of its agents and to protect information which would do genuine damage to national security'. He said, 'The government has also been advised by the Security Service that some of the information contained in your edition of 24 August 1997 has caused serious harm to the national security of the United Kingdom and to the operations of the Security Service by disclosing among other matters the workings of the Security Service in relation to particular countries. o judge whether he was compromising ongoing operations. He commended Holborow for going along with Shayler's strictures that nothing should appear that contained unnecessary details of operations, but said that this clearly illustrated the need for his articles 'to be properly scrutinised by the responsible authorities'. Presumably he meant MI5.

Phillips asked, once again, for a formal undertaking that the *Mail on Sunday* would not publish further material from Shayler without first giving the government the opportunity to assess whether it would be damaging to national security. 'Unless I hear from you by 17.30 today giving an undertaking in those terms, then I am instructed to apply for an injunction against Associated Newspapers Ltd.'[9] Campbell had been right. Unless the newspaper gave in, they would send in the heavies.

The deadline passed and solicitors for the *Mail on Sunday* were told to expect a hearing before Mr Justice Keene at the High Court in the Strand at 6 p.m. At the last minute it was cancelled at the request of the Treasury Solicitor.

Holborow's response to Phillips's letter, sent back the same evening at 9.45 p.m., was firm.

> I must say that in view of its contents, I regret your suggestion that any further details I publish from David Shayler should be 'properly scrutinised by the responsible authorities', and I regard it as political censorship.
>
> In my view the pressure applied by the Prime Minister through his Chief Press Secretary, when I was told that if I did not disclose the contents of this weekend's *Mail on Sunday*, 'the heavies would be brought in', constitutes a clear attempt to muzzle free reporting before publication on an issue of public interest.
>
> I am particularly concerned the actions being sought against the *Mail on Sunday* come from a government committed to freedom of information.
>
> You may rest assured that the *Mail on Sunday* will publish nothing that affects national security.[10]

Holborow was not going to give in without a fight. The bullying had made him more determined than ever to press ahead with publication. Nothing further was heard that night. The second series of articles, updated with a piece by Annie Machon stating why she supported Shayler's stance, was ready for printing.

During that Friday Special Branch had also been busy. They had applied at Middlesex Guildhall Crown Court before His Honour Judge Fabyan Evans for five production orders under section 93H of the 1988 Criminal Justice Act. The purpose of the orders was to find out whether or not Shayler had benefited financially from his disclosures. Shayler had committed an offence simply by communicating information as a result of his employment by MI5. If it could be shown that he had benefited financially, then any proceeds could be regarded as having derived from the crime and were liable to seizure. The payments themselves were not criminal, but were evidence that he had passed on information. The production orders required their targets to furnish the police with details of any payments or other benefits made to Shayler. They were directed against the *Mail on Sunday*, the BBC and three banks. All five were granted and immediately complied with. Only the *Mail on Sunday* gave notice that it intended to apply to set aside the order.

At 11.34 a.m. on Saturday morning Phillips sent his reply to Holborow's defiant letter of the night before, noting that he had been in touch with David Smythe of Kingsley Napley informing him of a hearing in front of the duty judge later in the day. Phillips once again reiterated that it was not the government's intention to prevent criticism of the Security Service. He asked who was the best judge of what was and was not a threat to national security and went on, 'In effect you are saying that you are. But you are simply not in a position to make such a judgement.' He added that Alastair Campbell entirely refuted Holborow's claim that he had said 'the heavies would be brought in'. What was said was: 'We have no desire to get heavy but we have a duty to protect our agents and national security,' said Mr Phillips. 'That gives his phrase a quite different meaning.'[11]

The hearing for a temporary injunction was held in the drawing-room of Mr Justice Keene's house. Present were Harvey Kass, the *Mail on Sunday*'s legal director, David Smythe for Kingsley Napley and barrister Geoffrey Robertson, QC, and Roland Phillips for the Treasury Solicitor. Ray Clancy, then assistant news editor on the *Mail on Sunday,* took notes.

In his judgment granting a temporary injunction against the *Mail on Sunday,* Mr Justice Keene noted the government submission, which alleged damage to national security in four areas:

(a) enabling targets of investigations to become aware of the particular surveillance used against them and therefore avoid them;

(b) enabling targets to identify sources from which information has come into the possession of the Security Service, thereby jeopardising the usefulness of such sources;

(c) jeopardising the confidence in the Service of those who assist it in operational matters;

(d) a similar loss of confidence on the part of potential future informants.

Against the arguments of the Crown over duties of confidence and so on, barrister Geoffrey Robertson for the *Mail on Sunday* argued that the paper was entitled to rely upon Article 10 of the European Convention on Human Rights, guaranteeing freedom of the press.

He said that there was no evidence that national security would be damaged by further revelations and that the plaintiffs had failed to provide any. Robertson argued that the court should be slow to intervene in a matter that would be prior restraint on publication by the press.

Mr Justice Keene took an even-handed approach in his judgment. Much of what had already been published, he argued, 'was very general, very old or both. There was no harm to the public interest by publication of those matters.'[12] However, he thought that some of the general material in the article 'Case That Made Me Quit' might potentially be of use to a hostile power. He concluded that a short-term injunction would cause no great harm to the public interest.

The temporary injunction restrained the *Mail on Sunday* from publishing further information Shayler had gained as a result of his work for MI5 and Shayler himself from disclosing to anyone such information. A full hearing was scheduled for 4 September.

The hearing at Mr Justice Keene's house finished at 4.30 p.m. on Saturday afternoon. Until that point no one at the *Mail on Sunday* offices in Derry Street, west London, knew for sure whether or not the paper would be published that night with its front page and story intact. When the news was phoned through by Harvey Kass, the staff swung into action to produce a special edition. The front page carried the one word 'GAGGED!' and inside was an account of how Alastair Campbell had tried to bully the editor into handing over copy prior to publication.

It also contained the article by Annie Machon outlining her reasons for sticking by Shayler. A Classics graduate from Cambridge, Annie Machon had joined MI5 about nine months before Shayler. 'I've only decided to speak out in the face of the totally unjustified smears which have begun to appear about David,' she said. Unlike him she was not prepared to talk about her own experiences in MI5 except in the most general terms.

Machon, who had received glowing reports for her work in MI5, also said she had witnessed management abuses and that director-general Stephen Lander was excruciatingly shy. 'Unlike his predecessor Stella Rimington, Lander has no presence or charm,' she said. She revealed that many recruits to the Service were leaving after a very short time: 'Fourteen people have left during the last year, when you would normally expect four or five to go through natural wastage. Many of these are young high-flyers like David who became disillusioned because the old guard blocked any initiative and suppressed new ideas. Management has ignored the problem.'[13]

In the newspaper world an injunction is normally seen as a 'winner-both-ways' bet. Either the injunction is not granted and the paper can print what it intended in the first place and crow about having defeated legal moves to stop publication, or the injunction is granted and the paper can tell the story of how it fought for press freedom but lost bravely. As the presses began to roll in the early hours of the evening, editor Jonathan Holborow was ecstatic. 'I've waited 30 years to be able to run a front page like that,' he told anyone who would listen.

Inside the paper, Holborow stated that the injunction represented a grim day for British freedom. He noted that Lander had told the Home Office that the articles had endangered national security. 'This is total rubbish,' said Holborow. 'What MI5 are frightened of is that the *Mail on Sunday* was going to further expose the inefficiencies and bureaucracy of a Secret Service that is virtually unaccountable.' That evening he was interviewed for television news and the story was firmly on the agenda for the following week.

However, shortly after midnight, in the early hours of the morning, in Paris, Diana, Princess of Wales, was killed in a car crash. (The paper changed its front page five times that night, so professionally that it actually won a British Press Award for design.) Her death, and the extraordinary events that followed with the outpouring of grief, completely changed the public agenda. It took weeks to get the Shayler story back on the front pages of the national press. One of the biggest stories of the year had been knocked out by one of the biggest of the century.

Meanwhile, as the legal process ground relentlessly through the courts, the police investigation was gathering pace. Immediately on publication of the first set of articles Detective Superintendent Martin Morrissey of the Met's Special Branch was appointed the senior investigating officer in what the police named 'Operation Oscillate' – their investigation into Shayler's possible breaches of the 1989 Official Secrets Act and other legislation. Special Branch officers now had permission to visit the *Mail on Sunday* offices, the BBC – because of the *Newsnight* interview – and the three banks to question them about possible payments to Shayler and what he had done with any money he had received. But they were not just involved in a paper trail.

On Friday 29 August, as the lawyers were still arguing about whether or not an injunction would be sought, a special team from Special Branch was busy breaking into Shayler and Machon's flat in St George's Drive, Pimlico, in search of incriminating evidence. An officer from the Special Branch at Scotland Yard had obtained a search warrant from Bow Street Magistrates Court. The warrant, under section 9(1) of the 1911 Official Secrets Act, allowed the officers to search for 'any sketch, plan, article, model, note or document or anything of a like nature or anything which is evidence of an offence under the Official Secrets Act'.[14] It specifically stated that the officers were permitted to 'enter the said premises on one occasion only within one month from the day of issue of this Warrant'. In fact, the search team spent three days in the flat, and was thus probably searching illegally for most of this time.

Its members arrived at the first-floor flat at 59 St George's Drive, Pimlico, at 4.30 p.m. that Friday: three plain-clothes officers and three members of the Metropolitan Police Public Services Department.

When no one answered the door, the policemen broke it down, splintering the door stanchion. When they found no one at home two of the six officers left. Then a police photographer arrived. After he had made a thorough record of the contents of the flat, which took about two hours, he left and the remaining officers began their search. An officer from the Met's computer-system branch arrived at 6.30 p.m. and stayed for around 45 minutes, presumably to copy the hard disks of the computers in the flat.

After a couple of hours the search was called off for the night due to poor lighting and the sheer amount of material that had to be examined. One officer stayed on guard all night before the search recommenced the following morning at 7.30 a.m. Once again, the officers were in the flat until late in the evening. They returned early on Sunday morning and by lunchtime they had finished. Once again, according to police, a full photographic record of the interior of the flat was made before the door was locked at around 4 p.m.

The results of the search were comparatively meagre: two staff-appraisal forms relating to Shayler's supervision of junior colleagues – but nonetheless covered by the Official Secrets Act – were found. Shayler said later that he had taken them home to complete them (not unusual for MI5 staff) and had forgotten about them. In addition, the police removed a number of other items, including personal letters between Shayler and Machon and photographs. For some inexplicable reason they also removed bed-linen and some of Annie's clothing. Even more strange, the police left a paper Machon had written for a management consultancy on MI5's personnel management in full view on the table.

The condition in which the police left the flat soon became a matter of controversy. Tipped off about the raid, Nick Fielding and photographer David O'Neill visited it the week after. It was in a mess. 'It looks like the work of a particularly vicious gang of burglars,'[15] Fielding reported. Slivers of wood from the shattered door frame lay on the floor with a broken chair. A lampshade had been discarded alongside an empty waste-paper basket, whose contents had been removed. The answering-machine had gone and the telephone had been disconnected. Undeveloped rolls of film had been removed, along with two laptop computers and a PC. Missing paperwork included insurance policies, private love letters, photos of holidays and dinner parties, old engagement diaries and bank statements.

From the two drawers of a small bedside cabinet all Shayler's personal papers had been removed. Even the carpet had been lifted to check the floorboards. The draft of his book had gone and Shayler later found out that his and Machon's mail had been intercepted at the postal sorting office.

Shortly after the *Mail on Sunday* published the story of what had happened to the flat, Jonathan Holborow received a letter from Commander Barry Moss, head of Special Branch. Moss complained that the photographs of the damage to the flat 'do not reflect the state in which the property was left when my officers vacated the premises nor the state in which the premises were found before the search'. He said his officers had taken photos both before and after and that the article 'unfairly reflects upon the professionalism of the police officers concerned'. He admitted there had been accidental damage to a chair and said, helpfully, that compensation was availabe to Shayler.[16]

The article was raised with Holborow by Jack Straw at a private meeting on 14 October. There was more than just a hint of a suggestion that perhaps Fielding and O'Neill had damaged the flat. However, when they visited it they assumed it was under observation, probably bugged, and filmed the entire incident with a video camera to protect themselves.

If neither the police nor the journalists were responsible for the damage, who was? Moss stated in his letter that his investigation officers had acted independently of any other department or agency in deciding to search the flat. Had MI5 been interested in it? The specialist teams from A4 would easily have been able to effect an entry into the building, keys or no keys. The matter has never been resolved.

The Special Branch visits to the BBC (on 29 August) and *Mail on Sunday* offices (on 2 September) were carried out by two officers, one of whom was a member of the Financial Investigation and Special Access Centre (FISAC), the part of Special Branch responsible for money-laundering and other financial investigations.

On 4 September, Mr Justice Hooper made an order by consent continuing the injunction granted the previous Saturday. It also included an undertaking that all documents and other records 'containing information obtained by Mr Shayler in the course of or by virtue of his employment in, and position as a member of, the Security and Intelligence Services' should be held in a safe in the *Mail on Sunday*'s legal department, with access only to Jonathan Holborow, Nick Fielding and legal advisers. In addition, all material held on the *Mail on Sunday*'s central computing system had to be removed and was stored on eight magnetic disks, which also went into the safe.

The production order previously obtained by Special Branch on 29 August had directed the paper to produce within 24 hours all documents 'concerning any transaction in relation to the dealings with David Michael Shayler'. Holborow decided to challenge this on the grounds that it was drawn in such wide terms that it caught not just financial documents but all documents in the possession of the paper, including journalistic material. In order to allow the appeal to go through, all the documents relating to Shayler's payment by the *Mail on Sunday* were placed in a sealed envelope and handed over to Special Branch, who agreed at that stage not to open the package unless someone was taken into custody.

The case was heard in front of Judge Inman at Middlesex Guildhall Crown Court on 8 September. Inman agreed that the original order was too wide and he discharged it. He replaced it with one that required the newspaper to produce within seven days documents covering 'any payments made to David Michael Shayler and/or any other financial benefit received by him from the *Mail on*

Sunday in relation to the article which appeared in the paper on 24 August 1997'.

From the documents they received, the police worked out that the *Mail on Sunday* had paid Shayler a total of £39,000. He had received an initial £19,000 as he left the country. Shayler's argument all along had been that publication of his revelations would necessitate him leaving the country if he was to avoid arrest. He and Machon, who had both given up potentially well-paid jobs with management consultancies, needed something to live on until they could establish themselves abroad. The second tranche of £20,000 had not been requested by Shayler, but was agreed by Holborow after the couple had gone. He took the view that they would have to be out of the country for some time and that the initial payment would not last long.

After Shayler and Machon had transferred the money to the accounts of three friends, including David's brother Phillip, to prevent its seizure, the three were arrested and bailed on money-laundering charges. They had handled what the police referred to as the proceeds of crime. Several months later all charges were dropped and no attempt was made to seize the money.

One of those arrested was Matt Guarente, a financial journalist. 'I didn't take it too seriously at first,' he said. 'I thought they would have to find David guilty of a crime first before they could charge me with anything, and as he was out of the country, it was a long shot. But it made my life a bit difficult at work, although Bloomberg's were very good. They accepted that I had simply helped a friend. If I had been charged, it might have been a different matter. They arrived at 7.00 a.m. one morning, a policewoman and two other officers, and started to search my flat. Once they had found the bank statements, they were happy. I was then taken down to Charing Cross police station and kept there until 2 p.m. They were all very apologetic and polite and did everything by the book. Two months later, I heard that they were not going to proceed with charges.'[17]

By the end of the first week following publication, Operation Oscillate had made considerable progress. The Treasury Solicitor had successfully applied for and won an injunction that stopped the *Mail on Sunday* publishing any further material from David Shayler. The police had won an order requiring various institutions to provide them with details of money transactions and the Special Branch search teams had done a thorough job in going over the flat in Pimlico.

We can only guess at what was happening at MI5's Thames House headquarters. Shayler himself had written a piece for the *Evening Standard* during that first week, which sought to answer that question. 'The Director General will be desperately trying to salvage some credibility with the government. The career bureaucrats will be trying to search out inconsistencies in my story. I imagine they will suggest I am a rogue male, the only malcontent in an otherwise happy Service, or besmirch my character. MI5 will probably try to assert that my revelations undermine their work, despite the fact that I was very careful not to compromise ongoing operations or the security of officers,' Shayler noted prophetically. He said they would be considering how to track him down and would have alerted the ports. His record-of-service file would be converted into a personal file for a target. 'But the last thing on the office's mind will be trying to learn a lesson from this whole episode. It does not take criticism well and is loath to get to grips with problems or difficult issues.'[18]

Tony Blair's government could, and should, have treated David Shayler's revelations about the Security Service as a godsend. Whitehall reviews had come and gone in the past, but MI5 and the rest of the intelligence community had remained almost untouched. Margaret Thatcher had fêted MI5 and MI6, and authorised the spending of hundreds of millions of pounds on new headquarters buildings for both organisations.

Blair had the perfect opportunity to bring the Services more closely under government control and parliamentary scrutiny. Here was a new government, pledged to openness, confronted with a series of revelations about the Security Service, most of which had occurred under the previous Tory administration. While no government likes to be seen as 'soft' on defence and security issues, it can be argued that the new government had little to lose by instituting a major overhaul.

There were some suggestions that both Straw and Blair had an open mind on the matter. Campbell's 'send in the heavies' comments in August can also be interpreted as an attempt by the government to avoid having to obtain an injunction against a national newspaper. The writ itself, when finally agreed by the court, was not as draconian as it might have been. It allowed the *Mail on Sunday* editor to approach the Home Secretary to approve particular stories. Although this was indeed a form of 'pre-vetting', it was less harsh than it might have been.

On 23 September, Jack Straw wrote to Holborow in conciliatory terms:

> The Government's response to the publication, by your news-paper, of material provided by the former Security Service officer David Shayler, has, throughout, been determined by our concern about the real damage which such disclosures might cause to national security and to the public interest.
>
> I thought you should know that since the publication of the article on 24 August, a number of Security Service agents and former agents have been in touch. Some of them have expressed real concern at the prospect that Shayler's disclosures might give some clues which – though not necessarily apparent to the untrained eye – might enable their targets to identify them, putting their lives and those of their families at risk.
>
> I am sure that if I could convince you that our concern about the damage which can be caused by publication of Shayler's stories was genuine and well-founded, you would think twice about publishing any further disclosures by Shayler or by other former officers of the Security and Intelligence agencies.[19]

Straw invited Holborow to contact him at the Home Office where he would be happy to discuss the issues with him in general terms. Two weeks later, on 14 October, Holborow met him at the Home Office. No one else was present in the room. Holborow had half expected a difficult meeting and was dreading being shown some devastating document that undermined the paper's case. It never happened. Straw was firm, but conciliatory. If there was any truth in the suggestion that Shayler had damaged MI5 operations, surely he would have used this opportunity to let Holborow know? Straw wanted to know what the paper's (at that time unpublished) 'big' story was and assumed, wrongly, that it was something to do with the IRA. Holborow simply told him it was a story connected to the Israeli embassy bombing.

Straw also told him that in the week following the first set of articles, he, Tony Blair, Alastair Campbell and Stephen Lander had spent two-and-a-half days discussing how they were going to deal with the problem of the MI5 whistleblower. Straw made no promises at his meeting with Holborow and at one point referred to Shayler as a 'criminal'. His main purpose was to get an undertaking – freely given – that Holborow would not print anything that would jeopardise the security of MI5's agents.

That evening, Holborow and the *Mail on Sunday*'s political correspondent, Chris McLoughlin, had a meeting with Nick Brown MP, then the government's Chief Whip. The subject of Shayler came up. When Holborow stated that it was not the paper's intention to attack the government, but simply to inquire into the Security Services and the return of Shayler to the UK, Brown said he would telephone McLoughlin the next day. He called at 8.45 a.m., having spoken to the Prime Minister. It was clear that the PM had been well briefed on the subject. Later that day McLoughlin met Brown and was told that he was happy to act as an 'honest broker' between the government and the paper over a solution to the issue. Brown's main concern as Chief Whip appeared to be that, unless the matter was quickly resolved, it would find its way on to the Commons agenda and threaten the government's legislative programme.

Brown added that he would be happy to see Holborow the next day at 12 Downing Street. The meeting took place at 3 p.m. Holborow was conducted to a meeting room in the building, which, he was told, was secure from the possibility of electronic eavesdropping. He was invited to sit in Winston Churchill's chair as Brown asked him to spell out what he wanted. Holborow said he wanted Shayler and Annie Machon to be able to testify to the Parliamentary Intelligence and Security Committee and, more fundamentally, that there should be a review of MI5. Brown agreed to pass on the message and call Holborow the following Monday.

On Thursday 24 October, Annie Machon came to Kensington to meet Holborow. She had arrived back in the UK for a bail hearing, but it had been put back until December. Later the same day, John Wadham, who was now representing Shayler on behalf of Liberty, also saw Holborow. He said that the Treasury Solicitor's office had approached him and that he was due to see Roland Phillips the following day. He had been told that the meeting was not to be publicised and any suggestion that negotiations were taking place would bring all discussions to a halt.

The following day, Friday 24 October, Nick Fielding and Mark Hollingsworth were told that Special Branch officers wished to interview them in connection with the case. Both agreed that they would not give a statement, because the only use to which it could be put was as part of a prosecution case against Shayler. Geoffrey Robertson, QC, who had been retained by the *Mail on Sunday*, agreed. A full legal conference was held the following Tuesday (28 October). Further discussion took place over whether or not the two reporters should make a police statement. Robertson even suggested they should consider making a statement to John Wadham, which would make both men defence witnesses and therefore immune to cross-examination at any future trial.

On the same day MI5 director-general Stephen Lander visited the editorial offices of the *Guardian* newspaper in Faringdon Road, where he met reporters Richard Norton-Taylor, Seumas Milne and David Leigh. His appearance may have been connected with the fact that the following day he was due to appear in front of the Parliamentary Intelligence and Security Committee to give evidence. On Shayler he appeared conciliatory, saying it was 'not necessary to use a sledgehammer to crack a nut'.

Lander's single public appearance did not mean that he was inact- ive behind the scenes on the Shayler affair. On several occasions he invited selected journalists to join him for informal discussions. One such meeting took place in early December 1997. *Guardian* journalist Richard Norton-Taylor was present, as were Michael Evans (defence correspondent of *The Times*) and Michael Smith (defence correspondent of the *Daily Telegraph*). The meeting took place in Lander's private office on the fifth floor of MI5 headquarters at Thames House, Millbank. The atmosphere was more like a gentlemen's club than a security organisation, said one of those present. Lander was characteristically nervous, shy and uptight, but as the drinks were served he became keen to talk. Strangely, he appeared unwilling or unable to put across MI5's point of view and over the next three hours appeared more interested in the opinions of the journalists. He was boiling with rage at Shayler and bristled every time his name was mentioned, but instead of briefing the press, he seemed to be seeking informal advice. 'What do you think we should do?' he asked. All those present told him that if Shayler was prosecuted the media would have a field day. Lander did not reply. He sat there stony-faced, brooding and thinking.

Frustrated by the injunction and convinced that MI5's bungling of the bombing of the Israeli embassy story was in the public interest, *Mail on Sunday* editor Jonathan Holborow decided to test out the terms of the injunction. The procedure required Holborow to submit to the Home Secretary any proposed story based on material already supplied to the newspaper by Shayler. Jack Straw, acting on advice from the Security Service, would vet the material and determine whether or not it was a threat to national security. If not – no matter whether he considered it to be true or false – Straw would allow it to be published.

This unusual procedure, by which the government was able to 'pre-vet' any proposed articles based on Shayler's material, did not sit easily with the notion of press freedom. It was debated at the *Mail on Sunday* at some length, but in the end everyone knew that unless the paper accepted it, nothing else would come into the public domain.

On Wednesday 29 October 1997, Nick Fielding hand-delivered a copy of a proposed article on how MI5 had ignored warnings about a bomb at the Israeli embassy to Straw's private secretary at the Home Office.

The following day, Jack Straw wrote personally to Jonathan Holborow: 'I am writing to let you know that the Government does not seek to restrain publication of the article in the terms of which you have given notice and, in accordance with the terms of the order, you will shortly receive a letter to this effect from the Treasury Solicitor.'[20]

Straw's letter did not end there. He added a second paragraph, which is worthy of analysis.

Having discussed with the Security Service the allegations contained in the draft article, I can say that it is not the case that such information as the Security Service had in their possession would have enabled it to prevent the Israeli embassy bombing from happening. I can, however, see how Mr Shayler, a junior member of the Service who was not involved in the relevant area of work at the time, could have gained this mistaken impression. You should be aware that if I am asked about the article, this is how I shall respond.[21]

This was clearly a tacit admission by the Home Seretary that Shayler's story was true. Shayler never said that the information itself could have prevented the bombing, but 'such information as the Security Service had in their possession' could have been acted upon, had senior officers known of its existence. There were many curious features of the bombing, which indicate that something had gone seriously wrong.

On Friday, a letter arrived from Roland Phillips at the Treasury Solicitor's stating formally that 'the information contained in an article proposed for publication in the *Mail on Sunday* is not information in respect of which the Crown seeks to restrain publication.'[22]

The story was published that Sunday and had an enormous impact.

That same week there was an incredible development. On 30 October the government announced that there was to be a comprehensive spending review of the intelligence agencies. The announcement was made by Treasury Chief Secretary Alastair Darling. For the first time, MI5 was to be brought under political control. A full-scale review, reporting to a senior Cabinet minister, had, as its overall aim, 'to determine how best the security and intelligence agencies may contribute to the achievement of the government's objectives, on the assumption that for 1997–98 and 1998–99 the existing cash limits and running costs control totals are unchanged.'

More specifically, the objectives were to 'review the intelligence agencies' – including MI6 and GCHQ – aims and objectives, their costs, and to examine the extent to which they were aligned with the government's overall objectives. It would also seek to establish whether the current system for deciding what the agencies did, what intelligence they collected and what resources should be allocated, was the most efficient or effective way of linking resources to tasking and capabilities. This meant that even the Joint Intelligence Committee could be overhauled. It was also a hint that the question of merging the three principal intelligence agencies would be considered.

The review would also look at the scope 'for changing the allocation and composition of the Agencies' programmes to maximise their contribution towards the government's objectives'.[23] Although this was not spelt out, it appeared to be a sign that someone was at last taking on the issue of who did what. For several years confusion had surrounded the separation between MI5 and MI6 and between MI5 and the police, particularly in relation to Northern Ireland. And so the review proposed 'to investigate whether there are any areas where the Agencies' programmes duplicate those of other departments or law enforcement agencies and, if so, to consider the rationale for this and the scope for efficiencies'.

Also to be looked at were the agencies' assets. It was well known that both MI5 and MI6 had large property interests in central

London, as well as a number of buildings in various parts of the country. The secrecy surrounding the budget and accounts of both organisations had allowed such assets to grow without any coherent overall strategy.

Only one thing grated about the decision to set up the review: it was to be conducted by John Alpass, the government's then Cabinet Office intelligence co-ordinator and a former deputy director-general of MI5 until 1994. The review was being conducted effectively by an 'insider', someone who had been part of the old regime and who had every interest in shielding the intelligence agencies from a too extensive an inquiry.

The breadth of the inquiry was unprecedented and was the first comprehensive examination by an elected government of what the Service actually did. It was a remarkable vindication of Shayler's criticisms.

Whether or not Alpass conducted a thorough review cannot be judged. In July 1998, nine months after the announcement that it would take place, a small report in *The Times* [24] noted that it had concluded with a decision not to merge MI5, MI6 and GCHQ. The other significant fact to emerge was that the total budget of all three agencies was effectively to be frozen for the next three years. It would be £743 million in 1999–2000 and rise by a mere £2 million in each of the following years.

Shayler's revelations provided the perfect excuse for the government to act and to that extent they should be grateful to him. They caused MI5 to shoot to the top of the political agenda. As one source at the time told the *Mail on Sunday*, 'MI5 was number 27 on our list of priorities before. Afterwards, the Service was being discussed by ministers at all levels.'

Lander himself was asked to appear before the Intelligence and Security Committee on 30 October 1997. Even though the committee was dominated by politicians – the chair was former Defence Secretary Tom King, and members included ex-military-intelligence officer Michael Mates and former MI6 officer Baroness Ramsay of Cartvale – this was still an important development. With newer, more radical members, like Labour MPs Dale Campbell-Savours and Yvette Cooper, there was a chance that things would change. Shayler had already written to the Committee on 10 October, asking it to take evidence from him. His lawyer, John Wadham, later wrote asking to submit evidence to the review.

During the private hearing, Lander was questioned over MI5's extensive files on so-called 'subversives'. He replied that MI5 closed down its anti-subversion work in 1992 and had begun to weed out the files. When the committee's third annual report[25] finally appeared in October 1998, it contained an extensive discussion on the question of Security Service files.

MI5 itself decides which files to destroy, although the committee felt that some form of independent check should be built into the process. There was little word on Special Branch files, often collected under the direction of MI5 officers.

As the committee continued its work, it became clearer and clearer that it would not take evidence from Shayler. No formal letter was ever sent to him, but Shayler realised after he had sent reminders that it was pointless to continue.

John Alpass appeared to be more accommodating. In December 1997, John Wadham wrote to him on Shayler's behalf asking for his client's views to be taken into account. Alpass wrote back on 13 January saying that he would be happy to hear Liberty's views, but that as far as Shayler was concerned, 'I felt it right to show your letter to the Treasury Solicitor, who will be writing separately about that aspect.'[26]

A letter duly arrived from Roland Phillips of the Treasury Solicitor's office, which proved to anyone who had doubted it that Sir Humphrey was alive and well and living in Whitehall. 'In so far as your client, in expressing his views to the Committee, would be drawing upon experience gained as a member of the Service, as seems to be inevitable, then he will I am sure have very much in mind the terms of the injunction which I have summarised above,' he wrote. 'You will need to consider this potential difficulty very carefully with your client and I should be grateful if you would confirm that your client will take care to observe the strict terms of the injunction.'[27]

In other words the government's legal officers were saying that Shayler could not speak to the Cabinet Office security co-ordinator because he would be breaking the terms of the injunction taken out against him and the *Mail on Sunday*, even though Alpass had the highest possible level of security clearance and had formerly been MI5's deputy director-general. As Shayler said at the time, 'It has all the elements of a Whitehall farce. They are too interested in fighting turf battles to care about the security of the country.'[28]

Despite this, in mid-February Shayler sent a 6,000-word submission on MI5 to the Alpass review. It covered management issues, such as grading, postings, the use of computers and other bureaucratic matters. In the covering letter, Shayler wrote that he had prepared another dossier covering operational malpractice. He did not want to send it via e-mail, fax or the postal service because they were not secure. He asked Alpass to find a way of securely receiving the information. There was no reply to his letter or acknowledgement of the submission.

It was, perhaps, a short-sighted decision. In the dossier Shayler had prepared, but not sent, he disclosed his knowledge of how MI6 had funded an assassination attempt on Colonel Gaddafi of Libya. In the face of Alpass's refusal to see it, Shayler decided to make the story public.

Bizarrely, just as this Whitehall farce was being conducted, Roland Phillips and the Treasury Solicitors had also opened up substantive negotiations with John Wadham. By mid-December 1997, Phillips had produced a 'heads of agreement' document which aimed at becoming the basis on which Shayler could return to the UK.

The nature of this document was an agreement between Shayler and the Attorney General. According to a draft, Shayler would meet representatives of the Crown and:

(a) provide them with full details of all information and documents from inside MI5 which he had disclosed to anyone at Associated Newspapers;
(b) return all such documents or, if impossible, say who had them;
(c) use his best endeavours to get back any such document;
(d) agree not to publish or disclose any further information without the consent of MI5's Director of Establishments. He would not give such permission if he thought it was against the national interest;
(e) agree to pay the Crown, within five years, the sum of £39,000, being the amount he had received from the *Mail on Sunday*.

In addition, in exchange for dropping the terms of the injunction against him, the agreement required Shayler to agree to assign world copyright in any future publication, whether fiction or non-fiction, to the Attorney General in perpetuity. This meant that, for the rest of his life, Shayler would not be allowed to be a copyright holder in his own right.

Throughout the first few months of 1998, negotiations beween John Wadham and the Treasury Solicitor continued. Wadham argued that the only matters on which the Attorney General needed to be concerned were those relating to security. If Shayler chose to write a book on fly-fishing, for example, why should he hand over copyright to the Attorney General? Why should it require govern-ment consent to be published? Wadham also sought an assurance that any information Shayler provided on his dealings with the *Mail on Sunday* should not be used as the basis for a prosecution against them. He also suggested that, 'It is necessary to recognise that most of this money has now been spent. Any agreement would have to ensure that the debt could not be enforced for five years.'[29] No mention was made in the document about whether or not Shayler would be prosecuted.

The negotiations dragged on for several weeks. In February 1998, Wadham wrote again to Phillips, complaining at the slow pace of the negotiations. He continued to press for an assurance that Shayler would not be prosecuted, and suggested that one way of building bridges would be for a member of the Security Service to go to Paris to meet Shayler. But things were not going well. As Wadham put it: 'Even with the amendments proposed, without more reassurance on how Mr Shayler will be treated on his return, no sensible lawyer would advise him to sign the agreement.'[30]

However, by this time there had been a significant development in the police investigation. On 29 January, a Special Branch detec-tive wrote to Nick Fielding and Mark Hollingsworth: 'Further to the continuing criminal investigation into alleged breaches of the Official Secrets Acts 1911–89 and related offences, it is proposed to make application for Production Orders under Schedule 1 Police and Criminal Evidence Act 1984 *for further material held by you* [our emphasis] in relation to David Michael Shayler . . . This includes any items held by you in relation to Shayler's former employment.' The policeman said that the order would be stayed if the relevant mate-rial was produced in response to his letter.

The letter, which threatened a new round of legal action, came as a bolt from the blue. Fielding and Hollingsworth knew exactly what it referred to and it was a worrying development. Two days before he had left Britain, Shayler had left a pile of documents for safe-keeping with the *Mail on Sunday*. In the confusion that previous August, the documents had been overlooked. The Special Branch officers and government lawyers had been satisfied with the terms of the injunction obtained at the time, which required all material in the possession of the *Mail on Sunday* to be stored in the legal department's safe. Presuming this was to cover journalistic material and computer tapes from the newspaper's editorial system, it appeared not to have crossed the minds of the Treasury Solicitor – or, for that matter, MI5 – that Shayler may have had documents in his possession when he left the Service.

The 28 documents were internal MI5 reports, many of them marked, in order of descending importance, in terms of security: 'Top Secret UK Eyes Alpha Umbra Gamma', 'Top Secret/Umbra/UK–US Eyes Only', 'Top Secret', 'Secret', 'Confidential', 'Restrict Covering Sheet', and so on. They included papers on IRA training in Libya, an assessment of the links between the IRA and Libya, an internal history of MI5 from 1909 to 1959, a document entitled 'Investigation of Subversive Organisations', numerous reports written about Libyan dissidents by Shayler, details of meetings between Foreign Office and Libyan officials in Cairo in 1994, an assessment of IRA arms-procurement efforts since the 1995 ceasefire and a set of documents relating to Operation Shadower – the MI5 surveillance operation against *Guardian* journalist Victoria Brittain.

Shayler had been careful not to take any 'raw' intelligence documents that might identify sources or informers and had never intended that the documents should be published. He had taken them simply to establish his *bona fides* with Fielding and Hollingsworth. Had he not done so, it is less likely that the *Mail on Sunday* would have had the confidence to publish his disclosures.

When the documents had arrived at the *Mail on Sunday* it quickly became clear that few, if any, could ever be published. With the exception of those on Operation Shadower, they were too sensitive. A decision had been taken to store them and hand them back when the opportunity arose. As the months had passed it had become more and more of a mystery to Fielding and Hollingsworth that MI5 had not requested them back. Although most were copies, one at least was an original document with a circulation sheet still attached. Why had they not been missed when MI5 prides itself on its internal security?

The other obvious question was why, after nearly six months, had Special Branch decided to come after the documents. If they had suspected their existence before, they would have acted immediately. It is safe to presume that they must have been acting on 'received information', although where this came from is unknown.

In the first instance, lawyers acting for Fielding and Hollingsworth wrote back to the Special Branch policeman pointing out a genuine difficulty. The amended High Court injunction granted on 4 September 1997 included an undertaking that any documents containing information obtained from Shayler should be held in secure storage in the legal department safe at the *Mail on Sunday*. 'Since the High Court has been seized of this matter and has issued an Order after argument that protects your position, you may wish to reconsider your decision to seek a Production Order in a lower court, as clearly all relevant material is safeguarded under the terms of the Injunction,' wrote David Smythe, of Kingsley Napley. 'In view of the Injunction any Production Order made clearly cannot be executed without the leave of the High Court.'[31]

So the original injunction had tied up all documentation and a production order requiring material to be handed over could not overrule it. Each side withdrew to consider their position. At the *Mail on Sunday*, a legal conference was called, with Geoffrey Robertson, QC, and Shayler's lawyer, John Wadham. It was decided that the best course of action was to devise a way of handing over the documentation in return for the police agreeing not to proceed with the production orders. Wadham contacted his client and on 18 February wrote to Associated Newspapers' legal director Harvey Kass.

Shortly before his departure from the UK my client left a number of documents for safekeeping with Nick Fielding at the *Mail on Sunday*. They were to be held securely until my client had sorted out his position with his former employers – he had no wish to take them overseas or to disclose their contents to others. He understands that a few days after his departure they were in any event made the subject of a High Court order, requiring them to be placed in your safe and effectively 'freezing' them.[32]

Wadham explained that Shayler now wanted the documents handed over directly to the Security Service, without being given to police officers or any other third party. Wadham asked Kass to arrange with the Treasury Solicitor to vary the terms of the injunction so that the documentation could be removed from the safe and passed on to MI5.

The package of documents was eventually handed over to a representative of the Treasury Solicitor who arrived, bearing a letter of authority, at the *Mail on Sunday* offices. In the presence of solicitor David Smythe and Harvey Kass, the package was taken out of the safe in the legal department where it had lain undisturbed since the previous August and given to the legal officer.

The return of the documents clearly had a major impact on the thinking of the Treasury Solicitor and, more particularly, on the thinking of those running Operation Oscillate in Special Branch and the Security Service. The timetable for negotiating an agreement with Shayler began to slip.

It was not until February 1998 that Wadham received a reply to his letter, which had started the negotiating process in December 1997. Knowing how Whitehall operates, Shayler had asked him to send a negotiating timetable to the government solicitors. On 15 March 1998, MI5 failed to meet the first of these deadlines, namely the dropping of all police action against Annie Machon, who was still, after seven months, on police bail.

Progress was eventually made on her case. Even though potential charges under the Official Secrets Act had been abandoned, she still faced charges for money-laundering because of her role in handling payments made to Shayler by the *Mail on Sunday*. But on 27 March, John Wadham was informed that the police were not going to prosecute her. She was now free, and could come and go from Britain as she pleased, no longer subject to police bail.

Even by early May no agreement had been reached. Wadham was told explicitly by Roland Phillips at the Treasury Solicitor's office that the recent delays 'had resulted from dismay about the contents of the documents that had been returned by the *Mail on Sunday*'. Yet the bones of an agreement for Shayler's return to the UK were in place. Wadham argued that although there could be no immunity from prosecution for his client if he returned, it would not be in the public interest for a court case to go ahead. The Attorney General, he said, had enough information to make a decision. Once he had given an assurance that a prosecution would not go ahead, arrangements could be made for Shayler to return.

Phillips told Wadham that instead of Shayler being arrested on his return he might possibly be interviewed by the police by appointment, possibly the day after.

Discussions continued about assigning Shayler's copyright, but differences were narrowing. Shayler had also agreed to be debriefed on his return by members of the Security Service, provided that none of his disclosures were used against him. He would remain silent in the face of questioning by the police.

A week later Phillips told Wadham that the Attorney General was not in a position to reach a conclusion on the question of prosecution. He also reiterated the point about the documentation: 'You have yourself inferred that the recovery of the material disclosed by your client to the *Mail on Sunday* led to an interruption in our discussions. Neither you nor I are aware of the overall effect of that material, but it has given rise to further inquiries and evaluations, which are not completed and which make it quite impracticable for me to meet any kind of deadline.'[33]

Events were rapidly heading towards an impasse. Negotiations that had originally been scheduled for two months had now stretched on for almost five. Something had to give.

9

EXILE, ARREST AND THE
GREAT ESCAPE

As I sit here in my prison cell, I can't help feeling that my only mistake
was being too open with you.

David Shayler, in an open letter to Stephen Lander,
director-general of MI5, 9 September 1998

As the *Mail on Sunday* battled through the courts in the days following publication of the first set of articles in August 1997, Shayler and
Machon, temporarily in Holland, were preparing to move yet again.
In the previous week they had stayed in four different hotels. There
were to be another four during the course of the next week.

On Saturday 30 August they took the 10 a.m. train from The
Hague to Paris. Three-and-a-half hours later they arrived at the Gare
du Nord, the only place in continental Europe where British policemen are stationed – because of the Eurostar connection. They made
their way out of the station and travelled across town to Paris
Montparnasse before boarding the TGV to Bayonne.

They arrived at Bayonne to find the station full of armed police
and feared the worst, but no one bothered them as they went on to
the Hotel Mercure, where they were booked in as Mr and Mrs
Dobbie. That evening, as news of the injunction spread throughout
Fleet Street, they ate on a terrace overlooking the swimming-pool.
Later that night, far from the whirlpool of events in London, they
had their first good night's sleep in days.

The following morning, Sunday, they learned of the death of
Diana, Princess of Wales. Shayler's first reaction was of relief that the
first series of articles had been published the week before. Because
Diana died in the early hours of the morning only a few of the
papers ran the story in their first editions. Many were still running

substantial pieces about Shayler. The *Sunday Telegraph* had printed a background article based on information from someone who had shared a flat in Darlington with Shayler's friend Graham Dunbar. 'In some kind of bizarre transference, this friend of Graham's attributed to me a number of his own outlandish acts, including phoning Edwina Currie pretending to be Peter Lilley and leaving obscene messages on Peter Cook's answering-machine,'[1] said Shayler.

Later that day Machon spoke to her father, Nick Machon, editor of the *Guernsey Press*. As a crusading journalist, he supported the idea of a whistleblower, but was unhappy with Shayler's decision to accept money to cover expenses while they were on the run. He told his daughter that the *Sunday Mirror* had offered him around £50,000 for a picture of her, but he had refused.

The *Sunday Times* also ran a background piece: it asserted that Shayler's main motive for his exposé was that he had not worked in MI5's prestigious T Branch. This provided evidence that off-the-record briefings were taking place: Shayler had spent two years in T Branch when MI5 took over responsibility from Special Branch for IRA investigations on the mainland.

Two days later, Tuesday 2 September, Shayler made contact for the first time with solicitor John Wadham, director of Liberty. Wadham told him that he would research the possibility of extradition from France to England. They agreed to keep in contact. That evening, around 7 p.m., Shayler noticed a middle-aged man wearing a blouson sitting in a white Peugeot 406 parked beside a telephone box he had used earlier. He looked every inch a plain-clothes policeman. He and Machon considered leaving their luggage in the hotel and taking a train out of Bayonne. They checked the railway timetable and decided they could catch a train late that evening to Lisbon. After an hour or so the car disappeared, and they decided to stay put.

The next few days were spent in re-establishing telephone contact with family members and friends, and waiting for their friend Matt Guarente to meet them in Bordeaux, which Shayler knew well as he had spent a year there as a student in 1986–87.

They spent the next few days with Guarente, touring the Basque country, changing hotels every couple of days, until he returned to London. Shayler called John Wadham to discuss Machon's legal status and situation. Wadham had been told by Special Branch that she could return to the UK as long as she gave a statement to the police. He said the agreement was that she could return but might be charged under the Official Secrets Act, which would involve bail and possible surrender of her passport. It might mean that they would spend a year apart. But Wadham was reassuring: the reality was that there was very little with which she could be charged. She had criticised MI5's management in general terms, but that was hardly likely to sustain a criminal prosecution. Machon was frightened to go back, but knew that she must to sort out their affairs. Any delay, Wadham advised, might count against her. Shayler and Machon agreed. The risk was minimal and a plan was organised.

In the meantime, Graham Dunbar, who had been holidaying in the Dordogne, arrived to stay for a few days, bringing with him a laptop computer. He left on Wednesday 10 September, and the following day Machon and Shayler left Bayonne for Toulouse. The following Saturday they took a train to Perpignan on the south coast where they had arranged to meet Nick Fielding, who was due to arrive on Thursday 18 September.

The following day John Wadham also arrived at Perpignan airport. It was the first time he had met his clients. He told them he had written to then Home Secretary Jack Straw asking for an assurance that his office phones were not being tapped as this would be an infringement of lawyer–client confidentiality. Straw's reply had been ambiguous.

By that evening, certain realities had begun to sink in: Shayler and Machon knew that her return to the UK might be the start of a long separation. The following morning, Saturday 20 September, everyone was up at 4.15 for the drive to Barcelona – the nearest international airport – and the 8.00 a.m. flight to Britain.

It landed around midday at Gatwick. As she, Wadham, Fielding and photographer Dave O'Neill walked into the main terminal, Machon noticed a Special Branch officer standing just inside the terminal. He gave an embarrassed smile when he realised they had spotted him. Annie knew him well as she used to work with him occasionally while she was still in MI5.

As soon as she had shown her passport to the immigration officer and walked through the barrier a group of plain-clothes officers appeared. Detective Superintendent Morrisey read Annie her rights and told her she was being arrested under the Official Secrets Act and the section of the Criminal Justice Act that dealt with money-laundering. She had not been expecting the second series of charges and immediately began to worry. As they led her away she sought reassurance from John Wadham, who stood beside her throughout the ordeal. The police moved with Machon quickly towards the escalators in an attempt to shake off Fielding and O'Neill. However, O'Neill went ahead outside the terminal and found the police cars – without a moment to spare. Seconds later, the exit door opened and out came Machon surrounded by a mêlée of six or seven large police officers. He snatched a photograph as she and her police escort moved towards the cars. Her face – as can be seen in the exceptional photos he shot[2] – was barely visible in the sea of grey serge.

The two police vehicles arrived at Charing Cross police station at 11.15 a.m. The police were thorough, even searching the car she had travelled in in case she had stashed any documents behind the seats. Once inside, she was frisked and her bags were emptied on to the floor in front of the officers. They confiscated her cigarette lighter. After a two-hour wait, she was given a cursory examination by a doctor to see that she was fit to be interviewed. A disagreement between John Wadham and the doctor ensued when Wadham insisted on being present for the medical.

The first interview began at around 1 p.m. and lasted 30 minutes. The two Special Branch officers present were clearly nervous, knowing that this was a politically sensitive case. Wadham noticed that their questions – which were mostly about her career in MI5 – had been typed in advance, presumably by MI5. Annie gave a polite 'No comment' to each. Her replies were then taken to DS Morrissey, the officer in charge of the case, who was waiting in another room. After the session was over she was taken to a cell and locked in for 90 minutes before a second interview in which the police exerted psychological pressure in an attempt to force Machon to incriminate herself or Shayler. They said this was her only chance to state her case, which was untrue, and dwelt on her exemplary career in MI5. They said they knew she didn't do it for financial reasons, but because she loved Shayler. One officer pulled out a love letter she had written to him – which had been removed from their flat during the search – and read out every word. Machon was outraged, but said nothing. She used the anti-interrogation technique of silently chanting a mantra as she gave no comment to the questions she was asked.

The police wanted to know where Shayler was now, but Machon said she could not tell them. There was a delay of 45 minutes while the officers consulted with their boss. When they returned they asked about money. Both men looked bored. They had known in advance that she would not speak voluntarily. The interview ended at 4.55 p.m. Half an hour later Machon was told she could go. She was bailed to return on 20 October.

During the next few days Machon returned to the flat in Pimlico and, with the help of David's brother, Jem, moved out their remaining possessions. She also saw her mother. On Monday 22 September she heard that Matt Guarente and Graham Dunbar had been arrested in Notting Hill and Norwich respectively in connection with the payments made by the *Mail on Sunday*. Both were questioned and released on bail. David's brother Phillip was also due to be arrested, but he was in Argelès-sur-Mer on the south-east coast of France with his girlfriend and two other friends. He turned himself in when he got back to Britain.

Shayler's main concern now was to try to find somewhere for him and Machon – if she was allowed to leave the UK – to settle for a while. They had now been on the run for three weeks. They were tiring of the constant move from hotel to hotel and the need to be vigilant.

Then, out of the blue, friends of friends offered them the use of a farmhouse in the remote Creuse area, about 350 kilometres south of Paris in the centre of France. It was large and isolated, about two kilometres from the nearest village. Shayler arrived there on 23 September 1997 and Machon four days later.

It was a far cry from their flat in central London: instead of the squares and plane trees of Pimlico, they were several miles off the main road in an area that, even in rural France, is considered remote. Rolling hills, forests and lakes dominated the scenery, but without beaches or mountains it was well off the tourist trail. Their lack of transport meant that they had to walk into the village of La Celle Dunoise or get a taxi into the nearest town, Dun-le-Palestel, where they sometimes ate at the Hôtel Joly or the Hôtel de France.

Nick Fielding and photographer Phil Ide visited them there in early October, to find Shayler working on the dossier he hoped to send to the Parliamentary Intelligence and Security Committee.[3]

Later in October friends arrived from the UK to visit the couple and in mid-November Shayler's parents also came. In early December, his brothers Phil and Jem and their respective girlfriends were there.

Annie returned to London for a bail hearing on 15 December 1997, to be told that it had been postponed. By this time the case against Matt Guarente and Phil for money-laundering had been dropped, although Graham Dunbar still faced the possibility of charges.

Shayler travelled to Paris to meet Annie on her way back from London and also to hold his second meeting with John Wadham to discuss the negotiations with the Treasury Solicitor over a possible deal that would allow him to return to the UK. Before the couple set off back to Creuse, they were joined by Annie's brother Richard, who stayed with them for Christmas. Christmas itself was subdued, although they put up decorations and cooked a turkey.

As the weeks turned into months they settled into their new lifestyle. Nothing much happened, nothing much changed. The neighbours had been told that David was a writer and showed little interest in the quiet English couple. They spent much of their time reading and writing, keeping in touch with their friends. Occasionally they were visited by a journalist, who would be picked up some distance from the house and escorted there blindfolded. 'It is a long drive, first straight and then winding. We nearly crash into an oncoming lorry. The blind lurching of the ride and the smell of the black coating on the sunglasses makes me nauseous, and we come to the place just in time,' is how Alan Franks described it for *The Times*.[4]

They made an occasional trip out of France. At the end of January 1998, they went to visit Shayler's father at Briele in Holland, where he was working. At the end of March 1998, they went to Amsterdam to watch the Coca-Cola Cup Final on satellite TV. Much to Shayler's chagrin, his team, Middlesbrough, was beaten. At Easter 15 friends joined them at the farmhouse for a party to celebrate the fifth anniversary of their first meeting, in the library of the old MI5 building. At the end of May they visited Barcelona for a friend's hen weekend. Throughout they used either cash or the occasional travellers' cheque to avoid their movements being traced electronically.

In late June 1998, the negotiations, which had now been going on for more than six months, between Wadham and the Treasury Solicitor became noticeably more fractious. A letter from Roland Phillips to Wadham in June expressed dissatisfaction that articles had appeared in the *Daily Telegraph*[5] and the *Spectator* with the explicit warning that their discussions should remain confidential. He wrote: 'The report in the *Daily Telegraph* was inaccurate in a number of respects, in particular in stating that your client had been promised freedom from prosecution if he were to enter into an agreement.'[6] Shayler agreed that the *Telegraph* article was inaccurate and had been printed without consultation with him.

As it turned out, this was the last exchange of letters between Phillips and Wadham for many months. In France, Shayler was becoming increasingly frustrated. He had agreed not to make any further disclosures, but as his evidence was not even considered by the Parliamentary Intelligence and Security Committee or the Alpass Review, he decided he would launch his own website on the Internet. He stated initially that it would contain full details of his published revelations and the text of the unsolicited submission he had made to the Alpass Review, detailing waste, inefficiency and mismanagement within the Security Service. Technically, anything Shayler published concerning his previous employment would be in breach of the government injunction against him, but as he told Fielding:

'Anthony Blunt got immunity and he was a KGB spy. All the disclosures I have made have been in the public interest in an attempt to improve efficiency in MI5 and better protect the public. When I initially made contact with the government through my lawyer, it was made clear that the chances of reaching an agreement would be improved if I kept quiet. Nearly a year later there has been no progress. The whole negotiation was an excuse to shut me up. The website is the answer. Nothing will threaten the security of MI5 agents or staff or compromise working methods. But there are vital matters that need a public airing and the Internet seems to be the only way out.'[7]

The website had been under development for a number of weeks, and Shayler had been helped by several friends still in the UK. Originally, it consisted of nothing more than a portrait of Shayler under the title 'shayler.com'. However, once the site went on-line, it appears to have caused a major sensation with the authorities in the UK. Shayler had been prevented under the terms of the injunction from speaking out in the UK – no newspaper would dare print his allegations and risk prosecution. The web was different. Here Shayler could disseminate information without going through a UK publisher. He was a mouse-click away from being able to distribute his message throughout the world.

It was a situation that could not be tolerated. On 22 July, Roland Phillips, the Treasury Solicitor – for whom dealing with Shayler seems to have become a full-time occupation – wrote to TABnet, the Californian Internet company that hosted Shayler's website. 'It appears likely that the website may be used to publish information in breach of the injunction . . . You should be aware that an attempt may be made by Mr Shayler to publish such information, thereby putting himself and any person reproducing that information in breach of the injunction and liable to action for contempt.'[8] Phillips went on to point out that the website carried the logo of the Security Service 'as though the website is somehow the official website of the British Security Service and has a connection with the Crown'. The notion that people logging on to www.shayler.com would somehow think that they were looking at official MI5 policy documents cannot have been missed by the Californians who received this statement. TABnet was asked to comply with the terms of the injunction against Shayler and confirm that the MI5 logo would be removed.

Phillips had clearly not understood the complexities of Internet business, and TABnet was in no mood to kowtow to the British government. Spokeswoman Kate Carrigan said, 'If the British go to court and win an injunction then we would shut down his site. But just so long as it is not pornography we take absolutely no responsibility for the content of people's sites. The Internet is free space. There have been a lot of upholdings of the First Amendment to the Constitution, which guarantees free speech on this matter. We do not get into the business of editing or controlling anybody's content. We will wait until it goes through the courts . . . until then we have no control over it and we refuse to get involved.'[9]

It was not the response Phillips was looking for. David Kerr, chief executive of the Internet Watch Foundation in the UK, offered him little comfort. 'Other countries will be reluctant to take action against a website which, for whatever reason, offends a particular government. Internet service providers would regard this as against the spirit and culture of the Internet. Technically, it is impossible to block the site. Blocking it in one place would simply mean it will pop up somewhere else.'[10]

His opinion was backed by Harold Stout, a New York-based constitutional lawyer: 'The constitution provides very strong freedom of speech protection – broadly, they would have to show that release of the information by the site constituted a direct threat to American national security.'[11] And as yet nothing had appeared on Shayler's website. It was merely a 'site under construction'.

Several sources have since told the authors of this book that it was the website more than anything else that prompted moves to arrest Shayler in Paris. It certainly stimulated MI5 to produce its own anodyne website within days of the furore breaking. (Needless to say, MI5's site contained nothing about their former officer David Shayler.) Just two days before his arrest, Shayler's website suffered a cyber-attack. Graffiti was scrawled across the site and the hacker's handiwork was signed 'Quasi'. Kate Corrigan said the only way the hacker could have done such damage was by intercepting Shayler's password – a sophisticated process. 'It seems that this guy has got people who want to screw with him. Maybe it was MI5. The person didn't just hack the page but somehow got hold of the password. We would have given Shayler the password via e-mail and that is pretty secure. But if you have the right technology and techniques you can get someone's mail.' Shayler now suspects that the e-mail containing his password was 'morticed'[12] – intercepted and kept by the authorities so that he never received it. For government agencies this is a simple matter, especially if you have access to GCHQ and can monitor phone calls and e-mails with impunity.

Under UK law the deliberate destruction of a website is treated as criminal damage and is illegal. If it was MI5 – and there were few other obvious candidates, considering the legal moves that were already afoot – it was just another of those breaches of the law that the public has been told countless times were now in the past. 'They would probably have justified it with a property warrant,' said Shayler. But even this shows the shortcomings in Britain's system of accountability. Politicians involved in a scandal could decide how their opponents' civil liberties might be curtailed.

Negotiations were still at a standstill with the Treasury Solicitor. John Wadham was forced to issue a press release on 25 July stating that MI5 and the government were refusing to offer Shayler immunity from prosecution in return for his co-operation. Shayler, said Wadham, was willing to submit any book he wrote about the intelligence services to the relevant authorities and had also agreed to return the expenses he had taken from the *Mail on Sunday* when he was able to do so, but there were sticking points. 'Under the terms of the proposed agreement, the authorities also demanded that Mr

Shayler tell MI5 what he told journalists, but would make no undertaking that his information would not be used to prosecute those journalists under the Official Secrets Act. Mr Shayler was very concerned not to get those who broke his story into the same kind of trouble he has found himself in,' said Wadham.[13] He also said that Shayler did not want to return to the UK to face prosecution: 'He has no income and is tempted to accept offers to make further disclosures either abroad or on the Internet (where the injunction cannot be enforced).'

Shayler backed up the statement: 'If they were really concerned about national security, they would not have put me in the invidious position of having to look at publishing further stories without the input of the authorities to support my life in exile. I can't help thinking that the injunction and the negotiations have been used as a way to silence my criticisms of a largely unaccountable and highly secretive government department and to spare the government any more embarrassment about which members of the Cabinet have been the subject of MI5 files.'[14]

At the same time Wadham issued his until-then secret correspondence with the Treasury Solicitor to show that substantial negotiations had been taking place. It was, indeed, a major breakdown of communication.

As MI5 officers involved in Operation Oscillate debated what they could do to stop Shayler, there was a dramatic development. At one of his earliest meetings with Fielding and Hollingsworth, Shayler had mentioned an attempt by MI6 to organise the assassination of Colonel Gaddafi. The *Mail on Sunday* editor Jonathan Holborow had baulked at publishing the story because it had not come directly from Shayler's own experience.

In contrast to other material Shayler had provided, the substance of the allegation was effectively hearsay. Shayler had been told of the plot by his counterpart in MI6, but had no personal knowledge of, or planning role, in the incident.

Holborow had adopted a conservative policy in relation to Shayler's revelations because he thought it would be easier to defend them if the paper was attacked. Even if Shayler had genuinely been told about such a plot, the reasoning went, it could be that he had been misinformed. If opponents could seize on certain articles and say that they had been proved to be false, all Shayler's revelations might be brought into disrepute.

However, the BBC's Mark Urban had heard the story directly from Shayler, at a hotel in Limoges, France, towards the end of 1997. Formerly defence correspondent for the *Independent*, Urban had covered the Gulf war for *Newsnight* in 1994 and had been the BBC's Middle East correspondent based in Israel. He had also written a well-respected and informed book on the British intelligence community called *UK Eyes Alpha: The Inside Story of British Intelligence*. For months on and off Urban had been digging away to try to confirm Shayler's story. He had followed up his initial conversation in Limoges with a filmed interview for *Panorama* in Paris in the spring of 1998, and by the end of July his programme was ready for transmission.

Once Urban had finished his programme, he then had to get it broadcast. The method adopted by the *Mail on Sunday*, of submitting material to the Home Secretary for approval, was the only possible one. He submitted the film in mid-July and BBC lawyers spent the following two weeks arguing over the script almost line by line with the Treasury Solicitor to get permission to broadcast it. Even conservative BBC bosses accepted that the story stood up and that it was in the public interest to put it out.

Jonathan Holborow had also had a change of heart and Nick Fielding was sent to France at the end of July to meet with Shayler and confirm the details of the story. He submitted his first draft to the editor in the afternoon of Friday 31 July. Within an hour it had been forwarded to the Home Secretary and by 10.40 that night a reply was received from the Treasury Solicitor's office. Again it was from Roland Phillips, who was already dealing with Urban's request to broadcast his story. 'I am instructed that the central claim of the story is false,' Phillips said. 'There are also significant inaccuracies amongst the various details in the article. Nevertheless, it contains a number of facts, publication of which would be damaging to the security of the United Kingdom, and for this reason I am instructed not to make the statement in writing which you would require to publish without breaching the injunction.'[15]

So, even though the story was denied, the *Mail on Sunday* was told that details of what Shayler had said could not be published. Negotiations continued throughout much of the following day. The Treasury Solicitor's final offer was to allow publication of a substantially amended article, which involved removing much of the detailed content. But so weak and bowdlerised was the result that

Holborow decided not to publish it and at 6 p.m. on Saturday 1 August Mr Phillips was told the *Mail on Sunday* would abide by the terms of the injunction and not go ahead with the article

The saga surrounding the Gaddafi story was not yet played out, but it was quickly overshadowed by events. Within two hours, David Shayler was seized in the lobby of a Paris hotel by French security police and spent the next three-and-a-half months in the Santé prison in Paris awaiting possible extradition to Britain. When *Mail on Sunday* deputy managing editor John Wellington phoned Roland Phillips at home at 8.45 p.m. that night to ask him if he was aware that Shayler had been arrested, Phillips was taken aback and said he had known nothing of any such plans.

The government was now involved in negotiations with the BBC over a *Panorama* special on the Gaddafi allegations while at the same time it had made it almost impossible for the *Mail on Sunday* to publish its version of the story. While rejecting the story as false, solic- itors acting for the government argued that details in Shayler's story could be damaging to national security. The following day, as Shayler was questioned in France, hints of a story about Gaddafi surfaced in the *Sunday Times*. It was clear that the story was beginning to leak out, but with the government injunction in force it would not appear in Britain. Lord Williams, the Home Office minister, appeared on BBC Radio 4 to deny that there had been an 'official plot' to kill Colonel Gaddafi. His comments only fuelled speculation that there had been an unofficial plot. The Foreign Office would say only that, 'The central claim that there was an official plot to kill Gaddafi is untrue.'

The following week, on Tuesday 3 August, the *New York Times* published a version of the story. Unencumbered by British law, their version was brief but accurate. Seizing on the fact that once it had been published abroad it was unlikely to be stopped in Britain, on Friday 6 August the *Guardian* reprinted the *New York Times* piece and, to all intents and purposes, the story was out. However, the Treasury Solicitor was not giving in that easily. The same evening, the BBC was told it could not run its programme and that the orig- inal High Court injunction would be applied against it. The BBC issued a statement that evening saying it had been investigating the story for many months. 'Some of the detail of the allegations was covered by an injunction which only the government or the courts had the power to lift,' it said. 'On Wednesday, in the light of foreign press disclosure of an assassination attempt, the BBC asked the government to lift the injunction so that the whole story could be told.' The Corporation said it was urgently considering the next step 'in the belief that the public interest now requires full examination of the allegations made by Mr Shayler'.[16]

The BBC also threatened to contest the original injunction in the courts. It had originally been granted as a short-term measure and had never been formally tested at a full hearing. Fearing the injunction might be removed by a judge and a rerun of the *Spycatcher* saga, the government decided to allow *Panorama* to reveal more details, although some were still suppressed. Finally, on the evening of Saturday 7 August, a week after Shayler's arrest, the *Panorama* special was broadcast.

Despite further denials of an 'official plot' by then Foreign Secretary Robin Cook on *Breakfast with Frost* on 9 August – he said Shayler's claims were 'pure fantasy' – the story continued to run. On 17 August the Libyan government announced that it had asked France to hand over Shayler. The demand came from Abdel Ati al-Obeidi, head of the Europe department of the Libyan foreign affairs ministry, and was made to the French Chargé d'Affaires in Tripoli. 'When receiving the French Chargé d'Affaires, Obeidi informed him about Libya's demand for the surrender of the British intelligence officer who is now in France or allowing Libyan judges to interrogate him according to legal ways agreed upon by both countries,' ran the Libyan official statement. The Libyan authorities also called on the British government to open an independent inquiry into Shayler's disclosures. They added that in December 1997 they had requested Britain to hand over four people who had committed terrorist acts and were being harboured in the United Kingdom. Obeidi said he had met with diplomats from Russia, China, Nigeria and Italy to tell them of Libyan government concerns.

Throughout the next two months, Libya continued to call for Shayler's extradition from France and at one point seemed poised to break off UN-brokered negotiations to hand over two intelligence officers accused by Scottish police of involvement in the Lockerbie PanAm bombing. The Libyans also asked to speak to former Foreign Secretary Malcolm Rifkind, the responsible minister at the time of the alleged assassination attempt.

On Wednesday 29 July 1998, Fielding received a message from former MI6 officer Richard Tomlinson. He didn't know it at the time, but Tomlinson had recently fled Britain three months after serving six months of a year's sentence for offences under the Official Secrets Act. In December 1997, he had pleaded guilty to breaking the Act by attempting to publish a book in Australia about his experiences in MI6. He was the first MI6 officer to be prosecuted for secrets offences since George Blake 36 years before. It was revealed at his trial that he had been in negotiation with Transworld Publishers in Sydney, and offered them a seven-page synopsis and a short preface outlining the first seven chapters of his proposed book. The synopsis contained details of 'training, operations, sources and methods', which Tomlinson had obtained from his four years in the agency. He had worked in Russia and Bosnia and had also infiltrated Iran's arms-supply network.

Tomlinson was dismissed from MI6 in August 1995. When he attempted to claim unfair dismissal through an industrial tribunal, the case was blocked by the then Foreign Secretary, Malcolm Rifkind. After his conviction in December 1997, he spent four months in Belmarsh top-security prison. He was released at the end of April 1998 and was on parole until the end of July that year.

He had decided to go to France after Special Branch officers called at his parents' house in Cumbria. Tomlinson told friends that he had hidden from the officers, fearing that he was going to be re-arrested. He travelled to Dover and caught a late-night ferry to Calais. Although he had no passport, he convinced French immigration officers of his identity by showing them his driving licence. They let him in.

By leaving the UK before his parole expired, albeit only by days, Tomlinson had committed a criminal act. Once in Paris, he booked into the two-star Britannia Hotel, near the Gare St Lazare, under his own name. Shortly afterwards, he sent faxes to his lawyer, John Wadham of Liberty, and to his MP, Kate Hoey, asking for their support. His intention was to obtain a New Zealand passport (he has dual nationality) and leave for that country as soon as possible.

He called Fielding because he wanted to be put in touch with David Shayler. Fielding passed the message to Shayler and by Thursday evening the two men had spoken. Tomlinson told Shayler he had broken his parole conditions and that he was now in Paris. Shayler agreed to meet him on Friday 31 August. He was due to come to Paris anyway to take part in a live broadcast on *Breakfast with Frost* that Sunday. Before he left for Paris, Shayler also had a call from a *Sunday Times* journalist, Nicholas Rufford, who wanted to speak to him about the Gaddafi story. It was unclear where he had heard about it. Rufford suggested that if Shayler and Tomlinson were to meet up in Paris, they should agree to be photographed – although a court order in force in Britain meant that no image of Tomlinson could be printed or broadcast in the UK.

On Friday morning, Fielding flew to Paris, met up with Shayler and Machon and took them to his hotel, the Golden Tulip. For the next 90 minutes Fielding and Shayler discussed the Libya assassination plot, which Shayler had first detailed to the reporter almost a year before.

Shayler and Machon left by taxi for their meeting with Tomlinson at 2 p.m. while Fielding filed his story to London. They arrived back at around 4.30 p.m. and said that Tomlinson had not appeared. Instead they had met two journalists from the *Sunday Times*, Nick Rufford and David Leppard, who had wanted details of the Libya story. When Tomlinson did not arrive, shortly after the meeting had begun Machon decided to leave the café in which they had met and call him at his hotel. Leppard left at the same time. When she got through, Tomlinson said he was willing to do the photograph, for which the *Sunday Times* would pay a fee, and urged her to persuade Shayler to do the same.

When Annie explained to Shayler what Tomlinson had said, he told the *Sunday Times* journalists that he would not agree to a photograph until he had spoken to the *Mail on Sunday*. Annie went back to the phone-box and rang Tomlinson's hotel. Her call was answered by the hotel receptionist, who told her that Tomlinson had just checked out. Leppard reappeared at this point and said he had been to Tomlinson's hotel. He had also been told he had checked out. 'Perhaps he's been lifted,' Machon joked.

In fact, that is precisely what had happened, although no one was to know it for a further 24 hours. As soon as he had put the phone down on Machon's call an armed team from the DST, the French Secret Service, had burst into his room, wrestled him to the ground – cracking his rib in the process – and taken him away.

When Tomlinson did not appear, the *Sunday Times* journalists offered to pay Shayler £300 for a brief talk and photos, and he was taken to a venue near the Eiffel Tower to pose, returning afterwards to the *Sunday Times* Paris office.

Shayler and Machon returned to Fielding's hotel where they discussed what might have happened to Tomlinson. It was clear that something was wrong.

The following morning, Saturday 1 August, Machon called Rufford to find out what was going on. He told her he expected to see Tomlinson that morning and that, if she wanted, she could come and collect the money he had promised to pay for the pictures. When she went to the *Sunday Times* office, Shayler stayed at the hotel.

At around midday Fielding began to have serious problems with his mobile telephone. Each time he made a call, he could hear someone at the other end, but they could not hear him. When he arrived back at the hotel, he found that he could not get into his room, which had a swipe-card entry system. The concierge could not explain it. The likelihood, he thought, was that someone had been in the room. From then on, there were constant difficulties with phones and it seems likely in retrospect that Fielding's calls were being monitored as the DST tried to locate Shayler and determine the best time to arrest him.

Unknown to Shayler, or anyone else outside the police and security services, the evening before, at 7.30 p.m., an arrest warrant had been issued by Mr Michael France, JP, at Horseferry Road Magistrates Court. According to the warrant, Shayler was wanted for two offences under section 1(1)(a) of the Official Secrets Act 1989, and the British authorities intended to seek his extradition. On Saturday 1 August at 6 p.m. London time, the arrest request was faxed via the National Criminal Intelligence Service to Interpol in France, but it was clear that the DST had been monitoring Shayler's movements for some time before the arrest occurred, and Special Branch officers had arrived in Paris on Friday night to liaise with their French counterparts.

At around 3 p.m. that afternoon, for example, Shayler spotted a small, scruffy man of Mediterranean appearance outside the hotel. He looked as if he was on surveillance duty and eventually turned up as one of the arrest team.

By this time, the *Mail on Sunday* in London had heard from the Treasury Solicitor that they would only be allowed to publish a much-truncated version of the Gaddafi story, which editor Jonathan Holborow would not accept. Fielding was asked to concentrate on putting together a story about Tomlinson and his apparent decision to go to New Zealand.

At around 5 p.m. Shayler said he was going out to a bar, Stolly's, just off the rue de Rivoli, to watch a football match on satellite TV featuring Middlesbrough. He left by taxi.

At 7.45 p.m. Shayler called Fielding from Stolly's to say he was on his way back and would be at the hotel in around 20 minutes. Middlesbrough had lost their match 1–0. The 20 minutes passed and at around 8.10 p.m. there was a knock on Fielding's door on the third floor of the hotel. Expecting it to be Shayler, he opened it. It was Annie Machon. She was clearly distressed and told him that three plain-clothes officers had come to her room and asked for Shayler's passport. She told them she did not have it and after further exchanges they had left telling her that Shayler had been arrested and that she could not see him.

The two of them rushed down to the lobby of the hotel where the desk manager told them that Shayler had just been led away by four or five men. Fielding filed his story of what had happened to Shayler immediately to London. The paper's front page was cleared and, anticipating that the story was hugely important, Jonathan Holborow released it to the Press Association, which put it out on the wire service within an hour. By the following morning it was the lead story in almost all the Sunday papers.

An hour later, Fielding learnt that Tomlinson had been arrested and released after 24 hours, but his priority was to find out what had happened to Shayler. Calls to French legal officials drew a blank. Worried that journalists would soon begin to arrive at the hotel, they packed up and moved out. The next morning he and Machon headed 200 miles south for the farmhouse at La Celle Dunoise. Machon wanted to collect Shayler's passport and clothing for them both. Surprisingly, the DST had not visited it, missing Shayler's computer which he had left behind.

As they set off back to Paris, Fielding's mobile rang with a recorded message his wife had left some hours before. His brother had been admitted to hospital where he had had an emergency operation, but had not been expected to survive Sunday night. He rang home to find that his brother was still alive, but very ill. There was no alternative but to head back to Paris and take a flight to London. Fielding called deputy news editor Ray Clancy, who arranged for a colleague, Sarah Oliver, to fly to Paris to meet Annie Machon.

Tomlinson resurfaced a week later in New Zealand. There, too, he was subject to injunctions, his room was searched and his computers were taken. On 7 August he was pulled off a plane as he tried to fly from New Zealand to Australia, where he had hoped to meet his brother, on the grounds that he did not have a visa. A few days later he returned to Geneva, Switzerland, and made headlines after a controversial documentary on the death of Diana, Princess of Wales, was shown on television. Tomlinson had visited the judge investigating her death, and claimed that Henri Paul, the chauffeur of the Mercedes that crashed killing the Princess and Dodi Fayed, had been in the pay of MI6. He also said that MI6 had previously developed a plan to kill Serbian leader Slobodan Milosevic in a tunnel, using bright lights to disorientate his driver – it sounded suspiciously like some of the more extravagant conspiracy theories being promoted by Dodi's father, Mohammed al-Fayed, to explain the deaths of his son and the Princess.

At the end of August, Tomlinson flew to America to appear on an NBC television show to discuss further his statements about Diana's death. He was arrested when he arrived at JFK Airport the day after the first anniversary of her death and deported to Switzerland. In a prepared statement a US Immigration Department spokesman said: 'Mr Tomlinson was applying to enter the US at JFK airport under a visa-waiver pilot programme, which permits certain foreign nationals to enter the US without a visa. Tomlinson was ineligible to enter the US under the waiver programme because he is a convicted felon, having served time in a British prison and subsequently having violated the terms of his parole this summer.'[17]

In a final twist to this story, had Tomlinson been allowed to enter the USA and appear on the NBC *Today* show, he would have flown back to Geneva on Swissair flight 211, which mysteriously exploded with the loss of all on board off the Canadian coast a day later.

A week after he was arrested, Shayler managed to get his first letter out to Annie. He described in detail the circumstances of his arrest:

Without a shadow of a doubt, the 24 hours at the depot in the bowels of the Palais de Justice were the worst of my life. The DST had arrested me in the hotel lobby when I was soaking wet. They took me to the police HQ, where I'd been before on MI5 business, would you believe? After a bit, I was laughing and joking with them and they gave me coffee and cigarettes, while they filled in the forms. When they first arrested me I thought they were terrorists trying to abduct me.

But the depot was terrible. I spent the night in a cell with two others. It was about 12 x 6 ft with a triple level bunk-bed arrangement and a hole in the ground to shit in. In addition, as I was last in, I had the top bunk under a 100W light bulb (protected from vandalism by three inches of Perspex). Needless to say, I didn't get any sleep at all. The next day I was brought before the judge who said she would get me a lawyer. I was then returned to the cells, where I languished until 10 in the evening. I had no watch, there was no window and there was nothing to do – can you imagine it? After just a few hours I was about ready to confess to anything, give up the ghost and submit myself to the UK authorities.

By the time I got to prison, I was relieved to find I wasn't sharing a cell with some of the psychopaths they drove me to La Santé with. I was glad to find a comfortable cell. The only problem was that I couldn't figure out how to turn off the light. The switch is outside the cell, but the others here showed me how to tie my laces to the switch and feed them into the cell so I can now turn it on when I want to.

My fellow incarcerates have been brilliant. They saw me on telly on Sunday before my arrival and since then, they've done everything to help me. The food here is bollocks but they do have a paid-for choice, which I've ordered and begins as of Monday. One bloke here is a fan of *The Prisoner* (not Blocko, but the cult series) and he has dubbed me 'Numéro 7'. By the way, my French has come on in leaps and bounds. I'm bloody brilliant now so no excuses in future, I'll book the glazier. Before I forget, I need a good French–English dictionary for those little words. I saw Liverpool v Inter on Eurosport the other night and then *Game On* was on. It was the one where Matthew wakes up in Mandy's bed in her panties. You remember it? I looked for the year and it was made in 1994, when our relationship was in its infancy.

I've just filled in my order for scram (food), sports gear, toiletries, stationery and mags. Trouble is, I won't get them until Monday 17 August. That's the trouble with this place, you're always waiting around for someone to open a door or to bring some grub or cigarettes or whatever. It's a pain in the arse.

Love Dave.[18]

Shayler had arrived at Santé. It had come as an unpleasant surprise. While he had been held at the depot, he had assumed that a lawyer would visit and advise him on his legal position. Instead he was taken to prison. Maître Anne-Sophie Lévy, the lawyer who had taken up his case in France, had spoken to a judge who claimed to know nothing of Shayler or his whereabouts.

Despite numerous requests from Annie, for the first six weeks of his imprisonment Shayler was allowed visits only from his lawyer, John Wadham, from a social worker and on one occasion from a British consular official. Wadham had to go to the Palais de Justice in Paris where he met Monsieur de Sariac, deputy chief of lawyers, who authenticated his Law Society credentials and wrote a letter to the prosecutor's department, who in turn issued him with a licence to visit Shayler.

Shayler was initially held under article 145.4 of the French Code of Criminal Procedure, which allowed him to be kept in isolation for up to ten days. A court might then approve a further ten days' isolation. 'My conclusion is that the French authorities assumed or were told that David should not be allowed to see his family,' said Wadham at the time. 'The British deny this and I have asked them to ask the French to allow David all the rights and privileges he would have had if he were detained in Britain.'[19] The Home Office denied that it had asked French prosecutors to take a tough line.

When Wadham left after his first visit he issued a statement from Shayler – now prisoner No. 269151F – which became his credo:

I am in prison for telling the truth. The matters that I have brought to the attention of the public are vital issues for our democracy. I should be protected, not prosecuted. Rather than suppressing whistleblowers, the government should set up an independent body to investigate these claims.

There should be a truly independent mechanism to investigate these disclosures. MI5 and MI6 should not be able to hide behind the secrecy legislation. If agents were paid for an assassination attempt that resulted in the murder of innocent people, those who paid them are the real criminals. If Libya had an extradition treaty with the UK they would be sent to Libya to stand trial for murder.

Presumably other people in MI5 and MI6 know the details of this story and they should now examine their consciences. It is clear that MI6 is acting outside government control. The government is too naïve in accepting one version of the story on trust

from MI6. The government has had a year to take action. Why
was it that just after the *Mail on Sunday* submitted the Libyan
story to the government for approval I was arrested? I find it
astonishing that the government has decided to prosecute me.[20]

Within days of Shayler going to prison, his brothers took on the job
of turning the tentative website into a reality. By the end of August,
it was up and running and carried details of his case, newspaper articles and letters of support. After three months on-line it had been
visited by more than 30,000 people, many of whom left messages in
the on-line guestbook and 85 per cent of whom were in support.
The rest were either insults or (a tiny number) rational defences of
the government's position. By the end of 1998, 55,000 people had
visited the site.

Shayler thought he would be in prison for only a few days before
a bail hearing. Apart from seeing a judge on the morning after his
arrest, it was two months before he had a chance to make an application for bail. When he did, it was refused.

In London, Wadham applied for legal aid to help fight the extradition case in England and to work closely with the Paris lawyers to
ensure that Shayler's interests were protected. Bow Street magistrates
refused even to consider the application on the grounds that there
were 'no proceedings' in England. Believing the decision to be unlawful, Wadham decided to challenge it with a judicial review in the High
Court. The hearing took place on 2 October, a few days before Shayler
was due to appear at the Palais de Justice to tell the French court that
he did not consent to extradition and that his lawyers were going to
fight the case. It ended in failure, with the High Court upholding the
earlier decision. Shayler's French lawyers, Anne-Sophie Lévy and
William Bourdon, took the case on an expenses-only basis, and most
of their costs were eventually paid by the *Mail on Sunday*.

As the weeks passed, Machon worked tirelessly to publicise
Shayler's case, speaking at public meetings and appearing on TV
and radio to keep up the pressure. She was now living in a rented
apartment in Paris, which enabled her to visit him regularly and
take him in the 'extras' that prisoners in France are allowed. She
was able to pay money into an account at the prison, which he
could use to buy paper, toiletries and magazines. Shayler kept up
a lively correspondence, writing to newspapers and emphasising
that he was being persecuted even though he had told the truth

about what he considered to be serious abuses in the way MI5 and MI6 were run.

While in Santé, he received over 300 letters of support. They came in three waves: first, *Guardian* readers, after his address was published in that paper; second, Middlesbrough fans; third, supporters of Liberty, who read about his case in their newsletter.

Football fans at Middlesbrough – where Shayler had a season ticket – heard about the case in their fanzine *Fly Me to the Moon*. 'During David's year in exile, the thing that he missed the most (apart from friends and family) was, without doubt, the Boro. He even renewed his season ticket in the hope that at some time during the season this would all have been sorted out in his favour and he would have been able to get to the Riverside,' wrote his brother, Phil.[21] Shayler even managed to get a piece about Boro published in the popular magazine *FourFourTwo*. 'It spoke volumes that MI5 played MI6 at cricket and rugby, but not at football,' he wrote.[22]

The fans reciprocated. After his release a Boro fan, butcher Martin Blackwell, flew over to Paris bringing with him one of his famous pies, with '007' baked into the crust. 'We saw him released from prison in his Boro shirt and thought that he couldn't be such a bad chap,' Mr Blackwell told his local paper. 'One thing led to another and we decided the British spy would be missing some great British pies.'[23]

He certainly was missing his freedom.

On the Eiffel Tower there is a huge clock counting down towards the Millennium. The day I was arrested, I remember, it was 518 days to go. When I came out it stood at 408 days. One hundred and ten wasted days. My dread was that I would be in prison for the Millennium. I was in the section of the prison reserved for what the French call '*fonctionnaires*', mostly former government employees. They included Algerian and Corsican terrorists and a few ex-cops. One of the ex-cops had been a leading light in the French National Front, an extreme right-wing organisation. He was in for armed robbery. He told me he had done undercover work for the French intelligence service in Tahiti. He was a big fan of the TV series *The Prisoner*, and he used to call me 'Numéro Sept'. I suppose he considered himself to be Number Six.

Another cop in there had killed his wife. Then there was a French Army officer, Pierre Bunel, who had passed Nato secrets to the Serbs. I was the only Englishman, as far as I know. They used to call me '*Perfide* Albion' as a kind of joke. None of them could understand why I was in prison.[24]

Shayler did not find it easy to settle into the prison routine. The refusal to allow him visitors for the first six or seven weeks of his imprisonment had one immediate consequence: 'The only way you get your washing done is to give it to your visitors,' he explained. 'As no one was allowed to come and see me, I had to wash everything by hand in my cell in cold water.' He began to use the small exercise room in the prison and found himself spending three hours a day on the rowing machine and weights. Gradually, as his French improved, his fellow prisoners began to talk to him.

They picked up on the fact – hard to miss, really – that I am a Middlesbrough fan. They all knew Gazza and that's what they started calling me. I was invited to take part in their card games – mostly playing a game called Tarot, which is played with a standard pack plus 21 Tarot cards. It's very addictive and by the end of my time there I was playing every moment I could. I think that to start with some of them were suspicious of me, because of my background, but it didn't last very long.

One person who tried very hard to talk to me was the terrorist Carlos the Jackal. He has been held in an isolation cell in Santé for several years without any contact with anyone, but his cell overlooked our exercise yard and not long after I arrived, even though he could not see us, he began shouting out my name when I was walking into the yard. He was asking about the Libyan story, about Gaddafi. He wanted to know who the British contacts were, all that kind of stuff. For days he was shouting out the window. To be honest, it frightened me. I refused to reply to his calls and told people to say I was not in the yard. It stopped after a while, so I suppose he must have given up. It seems bizarre to me that the only reason I was in a position that someone like Carlos the Jackal – the world's most infamous terrorist – could get in contact with me was because of the action of the British government.

In my own section of the prison there was another spy, a French Algerian, also in on terrorism charges. He too tried to get close to me. I don't know if he had any agenda, but all these things had to be considered.[25]

Shayler had more reasons than most not to spend too much time in the Santé Prison.

Ten days after his arrest he wrote an open letter to MI5 director-general Stephen Lander. 'So you finally have me where you want me – locked up, virtually silenced and denied the rights normally granted to prisoners in the French penal system, visitors and a word-processor,' he began bitterly.[26]

As I sit here in my prison cell, I can't help feeling that my only mistake was being too open with you. After two government bodies refused to take my evidence, including the details of the Gaddafi plot, I told you I intended to put my disclosures on the Internet. I didn't want to do this but I couldn't see how else I could encourage you to take that evidence . . . My prosecution and persecution serve nobody's interests, least of all yours. You would be better off using this situation as an opportunity to demonstrate to the public that you can be reasonable, respons-ible and capable of good judgement. So stop your prosecution of me and reform the Official Secrets Act.[27]

His appeal fell on deaf ears.

The full hearing of the case in Paris was scheduled for 21 October 1988. As the day approached it became clear that it would turn on whether or not the offences against the Official Secrets Act would also be considered offences in France. Shayler's lawyers planned to argue that his arrest was contrary to international human-rights law. David Feldman, dean of the Faculty of Law and Barber Professor of Jurisprudence at the University of Birmingham, was commissioned to explore the compatibility of Section 1 of the Official Secrets Act with international law. He argued that the wide-ranging nature of Section 1, which bans communication of any information about the Security Service, not just information damaging in itself to national security, cut across Shayler's human rights. He also argued that the Act violated Shayler's human rights under Article 13 of the European Convention of Human Rights in that it gave him no effective remedy.

'I conclude that the provisions of Section 1 of the Official Secrets Act 1989, both generally and in their application to the case of Mr Shayler, violate Mr Shayler's rights under Articles 10 and 13 of the European Convention on Human Rights and under Article 19 of the International Covenant on Civil and Political Rights.'[28]

Shortly before the hearing, the thrust of the British government's extradition case began to unfold. They argued that Shayler should be brought back to England and prosecuted, primarily because he had passed documents to Nick Fielding and Mark Hollingsworth, even though the documents had never been disclosed, had been kept in a safe and handed back to the government on Shayler's own instructions.

> This shows real cowardice on the part of the government [said Shayler in a statement released from prison on the day of his trial]. If they really believe I should not have made my disclosures in the press, they should prosecute me for those. Nevertheless, I have nothing to fear from the trial. I showed documents to journalists because I wanted to convince them that I worked for MI5, to prove the allegations that I was making and for their assessment of what was in the public interest. The documents were kept safe and then handed back to the government. Without that proof, the stories about MI5 malpractice might never have been told.[29]

Wadham backed Shayler's statement. He said, 'The government are using a tactical ruse to try to convict David without confronting the real issues. The disclosures in the media caused no damage. I challenge the government to put David on trial for what was reported in the media. This ruse is only possible because the Official Secrets Act is so draconian. When the Act was going through Parliament the current Prime Minister, Home Secretary, Attorney General and others in Cabinet and government voted against it for this very reason, yet they are still happy to use it.'[30]

The main affidavit backing the government's extradition claim came from Detective Superintendent Martin Morrissey of the Special Branch, who had been in charge of Operation Oscillate from the outset. He outlined Shayler's MI5 career, then the circumstances surrounding Shayler's first series of disclosures in the *Mail on Sunday* in August 1997. He said one article – 'The Case That Made

Me Quit' – might have contained material 'which could have been drawn from the classified documents disclosed to the newspaper by Mr Shayler'. As for the other articles, he said, 'It is assessed that these disclosures would not cause serious damage to the work of the Security Service or national security.'[31]

In fact, Morrissey's statement was incorrect. Nothing in the article he mentioned had been drawn from any of the documents Shayler left at the *Mail on Sunday*.

At the Palais de Justice, in the packed Première Chambre d'Accusation, Shayler's lawyers made impassioned speeches on behalf of their client. They argued that no damage had been done by his revelations, that his arrest was politically motivated and had been timed to stop publication of his allegations concerning the plot to kill Colonel Gaddaf. They added that Section 1 of the Official Secrets Act was political and contravention of it was essentially politically motivated, as was the prosecution of those who violate it. It was a crime against the state in its purest form.

They also argued that, if the case was so serious, why had government lawyers spent months trying to negotiate with Shayler and why had the deal included the possibility that he would not be prosecuted in exchange for copyright over anything he ever wrote? They cited Professor Feldman's expert opinion to the court that the Official Secrets Act violated the freedom of expression in the European Convention on Human Rights. Bourdon noted that under Article 5.2 of the law of 10 March 1927, someone could not be extradited if the alleged crime was political or if extradition was demanded as a political goal. He also told the court that the British authorities had known for many months where Shayler had been living in France yet had made no attempt to extradite him. Why had they chosen that moment? It could only have been because of the impending revelations about Gaddafi and was therefore clearly a politically motivated action.

Shayler, who throughout the hearing was in a dock behind glass in a corner of the courtroom, was clearly stressed by the whole procedure. At one point he was asked to make a statement, which he did, in French. The hearing was over in less than half an hour and soon he was back in prison. The court said it would give its decision in a month, on 18 November.

Nearly two weeks later, as Shayler waited in the Santé prison, unsure of his fate, the House of Commons was making history. On

2 November it conducted its first debate on the Intelligence and Security Committee, which had produced its third annual report during the summer. Both the report and the debate are remarkable for one simple fact: despite the acres of newsprint devoted to the affair and hours of television debate, neither mentioned David Shayler. He had alleged that senior members of the present government had been bugged, that MI5 was keeping files on them, mounting invasive surveillance operations and conducting other activities beyond the control of Parliament. His allegations had caused a major sensation that had hardly been out of the news for a year, yet MPs could not bring themselves to mention his name.

The Intelligence and Security Committee had been appointed in July 1997, had met on 30 occasions and had taken witness statements from 26 people including the Foreign and Home Secretaries, the heads of MI5, MI6 and GCHQ and their staff, and had certainly discussed Shayler on several occasions. Yet the committee members – Tom King, Lord Archer of Sandwell, Kevin Barron, Alan Beith, Dale Campbell-Savours, Yvette Cooper, Barry Jones, Michael Mates and Allan Rogers – had refused to accept evidence from him even though he was the most important whistleblower ever to come out of the security and intelligence community.

Many of the issues they had discussed – the vetting of MI5 staff, the retention and destruction of files, recruitment, dealing with problem cases and developing oversight – had been raised by Shayler in great detail. In retrospect, their refusal to take his evidence can only be seen as a monumental failure of the committee and evidence of its lack of independence from the intelligence community.

The debate on 2 November was similar. Then Foreign Secretary Robin Cook set the tone. Not so long ago, he said, no government would even recognise the existence of MI6 and it would have been inconceivable that Parliament should debate its functions. Even the location of the MI5 and MI6 headquarters had been protected information. 'It is perhaps a measure of the new openness that, when I last visited those headquarters,' said Mr Cook with pride, 'I noticed that the nearest bistro has been named "Miss Moneypenny's" – which is an interesting case of fiction invading real life.'

The closest Cook could bring himself to mentioning Shayler (and Tomlinson) was when he said: 'The members of the committee are familiar with the difficulties caused to SIS and the Security Service by former members of staff who present a cocktail of fact and fiction as a portrait of the work of the services. Considerable investment has been made to reduce the possibility of such cases in future by improving the vetting and recruitment procedures and strengthening the monitoring of staff in post.'[32] This from someone who, in the Sandline fiasco, when a British mercenary company claimed it had government agreement to break a UN arms embargo covering Sierra Leone, had been badly served by his own MI6 staff.

The committee chairman, Tom King, weighed in: 'People have breached their contracts and the Official Secrets Act in return for money. Staff have become disaffected because of grievances of one sort or another. The Foreign Secretary referred to two recent cases. People may, or may not, have been seeking payments from national newspapers for information or hearsay.'

The committee had not been interested in individual cases, said King. It was important that there was an internal method of identifying problems and dealing with them. 'That is why the report deals with recruitment, as care must be taken to ensure that people are suitable for employment in the agencies in the first place.'[33] To King's way of thinking, it was not important that a former MI5 officer had alleged an assassination attempt against the head of state of another country, or that MI5 had had a warning about the Israeli embassy bomb, or that the handling of files at MI5 was out of control or that a journalist on a national newspaper had been subject to outrageous surveillance and intrusion into her private life. No, the problem was that 'unsuitable' people were somehow working in the intelligence services, people who would not hold their tongue when they saw things happening that were not compatible with democracy.

King and the committee's only concessions were to accept the need for security staff to have access to an industrial tribunal if they felt they had been unfairly dismissed, and that the committee itself should have an investigative arm: 'We shall not be able to help matters unless we can say that we have investigated the allegations, with full access to all the relevant information, and that we are satisfied either that a charge needs to be answered or that the charge is merely malicious and unfounded. Then we can speak with the unanimous, all-party voice of our committee, which will carry the authority that the agencies are entitled to expect.'[34]

Committee member Allan Rogers was more realistic: 'We have a question-and-answer system and we can investigate, but if the agencies hide behind reasons of national security or endangering the lives of agents in operations, we have to accept that and go no further. In that sense, we cannot perform our task of oversight properly, but the system is evolving and slowly moving forward.'[35] However, Rogers, in an oblique reference to Shayler, referred to 'chequebook treason'. 'If the individual to whom I have referred had wanted to speak purely for the love of country, there are mechanisms by which he could have done so,' he said, while at the same time acknowledging that such mechanisms that existed were in need of a major overhaul.

Perhaps MPs had been warned not to speak about Shayler, but the debate proved conclusively what a dramatic impact he had had on security policy. He was like Banquo's ghost, ever present in the debate, but unacknowledged.

The few remaining days before the Paris court's final adjudication passed uneventfully. Shayler was unsure of what the outcome would be. The consensus in Britain was that it was an open and shut case: he would be back in Britain before Christmas, with the trial set for April or May. It was unlikely he would be allowed bail, so would probably spend time at Belmarsh high-security prison in south-east London. Annie Machon had already begun to think about where she could live to be near the prison.

Wednesday 18 November was bitterly cold in Paris. From 10.30 a.m. Machon, with Phil and Jem Shayler, waited outside the Palais de Justice to try to catch a glimpse of Shayler as he was brought in from prison but missed him. By 2 p.m., when the court was due to convene, a large crowd of reporters had gathered outside. Even the French press had become interested in the case and Shayler's face was recognisable to many French people.

When the court doors opened there was a scramble as people rushed for seats. But even before most had found one, the hearing was over. Madame Ponroy, president of the court, Madame Foulon and Monsieur Buisson, the two court counsellors, had hardly finished speaking when the court erupted. 'You are free,' Madame Arari, the court-appointed translator whispered to Shayler, as he stood in the glass-bound dock. Bemused as a court official asked him his name, age, place of birth, he had missed the single sentence that had come from Madame Ponroy.

Few of the journalists in court that day had believed Shayler would win his case. He himself had had mixed feelings. That morning, he had been unwilling to pack his bags, yet neither did he want to leave his cell untouched, as if it was just another day. Instead he opted to tidy it, knowing that if things went his way he could quickly gather up his few belongings.

Later that morning, at the Palais de Justice, he had been taken out of the prison van, handcuffed, and led through the bowels of the building on a chain. It brought back bad memories of the 24 hours he had spent in the holding cells there following his arrest by the DST. 'That first night was terrible,' he told Fielding later. 'I was put into a filthy shared cell. My requests for a lawyer had been laughed at. I had been arrested without having a chance to speak to Annie and the French secret police gave me the impression they had been told I was passing secrets to terrorists. I was fingerprinted, photographed, searched and asked my height. That was embarrassing, because I only knew it in feet and inches. They must have thought I was stupid.'[36]

Now he was back for a second time. As he sat in the 'mouse cage', the tiny wire cells used to hold prisoners awaiting an appearance in court, he reflected on the time he had spent in prison. It had been a strange experience for a grammar-school boy used to tracking international terrorists and criminals.

As the seconds ticked by towards the hearing, he thought of the consequences of being extradited: 'The irony is that even if I had been extradited and then found guilty at trial in Britain, the maximum sentence for my alleged offence is two years. By that time I would have served almost half of that and would have been due for almost immediate release. What would the government have done then? I would have served my time and could have left the country and said what I liked. It surely makes much more sense for the government to come to an agreement with me. I had hundreds of letters from people while I was in prison. Many of them could not understand how this government, which pledged itself to reform of the Official Secrets Act, could act in the way it has done.

'What happened to people like Jack Straw and Tony Blair when they went into government? I thought they were strong supporters of open government. Why do they slavishly follow the line given to them by the Security Service? Why has there never been an inquiry into any of the allegations I have made. No one has officially denied them, but they won't call anyone to account. Allegations about me are fed to the press, who repeat them without checking the facts. But

I stand by everything I have said. Why should I lie? And now look at the mess they have got themselves into. I understand that this is the first time for 50 years that the French have refused to extradite someone to the UK.'[37]

Shayler was right. The court had made a landmark decision. Madame Ponroy's judgement noted that the extradition arrangements between Britain and France were governed by the 1957 European Extradition Convention. According to this law, she stated, extradition cannot be considered for political offences. Similar points apply in relation to France's own 1927 law on extradition. She also made the point that criticism of the function of state organisations, in French law, was clearly a political action. Having judged that Shayler's offence in criticising the Security Service was political, it followed under Article 3 of the European Extradition Convention that Shayler could not be extradited. It was as simple as that. 'The court's decision is unequivocal,' Shayler later told Fielding. 'It says that Britain's attempt to extradite me fails because the nature of what I did is political. You cannot be extradited from France for political offences. The full impact of this decision has yet to become apparent. It has driven a coach and horses through Britain's secrecy laws and I am sure that the law will now have to be changed. No one has ever challenged the Official Secrets Act from abroad before and now, on its first test, it has collapsed.'[38]

As the translator's words sank in, David Shayler was visibly shaken. The weight of the months inside Santé fell from his shoulders. Outside the courtroom, as he waited to be taken back to prison to collect his belongings, word had begun to circulate. 'The police officer asked me about the case. Then he opened the cage door and offered me a cigarette. It was very human. Back on the wing there was jubilation. "You should never have been here," they said. They were right and so was the court.'[39]

Later that afternoon, outside Santé prison, Shayler eventually emerged, with his belongings in two cardboard boxes, at around 4.30 p.m. to be greeted by his brothers. Annie was waiting nearby in a car and within minutes they were on their way to the Hôtel Raphael near the Arc de Triomphe for a celebration. Later John Wadham arrived, to be followed by Shayler's French lawyers William Bourdon and Anne-Sophie Lévy.

The following days were spent at a small hotel near Chartres as Shayler began to unwind and talk through his prison experience. He was still very nervous, unsure of his freedom and fearful of another spell in prison. His legal position was uncertain. He had defied the threat of extradition, but he could still be deported – a political decision that could be made without reference to the courts.

Shayler still had plenty to say, but was guarded and unwilling to take further risks with his liberty. 'Before I went to prison I had a place to stay in France. I thought I was beyond the reach of MI5 here. It was a beautiful French farmhouse out in the sticks. But now there is no way I can go back there. I would be at risk from anyone who wanted to have a go at me. And leaving France makes me a target for arrest on behalf of the British authorities. They have a warrant for my arrest anywhere in Europe. What can stop them? It is getting to the point of persecution. I won the court case, yet they continue to haunt me. And what can I say about what I know? Nothing. My words could put me back behind bars. I am trapped. The more time goes by the more frustrating it will be.'[40]

One particular incident brought home to Fielding just how much the whole experience had affected both Shayler and Machon. As they sat talking at the hotel, Shayler tried to make an outgoing call, but even as he was waiting for an outside line, he began to panic, although it was nothing more than an innocuous mistake by the operator.

Only a few seconds later, Machon came into the room, saying she had seen someone she did not recognise outside one of the rooms. This, too, was easily explained, but the effect on Shayler was dramatic. 'It took me straight back to the day I was arrested,' he said. 'I now know I was being watched before they took me in. Then, too, I had problems with the phones and strangers watching our hotel. For a moment there I was back down again. I felt I was producing samizdat literature in the old Soviet Union. Any moment they could burst in and take me away. It was terrifying.'[41]

Shayler knew that in some ways he was still a prisoner. 'I have very little money, nowhere to live and I am on strict warning to be extremely cautious in what I say. It is almost like starting all over again. I still feel extreme anger and frustration about what happened to me, but have very few avenues through which I can express it. I spent four months in prison for telling the truth about the failures of the British intelligence services. I may be bloodied, but I am certainly unbowed. Britain has been shown up in front of the rest of Europe by this week's decision and I feel it has been a complete vindication of everything I have done so far.'[42]

Just how much danger Shayler was in became evident a week later, after he and Machon had moved into a small, rented apartment in Paris. That week he received a fax from the BBC Arabic Service requesting an interview. It came from an ex-journalist, who said his name was Souhail Rasheed. In the same week, Anne-Sophie Lévy, Shayler's French lawyer, received a number of calls from the same person offering him £50,000 to do a television interview. Shayler and his lawyer discussed the political sensitivities of giving an interview to an Arab journalist, but decided that there was little anyone could do about it as long as he made no new disclosures. Shayler called Rasheed on a French mobile number and agreed to meet him in the Café Beaubourg in Paris at 4 p.m. on Thursday 25 November 1998.

Shayler and Machon arrived at the meeting about ten minutes early and sat in a corner. A waiter approached them and said that Rasheed was waiting for them on the first floor. In fact, he was sitting just by the spiral staircase, with an excellent view of both entrances to the café. 'I remember thinking at the time that if I had been an intelligence officer waiting to meet a target, I would have chosen the same position,' said Shayler. Rasheed, in his 50s, was wearing little round tortoiseshell-rimmed glasses, was grey and balding and sported a pointed beard that barely covered his chin. His look was completed by a pipe, which he constantly relit.

As soon as the waiter had taken the order, Rasheed told the couple he wasn't going to beat about the bush. He declared he was 'a representative of the Libyan intelligence services' and was licensed to carry a firearm. As he announced this he patted a large bulge just below his armpit. As he spoke, slowly and deliberately, he kept sparking up his lighter. Rasheed said that the Libyans wanted Shayler to go to Tripoli because he had information they wanted. In return, Shayler could name his price. At one point, when Shayler looked as if he was wavering, he added, 'We are talking millions of pounds. We have bank accounts already set up in Switzerland for this sort of thing.'

Shayler was not wavering. He was just too scared to say no. He wondered if the lighter was a recording device. Rasheed, perhaps worried that he had frightened Shayler, backtracked. If Shayler went to Libya, he said, it would only be to meet Colonel Gaddafi for tea. He could give his evidence about the assassination plot and Lockerbie in writing. And the Libyans would, of course, help him to get a book published. Thinking he could tread a fine line between outright treachery and helping the Libyan authorities with their inquiries into the Gaddafi plot, Shayler discussed the possibility of giving some sort of statement, but without leaving France.

Rasheed said that any book deal or payment was dependent on his going to Libya. 'Don't worry,' he said. 'No one there thinks you were involved in the plot.' They wanted him in Libya to answer questions – not as a witness but as a co-conspirator. Shayler told him he had had nothing to do with the plot, other than being briefed on what was happening: 'For a second or two,' he said later, 'I left the conversation and let my mind follow all this through to its logical conclusion, which was torture, show trials and execution. The cynical might think I am over-dramatising the situation, but, remember, I've studied these people. I spent two years reading about atrocities committed by the regime that would have embarrassed medieval despots. There was no way I was going to Libya. Of that I was sure.'[43]

Rasheed, although he could sense Shayler's unease, ploughed on. He switched tack. He asked if Shayler would be prepared to give a statement about the Gaddafi plot to a lawyer in Paris. Shayler said he would have to consult his own lawyer first. Rasheed switched to Lockerbie. He began to spin theories about where the real responsibility lay, suggesting other Arab countries. Shayler smiled limply, hoping that the meeting would soon end. Of course, continued Rasheed, if he could prove that Libya was not responsible for the attack, he would also be handsomely rewarded. Shayler remained silent.

Eventually Shayler agreed to get back to Rasheed within a week, although he had no intention of doing so. When asked for contact numbers, Shayler said he didn't have any because he was in the process of moving to a new flat. 'Don't you have a mobile?' said Rasheed. Shayler tried to show no fear. That morning he had bought a no-subscription, no-bills mobile phone at a shop not far from the new flat. Did they have him under surveillance? No, he said. Instead he gave him an e-mail address, although the account had been closed while Shayler was in prison.

Before Rasheed left, Shayler managed to get him talking. He said he was a Jordanian by birth but had become a naturalised French citizen. With that, Shayler and Machon got up, shook hands with him and left.

It was only when they came out of the Café Beaubourg that Shayler realised they had been in there for 51 minutes. They talked casually, trying not to look worried, and agreed not to return directly to their flat. They walked towards Les Halles, in the opposite direction to the flat, then turned towards Place de Châtelet, thinking they were probably being followed. Shayler had to make a call from a phone-box on an unrelated matter, and as he did so, Machon crossed the road to see if anyone was following them. An Arab stopped, looked across at the phone box Shayler was using, paused, then went on his way. A couple of others hung around the square for no apparent reason.

Shayler and Machon decided to find a café and sit down to analyse what had just happened. First they had to put some distance between themselves and those they suspected were following them. They headed up avenue Victoria, then turned right into rue des Lavandières. As they turned, they both glanced behind them. One of the Arabs had moved off in their direction and was using a mobile phone. The couple scurried towards rue de Rivoli, doubled back on themselves a couple of times and eventually found a café where they thought they would be safe.

They sat and drank kir for an hour or so, trying to calm down, but viewing everyone who came into the café with suspicion. They did the same in each café they entered that night until, nervous and exhausted, they decided to stay the night at the Septième Arts Hôtel – which they had used regularly in the past – rather than return to the flat and risk blowing its location to the Libyans.

As soon as they could, they called John Wadham, who came over to meet them the following Friday, 2 December. On the Wednesday before Wadham arrived, Shayler wondered if Rasheed would attempt to contact them again, now that the week was up. That night, about midnight, the door buzzer sounded in the flat. As only one other person knew where they were living at the time, the couple froze. Not even the letting agency knew they were David Shayler and Annie Machon. The paperwork had been made out in the names of David and Anna de Carteret. Was it drunks? It buzzed again. They turned off the TV and the lights, even though they weren't visible from downstairs. The buzzer sounded a third time, but on this occasion whoever it was just left their finger on the button for around 30 seconds. Shayler and Machon cowered in the flat. At about 1 a.m. the same thing happened again, just as they were dropping off to sleep. And again at 8 a.m. and then again an hour later.

When they met Wadham the following day, it was agreed that Shayler should inform MI5 of what had happened. Officers and former officers alike have a duty to report approaches from foreign intelligence services. Wadham called the press liaison officer at MI5, while Shayler and Machon listened. MI5 said it was none of their concern until Wadham pointed out that the couple were simply following Service guidelines. The press liaison officer spoke to Stephen Lander, then called back. They had agreed it was a matter for the French intelligence services. Wadham pointed out that it was a threat to national security as Shayler had details that the Libyans clearly wanted, including the names of agents in Libya who worked for MI5 and MI6.

Nothing was heard for two weeks, when Wadham phoned to say that MI5 wished to pass on an 'unconfirmed rumour' that the Libyans wanted to kidnap Shayler in connection with the 'so-called Gaddafi plot'. Shayler was told that MI5 were doing nothing about this threat, but if he were to return to the UK he could rely on the protection of the authorities. Otherwise he was on his own. Wadham says he asked MI5 to pass on the information to the French authorities, which they reluctantly agreed to do. To be sure that this happened, Shayler's French lawyer, William Bourdon, also phoned the DST. They said it was a problem for the British. Bourdon then wrote formally to the DST.

A week later, the press liaison office at MI5 phoned Wadham again with similar information. Again, MI5 stated it could do nothing to help.

For the next three years Shayler remained a spy left out in the cold. The parliamentary Intelligence and Security Committee refused to even discuss his allegations, although they represented the biggest intelligence scandal for over a decade. MI5 and the government also chose to ignore them and instead threatened the whistlebloer with criminal prosecution. The security establishment hoped that Shayler would disappear into frozen isolation and be silenced and marginalised as a lone discredited voice in the wilderness.

In fact, the reverse occurred. The inevitable consequence of the legal harassment and absence of an inquiry was embarassing new revelations about the Gaddafi plot, avoidable IRA atrocities and the bombing of the Israeli embassy. Most damaging of all was an interview by a second former MI5 officer, Jestyn Thirkell-White, to the authors. He spoke out because of the absence of any independent inquiry into Shayler's claims. He also objected to the harassment of his former colleague's supporters. 'MI5 and Special Branch were acting like the very police state they are supposed to be protecting us from,' he said. An MI5 officer from 1991 until 1996, the modest, carefully-spoken Thirkell-White corroborated many of the allegations of mismanagement and bungling of operations made by Shayler. And, crucially, he concluded: 'I do not accept Jack Straw's statements that Shayler's revelations have in any way damaged national security.'

Allied to the new disclosures, Shayler became more prominent and vocal than ever through the media and addressing public meetings. He even appeared in a link-up to Paris on the popular satirical TV show *Have I Got News for You?* His relentless campaign, expertly marshalled by Annie Machon and with substantial report from Liberty director John Wadham, resulted in the government making significant concessions. The most dramatic was the Attorney General's decision not to oppose bail when Shayler returned to the UK on 21 August 2000.

On his home-coming, Shayler declared that he intended 'to challenge the cover-ups and complacency that have followed my disclosures'. As soon as he arrived at Dover on the ferry, he was charged and bailed under the Official Secrets Act.

The charges against the whistleblower were notable for being restricted to his original disclosures in the *Mail on Sunday* in 1997 about secret files on politicians and operations about Libyan intelligence activities in the UK. The more serious allegations on how MI5 negligence failed to prevent several IRA bombings on the mainland, the Israeli embassy in London and how MI6 financed a plot to assassinate Colonel Gaddafi were ignored by the prosecution.

Before his trial, the insidious nature of the Intelligence establishment was starkly exposed when Dame Stella Rimington, head of MI5 throughout Shayler's service, sought to publish her memoirs. 'I have always wanted to bring some daylight into the workings of the secret state,' she told the BBC's Michael Cockerell for his documentary *The Spying Dame*. Rimington was not prepared for the backlash. After submitting her book for government vetting, she was summoned by Sir Richard Wilson, the Cabinet secretary, and given what she called 'a polite bollocking – mostly polite but sometimes pretty sharp.' He told her that 'anything' said by a former head of MI5 – however, apparently innocuous – could be useful to enemies of the state.

The the dirty tricks started. Her draft manuscript was leaked to the *Sun* in order to destabilise and discourage her publisher. Stories from anonymous official sources suddenly appeared in the press with damaging allegations about her private life and professional competence. Like Shayler, she was accused of vanity and venality. One official accused her of a 'grotesque act of betrayal'. Rimington called it a 'laddish, covert operation' and believes the culprits were Ministry of Defence civil servants. 'I felt a bit like a character in a Kafka novel who cannot quite understand what the bureaucracy that is dealing with is all about and what the machine is doing to him,' she recalled.[44]

The establishment which Rimington had long served loyally and diligently had turned against her and twisted the knife. 'We all thought she was a chap and chaps just don't do that,' said one mandarin. The hysterical and needless over-reaction of 'Operation Rimington' was exposed when her book *Open Secret* was published in 2001: it was a bland, harmless account of her life inside MI5, which apart from some entertaining anecdotes, barely contains anything that is not already on the public record. But it showed just how far MI5 would go to suppress even the slightest criticism (in Rimington's case that the agency was too secretive). For Shayler, the experience of his former boss revealed again that he was not just a lone critical voice or a loose cannon.

A year later, Shayler's case came to trial at the Old Bailey. From the beginning the legal dice was loaded against the defendant. All the prosecution needed to show was that Shayler had provided information and MI5 documents to the *Mail on Sunday* – a fact that he did not deny. He was prevented from demonstrating that his disclosures did not damage national security or introduce evidence of MI5 wrongdoing. In effect, he had no defence. 'I am put in a position where it is a crime to report a crime,' he said during the proceedings.

On Friday 4 October 2002, three days before the trial started, two Cabinet ministers demanded that part of the case be held in secret. David Blunkett, the Home Secretary, and Jack Straw, the Foreign Secretary, signed public interest immunity certificates. They were in effect gagging orders because they asked the judge to agree in advance that the court should go into secret session if the activities of MI5 were introduced by the defence. The certificates were issued without providing evidence to substantiate their case. Media lawyers accused the government of trying to intimidate the trial judge, Mr Justice Alan Moses, and of interfering in the criminal process.

Ministers and the intelligence agencies were concerned that Shayler, who had chosen to represent himself in court in order to address the jury directly, would make his most devestating claim yet: that the Libyan Islamic rebels paid by MI6 to assassinate Colonel Gaddafi in 1996 were members of Al Qaeda. One of the Libyan conspirators, Anas al-Liby, is reported to be one of Osama bin Laden's most trusted lieutenants and is on the US government's most-wanted list with a reward for $25 million for his capture. Al-Liby lived in Manchester until May 2001, when he eluded a police raid on his house and fled abroad. Among the documents left behind was a 180-page 'manual for jihad' containing instructions for terrorist attacks.

If this allegation was made during the case, it would have been highly embarassing for the security establishment, barely a year after 11 September. Hence the gagging orders which were submitted to the court on Monday morning. And the judge ruled that the media could not even report that the gagging orders had been issued. Lawyers advised newspapers that they could be in contempt just for publishing that reporting restrictions were enforced. 'The judge ruled that they (legal arguments) cannot be reported,' was all the *Guardian* could state.

Once the trial got underway, Shayler was repeatedly prevented by the judge from explaining why he passed 28 secret MI5 documents to the *Mail on Sunday* – the central feature of the prosecution's case. When he told the court he was on trial for damaging national security which was 'at the very heart' of the case, Mr Justice Moses immediately interrupted. 'Don't treat the jury as fools,' he told Shayler. 'You are not being tried for national security.'

At one point the former MI5 officer said: 'Towards the end of my time in (MI5), I saw something so heinous . . .' but the judge cut in: 'You may or may not have done, and you have already written about it in newspapers. You are not going to do it again in court.'

Shayler responded: 'I was put in a situation where I feared for my life. As a result I contacted journalists (the authors),' but the judge warned him: 'Be careful. This is not really relevant, although the fact that you went to some journalists is relevant and you have now admitted it.'

During heated exchanges with prosecution counsel Nigel Sweeney QC, Shayler told the jury: 'I cannot tell you the one thing that explains why I did this. The cards are stacked against me here. There is something so serious that if you knew you would take a different view.' After referring to 'unlawful bugging', he added: 'I am put in a position where it is a crime to report a crime.'[45]

The prosecution focused almost exclusively on their claim that Shayler showed copies of MI5 documents to the authors and was later paid a total of £39,000. Stamped 'Top Secret', the documents included a 135-page report on IRA-Libya links between 1971 and 1996, an investigation of 'subversive organisations' in the UK and a note, headlined *Moscow Gold*, on Soviet funding of the Communist Party of Great Britain.

This issue was taken up by most of the press who claimed that Shayler 'traded state secrets for cash'. In fact, his revelations were made to us long before the documents were even mentioned. A contract was signed and the former MI5 officer agreed to go on-the-record solely on that basis. He was later paid limited amounts of money because he needed to leave the country and that required financial support while living abroad. Even the judge later accepted that he was not motivated by financial reward. 'If I'd wanted to make money, I could have sold the documents for £10 million to Libyan intellgence,' said Shayler during the trial.

The issue of documents arose only two days before publication in August 1997. They were never part of the arrangement and were immediately placed in a *Mail on Sunday* safe and later returned to MI5. None of the material from the documents appeared in any of our articles. The prosecution knew this full well, but chose not to address this point.

It was inevitable that Shayler would be found guilty. The Official Secrets Act imposes a life-long duty of confidentiality on MI5 officers, bans them from making any disclosures without legal authority and provides no public interest defence. The prosecution does not need to show that any damage to national security – merely that the information has been published.

Shayler faced a maximum of six years in jail, but on 5 November 2002, only received six months. 'There are factors which mitigate the severity of your conduct,' said Mr Justice Moses. 'I do take into account yur good character and your service for the Security Service . . . I do accept that your motive for your actions was not greed or the desire for financial gain. I am prepared to accept that, in part, you did so because you wished to expose alleged illegality and inefficiency.'

The Judge took into account the three-and-a-half months Shayler spent in prison in Paris, that he returned to London voluntarily and instructed his lawyers to return the MI5 documents. And he was persuaded by Annie Machon's submission and evidence that her partner was not motivated by ambition and careerist intentions.

Shayler was then taken to Belmarsh high-security prison in south-east London where he was assessed for which category of prison he should be sent to. Most of the inmates were supportive and he was given the prisoner's number HP6007 as a mocking reference to James Bond, but it was a very tough, stressful and difficult time for the whistleblower. He was frequently locked up 24 hours a day (known as a 'lock-up'). He was threatened and finished up sharing a cell with a convicted murderer who had smashed a man's head open with a hammer.

After three weeks in one of Britain's roughest jails, Shayler was transferred to Ford open prison in west Sussex. This was far more humane with plenty of activities. A month later, on 23 December 2002, he was released and returned home to Osea, an island off the Essex coast, accessible from the mainland for about three hours a day at low tide. But it was on the condition that he was electronically tagged for a month and adhered to a 12-hour curfew from 7 pm to 7 am.

The future for Shayler and his partner Annie Machon is unclear. They are angry about the press coverage of the case which portayed their actions as financially motivated – a claim which the judge dismissed as untrue. The former MI5 officer may have been convicted, but his disclosures and subsequent campaign has resulted in considerable reforms. MI5 has made their secret files more accessible, admitted that its operational techniques against terrorism has been far too slow and become more open and accountible than it was before Shayler's revelations. There is now far more open debate about the secret state than before August 1997.

Senior judges have also indicated that the Official Secrets Act is far too restrictive and censorial, particularly how it relates to the media. In 2001, in a judgement concerning one of Shayler's allegations, the Court of Appeal ruled that 'unless there are compelling reasons of national security, the public is entitled to know the facts and as the eyes and ears of the public, journalists are entitled to investigate and report the facts'. Later that year the Law Lords attacked a sweeping injunction obtained by government lawyers which was designed to prevent the media from publishing information based on Shayler's evidence. Such injunctions, said Lord Nicholls, 'may well in practice have a significant "chilling" effect on the press and the media generally, inhibiting discussion and criticism of the Security Service . . . Parts of the media may well be discouraged from publishing even manifestly innocuous material which falls within the literal scope of the order.'[46]

Shayler's legacy – at huge personal sacrifice – is that MI5 has reluctantly dragged itself out of the shadows and into the 21st century. MI5 will never admit it, but its most controversial whistleblower may well have woken up a sleeping giant in time to confront its greatest challenge – international terrorism.

10

WHO WATCHES THE WATCHERS?

If we are setting up a committee of parliamentarians that cannot even report to Parliament, people are bound to question the worth and value of the committee [Intelligence and Security Committee].

Peter Mandelson, House of Commons, 29 March 1994

To minimise the differences between the political police and the ordinary civil police in a democracy gives hostages to fortune. Political police seek to infiltrate agents and informers into all aspects of social and political life. What we would end up with is a secret police force.

John Alderson, former chief constable of Devon and Cornwall police force, letter to the *Observer*, 13 November 1994

The threat of Al Qaeda and Islamic-sponsored terrorism may have given MI5 a new and enhanced role and a larger budget, but it remains a politically insecure organisation. A tremor of unease still runs through the corridors of its extravagantly restored Edwardian headquarters at Thames House on London's Millbank. The inarticulate, introspective directors show no trace of their real feelings but the atmosphere is dominated by uncertainty. David Shayler's revelations and views have encapsulated what his former fellow officers think but dare not say: the Security Service remains in crisis. If it fails to reform sufficiently, to modernise and acheive real results in countering terrorism, then there are no guarantees about its future status and existence in its current form.

Under Dame Stella Rimington's leadership (1992–96), MI5 gradually, if rather tortuously, transformed itself from a counter-subversion and espionage agency to one dedicated to investigating Irish and Islamic-inspired terrorism. Externally, it has redefined itself with new parameters and roles, and the quality of its surveillance techniques and intelligence-gathering operations remains high.

But, crucially, it has failed to adapt or change its internal procedures for dealing with and acting on incoming intelligence on those new targets. MI5's traditional management methods remain largely unaltered and inflexible. The obsession with bureaucracy and analysis and the culture of excessive secrecy have rendered the Service ineffective against its new targets.

For the new, keen, young officers, recruited after the Cold War, this created enormous frustration and caused an exodus in the mid-1990s. 'Over the past 18 months the number of middle-ranking officers leaving the Security Service has increased dramatically,' revealed Annie Machon in August 1997. 'Fourteen people have left during the past year, when you would normally expect four or five to go through natural wastage. Many of these are young high-flyers like David [Shayler], who became disillusioned because the old guard blocked any initiative and suppressed new ideas. Management has ignored the problem.'

Machon, an MI5 officer from 1991 until 1996, who served in both counter-subversion and anti-terrorist branches, added, 'I still see serving officers socially and all they talk about is how fed up they are and their latest job application so they can leave.'[1]

Many of those remaining at Thames House are not there by choice. Working in the secret world for so long has made them unattractive to the private sector. There are not many job options for people who have spent their lives immersed in the twists and turns of Communist Party ideology. Unless radical change is imminent, the Service will find itself redundant or absorbed into other agencies. Playing the Whitehall game has produced short-term benefits, but the final whistle might yet be blown when there are no teams to play against.

MI5's weakness is that it had always been an inherently insecure and introverted organisation. Ever since its foundation, it has felt unprotected politically. The British public has always considered the notion of a secret police as distasteful, alien and intrusive. There has never been underlying popular support for its existence.

During the Cold War, the Service was secure because there was an ostensible threat to the security of the state. Protected from parliamentary and journalistic scrutiny, it was virtually unassailable, but when the trusted old enemy disappeared, MI5 felt isolated and undefended as its critics argued that it had no place in law enforcement and counter-terrorism. The Service searched for new components to rebuild its empire.

Despite their instinct for secrecy, MI5's directors now care deeply about their public image and reputation. They are largely mild-mannered, cautious individuals, who much prefer paper to people. Under threat, their reaction is to be pedantically correct in everything they do and hide behind bureaucracy to protect themselves. Frightened of making mistakes, they have become more mandarin than the mandarins, desperately anxious not to offend anyone in the Home Office or 10 Downing Street. This legalistic approach explains the endless redrafting of warrant documents and the cautious approach to intelligence operations that so frustrated and disillusioned David Shayler.

Stella Rimington recognised MI5's limitations and to some extent broke out of the strait-jacket. She promoted more openness and accountability and realised that MI5 needed extra resources to fulfil its new functions. She sought out new targets, but after Stephen Lander became director-general in April 1996, MI5 reverted to its old intransigent stance. The train of change was stopped in its tracks. Lander lacked the dynamic and flexible leadership qualities required to constantly reinvent and revitalise the Service in a constantly changing world.

Lander retained the Service's bureaucratic culture whereby officers spend most of their time writing briefings, copying out reports and drafting and redrafting warrants. These are all important functions, but in a fast-moving world where MI5's new targets are terrorists and, potentially, drug-dealers and organised crime, time is precious. Delaying recommendations and failing to distribute intelligence to law enforcement agencies because of bureaucratic restrictions and 'analysis' can have tragic consequences. In the more static world of counter-espionage, there was time to analyse and peruse scenarios, but in the fast, fluid reality of crime prevention, initiative, not inertia, and flexibility, not navel-gazing, are the determining factors.

The appointment of Lander was a pivotal moment for the Security Service. When Rimington, aged 60, announced her retirement in October 1995, it was presumed that Julian Hansen, her unassuming, taciturn deputy, would succeed her. But Lander and Eliza Manningham-Buller, a senior MI5 director, worked to undermine his chances of appointment in a style worthy of a John le Carré novel.

Both were in powerful positions. Lander was then director of Corporate Affairs, responsible for the Registry, information technology, finance, and relations with Whitehall and other security agencies. Hence he had a detailed overview of its workings. Manningham-Buller was principal operations director, which included surveillance, mail interception, telephone tapping and covert searches. This gave her a comprehensive and up-to-date knowledge of the Service and its intelligence requirements.

Lander used his prominence and power ruthlessly, according to informed sources. He told Rimington he would resign if Hansen became director-general. In a second meeting Lander and Manningham-Buller said they had no confidence in Hansen, who was described as 'ineffectual' with 'no presence'. Lander proposed himself as the best candidate. He promised Manningham-Buller that she would be his deputy and would eventually succeed him as director-general.

Rimington tried to persuade the two to back down, but she was trapped: if Lander and Manningham-Buller resigned, it would have been very difficult for the other four directors to run MI5, especially as it was poised to gain responsibility for organised crime. In a series of meetings in Rimington's private office, a deal was carved out. Hansen was told he had no support and would be deeply unpopular as the next director-general. Rimington then informed the Cabinet Office that Hansen had withdrawn his application. This was deeply economical with the truth, if not untrue. He had been forced out.

After Lander's elevation in April 1996, Hansen remained deputy director-general for a year and was then given a 'retread' – a part-time consultancy with the Service. He was succeeded by Eliza Manningham-Buller. The *coup d'état* was complete.[2]

The Manningham-Buller/Lander power axis was regarded as a triumph for the 'old guard' and Civil Service culture inside MI5. The new, young meritocratic intake were horrified by the appointments: they viewed Lander as a hidebound administrator incapable of modernisation. 'He is a bureaucrat, not an innovator or a manager,' said one officer. 'His success was due to Whitehall networking.'[3]

The irony of Lander's ascent was that he shared many of the personal characteristics of his rival Julian Hansen. Both were capable analysts and meticulous collators of intelligence, but hopeless with people. Reclusive, retiring and dull, they both lacked the charisma and warmth of personality to inspire their troops.' Unlike his pre-decessor Stella Rimington, Lander has no presence or charm,' said Annie Machon.[4]

Like his deputy, Manningham-Buller, Lander is from MI5's Cold War generation. Born in 1947, he was educated at Bishop's Stortford College, Hertford, and Queens' College, Cambridge. While at Cambridge in the early 1970s, Lander flirted with an academic career in history. He was riveted by the arcane world of the Tudor Church. For his doctoral dissertation he wrote a formidable 420-page tome entitled 'The Diocese of Chichester'. At first glance, it was a bizarre subject for a future head of the British Secret Service, but the Church in the 16th century was full of Machiavellian intrigue and plotting and the thesis provides an insight into Lander's character.

The *Sunday Times* asked experts to assess the dissertation. 'Rather revealingly, much of the thesis is devoted to Bishop Sherburne, a cunning, canny chap who Lander clearly regards as a role model and a hero,' said Oliver James, a clinical psychologist. Sherburne ran the legal system in Chichester in the early 1500s and Lander praised him for the way he made the courts 'more efficient at extracting information'.[5]

Dr David Starkey, the historian, who was with Lander at Cambridge, also believes the MI5 director-general has modelled himself on the Bishop. 'Sherburne had an impressive record at Oxford, winning a clutch of degrees, and was a man of high culture,' said Dr Starkey. 'But he quit the groves of academe for a career as a leading Civil Servant and then as a reforming disciplinarian bishop. The parallels with Stephen are striking. Sherburne was even involved in counter-insurgency, putting down the supporters of the pretender Perkin Warbeck, who had strong Irish connections.'[6]

In the dissertation, Lander revealed characteristics that he was later to demonstrate as head of MI5: his obsession with detail at the expense of the bigger picture, the labyrinthine sentences that complicate rather than elucidate, the stony lack of warmth and humour.

On the other hand, he displayed scholarly and forensic skills. He cultivated a range of inaccessible sources and carefully assessed their credibility. 'He's rigorous and he's sleuthed his way into the papers,' said Oliver James. 'He's properly examined the evidence.'

At Cambridge, Lander was a detached, sullen postgraduate

history student. While many of his contemporaries were akin to Howard Kirk – the hedonistic 'History Man' of the mid-1970s satirised in Malcolm Bradbury's notorious novel – Lander was remote and reserved. 'Stephen was a fringe figure, interested in boring bishops,' recalled Dr Starkey. 'He was the classic example of a student who observed everything, soaked it all up but rarely participated in the fun. He was very quiet, unassuming and serious and was not inclined to get involved in anything too subversive. He was almost boring, perfect for the security services.'[7]

After successfully obtaining his Ph.D., Lander worked for the Institute of Historical Research at the University of London. A year later, in 1975, he joined MI5, based on a recommendation by his careers adviser. 'Stephen's was regarded as a good Ph.D.,' claimed Dr Starkey. 'But it wasn't outstanding. The truth is he went into spying because he didn't get an academic job.'

Lander's MI5 career mirrored that of his predecessor, Stella Rimington. Shortly after the 1984–85 miners' strike, he became head of the infamous F2 section, responsible for monitoring Communist subversion. In 1986, he was seconded to the Foreign Office, working in the Near East and North Africa department. A year later he returned to MI5 as head of the Registry, where he introduced the new classification of files known as 'traffic-lighting'. Between 1988 and 1994 he was head of the section that countered IRA operations on the European continent and was then promoted to director of T Branch, where he managed investigations into world-wide IRA terrorism.

While there is no doubting his intellect and analytical qualities, Lander is entirely unsuited to management. Prickly and over-defensive, the diminutive director-general is prone to the sort of petulance that routinely bedevils those who have little or no natural authority. In a crisis, he is quick to blame subordinates. His chronic inability to communicate, witnessed by journalists during private briefings, is a major flaw for leading an organisation that constantly lives in the shadow of bad publicity. Unlike Rimington, who gave four lectures and one press conference, Lander has only spoken once on the public record.

He shows little enthusiasm for reform and adapting to new world realities. In the autumn of 1996, he attended a private meeting of academics and intelligence experts at the Institute of Historical Research, where he used to work. Hosted by Professor Peter

Hennessy, the discussion focused on the conditions for releasing historical documents.

Mark Urban, the BBC's diplomatic correspondent, argued that the notion of what constitutes a secret should now be reassessed. He quoted from Ministry of Defence official statements that there was now 'no immediate threat to national security' to the UK. 'We have to take on board the information implications of this,' he said, 'and accept that more documents and files can now be released through the Public Record Office.'

As Urban made his point, Lander looked across with a frown and was increasingly irritated. 'Well, all this releasing of records is still a problem,' he snapped. 'We have to check carefully whether that mat-erial should be released. Some of it reveals our tradecraft and some of our methods have not changed since the Second World War . . . I have to employ two officers who are responsible for examining the documents and it is a drain on my budget. They are full-time and they have better things to do than deal with half-baked, tomfoolery questions from journalists.'

Even more significant, Lander's intensely bureaucratic and almost academic approach to counter-terrorist operations has hindered MI5's talented agents, surveillance units and desk officers. According to a source formerly close to the director-general, his weakness is his lack of tradecraft and experience of intelligence-gathering fieldwork:

'Lander has never held a proper agent-running or direct source-handling post. He never had to stand on street corners for surreptitious meetings or take late-night phone calls from a distressed agent who needed urgent help. Lander's only experience in the field was advising Special Branches on agent-handling, which usually didn't involve direct contact with the great unwashed – the agents themselves.

'Even then, Lander was happier sitting behind his desk in Curzon Street, Mayfair. A senior Special Branch officer in Merseyside once reported that Lander, in his capacity as an adviser to agent-runners, seldom visited the regions, even though he was responsible for those regions. On the rare occasions that he did, he seemed more interested in getting his train back than the meeting itself.'[8]

The Honourable Eliza Manningham-Buller personified the old guard.

Born in 1948, she is the daughter of Sir Reginald Manningham-Buller, later Viscount Dilhorne, who served as Attorney General and Lord Chancellor in Harold Macmillan's Conservative governments. In 1958, he threatened to prosecute Weidenfeld and Nicolson for publishing Vladimir Nabokov's novel *Lolita*, which features sex with minors. He was not always highly regarded. The law lord Lord Devlin once described him as a man 'without a grain of judicial sense'.

The young Eliza received an Establishment education and her early life has been likened to a character out of an Agatha Christie novel. She went to Benenden school for girls in Kent where her contemporaries included Princess Anne and Veronica Wadley, editor of the *Evening Standard*. At Oxford she read English at Lady Margaret Hall, but was also an enthusiast for amateur dramatics. She joined the dramatic society and played the role of the Fairy Queen in a pantomine produced by Gyles Brandreth, later a Conservative MP and junior government whip. Photographs from her student days show her as an effervescent and strident young woman.

After Oxford, Manningham-Buller spent three years as an English teacher at Queen's Gate school, a private girls school in South Kensington, London, that served as a conveyor belt for young, upper-class women making their first formal appearance in society. One of her pupils was the celebrated TV chef Nigella Lawson. She is remembered for having 'a charmless manner' and an aggressive personality.

True to her Establishment credentials, the Hon Manningham-Buller was recruited by MI5 in 1974 in a style typical of that period: at a smart cocktail party in Chelsea. She became a spy at a time when women were heavily discriminated against and their duties were confined to transcribing tapped telephone conversations and low-grade clerical work. But she worked ferociously hard and was fiercely ambitious.

In contrast to her predecessors, Manningham-Buller's career is notable for its operational experience. She began in counter-espionage, spending the early 1980s monitoring the Soviet Union's spy network in Britain. In 1988, she became head of MI5's Middle East section and was involved in the Lockerbie investigation. She was then posted to Washington DC as the liaison officer with the US which involved exchanging intelligence with the CIA and FBI – a bureaucratic job which she hated. However, it was in Washington DC where she met her husband, David Mallock, a university lecturer in moral philosophy who became disillusioned and later turned to carpentry. The couple now live in Kensington and have a country house in Wales where her favourite hobby is breeding chickens.

Between 1992 and 1993, the new MI5 boss was head of T2 section, which had the primary role in countering Provisional IRA terrorism on the British mainland. This had previously been the responsibility of the Metropolitan Police Special Branch. She was successful at ensuring the Met abided by the new arrangement, but was not so effective on the operational side. As we revealed in Chapter 5, a number of IRA bombings took place on the mainland, some of which could have been avoided if it were not for MI5 management incompetance.

By the time she became operations director in 1994, Manningham-Buller was regarded by her staff as a formidable administrator who did not suffer fools gladly. She is forceful, opinionated and even lost her temper during the three-hour psychological examination when she formally applied for the top job. Some officers have nick-named her 'Bullying-Manner'.

Her supporters describe her as 'a feisty lady, full of character and intellectual drive'. They say she is determined, unpretentious and hates the paper-shuffling management culture of MI5. She is certainly an improvement on Lander and has already introduced more openness and accountability to appease critics, notably Treasury officials who do not believe MI5 provides value for money. Calm under pressure, the challenge for Manningham-Buller is whether she can shake off the legacy of the Lander regime.

MI5's *bête noire* is internal dissent and criticism. The prevailing atmosphere, according to Shayler, is 'Stalinist'.[9] After Lander's appointment as director-general, an enthused assistant director told a horrified Annie Machon: 'This is great. He is Stalinesque and that's what the Service needs – centralised control.'[10] A culture of unthinking conformity and compliance has been enforced. One officer was told he was 'too enthusiastic' and 'needed to curb his independent traits'.[11]

Staff have long felt bereft of protection with no access to industrial tribunals. In November 1987, MI5's personnel policy was so dysfunctional that a staff counsellor was imposed by the government. This was after a devastating critique by the Security Commission. Their report focused on MI5's treatment of Michael

Bettaney, who was under so much pressure that he became an alcoholic and had a nervous breakdown.

The Commission found that his stress had gone unrecognised and untreated by his superiors, and eventually he became a traitor, throwing top-secret information over the wall of the Soviet embassy. 'Stress is endemic in intelligence work,' said Miranda Ingram, a former MI5 officer who worked with Bettaney. 'You are trained to be suspicious, to assume the worst motive in the simplest of actions. Those attitudes can be very difficult to shake off at the end of the day, and you may find yourself doubting the honesty of a friend who tells you he is going out to buy a pint of milk, particularly as you are expected to lie to this same friend about the nature of your work.' Ingram argued that only a genuinely independent body could deal with such pressures.[12]

The Security Commission recommended a more open style of management by MI5 and that outside professionals should be recruited to the personnel section. The proposals were never implemented. Officers have been wary of approaching the staff counsellor, who is currently Sir Christopher France, permanent secretary at the Ministry of Defence. 'This was supposed to be a confidential service,' said Shayler. 'In practice, this was not the case. Although the subject of complaint was kept secret, officers were expected to inform personnel that they had seen the counsellor and this was widely believed to be a black mark on their records.'[13]

The mere existence of a staff counsellor was an indictment of substandard management, according to John Day, a former senior MI5 officer. 'I can see no merit in this appointment,' he said. 'If the recruiting procedures for the Service are sound and if the management is of a degree of competence and fairness, such an appointment is unnecessary. Either the government lacks confidence in the senior management of the Service, which I find hard to accept, or, when introduced, it was intended solely to defuse parliamentary and public concern.'[14]

Many officers feel there is no outlet for their frustrations and opinions both on personnel and the ethics of their work. 'During my time inside MI5,' said Shayler, in 1997, 'I regularly raised issues with senior officers. But such is the obsession with secrecy that my complaints were never taken seriously. The only forum is the Staff Consultative Group, which is filled with management stooges. To make matters worse, Lander has recently abolished the management steering group, which offered some scope for discussing and resolving problems.'[15]

The prospect of management victimisation is very real. According to Shayler: 'Another officer, who raised his very legitimate concerns about the deaths of three IRA suspects in Gibraltar at the hands of the SAS, was given a black mark on his office file. The fact that he had made these comments was passed to his new manager each time he moved section – with a clear implication that the officer was not to be fully trusted.'[16]

The danger of not openly dealing with an internal grievance or an operational disagreement is immense. 'What might begin as a moderate dissent will be silently nurtured and will fester until it grows into a much more serious dissent,' said Miranda Ingram. 'Because it is not drawn out into open debate, it may eventually seek a clandestine outlet. This might be a leak. Or, in a more extreme case, it can grow into a desire to seriously undermine the Security Service itself.'[17]

Even that most cautious of former officers, John Day, has sympathy for an MI5 whistleblower. 'To a degree,' he wrote in 1993, 'I sympathise with the motives of those who have made such disclosures because, in default of any other forum, they felt that this was the only way to ensure that essential reforms were made.'[18]

This is what happened to David Shayler. Despite a successful five-year career in MI5, he felt that management was unprepared to deal with staff concerns. Its reaction to a staff problem was to delay, defer or downgrade it rather than debate and work out a solution. Fortunately, when he aired his concerns with a wider audience, Shayler did not disclose genuine security secrets, sensitive operations or the identity of agents and informants, but a less stable officer, whose grievances and opinions were ignored or dismissed, might have taken that formerly unthinkable step of betraying real secrets to a hostile foreign power – as in the Bettaney case.

MI5 did respond to Shayler's allegations and proposals – but only after he went public in August 1997. Two months later, the Cabinet Office launched a review of the management of all the intelligence agencies, but it was hardly independent: the inquiry was conducted by John Alpass, who was investigating areas of MI5 for which he himself had been recently responsible.

A major reason why Shayler blew the whistle was that he believed MI5 was 'trapped in a culture which is damaging to the Service and undermining national security' with no mechanism for independent scrutiny. In a published message to Prime Minister Tony Blair, he said: 'Its obsessive secrecy means there is little or no public overview of its activities or the profligate waste of tens of millions of pounds. The press still acts as a brake on the worst excesses of government, but in MI5 management is not accountable for its actions, even though it is responsible for guarding national security . . . I know how MI5 works, how it protects its image by resisting independent scrutiny, even from the rest of the Whitehall establishment.'[19]

Despite some limited forms of parliamentary oversight, MI5 remains one of the least accountable secret services in the Western world. For most of its existence, ministers have been blissfully ignorant of the agency's budget and activities. MI5 was virtually immune to the law and had no legal status. It was, in effect, a law unto itself and a state within a state. 'I certainly didn't, and most people in MI5 didn't, have a duty to Parliament,' said Peter Wright. 'Officers were not government employees. I do emphasise this. It's a very real point.'[20] This was reinforced by John (now Lord) Cuckney, a former senior MI5 director, who told new recruits: 'The Security Service cannot have the normal status of a Whitehall department because its work very often involves transgressing propriety or the law.'[21]

Instead, there was a vague allegiance to 'the Crown' – a rather nebulous entity which is part of the state (or 'permanent government', as the historian Peter Hennessy refers to it). MI5 officers were told by their managers that they could break into, enter, search and place bugs in private premises under the power of the Royal Prerogative. This mysterious ancient power gave the Service a source of special legal authority outside the confines of the criminal law. It enabled officers like Wright to 'bug and burgle our way across London at the state's behest while pompous bowler-hatted civil servants in Whitehall pretended to look the other way'.[22]

MI5's protective Prerogative shield was confirmed in 1988 by Sir John Donaldson, then Master of the Rolls. 'It is silly for us', he said, in the Court of Appeal during the *Spycatcher* affair, 'to sit here and say that the Security Service is obliged to follow the letter of the law. It isn't real . . . The Security Service is bound by a strict rule of the law, but always bear in mind there is a prerogative power not to pursue criminal proceedings and a statutory power in the DPP to stop criminal prosecutions.' He claimed that it was in the public interest for MI5 officers to break the law, and that such breaches would not be pro-secuted, although he did draw the line at one crime: 'Murder is an entirely different matter,' said the judge.[23]

When asked about parliamentary oversight, ministers always replied that MI5 was accountable to the Home Secretary and ultimately the Prime Minister. This was based on a directive issued in 1952 by David Maxwell Fyfe, then Home Secretary, who jotted down six points on a napkin over lunch while he was out of the office.[24] It was handed to Sir Percy Sillitoe, a former chief constable but by then director-general of MI5, and concluded: 'Ministers do not concern themselves with the detailed information which may be obtained by the Security Service in particular cases, but are furnished with such information only as may be necessary for the determination of any issue on which guidance is sought.'

That remained the position for the rest of the Cold War. MI5 was not even part of the Home Office, according to the directive. Instead, according to MI5, the Home Secretary was 'kept informed about Service plans and priorities, as well as matters of current concern'.[25] Most Home Secretaries are adamant that they know what MI5 are up to. 'I go round their building and talk to people,' said Jack Straw, the former Home Secretary. 'I will say, "What are you doing? Show me the file," or "What's this bit of kit for?" I will go through their budget . . . I see it through the warrant applications [for telephone and mail interceptions] I get and the discussions I have with Stephen Lander.'[26]

However, as John Day acknowledged in 1993: 'Experience has shown that the Home Secretary on his own simply cannot carry out an oversight of MI5.' This was principally because, he said, 'Accountability depends on accurate, timely information, and it is questionable to what extent this has been made available to ministers in the past.'[27] Withholding material from Cabinet ministers was experienced by Gerald Gardiner, Lord Chancellor during the 1964–70 Labour government.

'I was once told that Cabinet ministers were allowed to see their own MI5 files,' recalled Gardiner, 'So I asked my department to get hold of mine, thinking that this would give me a good opportunity to judge the efficiency of MI5. After all, I would be able to judge what they said about me in comparison with what I knew about myself.

'However, the civil servants hummed and hawed a lot and I

kept saying to them, every week or so, "Where is my file?" In the end they said I would have to see the Home Secretary. Frank Soskice was embarrassed and said that he couldn't agree and that he wasn't allowed to see the files either. When they [MI5] wanted to show him [Soskice, Home Secretary, 1964–65] anything, they photographed a page and gave it to him but he never saw the complete file. He was so upset about it that I just let it drop.'[28]

MI5 regards ministers as largely transitory figures and view their occasional visits with scant respect. 'He [the Home Secretary] hasn't got a clue what's going on,' said a former officer. 'If he comes round, you lock away any sensitive files and set up a display file specially for him to look at – a spoof file on some imaginary subversive with lots of exciting material in it. He's not going to know any better.'[29]

Lord Jenkins, twice a Labour Home Secretary, largely conceded that this was true. 'It was a very difficult responsibility to exercise,' he said. 'I experienced in the Security Service what I can best describe as an inherent lack of frankness, an ingrowing mono-culture and a confidence-destroying tendency to engage in the most devastating internal feuds . . . There was naturally a secretive atmosphere, but this meant they were *vis-à-vis* the government as well as the people who might be enemies of the state.'[30]

Jenkins's successor Lord Callaghan, Home Secretary (1967–70) then Prime Minister (1976–79), was more circumspect: 'The relationship between ministers and the Secret Service should be familiar, but not intimate.'[31] But he admitted that inforzmation was kept secret from Whitehall. When asked if MI5 was 'out of control' in the 1970s, he replied: 'If it means do they take initiatives of their own kind without clearing everything with a minister, the answer is yes.'[32] Lord Rees, the last Labour Home Secretary before Jack Straw, flatly contradicted his young successor. When asked if he had known what MI5 was up to, Rees replied: 'No. And neither does any Home Secretary . . . Can't possibly.'[33]

The Prime Minister remains ultimately responsible for overall security policy and, if minded, can exercise this power through the Cabinet Secretary. MI5 works on the principle of studied ignorance for Prime Ministers: the less they know the safer they will be if they are questioned in the Commons. And if informing 10 Downing Street is unavoidable, there are *Yes, Minister*-style ways around the problem, according to the late George Young, former deputy director of MI6. 'There is a curious convention in Whitehall – you can inform the Prime Minister without telling him,' said Young. 'The Cabinet Secretary can wait for "an opportune moment" which "may never come".'[34]

MI5s relationship with Prime Ministers has varied. The Conservative Sir Alec Douglas-Home (1963–64) was wary of MI5 and once said it was 'very easy to cross the line between a free society and a police state'.[35] Labour's Harold Wilson (1964–70 and 1974–76) was fascinated by MI5 until some of its officers conspired to destabilise his government. The Conservative Edward Heath (1970–74) was sceptical of its value, but its most devoted admirer was Margaret Thatcher (1979–90), who was mesmerised by the secret state. During her premiership, MI5's budget doubled. She was also an assiduous reader of intelligence material: every day she received a digest of Box 500 reports which she would return to the Cabinet Office with her comments and sections underlined in bright blue pen.

During her tenure in Downing Street, MI5 went from being a shadowy bureaucratic backwater to an integrated part of the Whitehall machine. According to Nigel Lawson, Chancellor of the Exchequer from 1983 until 1989: 'The Security Services, their establishments and their hardware, were one of the few areas of public life virtually untouched by the rigours of the Thatcher era. Most Prime Ministers have a soft spot for the Security Services, for which they have a special responsibility, but Margaret, an avid reader of the works of Frederick Forsyth, was positively besotted by them.'[36]

Thatcher was the only Prime Minister to attend the highly secret meetings of the Joint Intelligence Committee (JIC). These were weekly sessions, held on the second floor of the Cabinet Office, of top security and military officials, including the director-general of MI5, to analyse incoming classified intelligence data. The JIC is the co-ordinating nerve centre of British intelligence. It formulates policy and is the command and control unit for MI5. Compared to the JIC, the Home Office is a mere postbox.

Between 1988 and 1990 Robin Robison worked as an administrative officer for the JIC, preparing the paperwork for the weekly meetings. But he became disillusioned by what he witnessed, mainly evidence of improper phone-tapping and collusion between the intelligence agencies and the government. 'I felt that I was sitting in the middle of something that really smelt,' he said, on Granada TV's

World in Action. 'Quite a lot of it was to do with the way in which government obtained information about a great deal of British life which was not strictly necessary and not really to do with defending the realm . . . In practice, the intelligence agencies were operating in a way which was deceitful at times and at best creating a fog around the whole situation so that ministers knew as little as possible and the public knows next to nothing. And MPs know really no more than the average man in the street.'[37]

Robison revealed that ministers never attended JIC meetings and did not even ask for information. When asked by *World in Action* what would happen if a minister demanded to see files to make sure there was proper oversight, the former JIC official replied, 'It wouldn't happen, because we had files which were specifically not for minis-terial eyes.' They were stamped 'Restricted Circulation' and only sent to the Prime Minister, the Chancellor, the Foreign, Defence and Home Secretaries and the Minister for Defence Procurement. This excluded a whole range of Cabinet ministers and ministers of state throughout the government. Most seriously, Robison told the authors of this book, some intelligence files are kept secret from the National Audit Office (NAO), which is supposed to oversee MI5's budgets and spending. Some dossiers are marked 'Not for NAO Eyes'. 'It just cuts across any pretence of democratic accountability,' he concluded.[38]

For the public there is little opportunity for redress if they believe MI5 has tapped their telephone, intercepted their mail, broken into their home, kept a secret file or blacklisted them for future employment. Ministers argue that the judiciary will protect citizens' civil rights, but the courts have rarely challenged the executive on matters of national security. In 1984, Lord Fraser, a senior law lord, stated: 'The decision on whether the requirements of national security outweigh the duty of fairness in any particular case is for the government and not for the courts. The government alone has access to the necessary information, and in any event the judicial process is unsuitable for reaching decisions on national security.'[39]

The lack of real accountability was demonstrated by legal action taken by Harriet Harman, the former Solicitor-General, and Patricia Hewitt, the DTI Secretary. Based on evidence from former MI5 officer Cathy Massiter, they claimed their phones were illegally tapped. Having no faith in the British judiciary, they took their case to the

European Court of Human Rights.

As the verdict loomed in the late 1980s, MI5 became increasingly anxious. The European Court had made clear in recent judgements that there should be effective oversight of security services to protect the rights of individuals. A defeat would be embarrassing but, more significantly, it would enable other victims to launch new lawsuits against the Service via the European Court.

The prospect of disclosures about past misdeeds and skulduggery horrified Home Office and MI5 officials. They lobbied the government to introduce a limited form of oversight and a mechanism for dealing with complaints. Their willing ally was Sir Antony Duff, MI5's director-general from 1985 until late 1987, a liberal-minded former diplomat and chairman of the JIC.

He discovered that the Service was living in the Dark Ages and failed to keep pace with the modern world. Charismatic and broad-minded, he personally toured every branch and spoke to staff in a civilised, urbane way. He introduced new measures to ensure that younger people were recruited who would introduce new ideas, and advocated more openness, accountability and more links with the media.

But his reforms were fiercely resisted by Margaret Thatcher, who was almost obsessive in her desire for secrecy. A Cold Warrior, she was a staunch defender of MI5's old guard and their freedom to investigate what she called 'the enemy within'. 'She was much opposed,' recalled Duff. 'Her instinct was not to reveal anything at all to anybody, ever. She didn't use any arguments – she just said no.'[40]

It was left to Duff's successor, Sir Patrick Walker, to implement the proposals. Although he agreed with change in principle, he was temperamentally and institutionally unsuited to be a visionary reformer. Unlike Duff, he was a consummate MI5 insider and tended to be over-defensive about the agency's controversial past. Born in 1935, he joined MI5 in the mid-1960s after serving in the Colonial Services. He was posted to Northern Ireland in 1979 when the province was dominated by hunger strikes, supergrass trials and shoot-to-kill controversies. He then expanded his experience by dealing with Arab and Irish terrorism in Britain. Before becoming director-general, he was head of F Branch, the counter-subversive division.

Colleagues found Walker quiet, shy and pleasant, with a sharp analytical brain, but lacking Duff's engaging personality. He was a skilled interrogator with an excellent memory, but instinctively reticent and introverted. His defining moment was the farewell party for Sir David Nicholas, the retiring chairman of Independent Television News, in October 1991, at the Savoy Hotel. Among the guests were Sir David Frost, the late John Smith, then Shadow Chancellor, Kenneth Baker, then Home Secretary, and the tycoon Richard Branson. Although he had known Walker for several years, Nicholas had never introduced the MI5 director-general to his friends. The invitation to the party posed a serious dilemma in a period of supposed reform for the Service.

After a period of protracted agonising, Walker decided to come out of the intelligence closet. He went to the party and introduced himself, rather formally and stiffly: 'My name is Sir Patrick Walker. I am the director-general of the Security Service.'[41] The guests were startled and their reaction was typically British. Some thought it was a private company like Securicor. Others had not heard of the Security Service, while the remaining guests shuffled their feet and changed the subject.

As MI5 officers had operated on the edge, if not the inside, of darkness, Walker's 'coming out' was seen as a meaningful new policy. But compared to other Western democracies, it was a minimal step towards enlightenment and accountability. That such a minor gesture was interpreted as a major breakthrough indicated just how far MI5 needed to progress.

To Walker's credit, he realised that reform was inevitable, if only because of external pressure from Europe. Eventually he persuaded Thatcher that legislation would head off demands for independent scrutiny and a compromise was agreed. This was the 1989 Security Service Act – four months before the European Court ruled that the British government had breached Harman and Hewitt's human rights.

The Act placed the Service on a statutory basis for the first time. Drafted by MI5 lawyers, it provided the agency with the legal powers – through a Home Office warrant – to tap phones, burgle houses and intercept mail. It also authorised a new Security Service Tribunal to review warrants and investigate complaints by the public. This consists of four lawyers who would examine cases and present an annual report to the Prime Minister.

The Tribunal's chairman is Lord Justice Sir Murray Stuart-Smith, a 75-year-old cello-playing pillar of the legal community. Educated at

Radley School and Corpus Christi College, Cambridge, he served in the Dragoon Guards before becoming a lawyer. 'If he is not of the establishment, he faces it on the periphery,' said a prom-inent QC . 'I would not think he knew how to think other than in terms of the establishment.' Another legal colleague thought he would 'not be looking for a case to strike at the establishment, but if it floats across his snout he will sniff harder'.[42]

In the past decade Stuart-Smith appears not to have sniffed at anything unsavoury and he sees his role as 'a reactor rather than an initiator'.[43] Between 1989 and 1997 his tribunal has received 275 complaints. Not one has been upheld. While it must appear inde-pendent, the tribunal remains within Whitehall's inner ring of secrecy. Applicants are not entitled to many of the rights they would have under normal tribunal or court proceedings. They have no access to any information, even if that material does not affect national security.

MI5's response is not made available to complainants, so they cannot challenge its version or mount a defence. If the case is rejected, the individual will not be given any reason for it and has no right of appeal. Even if it concludes there has been wrongdoing, the tribunal will refuse to state whether or not an unauthorised tele-phone or mail interception has taken place. Faced with these obsta-cles, the complainant is placed in an almost impossible position and it is hardly surprising that no cases have been upheld.

The prevention of citizens from participation during the tribunal's inquiry was later raised by Peter Mandelson, who at that time was unaware that he had been placed under surveillance by MI5 in the 1970s. He argued that it was only 'right and proper for the complainant' to have access to basic data. For the Home Office, David Davis rejected this proposal, claiming that merely revealing the recording category of the individual's file 'would undermine the basis of the Security Service'.

This was rejected by Mandelson, who told the Commons in 1994: 'If the complainant has no opportunity to correct, add to or subtract from that information in ways that could alter the tribunal's view and judgement, the tribunal will simply carry on in its merry way – taking certain facts as axiomatic and leading to what appeared to be safe conclusions but which were not.'[44]

The tribunal is also prohibited from investigating any cases that occurred before 18 December 1989 – even though MI5 are most likely to have retained files that may still be in use. This was not included in the Home Office guidelines 'Complaints Against the Security Service' and the loophole was greeted with dismay by some Tory MPs. 'This entirely goes against the spirit of the Act, which was designed to give people an opportunity to have their complaints investigated,' said Rupert Allason, who under the pen-name of Nigel West has written several authoritative books on the intelligence agencies. 'There was certainly never any question, when we debated this in the Commons, of there being a time limit.'[45] His colleague Richard Shephard, a Freedom of Information campaigner, said: 'The government is in extraordinary awe of the Security Service. What we are seeing is subservience.'[46]

While many MPs felt the Act was largely cosmetic and lacking in substance, at least MI5 was now out of the closet. Under Patrick Walker's benign leadership, semi-official lines were opened to selected journalists and editors, notably at the *Independent*. As James Adams, then defence correspondent of the *Sunday Times*, recalled: 'The conversation was polite but reserved. To the guests, it often appeared as if the hosts knew little about the world outside their own. To the [MI5] directors, the journalists appeared irreverent, informal and, on the whole, remarkably ill-informed about the kind of work MI5 does.'[47]

The point of contact was David Bickford, the Service's legal adviser from 1987 until 1995. A former Foreign Office lawyer, Bickford was congenial, open and had little patience with the *ancien régime*. He was a strong believer in the rule of law and would later criticise MI5 for not modernising itself sufficiently. Transparency was crucial, advised Bickford, and small shafts of light appeared through the darkness. Officials at the Commons who vet MPs' questions now allowed, for the first time, inquiries on 'certain matters' about MI5.

In December 1992, the director-general, Stella Rimington, was named. A year later she hosted a press conference to launch a booklet about MI5's origins and work. She even made herself available for a photo-opportunity at her desk, but there were still limits. A peculiar dichotomy occurred whereby Rimington was happy to talk to journalists but the Home Secretary refused to let her appear before the Commons Home Affairs Select Committee (although she later lunched privately with six committee members at MI5's headquarters).

However, public relations was never going to be sufficient to address the real issue: the lack of broader and more independent oversight. Rimington was adamant that the 1989 Act provided adequate controls. 'Accountability lies at the heart of the tension between liberty and security,' she said, during the 1994 Richard Dimbleby lecture, delivered in the Banqueting Hall at Whitehall. 'A delicate balance must be struck within the framework of government in determining how far the Security Service should be allowed to go in invading the privacy of the few in the interests of the nation as a whole . . . The Security Service must operate within a clear framework of law . . . We give absolute priority to ensuring that everything we do is carried out with the proper authority.'[48]

For some experienced former MI5 personnel, the new measures were far too weak. While the Act was being debated in 1989, John Day, a senior and ultra-loyal officer from 1958 until 1982, sent a memorandum to selected members of the House of Lords:

> The Security Service Act is disappointing in that it does nothing to improve the efficiency or effectiveness of the Service . . . All government organisations are prone to bureaucratic self-interest. Without any effective form of external scrutiny the Security Service – free from the scrutiny of press and Parliament and protected, by threat of legal action, from any disclosures by members of the Service – must be particularly prone to this occupational disease.[49]

Despite ministerial and Cabinet Office reassurances over the next four years, Day remained unconvinced. In 1993, he broke cover again and said that supervision of MI5 remained inadequate. In a privately published memoir, part of which was censored by the government, Day rejected a committee of parliamentarians or Privy Counsellors. Instead he argued for an outside independent monitoring body. This would consist of three security commissioners who might include a former senior member of the armed forces, a retired civil servant or diplomat, an academic or a former trade-union leader. 'They [the Commissioners], and their small staff, would require free access both to the records and staff of the Security Service. Their role would be an advisory one, not executive.'[50]

Later that year the government opted for a parliamentary oversight committee as part of its new Intelligence Services Bill.

Launched in late 1994, the committee consists of MPs who 'examine the expenditure, administration and policy' of MI5, MI6 and GCHQ, but its nine members are appointed and replaced by the Prime Minister rather than through the usual Commons procedure, which involves wider consultation.

Chaired by Tom King, the former Defence Secretary and Northern Ireland Secretary, the Intelligence and Security Committee (ISC) meets weekly in secret session in Room 130, a secluded and secure room in the Cabinet Office. After taking evidence from the Security Service, it produces 'issue reports', which are submitted through the connecting door to 10 Downing Street for vetting. Before any ISC document is tabled in the Commons, Tony Blair has the right to excise and censor anything he believes is prejudicial to national security or confidential. It is a blanket veto on its contents and the timing of its publication.

The ISC's allegiance to Downing Street rather than Parliament has caused some controversy. Its strongest critic was Peter Mandelson, a member of the Commons Standing Committee which scrutinised the Bill and later a Cabinet Office minister himself. 'If we are setting up a committee of parliamentarians [the ISC] that cannot even report to Parliament,' he said, on 29 March 1994, 'people are bound to question the worth and value of the committee.' Mandelson, who is fascinated by the secret world, was bitterly opposed to so much power invested in the Prime Minister: 'If something in the report was embarrassing to the Prime Minister and the government, he could try to delay its publication, possibly until after a general election.'[51]

Clearly, the ISC needed to strike a balance between monitoring MI5's policies and value for money and not disclosing sensitive operations and sources of intelligence. Its critics argue that excessive secrecy has prevented the ISC from fulfilling its function. 'You can't let out too many secrets,' said David Shayler, who worked for MI5 for the first two years of the committee's existence. 'But the problem is that MI5 is paranoid about secrecy. It really is over the top . . . You've got to keep politicians out to the extent that we don't want MI5 being directed by a political party, but at the same time it needs to have effective scrutiny of what it's doing and that doesn't happen at the moment. The problem with the committee is that as I understand it, they've come to MI5 a few times, but all they've done is seen the director-general and top management. It's very easy for the DG to say, a bit like Stalin, "They're all happy workers in the fields." Whereas if they had actually talked to people on the ground, they might get a bit more feedback of what people really think.'[52]

One of the ISC's most distinguished critics is Sir Anthony Duff, former director-general of MI5 and before that chairman of the Joint Intelligence Committee. 'Where this is not adequate', he said, 'is that they [ISC] report to the Prime Minister. They ought to be reporting to Parliament, like a normal select committee.'[53] This was reinforced by Lord Gilbert, the Defence Procurement Minister in Blair's government, when the ISC was debated in Parliament: 'If the oversight committee will not have the power to send for persons and papers and if the people before it will suffer no sanction if they lie until they are blue in the face, the committee will be a laughing stock . . . The committee must have the power to sweat witnesses, and its proceedings must be protected by the perjury laws. Those are the proceedings of every select committee in the House.'[54]

The current Labour regime is full of ministers who opposed the ISC at it now operates. 'It should be a select committee,' said Dr John Cunningham in 1994, then Shadow Leader of the Commons and later Cabinet Office minister responsible for co-ordinating government policy with 10 Downing Street. 'It is proposed that the committee should not report to Parliament but to the Prime Minister. I do not regard that as parliamentary scrutiny or oversight, because the PM has the right to veto sections of its report – I call it prime ministerial scrutiny and oversight.'[55]

Labour's policy in opposition was for the ISC to be accountable to Parliament, not 10 Downing Street – as a select committee. In 1994, Labour MP Allan Rogers attacked the ISC: 'It is nonsense to suggest that those are accountable structures.' He predicted that the committee 'will be a charade, a pretence at accountability' and promised that 'when the Labour government comes in, we will make changes to the Bill'.[56] That pledge was never implemented, and on 31 July 1997, three months after Labour's election victory, Rogers became a member of the Intelligence and Security Committee.

The ISC has become a patsy for MI5. It was conceived, in effect, by the intelligence community, as Rogers discovered when he spoke to Sir Colin McColl, then head of MI6. 'I suppose you wrote this Bill, Sir Colin,' said the MP, during the debates on the Intelligence Services Bill. 'No. I didn't write it,' replied the MI6 director. 'But I did give a job description.'[57]

The ISC has become absorbed as a creature of the executive. It has no power to call up papers or summon witnesses. Its only source of information is what MI5's director-general chooses to disclose. Then its reports are censored and rewritten by 10 Downing Street before they are presented to Parliament. 'The ISC has insufficient access to information to hold the secret agencies fully to account,' said Yvette Cooper, a Labour member of the ISC. 'Although we are privy to secrets, it is at the discretion of the agency chiefs. How can you have effective oversight if the people you are supposed to be overseeing are the very people who decide how much information you get?'[58]

Successive Home Secretaries have refused to reform the current apparatus. 'We want to see fully how the existing arrangements work out in the new Parliament before making any decisions about change,' he said.[59] But the ISC has been operating since 1994 and some members feel compromised and frustrated by its restrictions. The only concession has been the appointment of a part-time investigator who examines specific complaints by having access to information kept secret from the ISC. This is desperately needed as the ISC is staffed by just three Cabinet Office civil servants, but the choice of John Morrison, former deputy chief of intelligence at the Ministry of Defence, only confirmed the lack of independent scrutiny. An intelligence officer has been appointed to investigate MI5 and MI6. 'Credibility depends on knowledge,' said Yvette Cooper, 'and knowledge depends on having the power to investigate and verify.'[60]

David Shayler's allegations provided the ISC's first substantial test of their ability to hold the agencies to account. While they interviewed Lander (then director-general) at length, the committee refused even to consider Shayler's detailed evidence in secret session – either in writing or orally. Its members formed a view of Shayler without hearing his case and based their opinion on the inevitably partial analysis of his former employers.

The inner ring of secrecy and lack of accountability that prevents the ISC from delving too deeply into the secret state is almost unique. Apart from France, virtually every other Western democracy has independent oversight of their intelligence agencies without compromising national security. In the United States, Canada and Germany, oversight committees have full access to information. Since 1981, there has never been a leak (with one US exception) from inside the oversight branch.

Most of these structures were set up after searching legislative and judicial inquiries. They found widespread surveillance of legitimate political activity where subversion was either ill-defined or misunderstood; systematic law-breaking where the agency deemed it necessary 'in the interests of national security'; and inefficiency due to years of operating in excessive secrecy without clear mandates.[61]

The most accurate role model for the UK would be in Canada, where they have a similar parliamentary and constitutional system. In 1981, a Royal Commission investigated their security services and published a report. It suggested the following principles: the rule of law is paramount; operational techniques must be proportionate to the gravity of the threat; these practices must be weighed against the damage they might do to personal freedom and privacy; the more intrusive the technique, the higher the authority should be to author-ise its use; except in emergencies, less invasive techniques must be preferred to more intrusive ones.

As a result of the Commission, Canada now has an inspector-general who has supervisory watchdog powers over its security service. He regularly assesses whether it is following the above directives or has indulged in 'an unreasonable or unnecessary exercise of its powers'.

There is also a Security Independent Review Committee (SIRC) which consists of between three and five Privy Counsellors, but not members of the Commons or Senate. They are appointed by the governor-general after consulting the Prime Minister and leaders of all parties which have at least 12 MPs in the Commons. The SIRC has an extremely wide mandate to examine security service reports. Its remit is to discern whether or not the service is efficient and effective 'without unreasonable or unnecessary intrusions on individual rights'.

Entitled to access to all relevant information held by the security service, the SIRC scrutinises ministerial directives, reports on the number of warrants issued, the individuals or groups targeted and the reasons for that surveillance. It also receives and adjudicates on complaints from individuals about 'any act or thing done by the service' and is answerable to the Federal Court of Appeal. It has the power to make complaints on behalf of individuals who have been denied security clearance and conduct an inquiry, whether the Solicitor General likes it or not.

After a number of scandals involving secret files, the Australian government also appointed an inspector-general. His job is to ensure all four intelligence agencies operate legally and do not infringe people's civil liberties, including the right to privacy. 'Intelligence agencies are protected to an extent no one else in this society enjoys,' said Neil McInnes, the first Inspector-General on his appointment in January 1987. 'It is natural in a democracy for these agencies to be subjected to a special form of control.'[62] He has the power to investigate a complaint and launch inquiries on his own initiative – for example on receipt of an adverse security report on an individual or a minister's request for the security service to collect and pass on information. He is also allowed to enter any intelligence agency and inspect files. If any officials try to obstruct him, they can expect a heavy fine.

In tandem is an all-party Joint Parliamentary Committee to monitor the Australian Security Intelligence Organisation (ASIO), the equivalent of MI5. Established in 1979, the committee's seven members – three from the Senate and four from the House of Representatives – are appointed by all party leaders. It has the power to conduct special inquiries. One of its reforms, welcomed by ASIO, was a new definition of 'subversion', which was seen as too broad. Instead, there were three new terms of activity: 'politically motivated violence', 'promotion of communal violence' and 'attacks on the Australian defence system'.

The ASIO must present a detailed annual report, which includes the phone numbers of its nine main offices and head office in Melbourne. Its director-general is answerable to the Attorney General, who has the power to issue new written guidelines. However, material considered security-sensitive about contemporaneous issues or operational methods is withheld from the committee and Parliament.

The United States has the most vigilant form of monitoring. There are powerful select committees on intelligence in both the Senate and the House of Representatives, with 15 members each to prevent abuse and law-breaking. They have a right to call for any people or papers. It is illegal for an intelligence agency not to disclose to Congress any operation, however secret (except for names, dates and places).[63]

Every new director of the CIA has to be approved by Congress. Its budget has also to be approved by Congress and is monitored by the

General Accounting Office, akin to Britain's National Audit Office. There are exhaustive hearings on their overt and covert operations, including telephone tapping and mail tampering. Wide-ranging freedom of information laws also allow considerable access to personal files and intelligence documents, particularly of a historical nature. Warrants have to be issued by the Attorney General and are subject to the courts' approval.

Although all members of the oversight committees are carefully security-vetted, some details of sensitive operations are withheld. Technically, this is illegal, so only the chairman and the senior minority members of the committees are informed. Congress has accepted that in reality it cannot receive prior notification of all covert CIA operations. Despite the extent of oversight, the US government goes to equally extreme lengths to protect genuine security secrets. Thick, sealed doors, protected by armed guards, show the degree to which these committees are committed to national security.

Unlike the CIA, the FBI has no charter, but its director answers to the Attorney General and the agency is accountable to three committees of each House of Congress and a judiciary sub-committee. The FBI also sends an annual report of its activities to Congress. This contains 150 pages of information on operations, ranging from police training and civil rights issues to drugs and terrorism.

The American experience shows that intelligence operatives are well protected and national security is not jeopardised by rigorous independent scrutiny, but the British are not so impressed. After a fact-finding trip to the USA in March 1998, ISC chairman Tom King complained there was too much accountability and it created a cumbersome bureaucracy. He was told by James Woolsey, director of the CIA from 1993 until 1995, that he gave evidence to a committee on Capitol Hill almost every day. 'We do not want to follow the model of oversight on that scale,' concluded King.[64]

For many years MI5 was content to restrict its role to combating subversion, foreign espionage and international terrorism., but since the IRA ceasefire of 1994–96, the Service has searched far and wide for new threats. After the Cold War, MI5 cunningly carved out roles to justify its existence. This was viewed suspiciously by some Cabinet ministers. 'We don't want to be inventing or appearing to invent new targets to keep busy when their old targets have disappeared,' said Geoffrey (now Lord) Howe, former Foreign Secretary

(1983–89), deputy Prime Minister (1989–90) and later a member of the ISC.[65]

One of MI5's most treasured new responsibilities has been investigating organised crime in support of the police. For years MI5 and the Home Office strongly denied they were interested in such activity. On 11 February 1993, Kenneth Clarke, then Home Secretary, said: 'The scale of drugs trafficking and other types of organised crime is not such that there is a current threat to national security. The Security Service therefore has no role in investigating these criminal matters and, contrary to recent press allegations, is not seeking one. The government have no plans to amend the Security Service Act to redefine the functions of the Service in this respect.'[66]

This was confirmed by Stella Rimington while director-general on 12 June 1994, during her Richard Dimbleby lecture: 'The Security Service Act makes clear that the work of the Service must be strictly limited to countering only threats to national security. We are not involved in countering drug-trafficking or organised crime. And we would only become involved if they came to pose such a threat to this country.'

Clarke accepted that organised crime was so serious in some countries that it did pose a national security threat – but not in the UK. In a letter to Tony Blair, then Shadow Home Secretary, in 1993, he stated: 'I do not consider that there is any question that it amounts at present to a threat to the security of the United Kingdom.' He added that it was 'most unlikely indeed' that drugs would reach such a danger point and so there were no security implications'.[67]

However, two-and-a-half months after Rimington stated her lack of interest the IRA ceasefire came into effect. That changed everything. Suddenly MI5 argued that organised crime was endangering national security and it was equipped to counter the threat. Rimington told the Home Secretary, Michael Howard, that the same skills used against IRA terrorism on the mainland could be adapted to investigate drug-trafficking, arms-smuggling and money-laundering. 'Whereas law enforcement intelligence is good for ordinary crime because of its short-term dynamic, in organised crime the relationships are more long-term, as with espionage,' claimed David Bickford, MI5's legal adviser at the time.[68]

As in her campaign to secure primacy against the IRA, Rimington played the Whitehall game superbly and Howard was persuaded. In

October 1995, he announced that MI5 was to support the police and other law enforcement agencies 'in the prevention and detection of serious crime'. The Service was so excited by its new role that a new section (D7) was immediately set up, staffed by six officers. But then they were told by the legal department that they could not start work until the legislation was actually passed. The officers sat at their desks for the next nine months 'researching the subject'.

MI5's new role dismayed senior members of MPSB, the National Criminal Intelligence Service (NCIS) and Customs and Excise, who already investigated organised crime. 'I employ analysts, so does NCIS, rather than sack them,' said Richard Kellaway, chief investigating officer of Customs and Excise, cuttingly. 'Maybe MI5 analysts should come and work for us.'[69]

In fact, the Service does have expertise in eavesdropping, covert searches and agent-handling which could be useful in combating organised crime. It can draw on an intelligent workforce who make a useful contribution to tracking down such criminals. The problem is its lack of accountability and oversight. The more MI5 becomes involved in criminal cases, the less convincing is its claim that it should retain its secrecy and be subject to less accountability than other law enforcement agencies. This means it will have to be less obsessed with secrecy and more transparent.

There is also a danger of an increased fragmentation of agencies which might affect co-ordination and impede investigations. The introduction of MI5 was not universally welcomed by NCIS, MPSB and Customs. They pointed to the fact that MI5 cannot deliver information on criminals with the same efficiency as police agencies. In 1995, NCIS employed 500 staff at a cost of £25 million – an estimated £25,000 for each employee. The Security Service had 2,000 staff on an annual budget of £150 million – about £75,000 per employee.[70]

In April 1998, yet another agency was established to counter organised crime – the National Crime Squad, which is now the lead police force in this area. Formed from six regional crime squads, it has 1,500 detectives and regularly uses hi-tech surveillance methods to monitor targets. Both this squad and NCIS have been effective and successful, and there is no evidence that MI5 is crucial to the law enforcement process.

In December 1999, MI5 was given primacy in investigating organised crime. Soon after the Northern Ireland settlement, the Home

Office was told by the intelligence services that Britain was facing a 'crime emergency'. The heads of MI5, MI6 and GCHQ were then summoned to a meeting at 10 Downing Street to discuss the threat from international organised crime. Tony Blair agreed to divert resources from counter-espionage and counter-terrorism so that MI5 could double its estimated £10 million annual budget on fighting 'serious crime'.[71] Apart from the traditional areas of drug trafficking, arms dealing and prostitution, this also involves investigating housing and child-benefit fraud.[72]

These areas have been the responsibility of the police, Customs and Special Branch. They deeply resent MI5 encroaching into law enforcement, because they claim that its officers are not equipped to convict criminals. MI5 operatives have been trained to gather and analyse intelligence. They are not adept at collecting evidence for a prosecution. Even if MI5 officers witness a crime, they will not always intervene, calculating that further useful information may be obtained by allowing events to continue. They tend to keep suspects in place rather than have them arrested and take detailed statements.

MI5 is particularly resistant to the openness of the criminal justice system, which requires them to give evidence and be cross-examined in court. In March 2000, a three-year case against three suspected Algerian terrorists collapsed at the Old Bailey when an MI5 informant refused to appear in court. Ministers had tried to stop details of Algerian government atrocities being introduced as evidence. That move failed and the MI5 witness then withdrew. The prosecution case promptly fell apart at an estimated cost of £20 million. MI5 was also criticised by the trial judge for bugging a conversation between the defendants and their lawyer at Belmarsh prison.

MI5 moving into crime detection and a quasi police role is a recipe for disaster. For much of its history, MI5 has flouted the law and its inexperience of gathering evidence for court cases is unlikely to succeed in complex prosecutions where adherence to the letter of the law is paramount.

It will also create inefficiency and turf wars between the police and the intelligence agencies. That has already started, according to a secret report in 2000 by the late Sir David Spedding, former chief of MI6, who found that a failure to share vital information was damaging the fight against organised crime.[73]

The main problem with MI5's involvement in the criminal justice system is its inherent secrecy. Under the 1996 Security Service Act,

MI5's function was extended to 'act in support of the prevention and detection of serious crime'. This was defined as an offence which 'involves the use of violence, results in substantial financial gain or is conducted by a large number of persons in pursuit of a common purpose'. This could include robberies and offences during demonstrations and Stella Rimington has spoken of the 'potential for integ-rating secret intelligence into the judicial process'. She told an audience of senior police officers: 'The Security Service is fully committed to supporting the police in detecting and preventing crime and preserving law and order. Criminal investigation can be a valuable focus for intelligence work, and equally intelligence can be converted into evidence.'[74]

This has enormous implications for the criminal justice system. A fair trial requires all evidence to be scrutinised in open court with witnesses being cross-examined, but the Service has relied on various immunities, exclusion orders and Public Interest Immunity Certificates (ministerial gagging orders) to prevent its operations being examined. As Lord Justice Simon Brown has stated: 'The very words national security have acquired an almost mystical significance . . . which instantly discourages the court from satisfactorily fulfilling its normal role in deciding where the balance of public interest lies.'[75]

Rimington claims it is wrong to make too sharp a distinction between the police detective and spy. But there are fundamental differences. Intelligence officers regard 'analysis' and a detailed comprehensive appraisal more important than preventing or even solving crime. And yet Crown Counsel are increasingly reading MI5 files for criminal cases. As John Alderson, former chief constable of Devon and Cornwall, said: 'These proposals are but tiny steps towards the fashioning of a police instrument which ultimately could damage even democracy itself. To minimise the differences between the political police and the ordinary civil police in a democracy gives hostages to fortune. Political police seek to infiltrate agents and informers into all aspects of social and political life. What we would end up with is a secret police force.'[76]

For MI5 to play a significant role in criminal investigations, it needs to accept new levels of accountability. This was pointed out by John Howley, the head of Special Branch, who supported the Service's new responsibilities: 'There would need to be a difference of attitude on the part of MI5 in coming to terms with the different standards of accountability.'[77]

However, so far MI5 continues to hide behind the cloak of secrecy in criminal trials: their officers give evidence in court anonymously behind screens in closed session. While this exists, there will always be a conflict between the principle of a fair and open adversarial trial and the secret workings of the Security Service.

The risk of the proliferation of weapons of mass destruction – nuclear, biological and chemical – has long been a serious threat to national security. An estimated 24 countries are trying to obtain the technology to manufacture such bombs. As some of these states sponsor terrorism, intelligence on such materials is invaluable and has become a high priority. Despite the various treaties on arms control and destruction, there are still thousands of nuclear missiles scattered among the former Soviet republics.

From the early 1980s, gathering intelligence on such proliferation was the sole responsibility of MI6 working alongside GCHQ. Then, in 1992, MI5 was brought in as the third agency. This was due to the collapse of the Soviet Union, which meant there was more danger of 'outlaw states' obtaining the raw materials to build these weapons. In addition to investigating the usual hostile powers like Iraq, China and Libya, MI5 also targets 'friendly' countries like India and Pakistan. Of most concern is nuclear proliferation in the Third World, which is at risk of catastrophic conflicts because of traditional rivalries.

As much of the material and technology required for such weapons can be found in the UK, MI5's role is to monitor foreign research students based at universities. 'Some governments will try every means – including enrolling their students at British universities – to bypass international agreements to obtain what they want,' said Stella Rimington.[78] The concern is that some students work undercover on behalf of foreign intelligence agencies. Based in G Branch, MI5 officers talk to university lecturers and hold seminars to make academics aware of the situation and explain the dangers.

In November 1997, two MI5 officers spoke to select members of the London Chamber of Commerce about this operation. 'If you know of any Iraqi students studying chemistry at a British university for more than three years, that would be of a great interest to us,' said one. This was followed up on 31 March 1998, when Stephen

Lander delivered a 'Counter-proliferation Briefing' at a 'Security Dinner' at the Dorchester Hotel. Sponsored by Resolution Security Ltd, a private security firm, Lander appealed to businessmen to 'work with the Security Service' and discover which countries were building up arms and nuclear supplies.

Once the intelligence is secured, MI5 passes it on to the government, which then applies diplomatic pressure to secure international agreement to prevent such proliferation. While MI5 can play a limited role in targeting 'students', most of this is overseas-based and Special Branch could easily oversee this work and avoid duplication.

Since 1994, MI5 has launched a propaganda campaign – largely by judicious leaks to the press – designed to persuade ministers that it is capable of a whole range of roles. Apart from serious crime and proliferation, the Service has 'let it be known' that it can counter social security fraud, police corruption, violent neo-Nazi gangs and Islamic terrorists. In truth, MI5 is desperately searching for new targets. The renewed ceasefire in Northern Ireland resulted in just 19.5 per cent of its resources being devoted to monitoring Irish terrorism. Proliferation, espionage and organised crime take up 19.1 per cent of the annual budget while 19.5 per cent is targeted at international terrorism and subversion. The rest is divided up between different areas (see Appendix One).

Some intelligence experts are not convinced that MI5 should be integrated into areas traditionally managed by the police, the time has come to consider closing down MI5 or transferring its responsibilities to other agencies. Such a radical view came from a most unexpected quarter just three months after David Shayler's revelations in the *Mail on Sunday*. In November 1997, David Bickford, MI5's legal adviser from 1987 until 1995, spoke at a conference on Business Crime and Risk. It was a remarkably candid and progressive speech.

Bickford stunned his audience of police and private intelligence specialists by launching into a withering attack on the Security Services, his main charge being that the £750 million a year cost of maintaining MI5, MI6 and GCHQ was completely unjustified. 'There was triplication of management, triplication of bureaucracy and triplication of turf battles,' he said. The former MI5 director added that the government 'should not finance three boards of directors, separate finance and contracts departments, separate research and development – and so the list goes on'.[79]

Speaking at the Royal Society of Arts in London, Bickford said a merger would save 'tens of millions of pounds' and provide for 'focused direction, integration, analysis of electronic and human intelligence to reduce risk'. He added that it was 'long overdue' for the ISC to instigate the amalgamation of the three organisations and replace them by a new national intelligence agency. British Intelligence, he said, 'is not doing its job properly.'

In effect, MI5's former legal adviser was calling for the abolition of MI5 because it was wasteful and incompetent. It was an astonishing statement, full of irony. For his analysis echoed precisely David Shayler's critique, which had been made public just weeks before. Like Bickford, Shayler argues that MI5 and MI6 often duplicate work because they do not communicate with each other and fail to devise a strategy to meet their objectives. Like Bickford, Shayler believes that it is impossible to reform the three intelligence agencies, given the intransigence of its management. 'The whole thing needs an overhaul,' he said. 'You have so many different organisations working in the area of intelligence, with sometimes duplicated roles and sometimes people not knowing who should be in the lead. You're creating this bureaucracy and creating the situation where departments can point to each other and say, "It wasn't our fault, it was their fault," and by doing that nobody is ever held to account.'[80]

Bickford and Shayler are not alone in their view of more centralised agencies to counter targets. In 1989, Sir Peter (now Lord) Imbert, then Commissioner of the Metropolitan Police, called for the establishment of a national detective agency to combat international organised crime. He was concerned at the fragmentation of groups and proposed an FBI-style national police unit to work as a unified investigative force. This was backed four years later when RUC Chief Constable Hugh Annesley argued for a national anti-terrorist task force, modelled on the FBI. A former Commissioner of Special Operations at Scotland Yard, Annesley believed such a body would be better suited to co-ordinate intelligence and train experts for that role.[81]

In practice, unification would not be a problem. In the United States, the FBI covers both counter-espionage (MI5) and police (Special Branch) functions. Alternatively, MI5's functions could be transferred to other agencies: vetting could go to the Ministry of Defence, counter-espionage and international terrorism could easily be absorbed by MI6, and organised crime could be reclaimed by NCIS.

Any new centralised agency would benefit from being staffed by the best of MI5, the police and Special Branch. In this fresh new environment, free of the bureaucratic restraints and old prejudices, officers would thrive. New ideas would prosper and proper independent oversight would be welcomed.

However, successive Labour Home Secretaries show few signs of even considering such a proposal. They back MI5's present regime as rigidly as any Conservative government. Despite their past opposition to the Official Secrets Act and oft-espoused commitment to freedom of information, the Labour government has not implemented any substantial reforms of the Security Service. Instead, the Home Office authorised a gagging order against the *Mail on Sunday*, the break-in to Shayler's flat and the arrest of Annie Machon and their friends.

During legal negotiations, Jack Straw, then Home Secretary appeared to be the conciliator while Blair wanted the MI5 whistleblower sent to the Tower. Shayler was allowed to negotiate possible terms for his return to the UK and got so far as a heads-of-agreement document. But this was short-lived. As soon as Shayler threatened to reveal details of the attempted assassination plot against Libyan leader Colonel Gaddafi, Straw authorised Special Branch to seek Shayler's arrest and extradition from France. It was a strategy that backfired on him in the most embarrassing fashion.

On several occasions in 1988 Straw voted against the Bill that became the current Official Secrets Act. He opposed the abolition of the public-interest defence for whistleblowers. But during his time as Home Secretary he was a staunch defender of the secrecy clause. In November 1998, in a letter to Frank Cook, the MP for Shayler's parents, Straw stated in the clearest terms his new stance:

> We have no plans to introduce a public interest defence into the 1989 Act. The Act deals with disclosures which cause specific kinds of harm to the national interest. That is a high threshold and goes far further than disclosure of material that is merely embarrassing. It is difficult to envisage how a public interest defence could be appropriately deployed in this very narrow range of circumstances. If there were a public interest defence, it would be open to any officer to decide for them-

selves when they thought the release of information was in the public interest – I do not see that that would be acceptable to any government.

Straw admitted that the Labour Party supported a public-interest defence in the past, but claims that MI5's operations have been changed, which makes such a defence 'much less desirable'. Naïvely, he said that the fact that the Security Service is now on a statutory basis means that there is no further need for a public-interest defence. 'In Mr Shayler's case,' concluded Straw, 'the right of free speech has to be weighed against the need, in the national interest, for effective security and intelligence services, something we intend to protect.'

Straw's close colleague Derry Irvine, the Lord Chancellor, has also had a change of heart since he became a minister. In 1996, Irvine criticised the inadequacy of the ISC. He also argued that the Official Secrets Act 'fails to recognise the public interest to know of abuses by government of its powers and is more repressive in practice than the previous Act'.[82] The Lord Chancellor was arguing that an MI5 whistleblower like Shayler should be protected by a public-interest defence.

For the moment MI5 is protected from reform and democratic oversight. It is allowed to retain its power base and its rigid bureaucracy and hides from public view by a secrecy culture backed to the hilt by New Labour. Its 'regulator', the ISC, has refused even to accept written evidence in private from Shayler.

But for what purpose? This obsession with secrecy has resulted in two young Palestinians languishing in top-security prisons after being falsely accused of committing the attack on the Israeli embassy after former Home Secretary Straw's refusal to release documents vital to their case that might reduce their jail term.

And what about Shayler's allegation about the MI6 plot to kill Gaddafi? If he is right, a state-sponsored murder was commissioned. Yet the government's own security adviser refused to receive his evidence on the matter.

Shayler has alleged that lives could have been saved if it was not for MI5 incompetence and bungling over IRA bombing campaigns in Britain. And yet, once again, no one in authority has sought to investigate his claims.

The closest we have come to an investigation is the Cabinet Office

review of MI5, MI6 and GCHQ set up in 1997 in the wake of
Shayler's initial revelations. It refused to accept evidence from critical witnesses – including Shayler – and effectively made no serious
recommendations for reform or change.

The Home Office has seldom been more authoritarian. New laws
governing terrorism, the Internet and encryption has massively
increased the power of the state. For the British people there
remains little protection from what is rapidly becoming a surveillance society. It is now frighteningly easy for state security agencies
to collate secret dossiers, tap telephones, intercept e-mails and place
people under surveillance. For most people, genuine access to their
MI5 file – their most important civil right – is still denied them. Even
the ISC has advocated that there should be independent scrutiny of
the way MI5 reviews its dossiers.

By a stroke of exquisite irony Cabinet ministers Jack Straw,
Patricia Hewitt and John Prescott have been victims of MI5. But they
refuse what every other western democracy apart from France has
enshrined in law: the right of the individual to inspect their file if
there is no danger to national security. Even the former Eastern bloc
regimes have published secret intelligence files from the
Communist era.

The main problem is that New Labour has acted very much like
Old Labour towards the Security Service: subservient, bewildered
and repressive against its critics. Just before the 1997 general election, the author Stephen Dorril wrote to Tony Blair asking about his
policy for the intelligence community. Blair suggested that he speak
to shadow Home Secretary Jack Straw. His office said he was 'thinking about it' but nothing appeared in the manifesto.[83] When they
entered office, Blair and Straw were clearly awestruck and
mesmirised by the power and mystique of MI5. In effect, MI5 formu-
lated its own policy and the government implemented it.

Despite taking steps towards more transparency, MI5 is still the
most secretive and unaccountible western intelligence agency
apart from perhaps the French secret service. It still relies on
excessive secrecy to intimidate and bamboozle senior ministers
and civil servants. Secrecy is MI5's most powerful and reliable
weapon and its directors can always fall back on it as a trusted
sword to resist further oversight and public scrutiny. As Malcolm
Muggeridge, himself a former intelligence officer, once wrote:
'Secrecy is as essential to Intelligence as vestments and incense to

a Mass . . . and must at all costs be maintained, quite irrespective of whether or not it serves any purpose.'[84]

The Labour government has hidden behind this veil of secrecy instead of confronting the fundamental problems facing the Security Service. While MI5 has taken on new roles and targets and expanded its power base, it has not dealt with the legacy of its past and the weakness of its internal structures, methods and management culture in a sufficiently radical manner. Unless it comes to terms with those inherent flaws, it will never truly be able to claim it is defending the realm.

Appendix One
STRUCTURE OF MI5

Senior Management

Director-general
Deputy Director-general
Director and Co-ordinator of Intelligence (responsible for Northern Ireland)
Legal Adviser

Departments

A Branch – Operational Support

A1A: Technical operations, covert entry, eavesdropping devices, CCTV coverage of premises
A1F: As above, but on longer-term targets like embassies and head offices of political parties
A2A: Transcription of intercept material
A3 and A5: Technical support for operations. This includes specialised covert photography and lockpickers to assist in covert entries
A4: Mobile and static surveillance units

B Branch – Human Resources

B1: Protective security for MI5, including security of buildings and vetting of MI5 staff
B2: Personnel
B7: Training and recruitment

D Branch – Non-Terrorist Organisations

D1: Vetting of people outside MI5
D4: Counter-espionage, notably on Russia and China
D5: Agent runners for this branch
D7: Organised crime

G Branch – International Terrorism

G2P: Counter-proliferation

G3A: Co-ordination of threat assessments

G3C: Countering threats from the Indian sub-continent, notably violent Sikh activists

G3W: Countering terrorism in other parts of the world not covered elsewhere by G Branch

G6: Agent runners for G Branch

G9A: Countering threats from Libya, Iraq, Palestinian and Kurdish groups

G9B: Countering threats from Iranian state terrorism and Iranian dissident groups

G9C: Countering Islamic extremists

H Branch – Corporate Affairs

H1 and H2: Liaison with Whitehall and the media. Covert financial enquiries with financial institutions. This section liaises with the police, customs, ports and immigration. It is also responsible for management policy, including information technology.

H4: Finance

The following sections are also part of H Branch

R2: Main registry

R5: Y-boxed files. These are files with restricted access within the Service.

R10: Registry for temporary files

R20: Responsible for administering GCHQ material

T Branch – Irish Terrorism

T2A: Investigates Republican and Loyalist terrorism on the British mainland

T2B: Liaises with local Special Branches and agent runners with responsibility for investigating Irish terrorism on the mainland

T2C: Assesses threats from Irish terrorist groups

T2D: Researches Irish terrorist groups

T2E: Liaises with Metropolitan Police Special Branch, based at Scotland Yard

T5B: Investigates arms trafficking

T5C: Counters Irish terrorism in continental Europe, including the Republic of Ireland

T5D: Counters Irish terrorism in the rest of the world

T5E: Studies terrorist logistics

T8: Runs agents for T Branch; includes a section based in Northern Ireland

PS: MI5 also has security and defence liaison officers based in Germany, Washington DC and Cyprus.

Appendix Two

DAVID SHAYLER'S SUBMISSION TO THE CABINET OFFICE REVIEW

Management issues

Background

- This document deals only with the management problems that MI5 faced when I was in the Service. Although it is possible the Service could have changed greatly, I doubt this is the case knowing the culture that prevails. An ex-member of MI5 recently told me that the Service had been obliged to carry out a survey of staff attitudes, as a result of my initial disclosures. To the surprise of senior management, the criticisms were greater and deeper than the points I had made.

- This document was initially submitted to the Cabinet Office Review of the intelligence agencies, ordered in October 1997. As far as I am aware, its findings were never made public, other than the fact that the review recommended a cut in budget for MI5, MI6 and GCHQ in real terms over the following three financial years.

- A former deputy director general of MI5, who was responsible for many of the problems that I discuss below, chaired the review. I believe this represented a clear conflict of interest which reflected very badly on MI5.

- Although my critiques apply to MI5, I know that Richard Tomlinson, the former MI6 officer, has many similar ideas about mismanagement in that Service.

Key points

- The 'Office culture' in MI5 accords no value to good management, efficiency and initiative. As a result, staff, particularly in the lower grades, have become demoralised and disillusioned.

- Management in MI5 are unwilling to embrace the change necessary to bring MI5 up to date with current management practice. As a result, particularly with regard to IT, it is inefficient and not as effective as it could be in protecting national security.

- MI5 should start modernising as quickly as possible. Many practices cost little to implement and staff have already been taught to use them on MI5 training courses.

- In areas where it does not have the expertise, MI5 needs to hire qualified consultants. It should not ignore this advice simply because senior managers feel their jobs are threatened.

- There should be a great deal more oversight of MI5's ability to provide value for money. Bureaucrats should not be allowed to build their own empires at the expense of the public purse.

General

Background

A1. When I joined MI5 in 1991, it was obvious that by failing to reform itself in the 1980s, the Service had fallen behind with management practice and information technology but still showed little concern with modernising itself. Given that its intelligence requirements had changed post-Cold War, MI5 seemed to have done little to adapt its management and working methods. However, in the early 1990s, the Service began to recruit GI officers from a wide variety of professional backgrounds in order, we were told, to bring new ideas and new perspectives to the Service. This was a departure from generally recruiting GIs direct from college with no experience of other organisational cultures.

A2. However, once this new intake joined, management ignored their views and ideas, expecting them to conform to 'Office culture' (the MI5 name for its rather quaint working methods). Those who had worked elsewhere, particularly in the private sector, were often surprised to find amateurish, outdated attitudes to management and change within MI5. The Service failed to see that it had to be managed efficiently, like any other private or public sector organisation, whether its end product was widgets, intelligence reports or arrests. In fact, management becomes more important when organisations have fewer resources and have to undergo change. When I was in MI5, my contemporaries saw few signs that anyone properly thought through the implications of change or how to make the resources go further. Senior management did not attempt to create 'buy-in' to change among the GI and the AG who became increasingly disillusioned with the Service as a whole.

A3. Some managers appeared to be more interested in protecting their own bureaucratic empires rather than helping MI5 to provide a more efficient service to its paymasters, the taxpayer. In fact, many staff had the impression that MI5 top management was deliberately trying to undermine change so the Service could claim that government policies weren't working and, by extension, that it needed more staff. During my time, managers from SM1 down to GI2 expressed their belief that management only applied to business and no one ever seemed concerned with saving money. Group leaders only discussed actual management issues with their staff when they had, as they saw it, nothing better to do.

A4. When Stephen Lander went on a walkabout to talk to staff in summer 1996, he sat and either looked out of the window or fidgeted around while they talked to him. In at least one case, he told an officer that her work was of little value as he never read the briefs she had to spend many hours co-ordinating and editing. It was quite obvious he had no interest in what his staff had to say. A responsible manager would use such an opportunity to listen and act where appropriate; he would not further demotivate his staff by openly ignoring what they had to say to him. I understand that Lander has also abolished the Management Steering group. If this is the case, it appears to show that MI5's commitment to management, and by extension, efficiency and effectiveness, is getting worse and not better.

A5. In fact, one example illustrates MI5's attitude to management rather well. One of my group leaders, a GI2, took an MBA in his own time and under his own initiative. When he finished it, the Service did not offer him promotion, even though he was a better-trained manager than many of MI5's directors. Disillusioned, the GI2 left when he was offered a post in local government, which recognised how it would benefit from his qualification. The Service did not, so it gained no benefit, despite partly paying for the officer's qualification.

A6. Although MI5 did change during my time there, the change was slow, ill thought out, and inefficiently managed not least because management opposed change, and by extension, greater efficiency. Only changes in government policy and funding forced MI5 to adopt new practices. But these were introduced without enthusiasm and in an amateurish way, which created bad feeling and demotivated staff. It was very obvious to many of the staff who had been recruited in the early 1990s or staff who had experience of professional work outside the Service that there was a number of obvious steps management should take. These are discussed below.

Training

A7. MI5's attitude to management was perhaps best illustrated by its attitude to training. MI5 would never let untrained officers be involved in operational activity on their own. For example, an officer would not be allowed to run an agent on his own, if the officer had not been on the agent-running training course. And quite rightly. However, training was optional for senior managers – many of whom chose not to go to the courses on offer – and personnel officers, most of whom fortunately did take up the opportunity. However, even these officers realised that their careers would be held back as they were not working in the mainstream of intelligence work while, due to MI5's posting policy, they were moved on after three years. In other words as soon as they became fully qualified. How did the Service expect untrained senior managers and part-trained personnel officers to do an efficient job?

A8. In addition, desk officers attended courses which their managers had not. On these, the desk officers were taught new ways of working, but were then discouraged from using these new skills and methods by ignorant managers. In some cases, GI2s even penalised desk officers in annual appraisals for doing what the officers had been taught on Service training courses. This was inefficient on three levels:

- The Service loses out, if there are more effective ways of working, and its trained staff are not using them.

- The actual training courses are a waste of time and money, if no one is allowed to use what they have learnt at them for the benefit of the Service.

- It is extremely demotivating and confusing for staff to find themselves penalised when they put into practice what they have learnt on a training course.

A9. The officers in middle management (GI3-2) were not given any special management training – beyond the basic GI4-6 and lower AG management courses. Many did not even follow the simple advice given on these courses. For example, GI3-2s were advised that they should have semi-formal meetings with individual members of their staff at least once every three months to discuss progress. During my time in the Service, I had to insist time and again that my group leaders held such meetings. Some simply refused. Others did so unwillingly and used them to mislead me about my progress towards promotion. Not one of my line managers ever sought to hold a progress meeting with me (although they always found time to pedantically edit written pieces I submitted to them).

Middle management

A10.   Middle management probably gave the most cause for concern to GI4-6s and the lower AG grades, as well as to personnel. Most organisations have a pyramid-style structure. In MI5, there were more GI2s than staff at the grades they managed, usually either GI4 or GI5. The vast majority, if not all, of those at GI2 (and many longer established GI3s) were promoted under the system which operated until the early 1990s. Most officers then went directly from GI4 to GI2. Although promotion was notionally on ability, many were effectively promoted according to their length of service in MI5.

A11.   When officers are promoted for time serving, it is inevitable that some will be promoted beyond their abilities. In addition to these officers, there are many GI2s in MI5 who were promoted using outdated criteria. These GI2s simply do not have the personality traits required to become managers – good interpersonal skills, self-confidence in front of an audience, leadership qualities, problem-solving ability, and organisational skills. Those who do have the right personality show little inclination to develop their management skills. Many of GI2s do little other than act as a conduit between their staff and senior line management (GI1 or SM4).

A12.   In other words, they act as an extra tier of bureaucracy without adding value. They certainly showed little inclination to carry out routine middle-management activities:

- They did not motivate staff.

- They did not measure performance or evaluate the length of time taken to perform routine tasks to establish if they had the right manning levels.

- They rarely developed and coached staff, partly because they were not trained but partly because they feared that capable GI4s could take their jobs. For similar reasons, they did not recognise the need to develop AG staff who, in some cases, had more appropriate skills for agent running than many of the more bookish GIs.

- They did not attempt to build teams. In fact, they were more likely to point the finger of blame at one of their staff than to take responsibility for the work of their group.

A13. As MI5 did not restructure or make staff redundant (see above), there were, during my time in MI5, far too many middle managers. Nearly all of them were untrained and many were incompetent. Too many of them held much sought-after positions, where they had responsibilities they could not meet. These middle managers interfered with routine desk work, often taking interesting cases off their staff, because they felt more comfortable carrying out desk work.

Proposals

A14. If it has not already done so, the Service needs to rationalise its structure. It is true that restructuring could mean there would be fewer promotion opportunities, although if MI5 were courageous enough to remove all of those who underperformed, it might open up positions to experienced GI4s. When I was in MI5, capable GI4s were often not even recommended for promotion because many of the GI2s were simply not trained, and had no idea how objectively to assess performance. They protected their own position by hiding behind the 'Office culture' which put a premium on conformity rather than problem solving and initiative.

A15. MI5 should assess which GI2s, GI3s and GI4s have the personal qualities and character which makes them capable of management. In order to ensure that this is done properly and objectively, MI5 should call in a human resources consultancy. The investment in consultants is sure to save money over time as the consultancy will select the managers of the future based on psychometric and management tests and interviews (see also the competency framework mentioned below). In addition, consultants will not be swayed by the rumour and hearsay which currently influences Promotion Board decisions.

A16. GI officers assessed to be capable of management should then be trained in management practice and skills. Again, this would probably be done more effectively if the Service hired a consultancy to conduct the training courses. Those assessed not to be capable of management should either be offered any one or more of the following:

- Policy posts, if they have demonstrated that they have the skills for this kind of work.

- Voluntary redundancy on attractive terms.

- Posts elsewhere in the Civil Service.

A17. The Service should also endeavour to provide staff with comprehensive and up-to-date outplacement services, advising them on how to prepare effective and modern CVs and actively using its contacts to help them find new posts, wherever they may be.

A18.   Of course, MI5 could take one simple step towards better assessing the capabilities of its middle managers. It could ask those who know best how well a particular GI2 or GI3 performs as a manager – their staff. Compulsory upward reporting is now the norm in the private sector. There is no convincing reason why MI5 should not introduce it.

A19.   As MI5 has chosen in the past not to make staff redundant or restructure its management organisation, this initiative is perhaps the most critical in terms of future efficiency and effectiveness. In other words, it is not a question of whether but when. The longer it takes to put this into effect, the more it will cost in terms of lost productivity now and higher severance payments in future.

Personnel

All-round desk officer
A20.   While I was in MI5, it maintained the policy of the all-round desk officer. While this may have looked like a good idea in theory, in practice it led to shy, reserved officers being forced into liaison jobs and, conversely, good communicators being posted to research jobs. Good writers were sent out to lecture and good speakers were put behind desks to edit drafts. I stress that individuals were not sent to posts where they had little experience so they could develop in areas where they showed aptitude. They were sent to jobs in which they had no interest, and no ability to carry out, in the vain hope this would make them develop new personality traits and skills. Staff at GI4-6 level believed this was one of MI5's most misdirected policies. I believe it was one of the biggest causes of resignation and disillusionment. Other organisations have found that they get better results by promoting those who show management capability, not those who have a comprehensive knowledge of the jobs at that grade.

Grading
A21.   GI4-6 officers were also disillusioned by the grading system. MI5 did not grade posts according to the skills and experience needed to meet the responsibilities but according to the importance of the work of the desk in the Service's priorities. Hence, GI4s and GI5s in F and G branches carried out a variety of responsibilities, including basic management, policy work and high-level representation of the Service, as well as carrying out the full range of desk work. GI4s and GI5s in T2A, however, mainly did the work

carried out by the former AG in G9 or F2: trace requests, reviewing GENs (tempor-ary files) and basic research and investigative work. There was very little real opportunity for officers in T2A to prove themselves as promotion material yet this did not stop the Service promoting them over G branch officers who had relevant experience and had demonstrated they had the skills required at GI3 or GI2.

A22. In fact, personnel officers used the grading system, particularly with regard to the former AG, as a simple way of posting staff. If the post was graded at AG6, the personnel officer seemed just to trawl through AG6s ready for a move and then send them to the post in question. The AG6 posts were extremely varied, ranging from filing and carding to similar work to GI6s, so staff at AG6 had a variety of skills and experience. B2A posted one AG6, who I had managed and developed to approaching desk officer stan-dard, to a filing job. This was a waste of resources on three levels:

- My time spent developing the AG6 (as I was taught to do on Service train-ing courses) was wasted and I had to devote further time to developing the replacement AG6;

- It was a waste of the AG6's potential as he was unable to use the desk skills he had learnt or develop his skills further while working as a clerk. He became demotivated as he had proved himself at what was, effectively, a higher level, but was then posted to work well below his capabilities;

- The Service wasted its ever-decreasing resources by not employing the AG6 to his full potential in the Office.

A23. When I pointed the above out during the AG6's annual appraisal, my group leader told me that I should keep such comments to myself and stop being a troublemaker.

A24. Fortunately, a forward-looking head of personnel (B2/0 in 1996), hired a firm of management consultants to help set up a competency frame-work when I was in the Service. Competency frameworks are now used routinely in the private and public sectors as they are a tried and tested methodology. They aim to assess the level of skills and personal qualities of each member of staff and to match these to the level of skills and personal qualities needed for each individual post. I, like many other staff, saw this as a very worthwhile exercise which, if done properly, would make a contribu-tion to the efficiency of the Service and would motivate staff by finding them jobs which matched their skills and personalities.

A25. B2/0 and many other staff, including myself, attended seminars, circulated documents, sought comments and so on. However, top management tried to undermine the framework by:

- Refusing to accept within the framework that GI4-6s should be rewarded for using their individual personality traits to persuade or influence outside contacts.

- Fiddling with the findings of the research to establish the framework.

- Not funding the survey properly in the first place.

- Not allocating resources to a Service-wide roll out of the new scheme to ensure staff buy-in.

A26. It was a clear indication of how far removed they had become from the staff they supposedly managed and how far out of touch they were with current management practice. B2/0 was as disappointed by this as others who had worked on the framework and complained that Stephen Lander himself had tried to undermine the programme.

Proposals
A27. MI5 should abolish its grading system. As it sees individuals as grades rather than matching their particular qualities to a specific post, it is counter-productive and bureaucratic. While I was in MI5, it abolished the distinction between AG and GI. There is no reason why the entire grading system should not follow.

Assessing performance
A28. When I joined MI5, staff did not have targets to meet. Their line managers assessed them against criteria like 'relations with contacts outside the Service', 'judgement' and 'analytical thinking' which were hopelessly subjective. No one ever bothered to set targets in advance so performance was not measurable against objective cri-teria. This was an open charter for any group leader to blacken the future of one of their staff, which many seemed to do with the pleasure of a Victorian schoolteacher. Staff were given 'general objectives', which could be measured, but meeting these did not count towards a good annual appraisal.

A29. I mention the above as that kind of appraisal was supposed to have been abolished in the Service with the introduction of performance-related pay. Group leaders (mainly GI2s and AG4s or AG3s) were supposed to set objectively measurable targets. Again, they were not trained to do this properly (although G14-6s and AG6s and below were taught these on Service training courses) and few ever bothered to set proper targets in agreement with individual members of their staff.

A30. In some cases, like my own, GI4-6s took the initiative and drafted and agreed measurable targets with their group leader. However, meeting these targets appeared to count for little compared to concepts like 'keeping your nose clean' and 'not rocking the boat'. In one case, an officer exceeded five management targets and was fully up to standard on all 'desk' targets but was not even recommended for promotion.

Proposals
A31. Training middle management will help in this area as will making redundant those who cannot adapt to new systems. MI5 needs to ensure it is fairly and objectively assessing staff as:

- It is ineffective to promote those who are not capable of management.

- Staff become extremely demoralised if their efforts are not recognised or objectively assessed.

Confidentiality
A32. When I joined MI5, staff were not allowed to see the final version of their annual report, which not only recorded the final verdict on that staff member's performance for the year but also made recommendations for their future in MI5. This changed while I was in MI5. However, there is still a culture of secrecy which is counter-productive. In 1993, my group leader wrote an appraisal of me which would have been actionable, had I not given up my legal right to take the Service to an industrial tribunal. Shortly after the whole debacle, I discovered on unofficial channels that loose minutes had been exchanged between my various line managers and between them and personnel commenting on my performance. I was not given a chance to comment on these and did not even know they existed at the time. In this case, management demonstrated here that they had little sense of good judgement when it came to natural justice. This is bad enough in any organisation. However, MI5 is charged with responsibility for investigating threats fairly and without bias. If it cannot manage this with its own staff, critics may wonder how it hopes to be considered fit to make such assessments with regard to other targets.

Proposals
A33. MI5 should allow staff to see their own personal files when they need to. This will encourage group leaders to take more responsibility for their

actions and ensure that staff have access to information held on them and will at least have a chance to reply to any criticisms.

Representation and redress

A34. I believe that much of the reason that line managers do such an appalling job in MI5 is that there is little redress and no repre-sentation. Police officers, who are crown servants like MI5 staff, have been known to take Police Federation lawyers into annual appraisals. While I do not suggest that this is the way forward, MI5 needs to look at the whole issue of staff representation and redress. When I was in MI5, there was no formal advice for staff in dispute with management. In fact, B2A specifically refused to become involved in these matters and line management closed ranks as they feared any dispute in their sections might reflect badly on them. Staff simply did not know which options were open to them if they felt they had been unfairly treated. Where staff knew avenues of redress did exist, managers encouraged staff not to use them by holding threats of long-term career damage over them.

Proposals

A35. If MI5 believes it cannot comply with English law and allow staff to take their cases to an industrial tribunal, the government must look at setting up independent arbitration specifically to deal with disputes in the intelligence services. Similarly, if the intelligence services do not feel that they can abide by the rules of natural justice and allow their staff to join a trade union, the government should set up a cross-services representational body, along the lines of the Police Federation. The representational body is particularly important as intelligence agency staff need to be represented in matters of pay since the abolition of collective bargaining in the Civil Service.

Office Culture

Conformity

A36. For reasons that appear to be outdated, MI5 models itself on the culture of the home Civil Service, except that it is the culture of the Civil Service before the reforms which began in the 1980s. MI5 does not explain this to its new recruits during the recruitment process. If I had known this, I probably would not have joined the Service as I had never had any inclination to work in this kind of repressive, conformist culture. There were times in MI5 when staff felt the whole organisation was geared to suppressing their individuality, initiative and drive. If a G4 took on greater responsibility than their grade would expect, their line managers actively sought out any minor problems encountered and used this against the officer concerned. One member of staff was told that he was 'too enthusiastic' in an appraisal report and that he had to 'learn to curb his independent traits' by the Promotion Review Board.

A37.   In fact, MI5 seems to combine the worst elements of the Civil Service with its gradism and bureaucracy (without, of course, the right to representation) and military culture where the junior ranks are expected to follow orders. Arguing your case in MI5 was seen as wrong. Line managers would record that this indicated a 'lack of judgement' on the part of the officer rather than an honest difference of opinion which had to be debated to be resolved. Staff gave up putting forward new ideas or arguing their point of view as they feared it would count against them. How can an organisation expect to modernise itself when open debate is at best discouraged and at worst suppressed?

A38.   Staff were often treated like children. When B2 proposed to allow staff to use the gym during core hours (08:00 to 12:00 and 14:00 to 18:00) as the gym was becoming too crowded at lunchtimes and after work, senior managers in G branch vetoed this initiative without reference to their staff. Although I appreciate that this is a small example, it demonstrates just how out of touch senior managers were with staff expectations and modern attitudes to empowering staff.

Proposals
A39.   MI5 should stop combining the worst elements of Civil Service and military culture. Again, removing managers who cannot or will not debate should help MI5 to become the dynamic organisation it should be. Similarly, the culture should change or recruiters should be more honest with applicants about the nature of the work and the attitudes of management.

A40.   Over-qualified recruits should not be taken on to do basic work, as happened when I was in the Service, just because it was expedient. This will only lead to further demoralisation of new recruits who may then leave, meaning the Service has seen little return on its investment in recruiting, vetting and training new officers.

Difference with other cultures
A41.   I have argued that MI5 should stop pleading special circumstances and adopt modern management practice. However, there are some areas where the intelligence agencies are different from the private sector and even the mainstream public sector. If you work for Shell and your career is not going well, you can always apply for jobs with BP, Esso etc. This option does not exist within the intelligence agencies, particularly with regard to

professional staff. In the past, when staff tended to be automatically promoted on length of service and had job security, these factors acted as compensation for the lower salary officers received compared with the private sector. Many officers were GI2s before they were 35 and therefore received moderately good remuneration.

A42.   There are now far fewer promotion opportunities so many officers will have to live off a GI4's salary, possibly for the rest of their careers in MI5. By the time they reach 40, these officers will be living off a pittance compared to graduates in the private sector and will probably have little more job security. It is likely that capable graduates who find themselves in these circumstances will wish to leave MI5. However, they will find it difficult to sell themselves in the private sector. Intelligence officers do not have relevant commercial experience and will have difficulty convincing potential employers that they can adapt their skills to other work. They will also experience 'culture shock' in adjusting to the outside world.

Proposals
A43.   The intelligence services have extensive experience of looking after resettled agents. They should use some of this experience to help former staff re-integrate with normal life. Personnel officers need to look at how they can help recruits with proper professional career planning and provide outplacement advice. MI5 also needs to develop contacts with the outside world to actively find jobs for officers who feel the need to move on, like the army does. Dedicated, properly trained personnel officers would make a valuable contribution here.

Information technology

Office management systems
A44.   When I worked for MI5, it was very much behind the times regarding office management and database IT. It seemed peculiar to me that an organisation whose entire work involved the processing of information could be so far behind commercial organisations in its introduction of IT. I appreciate that since I left, MI5 has taken some steps to rectify this, but only after spending many years trying to introduce an in-house system, which had reportedly wasted £25 million and was still not fully up and running when I left MI5. Again, MI5 appeared to adopt the way of the gentleman amateur, using intelligence officers with little or no experience of IT, who were untrained in project management techniques, to develop this system. In the end, MI5 was forced to buy an off-the-shelf office management system based on Windows 95 which it adapted to its own needs and rolled out as CORONA.

A45.   The costs of overmanning and general inefficiency as a direct result of not introducing IT into office management are incalculable, especially when we bear in mind how MI5 worked. Desk officers wrote material in draft, much of which would be copied by hand from incoming paper reports, then sent it to secretaries in draft. The officer would get it back, correct it, send it back to his secretary, receive another version (which might need further corrections) before disseminating the document to management. The document, especially if it were a warrant, might then be altered by the group leader, the assistant director, the director, H1A or the DDG. That this happened was bureaucratic enough, but without IT the whole process was made exponentially more complicated as each new draft had to be re-typed and printed out again.

Databases
A46.   When I joined F2 in 1992, some staff had just started to use HAWK, a database dedicated to recording subversives. Like with so much IT in MI5, it had been developed over a number of years but was only rolled out when the subversive threat was virtually over. As it was designed specifically for subversives, it could not be used to record other MI5 targets. MI5 now devotes half a desk to the study of subversives so I presume this database is not used to anywhere near its capacity. It would be interesting if the review could establish shelf database software, which was proven and could have been adapted to F2's needs and the requirements of other sections in the Service. This assessment would also have to take into account the cost of man-hours wasted by staff using the paper-carding system during the development of HAWK.

A47.   When I joined T2A, I found that there were similar problems with DURBAR, a system which could not cope with the amount or variety of data on it and was probably over five years out of date, even in 1992. I appreciate that DURBAR II was rolled out in my time in MI5 but the review might like to consider:

• What resources were wasted developing this system, when – again – commercially available software could have fulfilled the requirement.

• How much intelligence on terrorist targets, particularly PIRA, was either lost or missed by not having proper quality control of information entered on DURBAR.

A48.   I know that in many vetting cases, the Service had to give a 'nothing recorded against' assessment even though DURBAR indicated that the applicant had terrorist traces, as the original intelligence could not be located. The implications for national security, especially in the all-important area of Irish Republican terrorism, were enormous.

Voicemail

A49.   In 1996, MI5 invested in a new top of the range Voicemail system not in response to staff demand – although that was there among the technologically competent – but because it had to use up a large surplus in one of its budgets. Voicemail is used by many businesses to save on the costs of employing support staff. As this was top of the range, it had many useful features, which staff weren't allowed to use for undisclosed 'security reasons'. In fact, staff were forbidden (on pain of a breach being entered on their record of service) from even indicating to a caller whether the caller had got through to the right extension. (Callers could only get through to the lines via the switchboard or via an unlisted number as long as they had the correct extension number.)

A50.   It was, therefore, difficult to see how: 'Hello, it's Dave here' or 'You are through to G9A/5' was going to compromise security. However, callers who got the standard voicemail message often had to phone through to the secretary anyway because they did not know from the standard message whether the member of staff was away from his desk in the toilet or on a two-week holiday in the Bahamas.

A51.   If MI5 is going to use new technology, it should either buy a system which matches its requirements or allow staff to use the system to its full money-saving potential, taking into account any realistic security implications. MI5 should not be allowed to waste its resources simply because it has not spent its budget.

Proposals

A52.   As technology continues to develop, MI5 cannot allow itself to be left so woefully behind again. The agencies should set up a cross-agency IT department, staffed with dedicated IT managers and programmers, to ensure that the agencies get value for money from their IT and that lessons learnt can be shared across the agencies.

Services

A53.   MI5 currently carries out vetting for free. It needs to consider whether:

- Firms who wish to do government work or List X companies with defence contracts should pay to have their staff vetted.
- Central government departments should also be charged.

A54.   This may reduce areas where vetting is required. At the moment departments, particularly in the Civil Service, have many of their staff vetted routinely, even if there is no clear reason. In the past the BBC required its staff to be vetted even though they had no access to classified information. In all cases, unnecessary vetting leads to unnecessary invasions of privacy. It may also lead to unnecessary infringements of civil liberties if individuals are refused jobs on the recommendations of MI5 or their employers, when they did not need to be vetted in the first place. In all cases, unnecessary vetting is an unnecessary waste of taxpayers' money.

A55.   MI5 currently provides physical security advice ranging from document security to the sort of physical defences required for military and industrial targets to a wide range of clients, many of whom are in the private sector. MI5 does not currently charge for this.

Proposals
A56.   In the US, agencies carry out vetting. In my experience, wherever commercial organisations take over from state institutions, they perform the same tasks more efficiently and effectively. The management of vetting and advice services should be put out to competitive tender. Safeguards could be put in place to allow those who have legitimate complaints to appeal to an independent tribunal. Any successful tenderer who failed to properly assess an applicant could then be fined or have his contract terminated.

NOTES AND REFERENCES

Chapter 1

1. *Sunday Times*, 7 March 1993.
2. Thomas Powers, 'The Trouble with the CIA', *New York Review of Books*, 17 January 2003.
3. Robert Baer, *See No Evil: The True Story of a Ground Soldier in the CIA's War on Terrorism*, Crown, 2001, p.271.
4. *Time* magazine, 30 December 2002.
5. *Mail on Sunday*, 23 September 2001.
6. *Guardian*, 10 August 1998.
7. *Sunday Telegraph*, 6 September 1998.
8. *Independent*, 13 February 1991.
9. Stephen Dorril, *The Silent Conspiracy*, Heinemann, 1993, pp122–23.
10. *Sunday Times*, 13 July 1994.
11. For a full account of the arrest, trial and detention of Alami and Botmeh, see *Justice Denied – the Israeli Embassy and the Balfour House Bombings*. This pamphlet is available from Box FOSA, London WC1M 3XX.
12. Press statement released by Freedom and Justice for Samar Alami and Jawad Botmeh, 21 February 1999.
13. *The Times*, 9 November 2002.
14. *Financial Times*, 5 March 2003.
15. *The Times*, 9 November 2002.
16. *Independent on Sunday*, 16 February 2003.
17. *Financial Times*, 11 January 2003.
18. Evidence to the Parliamentary Intelligence and Security Committee, annual report, 2001–02.
19. *Guardian*, 1 March 2003.
20. Ibid.
21. *The Observer*, 25 August 2002.
22. From the Preface of the paperback edition of *Open Secret: The Autobiography of the Former Director-General of MI5* by Stella Rimington, Hutchinson, 2002.
23. Bernard Porter, *Plots and Paranoia*, Unwin Hyman, 1989, p.13.
24. Ibid.

25. Ibid., p.15.
26. Ibid., p.19.
27. Ibid., p.15.
28. Duncan Campbell, *New Statesman*, 21 October 1988.
29. Christopher Andrew, *Secret Service*, Hodder and Stoughton, 1987, p.23.
30. Porter, p.21.
31. Ibid., p.25.
32. Ibid., p.33.
33. Ibid., p.44.
34. Ibid.
35. Ibid., p.69.
36. Andrew, pp.41–4.
37. Ibid., pp.45–7.
38. Sir Alphew Morton, Hansard, Commons, 18 August 1911, col. 2252.
39. Andrew, pp.108–20.
40. Phillip Knightley, *The Second Oldest Profession*, André Deutsch, 1986, p.41.
41. Porter, p.137.
42. Ibid., pp.137–8.
43. Ibid., p.135.
44. Ibid., p.169.
45. Andrew, p.368.
46. Ibid., pp.390–91.
47. Ibid., pp.425–7.
48. Porter, p.167.
49. Andrew, p.455.
50. Ibid., p.479.
51. Ibid., pp.575 and 619.
52. Ibid., pp.544 and 645.
53. Michael Smith, *New Cloak, Old Dagger*, Victor Gollancz, 1996, p.56.
54. Mark Hollingsworth and Richard Norton-Taylor, *Blacklist*, Hogarth Press, 1988, p.27.
55. Ibid., p.30.
56. Michael Smith, *Daily Telegraph*, 3 August 1998.
57. Knightley, p.346.
58. Hollingsworth and Norton-Taylor, p.30.
59. Anthony Glees, *The Secrets of the Service: British Intelligence and Communist Subversion 1939-51*, Jonathan Cape, 1987, p.399.
60. Hollingsworth and Norton-Taylor, p.33.
61. Knightley, p.351.
62. Wright, p.369.
63. 'Harold Wilson: The Final Days', *Secret History* series, 3BM Television for Channel 4, 15 August 1996.

64. Hollingsworth and Norton-Taylor, p.33.
65. Hansard, Lords, 9 December 1993, col. 1034.
66. Tony Benn, *Diaries – Against the Tide, 1973–76*, Hutchinson, 1989, pp.298–9.
67. Hansard, Lords, 16 March 1988, col. 1150–51.
68. *MI5's Official Secrets*, 20/20 Vision for Channel 4, 8 March 1985.
69. *Mail on Sunday*, 24 August 1997.
70. *MI5's Official Secrets*.
71. *File on Four*, Radio 4, 10 August 1982.
72. Michael Herman, *Intelligence Power in Peace and War*, Cambridge University Press, 1996, pp.241–6.
73. Mark Urban, *UK Eyes Alpha*, Faber and Faber, 1996, p.193.
74. Smith, p.63.
75. Urban, pp.20–23.

Chapter 2

1. Chapman Pincher, *Daily Express*, 10 January 1971.
2. Wright, p.39.
3. Mark Honigsbaum, London *Evening Standard*, 20 May 1997.
4. Hansard, Lords, 16 March 1988, col. 1154.
5. Porter, p.213.
6. Peter Hennessy, *The Times*, 25 March 1981.
7. Urban, p.44.
8. Investors in People Annual Lecture, 1998.
9. Hansard, Lords, 16 March 1988, col. 1150–51.
10. Hansard, Commons, 21 November 1979, col. 506.
11. Michael Evans, *The Times*, 21 May 1997.
12. Stephen Dorril, *The Silent Conspiracy*, Heinemann, 1993, pp.130–31.
13. Caroline Phillips, *Mail on Sunday*, 15 May 1994.
14. Ibid.
15. Ibid.
16. Mark Honigsbaum, London *Evening Standard*, 20 May 1997.
17. Sarah Helm, *Independent*, 5 September 1989.
18. Adams, p.107.
19. Ramsay Smith, *Daily Mirror*, 3 January 1994.
20. Hansard, Commons, 2 November 1998, col. 637.
21. Urban, p.255.
22. Ibid.
23. *Computer Weekly*, 8 November 1994.
24. Urban, p.257.
25. *The Times*, 10 December 1919.
26. Dorril, p.257.

27. Intelligence and Security Parliamentary Committee, Annual Report, 1997–8, p.10.
28. Urban, p.258.
29. *Financial Times*, 20 July 2002.
30. *Punch*, 15 March 2002.
31. *Economist*, 29 March 2001.
32. Martyn Lewis, *Reflections on Success*, Lennard Publishing, 1997, p.813.
33. Michael Crick, *Newsnight*, BBC2, 26 August 1997.
34. *New Society*, 31 May 1994.
35. *Observer*, 2 February 1992.
36. *Mail on Sunday*, 24 August 1997.
37. Ibid.
38. Urban, p.263.
39. *Mail on Sunday*, 24 August 1997.
40. Ibid.
41. Ibid.
42. David Leigh, *Observer*, 10 August 1997.

Chapter 3

1. From Preface of paperback of Open Secret by Stella Rimington, Hutchinson, 2002.
2. Nick Davies and Ian Black, *Guardian*, 18 April 1984.
3. Ibid.
4. *FHM* magazine, June 1999.
5. David Nicholson-Lord, *Sunday Times*, 24 January 1982.
6. 20/20 Vision.
7. Ibid.
8. Peter Wright, *The Encyclopedia of Espionage*, Heinemann, 1990, p.49.
9. Urban, p.51.
10. Ibid., p.52.
11. Dorril, p.155.
12. Michael Evans, *The Times*, 6 May 1996.
13. Wright, *Encyclopedia*, p.255.
14. *FHM*, June 1999.
15. Nick Davies, *Observer*, 10 March 1985.
16. Stewart Tendler, *The Times*, 6 May 1996.
17. Duncan Campbell, *New Statesman*, 21 October 1988.
18. Wright, *Spycatcher*, pp.54–5.
19. 20/20 Vision.
20. Associated Press, 9 February 1999.
21. Porter, p.15.
22. *Newsnight*, 26 August 1997.

23. Affidavit sworn by Cathy Massiter, quoted in *Independent*, 13 May 1987.
24. Hansard, Commons, 7 February 1985, col. 1125.
25. Tony Benn, *Diaries – Conflicts of Interest, 1977–80*, Hutchinson, 1990, p.379.
26. Dorril, p.149.
27. Hansard, Commons, 12 March 1985, col. 184.
28. *How to be Home Secretary*, BBC2, 24 January 1999.
29. Hansard, Lords, 9 December 1993, col. 1035.
30. Hansard, Commons, 7 February 1985, col. 1125.
31. Hansard, Commons, 12 March 1985, cols. 210 and 241.
32. *Punch*, 3 December 1999.
33. Ken Hyder, *Guardian*, 14 June 1991.
34. Annual report by the Commissioner of Interception of Communications, 1991.
35. Ken Hyder, *Guardian*, 14 June 1991.
36. Rachel Sylvester, *Independent on Sunday*, 14 February 1999, and Ken Hyder, London *Evening Standard*, 20 January 1999.
37. 'Defending the Realm', *World in Action*, Granada Television, 15 July 1991.
38. Annual report by the Security Service Commissioner, 1997. Presented to Parliament by Prime Minister, July 1997. Cm. 4002, p.2, para 8.
39. Tony Benn, *Diaries – Out of the Wilderness – 1963–67*, Hutchinson, 1987, p.488.
40. Tony Benn, *Diaries – Office Without Power – 1968–72*, Hutchinson, 1988, p.106.
41. Wright, *Encyclopedia*, pp.47 and 105.
42. *The Profession of Intelligence*, BBC Radio 4, 10 February 1982.
43. 20/20 Vision.
44. Ibid.
45. Benn, *Diaries – Office Without Power*, p.408.
46. 20/20 Vision.
47. *Mail on Sunday*, 24 August 1997.
48. 20/20 Vision.
49. Ibid.
50. Evidence to the Commons Treasury and Civil Service Select Committee, 12 February 1986.
51. 'Defending the Realm', *World in Action*, 15 July 1991.
52. 20/20 Vision.

Chapter 4

1. *Esquire*, March 1999.
2. Hansard, Commons, 25 February 1999, col. 347.
3. *Newsnight*, BBC2, 26 August 1997.

4. Stephen Grey, *Sunday Times*, 18 May 1997.
5. From US State Department files quoted by author Stephen Dorril in letter to the *Guardian*, 6 August 1998.
6. *Mail on Sunday*, 24 August 1997.
7. Ibid.
8. Liam Clarke, *Sunday Times*, 5 October 1997.
9. Urban, p.90.
10. *Mail on Sunday*, 31 August 1997, and *FHM* magazine, June 1999.
11. Hansard, Lords, 9 December 1993, col. 1034.
12. Peter Hennessy, *Muddling Through*, Gollancz, 1996, p.276.
13. Hansard, Commons, 15 January 1988, col. 612.
14. Urban, pp.90–91.
15. *Mail on Sunday*, 31 August 1997 and *Guardian*, 18 December 2002.
16. Ibid.
17. Annual report of Intelligence and Security Committee, 1997–98, p.19.
18. Duncan Campbell, *New Statesman*, 21 October 1988.
19. *Mail on Sunday*, 24 August 1997, and *Newsnight*, 26 August 1997.
20. Affidavit sworn by Cathy Massiter on behalf of CND, 1986.
21. Nick Rufford, *Sunday Times*, 15 November 1998.
22. Nick Fielding, *Mail on Sunday*, 25 October 1998.
23. *Newsnight*, 26 August 1997.
24. *Mail on Sunday*, 24 August 1997, and *Newsnight*.
25. *Observer* profile, 26 July 1987.
26. Alan Travis, *Guardian*, 15 September 1997.
27. *How to be Home Secretary*, BBC, 24 January 1999.
28. Paul Foot, *Private Eye*, 29 November 1997.
29. *How to be Home Secretary*.
30. Paul Routledge, *Mandy*, Simon and Schuster, 1999, p.37.
31. Michael White, *Guardian*, 26 August 1997.
32. *Newsnight*.
33. Ibid.
34. Routledge, p.55.
35. *Mail on Sunday*, 24 August 1997.
36. *Mail on Sunday*, 28 September 1997.
37. *Mail on Sunday*, 24 August 1997.
38. *Mail on Sunday*, 28 September 1997.
39. Ibid.
40. Ibid.
41. Michael White, *Guardian*, 26 August 1997.
42. House of Commons Standing Committee E, 3 March 1994, col. 87.
43. Seumas Milne, *Guardian*, 22 September 1997.
44. *Mail on Sunday*, 28 September 1997.
45. Robert Preston, *Financial Times*, 30 September 1997.

46. Peter Mandelson and Roger Liddle, *The Blair Revolution – Can New Labour Deliver?*, Faber and Faber, 1996.
47. *Woman's Hour*, BBC Radio 4, 27 April 1999.
48. *Newsnight.*
49. Alan Clark, *Diaries*, Weidenfeld and Nicolson, 1993, pp.17–18.
50. Hansard, Commons, 28 June 1955, cols. 42 and 1603.
51. *Guardian*, 28 June 1989.
52. Hansard, Commons, 11 December 1979, cols. 1089–90.
53. Maurice Frankel, *Guardian*, 27 August 1997.
54. Hollingsworth and Norton-Taylor, p.100.
55. Hansard, Commons, 15 December 1994, col. 766.
56. Ibid.
57. Ibid.
58. Dorril, p.157.
59. Ibid., p.138.
60. Ibid., p.133.
61. Stephen Grey, *Sunday Times*, 25 May 1997.
62. Richard Norton-Taylor, *Guardian*, 9 September 1987.
63. Stephen Grey, *Sunday Times*, 25 May 1997.
64. Richard Norton-Taylor, *Guardian*, 3 September 1997, and interview with *Pink Paper*, 5 September 1997.
65. David Northmore, *Pink Paper*, 12 September 1997.
66. Hugh McManners, *Sunday Times*, 3 January 1999.
67. *Mail on Sunday*, 24 August 1997.
68. *Sun*, 25 August 1997.
69. *Mail on Sunday*, 24 August 1997.
70. Seumas Milne, *Guardian*, 22 September 1997.
71. *Spectator*, 28 March 1998.
72. Hansard, Commons, 25 February 1998, col. 341.
73. Ibid., col. 342.
74. Press statement issued by Home Office, 3 February 1999.
75. Hansard, Commons, 20 January 1998, 513w, 514w.
76. Ibid., 28 October 1992, 650w, and 22 February 1993, 514w.
77. Richard Norton-Taylor, *Guardian*, 28 August 1997.
78. Hansard, Commons, 29 July 1998, 251–2w.
79. Alan Travis, *Guardian*, 15 September 1997.
80. *Independent on Sunday*, 9 April 1998.
81. *Mail on Sunday*, 11 January 1998.

Chapter 5

1. Dorril, p.126.
2. Lewis, p.810.

3. Ibid.
4. Ibid., p.809.
5. *Observer*, 2 February 1992.
6. Investors in People, Annual Lecture, 1998.
7. Seumas Milne, *The Enemy Within*, Verso, 1994, pp.260–61.
8. Dorril, p.128.
9. Lewis, p.816.
10. *Independent*, 17 December 1991.
11. Lewis, p.810.
12. Dorril, p.225.
13. COS (66) 15th meeting, Confidential Annexe, 'Irish Republican Army Threat', 17 March 1966, DEFE 4/197, Public Record Office. Quoted in Richard Aldrich, *Espionage, Security and Intelligence in Britain 1945–70*, Manchester University Press, 1998.
14. Dillon, p.257.
15. Ibid., p.86.
16. Tony Geraghty, *The Irish War*, HarperCollins, 1998, p.148.
17. Urban, p.199.
18. Dillon, p.238.
19. Hansard, Commons, 8 May 1992, col. 297.
20. Lewis, pp.810–11.
21. Dorril, p.251.
22. Dillon, p.261.
23. *Sunday Telegraph*, 9 February 1992.
24. Geraghty, p.135.
25. Ibid., p.143.
26. Ibid., p.144.
27. Ibid., p.145.
28. Ibid., p.146.
29. Lewis, pp.810–11.
30. *FHM* magazine, June 1999; *Mail on Sunday*, 24 August 1997; *Spectator*, 20 June 1998.
31. Michael Smith, *Daily Telegraph*, 3 August 1998, and *Spectator*, 20 June 1998.
32. James Adams, *The New Spies*, Hutchinson, 1994, pp215–16.
33. *Sunday Times*, 25 April 1993.
34. Ibid.
35. Ibid.
36. Martin Dillon, *25 Years of Terror*, Bantam, 1998, p.293.
37. *Spectator*, 20 June 1998 and *Daily Telegraph*, 3 August 1998.
38. *News of the World*, 2 May 1993.
39. *Sunday Times*, 5 May 1996.
40. Richard Dimbleby Lecture, 12 June 1994.

41. *Mail on Sunday*, 24 August 1997.
42. *Punch*, 7 April 2000.
43. *Newsnight*, 26 August 1997.
44. *The Times*, 26 September 1993.
45. Richard Dimbleby Lecture, 12 June 1994.
46. Ibid.
47. Urban, pp.280–81.
48. Geraghty, p.155.
49. Philip Johnston and Michael Smith, *Daily Telegraph*, 6 March 1996.
50. Geraghty, p.154.
51. Henry McDonald and Yvonne Ridley, *Observer*, 14 February 1999.
52. John Mullin, *Guardian*, 16 July 1996.
53. Mark Honigsbaum, *Observer*, 31 July 1997.
54. Adams, p.207.
55. *The Times*, 10 June 1993.
56. *Mail on Sunday*, 24 August 1997.
57. Lewis, p.805.
58. *Punch*, 27 March 1999.
59. Lecture to the English Speaking Union, 4 October 1995.

Chapter 6

1. Quoted in *Kidnapped – A Money Programme Special*, BBC Two, 21 November 2001.
2. Leaflet: 'MI5 target Muslims for fulfilling their duty of supporting the Jihad in Chechnya', issued 1 March 2000.
3. 'Radical Islam in the UK', Institute for Counter-Terrorism, 20 October 2001, see www.ict.or.il/articles/articledet.cfm?articleid=398.
4. Quoted in *Al-Sharq al-Awsat*, 6 March 2002.
5. USA v Earnest James Ujamaa, Indictment, US District Court, Western District of Washington at Seattle, 28 August 2002.
6. *Guardian*, 10 August 2002.
7. 'Extradition to US of Al Qaeda suspect fails', *Guardian*, 30 July 2002.
8. Jake Tapper, 'Muslim Spy who infiltrated bin Laden's terror network in London,' *The Times*, 16 January 2003.
9. See Emerson Vermaat *Al Qaeda Networks in Europe*, June 2002, p37.
10. See Nick Fielding and John Elliot, 'Bin Laden called UK 260 times: Al Qaeda's phone records', *The Sunday Times*, 24 March 2002.
11. Published on the website www.cryptome.org
12. 'British-based plotters are jailed for market bomb plan,' *Guardian*, 11 March 2003.
13. ISC Annual Report 2001-2002, Cm 5542, p22.
14. Ibid. p22.

15. The report can be found at www.cabinetoffice.gov.uk/intelligence/CM5724.pdf.
16. *Muslim News*, 24 August 2002.
17. Amnesty International, *Rights Denied: the UK's response to 11 September 2001*, 5 September 2002.
18. 'Head of MI5 admits lapses in security,' *Guardian*, 9 July 2002.

Chapter 7

1. *Financial Times*, 26 April 1986.
2. Adams, p.223.
3. 'Terrorism and Unconventional Warfare', US Congress, 1998.
4. *Panorama* Special, 8 September 1998.
5. Ibid.
6. Ibid.
7. Quoted by Associated Press, 11 September 1998.
8. *Sunday Times*, 13 February 2000.
9. *The Observer*, 19 March 2000.
10. *Guardian*, 30 March 2000.
11. *Punch*, 15 November 1998.
12. Stephen Dorril, *MI6: Fifty Years of Special Operations*, Fourth Estate, 2000, p.787.
13. Mail on Sunday, 24 August 1997.
14. *Spectator*, 27 September 1997.
15. Quoted by John Willis in his report as *Guardian*'s ombudsman, 12 October 1997.
16. Ibid.
17. Ibid., p.7.
18. Ibid.
19. Ibid., p.8.
20. Ibid.
21. Ibid., p.9.
22. Unpublished interview with Nick Buckley, *Mail on Sunday* reporter.
23. Willis, p.11.
24. Ibid.
25. *Mail on Sunday*, 24 August 1997.
26. Ibid.

Chapter 8

1. Hollingsworth and Norton-Taylor, p.48.
2. Legal opinion by Geoffrey Bindman, 8 May 1997.
3. Interview with authors.

4. Ibid.
5. Ibid.
6. Ibid.
7. Ibid.
8. Ibid.
9. Letter from Roland Phillips to Jonathan Holborow, 29 August 1997.
10. Letter from Jonathan Holborow to Roland Phillips, 29 August 1997.
11. Letter from Phillips to Holborow, 30 August 1997.
12. Note of the Judgment of Mr Justice Keene at the Hearing on 30 August 1997, High Court document, 1997 A No. 1337, QB.
13. *Mail on Sunday*, 31 August 1997.
14. Warrant No. 2641, Bow Street Magistrates Court, 29 August 1997.
15. *Mail on Sunday*, 21 September 1997.
16. Letter from Barry Moss, QPM, to Jonathan Holborow, 10 October 1997.
17. Interview with authors.
18. London *Evening Standard*, 26 August 1997.
19. Letter from Jack Straw to Jonathan Holborow, 23 September 1997.
20. Letter from Straw to Holborow, 30 October 1997.
21. Ibid.
22. Letter from Roland Phillips to Jonathan Holborow, 31 October 1997.
23. Terms of Reference for the Comprehensive Spending Review of the Intelligence Services, House of Commons, 30 October 1997.
24. *The Times*, 15 July 1998.
25. Intelligence and Security Committee, Annual Report 1997–98, Cmnd. Paper 4073.
26. Letter from John Alpass to John Wadham, 13 January 1998.
27. Letter from Roland Phillips to John Wadham, 12 January 1998.
28. *Mail on Sunday*, 25 January 1998.
29. Letter from John Wadham to Roland Phillips, 23 December 1997.
30. Letter from John Wadham to Roland Phillips, 27 February 1998.
31. Letter from David Smythe to Special Branch, 2 February 1998.
32. Letter from Wadham to Harvey Kass, 18 February 1998.
33. Letter from Phillips to Wadham, 15 May 1998.
34. Michael Cockerell, *The Times*, 1 December 2001.
35. Jason Lewis, *Mail on Sunday*, 3 November 2002.
36. *Guardian*, 14 December 2002.

Chapter 9

1. Interview with authors.
2. *Mail on Sunday*, 21 September 1997.
3. *Mail on Sunday*, 12 October 1997.

4. *The Times*, 4 April 1998.
5. *Daily Telegraph*, 20 June 1998.
6. Letter from Roland Phillips to John Wadham, 24 June 1998.
7. *Mail on Sunday*, 19 July 1998.
8. Letter from Phillips to TABnet, 22 July 1998.
9. *Mail on Sunday*, 26 July 1998.
10. Ibid.
11. Ibid.
12. *Mail on Sunday*, 9 August 1998.
13. Liberty press statement, 25 July 1998.
14. Ibid.
15. Letter from Phillips to Jonathan Holborow, 31 July 1998.
16. BBC press statement, 6 August 1998.
17. Statement by US Immigration Department, August 1998.
18. Letter from Shayler to Machon, 7 August 1998.
19. Statement by Liberty.
20. Statement issued from La Santé Prison, 7 August 1998.
21. *Fly Me to the Moon*, Middlesbrough Football Club fanzine, August 1998.
22. 'The Spy who loved Merse (yes, really!)', *Four-Four-Two* magazine, September 1998.
23. *Middlesbrough Evening Gazette*, 26 November 1998.
24. Conversation with author.
25. Ibid.
26. 'An Open Letter to Stephen Lander', 9 September 1998.
27. Ibid.
28. Professor David Feldman, 'Compatibility of Official Secrets Act (UK), Section 1 with International Human Rights Law', September 1998.
29. Statement, 21 October 1998.
30. Liberty press statement, 21 October 1998.
31. 'Re: The Extradition of David Michael Shayler from France', p.8 of Morrisey's statement to French courts.
32. Hansard, Commons, 2 November 1998, col. 584.
33. Ibid., col. 593.
34. Ibid., col. 594.
35. Ibid., col. 596.
36. Conversation with author.
37. Ibid.
38. Ibid.
39. Ibid.
40. *Mail on Sunday*, 22 November 1998.
41. Ibid.
42. Ibid.
43. Conversation with author.

Chapter 10

1. *Mail on Sunday*, 31 August 1997.
2. *Observer*, 10 August 1997.
3. Ibid.
4. *Mail on Sunday*, 31 August 1997.
5. *Sunday Times*, 20 October 1996.
6. Ibid.
7. Ibid.
8. *Punch*, 27 March 1999.
9. *Mail on Sunday*, 24 August 1997.
10. Ibid., 31 August 1997.
11. Ibid., 24 August 1997.
12. *Observer*, 12 May 1985
13. London *Evening Standard*, 26 August 1997.
14. John Day, *A Plain Russet-Coated Captain*, privately published, 1993, pp.193–4.
15. *Mail on Sunday*, 24 August 1997.
16. London *Evening Standard*, 26 August 1997.
17. *New Society*, 31 May 1984.
18. Day, p.191.
19. *Mail on Sunday*, 24 August 1997.
20. See David Leigh, *The Wilson Plot*, Heinemann, 1988.
21. Wright, *Spycatcher*, p.31.
22. Ibid., p.54.
23. Richard Norton-Taylor, *Guardian*, 23 January 1988.
24. Dorril, p.172.
25. 'Myths and Misunderstandings', MI5 Official Booklet, 16 July 1993.
26. *How to be Home Secretary*, BBC2, 24 January 1999.
27. Day, p.194.
28. Tony Benn, *Diaries – Out of the Wilderness – 1963–67*, p.328.
29. Nick Davies and Ian Black, *Guardian*, 18 April 1984.
30. *How to be Home Secretary*, and Hansard, Lords, 9 December 1993, col. 1034.
31. Hansard, Lords, 9 December 1993, col. 1041.
32. Evidence to the Civil Service and Treasury Select Committee inquiry. Quoted in Dorril, p.174.
33. *How to be Home Secretary*.
34. Dorril, p.175.
35. Quoted by Lord Callaghan, Hansard, Lords, 9 December 1993, col. 1039.
36. Nigel Lawson, *The View from Number 11*, Bantam, 1992, p.314.
37. 'Defending the Realm', *World in Action*, Granada Television, 15 July 1991.

38. Ibid.
39. House of Lords Judicial Committee, 22 November 1984. Quoted by Morris Riley in volume 26 of *Lobster* magazine.
40. Urban, p.52.
41. Adams, pp.88–9.
42. *Independent*, 20 May 1992.
43. *Observer*, 21 July 1991.
44. Standing Committee E, Commons, Intelligence Services Bill, 22 March 1994, cols. 202–3.
45. Anthony Bevins, *Independent*, 27 June 1990.
46. Hansard, Commons, 17 January 1989, col. 289.
47. Adams, p.97.
48. Richard Dimbleby lecture, 12 June 1994.
49. Reproduced on p.195 of Day.
50. Day, p.197.
51. Standing Committee E, Commons, Intelligence Services Bill, 19 March 1994, cols. 258–69.
52. *Newsnight*, 26 August 1997.
53. Urban, p.296.
54. Standing Committee E, 22 March 1994, col. 279.
55. Hansard, Commons, 22 February 1994, col. 171.
56. Ibid., 27 April 1994, col. 351.
57. Ibid., 2 November 1998, col. 295.
58. *Guardian*, 22 October 1998.
59. Evidence to the Commons Select Committee on Home Affairs, 29 July 1997, Paragraph 92.
60. *Guardian*, 22 October 1998.
61. Professor Peter Gill, Liverpool Polytechnic, letter to *Guardian*, 17 September 1988.
62. *Guardian*, 2 December 1986.
63. Norton-Taylor, *In Defence of the Realm?*, Civil Liberties Trust, 1990, p.109.
64. Hansard, Commons, 2 November 1998, col. 594.
65. *Panorama*, BBC1, 'On Her Majesty's Secret Service', 22 November 1993.
66. Hansard, Commons, 11 February 1993, 770w.
67. Urban, p.282.
68. Ibid., p.283.
69. Ibid.
70. Ibid.
71. *Sunday Times*, 5 December 1999.
72. *Financial Times*, 26 January 2000.
73. *Independent*, 28 August 2001.

74. James Smart Lecture, City of London Police Headquarters, 3 November 1994.
75. *Observer,* 18 September 1994.
76. Letter to *Observer,* 13 November 1994.
77. *Sunday Telegraph,* 12 March 1995.
78. Richard Dimbleby Lecture, 1994.
79. *Guardian,* 23 November 1997.
80. *Daily Telegraph,* 3 August 1998.
81. Dillon, p.245.
82. Briefing document issued by Liberty, October 1998.
83. *New Statesman,* 27 March 2000.
84. Quoted by Frances Stonor Saunders, author of *Who Paid the Piper? The CIA and the Cultural Cold War* (Granta, 1999) in the *New Statesman,* 17 September 2001 .

BIBLIOGRAPHY

Adams, James, *The New Spies – Exploring the Frontiers of Espionage* (London, Hutchinson, 1994)

Aldrich, Richard, *Espionage, Security and Intelligence in Britain – 1945–1970* (Manchester, Manchester University Press, 1998)

Andrew, Christopher, *Secret Service* (London, Hodder and Stoughton, 1987)

Baer, Robert, *See No Evil: The True Story of the Ground Soldier in the CIA's Cold War on Terrorism* (New York City, Crown, 2001)

Benn, Tony, *Diaries – Out of the Wilderness, 1963–67* (London, Hutchinson, 1987)

Benn, Tony, *Diaries – Against the Tide, 1973–76* (London, Hutchinson, 1989)

Benn, Tony, *Diaries – Conflicts of Interest, 1977–80* (London, Hutchinson, 1990)

Clark, Alan, *Diaries* (London, Weidenfeld and Nicolson, 1993)

Davies, Philip, *The British Secret Services* (Oxford, ABC-CLIO Ltd, 1996)

Day, John, *A Plain Russet-Coated Captain* (Dorking, privately published, 1993)

Dillon, Martin, *25 Years of Terror – The IRA's War Against the British* (London, Bantam, 1998)

Dorril, Stephen, and Robin Ramsay, *Smear!: Wilson and the Secret State* (London, Fourth Estate, 1991)

Dorril, Stephen, *The Silent Conspiracy – Inside the Intelligence Services in the 1990s* (London, Heinemann, 1993)

Geraghty, Tony, *The Irish War* (London, HarperCollins, 1998)

Hennessy, Peter, *Muddling Through – Power, Politics and the Quality of Government in Postwar Britain* (London, Gollancz, 1996)

Hollingsworth, Mark, and Richard Norton-Taylor, *Blacklist – The Inside Story of Political Vetting* (London, Hogarth Press, 1988)

Knightley, Phillip, *The Second Oldest Profession: The Spy as Bureaucrat, Patriot, Fantasist and Whore* (London, André Deutsch, 1986)

Leigh, David, *The Wilson Plot – The Intelligence Services and the Discrediting of a Prime Minister 1945–1976* (London, Heinemann, 1988)

Lewis, Martyn, *Reflections on Success* (Harpenden, Lennard Publishing, 1997)

Macintyre, Donald, *Mandelson: The Biography* (London, HarperCollins, 1999)

Milne, Seumas, *The Enemy Within – MI5, Maxwell and the Scargill Affair* (London, Verso, 1994)

Norton-Taylor, Richard, *In Defence of the Realm? The Case for Accountable Security Services* (London, Civil Liberties Trust, 1990)

Porter, Bernard, *Plots and Paranoia – A History of Political Espionage in Britain 1790–1988* (London, Unwin Hyman, 1989)

Rimmington, Stella, *Open Secret: The Autobiography of the Former Director-General of MI5* (London, Hutchinson, 2002)

Routledge, Paul, *Mandy – The Unauthorised Biography of Peter Mandelson* (London, Simon and Schuster, 1999)

Smith, Michael, *New Cloak, Old Dagger – How Britain's Spies Came in from the Cold* (London, Gollancz, 1996)

Urban, Mark, *UK Eyes Alpha – The Inside Story of British Intelligence* (London, Faber and Faber, 1996)

Wright, Peter, *Spycatcher – The Candid Autobiography of a Senior Intelligence Officer* (Melbourne, William Heinemann, 1987)

Wright, Peter, *The Encyclopedia of Espionage* (Melbourne, William Heinemann, 1990)

INDEX

A Branch 59, 74, 195
Aaronovitch, David 129
'ABC' system 146-7
accountability 30, 248, 284, 287, 293-4, 297, 302, 305, 310, 312
Adams, James 301
agents 69-74, 92, 134, 143-5, 290
Al Quaeda viii, 9, 11, 13-15, 165-81, 278, 282
Alami, Samar 8-9
alcoholism 28, 42, 64-5, 100, 290-91
Alderson, John 36, 282, 312
Allason, Rupert 301
Alpass, John 149, 232, 233, 234, 292
Andrew, Christopher 25
Annan, Lord 40
Annesley, Hugh 315
Anti-Terrorist Squad 132, 139, 152, 175
Arab terrorists 4-15, 59, 66
arms trafficking 60, 309
Armstrong, Hazel vii
Armstrong, Robert 115, 121
arrest powers 22
Attlee, Clement 27, 116
Australia 307

B Branch 59
Baker, Kenneth 6, 57, 299
Baker, Norman 127
Baldwin, Stanley 57
Bali bombing 178
Banner, Paul 176
Barayev, Arbi 167
Bazelya, Khalifa 185, 194, 198, 201-3
BBC 37, 74, 81, 83, 99, 101, 107, 117, 165, 183, 185, 187, 213, 221, 249-52, 276
Beloff, Lord 40
Benn, Tony 33-4, 87, 106
Bettaney, Michael 42, 64, 290-91
Bickford, David 301, 309, 314-15

bin Laden, Osama 165-8, 175, 177-8
Bindman, Geoffrey 195-6, 198, 205-7, 210
Blacklist (Hollingsworth) 205
Blacklisting 27-8, 44, 116-17
Blackmail 28, 64, 70, 114
Blair, Tony 34, 104-5, 112-13, 226, 227-8, 293, 303, 311, 316, 318
Blake, George 253
Blunkett, David 13-14, 128, 180, 277
Blunt, Anthony 28-9, 41, 121
BNP *see* British National Party
Boggan, Steve 213
Bolton Street 50, 64, 93, 104, 210
Bombings 152; Bali 178; Canary Wharf 161; City of London 141, 149-53; electricity-supply stations 162; Enniskillen 138; Israeli embassy 7-9, 230, 275; Rimington's appointment 287; Soho 140-4; Warrington 151; *see also* terrorism
Botmeh, Jawad 8-9
Bourdon, William 260, 270, 275
Box 500 documents 100, 101, 103, 134, 153, 296
Breakfast with Frost (television) 188, 252-3
bribery 118
Bridge, Lord 89
British National Party (BNP) 72, 101
British Telecom 77, 84-5, 166
Brittain, Victoria 182, 193-201, 207, 210, 236
Brittan, Leon 82, 89
Brook, Sir Norman 28
Brown, Gordon 178
Brown, Lord Justice Simon 312
Brown, Nick 228

BT *see* British Telecom
bugging devices 77-9, 87, 195
Burgess, Guy 28, 41, 121
burglary 22-3, 31, 59, 76, 91, 195-6, 299, 316; *see also* covert searches
Bushell, Garry 123-4

C Branch 117
Callaghan, Lord 41-2, 82, 295
Cambridge University 28, 40, 100
Campaign for Nuclear Disarmament (CND) 35-6, 89, 93, 105, 124
Campbell, Alastair 204, 215-17, 219-20, 226-7
Canada 129, 305-6
Canary Wharf bombing 161
Canning, James 141
Carlisle, Lord 15
Carlos the Jackal 262
Carr, Lord 108
Carrigan, Kate 247-8
cars 74-5
Carver, Lord 34, 41
Castle, Barbara 107
Chamberlain, Neville 26
Chandler, Adrian 69-70
Chechnya 1-2, 167
Chesterfield pub, Shepherd's Market 64
Churchill, Winston 21, 26-7
CIA 3, 29, 31, 182, 184, 308
City of London bombing 141, 149-53
Clark, Alan 114-15
Clarke, Kenneth 57, 103, 141, 309
Class War 101, 104
CND *see* Campaign for Nuclear Disarmament
Cockerell, Michael 83, 107, 276
Cold War 27, 36-8, 59, 71, 75, 77, 79, 86, 108, 116, 142, 294

Coleman, George Churchill 139

Coles, Sir John 187

Collins, Michael 19, 24

communism/communists 24-5, 27, 30, 32-5, 40, 77, 87-90, 100ff.

computer systems *see* information technology

Computer Weekly 56

Conservative Party 25, 103

Cook, Frank 316

Cook, Robin 115, 188-9, 193, 252, 266-7

Cooper, Cyril 30

Cooper, Yvette 232, 266, 305

Cornwell, David *see* Le Carré, John

Coughlin, Con 191-2

counsellors 290-91

counter-terrorism 1-38, 178, 179, 282-90

covert searches 75-9, 285; *see also* burglary

Cox, John 35, 89

Crass 123

creation, MI5 21

Crick, Michael 213

Cuckney, Lord 293

Cumming, Captain Mansfield 21

Cunningham, Dr John 304

Curwen, Christopher 139

Curzon Street, Mayfair 50, 64, 93, 156

Customs and Excise 69, 85, 310-11

CX report 186-90

Czech surveillance fiasco 65

D Branch 59, 130

Daily Mirror 52

Daily Telegraph 144, 214, 245-6

Daly, Patrick 145

Dalyell, Tam 106

Darling, Alistair 231

Davies, Julie-Ann 190

Davis, David 300

Day, John 291-2, 294, 302

de Valera, Eamon 97

Defence of the Realm Act 22

Denning, Lord 76

Devlin, Lord 286

Diana, Princess of Wales 221, 232, 257

Dillon, Martin 140, 144

Diplock, Lord 32

Dobbie, Peter vi, 214-15

'dodgy holidays' 146

Donaldson, Sir John 293

double agents 26, 30, 73

Douglas-Home, Sir Alec 296

Downing Street attack 139

drinking *see* alcoholism

drug-trafficking 309

DST *see* French Secret Service

Duff, Sir Anthony 99-101, 131, 298, 304

Dunbar, Graham 211, 241-2, 244-5

Durbar system 55

e-mails 10, 85, 248, 318

The Economist 42

electricity-supply stations plot 162

Elizabeth II 157

Elwell, Charles 34, 136

encryption 85, 318

Enniskillen bombing 138

European Court of Human Rights 34, 37, 117, 298-9

Euston Tower 51,75, 84

Evening Standard 226

extradition proceedings 241, 251-2, 255,268

F Branch 34, 55, 94, 101ff., 117, 121, 129-30, 133, 136

Fayers, Raymond 151

FBI 3, 98-9, 174-5, 308, 315

Feldman, David 263, 265

Fhimah, Lamin 185

Fielding, Nick v, 204-5, 208-10, 213-14, 223-4, 228-30, 235-7, 242-4, 246, 250, 252-6, 264, 269, 271

filing systems 93-100; access rights 95-7, 116, 129, 318; destruction 97-8, 101, 124-6, 129, 233; microfiche 96, 98; overlooked documents 236, 278-9; 'Pink List' 122; procedures 93-4, 233; retention period 96-7, 115; statistics 116, 126-7; vetting 96, 116-25, 289-90, 318

Financial Times 11, 13

First World War 22, 26

Fleming, Ian 60

Fletcher, Yvonne 140, 182

flexibility 142

Ford 87-8

Fouché, Joseph 20

France 17, 240-46, 251, 253-6, 268-72, 305

France, Sir Christopher 291

Frankel, Maurice 116

Fraser, Lord 297

French Secret Service (DST) v, 20, 254-6, 269, 275, 318

Fuchs, Klaus 28

funding, MI5 18, 32, 53, 66, 105, 162, 226, 231-3, 293

G Branch 5, 7, 58-9,134, 313

Gaddafi, Colonel 182-7, 190-93, 234, 251, 275; *see also* Libya

Gaddafi, Saif 190-93

Gagging orders 277-8, 312, 316

Gardiner, Lord 87, 294-5

Gatwick airport 67

GCHQ *see* General Communications Headquarters

General Communications Headquarters (GCHQ) 10-11, 36, 54, 57-9, 84, 86, 122, 134, 140, 152, 170, 178, 231-2, 248, 311, 313

General Strike 25

gentlemen's club culture 40

Geraghty, Tony 145-7, 160

Germany 21, 26-7, 305

Ghana 194, 196, 200

Gibraltar shooting 138

Gifford, Gilbert 16

Gilbert, Lord 196, 304

Gill, Ken 77

Glover, Stephen 197, 199

Gordievsky, Oleg 30, 37, 101

Gordon, Betty 71-2

Gower Street 50, 135

Grant project 554, 56

Greene, Graham 26

Greenham Common 105

Grey, Earl 19

grievance procedures 292

Grosvenor Street 76, 210

Guardian vii, 12-13, 70, 122, 182, 189, 193-201, 205, 209, 229, 236, 251, 261, 278

Guarente, Matt 213, 225, 241, 244-5

Guernsey 208

Gulf War 5-7

H Branch 54, 59, 81

Hain, Peter 189

Hamza, Abu 168-70, 172-3

handlers 70-71

Hanley, Michael 31, 42

Hansen, Julian 284-5, 287

Harman, Harriet 34, 105, 115, 297-8, 299

Harraway, Syd 88
Hassaine, Reda 172-3
Hassan, Abu 168-9
Hattersley, Roy 111
Hawk system 55
Heath, Sir Edward 93, 100-101, 114, 163, 213, 296
Heathrow airport 10, 181
Hennessy, Peter 93, 293
Henty, Edward 150
Herman, Michael 36
Heseltine, Michael 35
Hewitt, Patricia 34, 297-9, 318
Hezbollah 7
Hickson, Alisdare 122-3
historical background 15-38
Hitler 26
Hodges, Andrew 21
Holborrow, Jonathan vi, 204, 207, 210, 215-19, 221-4, 227-30, 249-50, 255-6
holidays 56-7, 146
Holland 211-15, 240
Hollingsworth, Mark 205, 208-10, 228-9, 235-7, 264
Hollis, Roger 29-30, 41, 51
Holt-wilson, Eric 97
Home Secretary, MI5 accountability 294
homosexuality see sexual activity
'honey-trapping' 73, 201
Hooper, Mr Justice 224
Hornsey, Tina 151
Howard, Michael 157, 194, 309-10
Howe, Lord 309
Howley, John 312-13
human rights 299
Hunt, Lord 31-2, 42
Hussein, Saddam 5

Ide, Philip vi, 214, 244-5, 268
Imbert, Lord 315
Independent 213, 250, 301
Independent on Sunday 45-6, 129, 197
information technology 53-6, 95-7, 285
informers 73, 137-8, 143-4, 191
Ingham, Bernard 214
Ingram, Miranda 61, 291-2
INLA see Irish Nationalist Liberation Army
Inman, Judge 224-5
Institute of Race Relations (IRR) 179
Intelligence and Security Committee (ISC) 59, 177-

9, 228-9, 244, 246, 266-7, 275, 282; 303-5, 309, 315, 317-18
Intelligence Services Bill 112, 303
Interception of Communications Act 85, 90, 194
International Sikh Youth Federation 179
Internet 85, 170, 189, 246-8, 260, 318
'Investors in People' 66
IRA 11, 14, 66, 73, 98-9, 131-64, 275, 287, 289; Canary Wharf bombing 161; ceasefire 161, 309; City of London bombing 141, 149-51; Collins, Michael 19, 24; Downing Street attack 139; Durbar system 55; electricity-supply stations plot 162; Enniskillen bombing 138; Gibraltar shooting 138; informers 73, 137-8, 143-4; Lennon's support 98-9; Libya 184, 236, 279; McNulty, Sean 154-8; MI5/MPSB power struggle 60-61, 69, 139-40, 143; MI6 137; Rimington's appointment 131, 287; Soho bombing 140-41; surveillance 91, 162; telephone warnings 150, 161; Thames House 96; Wallsend bombing 154; Warrington bombing 151
Iraq 59, 184, 313
Ireland 19-24
Irish Nationalist Liberation Army (INLA) 145
The Irish War (Geraghty) 145
IRR see Institute of Race Relations
Irvine, Derry 317
ISC see Intelligence and Security Committee
Israeli embassy bombing 7-9, 230, 175
IT see information technology

Jack, Hugh 155-7
James, Oliver 288
Jenkins, Lord 32-3, 83, 89, 100, 295
JIC see Joint Intelligence Committee
Joint Intelligence

Committee (JIC) 5, 10, 36, 103, 114, 136, 178, 231, 296-8, 304
Jones, Jack 88
Jones, Martin Furnival 136

K Branch 134, 136
Kass, Harvey vi, 219, 237-8
Keelan, Kevin 211
Keene, Mr Justice 217, 219-220
Kell, Captain Vernon 21, 24, 27
Kellar, Alex 121
Kellaway, Richard 310
Kent, Bruce 89, 93, 105
Kerr, David 247
KGB 2, 27-8, 30-31, 37, 73, 75, 101
King, Tom 232, 266-7, 303, 308
Kinnock, Neil 34, 93, 104-5, 108, 297
Knight, Maxwell ('M') 25
Knightley, Phillip 29
Kohl, Helmut 184
Kosygin, Alexei 86-7
Kuzichkin, Vladimir 37
Kwei, Amartey 197

Labour Party 25, 31, 57, 102, 108-9, 111, 317-18
Lander, Stephen 54, 63-4, 106, 112-14, 126-7, 139, 157, 163, 181, 201, 215, 227, 229, 232-3, 240, 283, 287-92, 314; appointment 284; background 287-9; inflexibility 126, 284; qualities 63-4, 220, 285-90; recruitment 288-9; ruthlessness 285; 'Stalinist' atmosphere 290
Lawrence, Lieutenant Robert 90
Lawson, Nigel 296
le Carré, John (David Cornwell) 40-41, 60, 67, 104, 119, 121, 285
Lenin, Vladimir 97
Lennon, John 98-9
Leppard, David 254
Lévy, Anne-Sophie 259-60, 270, 272
Lewis, Julian 124-5
Liberty vi, 34, 36, 105, 241, 261
Libya 14, 59, 201-3, 252, 313; Brittain, Victoria 193-201; Gaddafi 182-5, 192-3, 278;

'honey-trapping' 201; IRA 236, 279; Rasheed 272-4; Tunworth 185-7, 190

Livingstone, Ken 105-6

Lockerbie disaster 106, 182-5, 252

Lustig-Prean, Duncan 122

McColl, Sir Colin 304-5

MacDonald, Ramsay 24

McGahey, Mick 88, 134

McGuinness, Martin 52

Machon, Annie v-vi, 101-2, 208-14, 218, 220, 238, 241-2, 268, 271-2, 280; arrest 242-3, 316; interviews 243-4; MI5 resignations 64, 220-22, 283; public meetings 277; Rasheed 272-4; Shayler's arrest 256; Tomlinson 254-5

McInnes, Neil 307

Mackintosh, Charles Rennie 22

Maclean, Donald 28, 41

McLoughlin, Chris 228

McNulty, Sean 154-8

McWilliam, John 84-6

Maguire, Air Marshal Harold 136

Maier, Karl 197

mail interceptions 34, 79-80, 91, 223, 285, 299, 308

Mail on Sunday v-vii, 43, 112-13, 123, 128, 197, 201, 260, 277, 316; Gaddafi 255, 264-5; injunction 220-21, 225, 237-8, 251-2; overlooked documents 236, 278-9; vetted article 230; whistleblowing 204-240, 276; writ 226

Major, John 104, 118, 157

management failings 66, 220-21, 246, 287, 290-92; grievance proceedings 292, 298-301; 'Operational Inefficiency' report 149, 153

Mandelson, Peter 93, 108-15, 124, 202, 300, 303

Mangan, Keith 166

Manningham-Buller, Eliza 10-11, 15, 284-7

Manningham-Buller, Sir Reginald 285-6

Marshbrook system 84

Marx, Karl 20

Massiter, Cathy 34-5, 73, 81-2, 87-9, 297

Masterman, Sir John 40

Maxwell Fyfe, Sir David 29-30, 294

May, Alan Nunn 27

Megrahi, Abdelbasset 185

Melville, William 22-3

Mensa, J. H. 200

merger proposals 24, 232, 315-16

Metropolitan Police Special Branch (MPSB) 1-3, 12-15, 20, 25, 42, 60, 70, 74, 76, 85, 103, 105, 115, 136-7, 155, 180, 221, 224, 242-3; files 36; IRA 11, 60, 73, 132, 139-41, 152; MI5 power struggle 6, 23-4, 60, 139-40; organised crime 310-11, 315; overlooked documents 236, 278-9

MI6 10, 36, 54, 57-8, 61, 69, 86, 178, 184-5, 192, 311, 313; Diana, Princess of Wales 257; I/Ops 190, 192-3; IRA 137; Libya 182, 192, 234, 278; merger proposals 24, 232; MI5 contrast 25, 137; review 231; Tomlinson 252-4, 257

microfiche files 96, 98

Middlesbrough fans 261

Militant Tendency (MT) 72, 90-91, 99, 101-3, 120-21

Milosovic, Slobodan 257

mobile phones 255

Mohammed, Omar Bakri 167, 174

Monson, Andrew, QC vii

Moore, Charles 191

Morning Star 33, 90

Morrissey, Martin 221, 242-3, 264-5

Morrison, Herbert 109

Moses, Justice Alan 278-80

Mosley, Oswald 26

Moss, Barry 223-4

Mousaoui, Zacarias 3, 169, 173

MPSB *see* Metropolitan Police Special Branch

MT *see* Militant Tendency

Muggeridge, Malcolm 26, 318-19

Mughrabi, Ridd 8

Munday, Anthony 16

Murphy, Joe vi

music industry 26, 123-4

Mussolini 26

National Audit Office

(NAO) 52-3, 57, 297, 308

National Crime Squad 310

National Criminal Intelligence Service (NCIS) 86, 178, 255, 310

National Front 72, 101

national security issues: courts 89-90, 279; organised crime 309-11, 315; Shayler's revelations 130, 206-7, 219-21, 251, 278, 292-3; weapons of mass destruction 313-14

NCIS *see* National Criminal Intelligence Service

New Scientist 42

New York Times 251

New Zealand 78

News of the World 150

Newsnight (television) 81, 129, 213, 221, 250

Nicholas, Mary Ann vii

Nicholas, Sir David 299

Norton-Taylor, Richard vii, 229

observation posts 75

Observer 117, 189, 282

Official Secrets Acts 21, 47-8, 60, 144, 189, 205-6, 215, 221-2, 238, 242, 253, 263-5, 276, 280, 316

O'Haidmaill, Feilim 160

Old Father Thames pub 207

Oldfield, Sir Maurice 42, 121, 137

Omand, Sir David 14, 179

O'Neill, David vi, 223, 242-3

'Operational Inefficiency' report, MI5 149, 153

organised crime 59, 309-11, 315

Orwell, George 124

Panorama (television) 165, 182, 250-52

Pereira, Lisa

Parkinson, Cyril Northcote 53

Pepper, David 122

Pereira, Lisa vii

Philby, Kim 28, 41

Phillips, Roland 217-19, 228, 231, 233-5, 238-9, 245-7, 250-51

Pierce, Gareth 8-9

'Pink List' 122

police *see* Metropolitan Police Special Branch, National Crime Squad,

National Criminal Intelligence Service
Ponroy, Madame 268, 270
Porter, Bernard 17-18, 22-3, 25
Post Office Bureau Services 79
Powell, Sir Charles 36
Prescott, John 115, 318
Prevention of Terrorism Act 60, 157
propaganda campaign 314
pub culture 64, 210
public interest defence 272-4
Public Order Act 26

Rasheed, Souhail 272-4
Rawlings, Jerry 196
RCP see Revolutionary Communist party
recruitment 25, 35, 38-66, 69-70, 73, 267, 283; advertisements 39-40, 42, 44-5, 72, 164; agents 69-72; gentlemen's club culture 40; Lander 288-9; overhaul 42, 44; personnel proposals 291; references 40; Rimington 133; Shayler 45-50; tests 43-4, 46; universities 40, 42-4
Redgrave, Vanessa 98
Rees, Lord 83, 111, 117, 295
'Reform Society' 19
reforms 41-2
Registry 50-51, 59, 93, 126, 289
'Registry Queens' 39, 95
Reid, Betty 72
Reid, Richard 169, 173
resignations 204, 283
Revolutionary Communist Party (RCP) 90, 101
Rifkind, Malcolm 187, 191, 252-3
Rimington, Dame Stella 14, 31, 41, 60, 69, 78, 93, 114, 131-5, 139ff., 148, 154, 163, 276-7, 282, 284, 289, 301-2, 312; amateur dramatics 133; background 132-3; bossiness 135; organised crime 309-10; qualities 134-5, 220; recruitment 133; retirement 284-5; tantrums 135
Robertson, Geoffrey, QC vi, 219-20, 229, 237
Robison, Robin 296-7
Robson, Nigel 122

Rogers, Allan 266-8, 304
Royal Prerogative 293
Royal Ulster Constabulary (RUC) 78, 91, 119, 136-7, 143-4, 159, 315
RUC see Royal Ulster Constabulary
Ruddock, Joan 89, 105
Rufford, Nicholas 253-4
Rusbridger, Alan 201
Russia, 59; see also Soviet Union

Sandline 267
SAS 138
Scanlon, Hugh 88
Scargill, Arthur 88, 134
Second World War 26
Secret Service Bureau 21-2, 97
Secret Service grant 17
Secret Service Tribunal 201
Security Service Act (1989) 76, 96, 194, 299, 302-9, 312
Security Service 15, 26, 44-5, 47, 84, 217, 282-319
sexual activity 28, 49, 73, 121-2, 201
Shayler, Anne 45-6
Shayler, David v-vi, 7, 14, 104, 194; agreement terms 234-5, 238, 248; Alpass review 232-4, 246, 292; arrest 248, 251, 255-8, 269, 276, 316; background 46; City of London bombing 149, 152-3; criticisms 202, 206, 226, 315; CX report leak 189; extradition proceedings 241, 251-2, 255, 268; financial benefits 218, 221, 224-5, 279; France 240-42, 244-6, 251, 253-70; freedom 270; Holland 211-15, 240; Internet usage 246-8, 260; kidnap threat 275; national security issues 130, 206-7, 219-21, 251, 275, 292-3; novel 207-8; 'Operational Inefficiency' report 149, 153; prison 257-70, 280; publication day 212-13; radio advert 216; Rasheed 272-4; recruitment 45-50, 62; resignation 204; return to UK 276; Sean McNulty 155; search warrant 222-3; whistleblowing 3-4, 204-39, 292

Sheikh, Omar 166, 176
Sheldon, Bernard 76
Shephard, Richard 301
Shepherd's Market, Mayfair 210
Sheppard, Olga vii
Sherburne, Bishop 288
Short, Edward 31
Sierra Leone 267
Sillitoe, Sir Percy 294
Single Intelligence Vote 57
Smith, Ramsay 52
Smythe, David vi, 219, 237-8
Socialist Workers Party (SWP) 72, 90-91, 99, 101-2, 105, 123
Soho bombing 140-41
Soviet Union 25, 27-30, 32, 36-7, 73, 102, 116, 313; see also Russia, Cold War
Spiro, Brian vi
Spycatcher (Wright) 47, 207, 252, 293
Staff Consultative Group 291
Star system 95
Starkey, Dr David 288-9
Stout, Harold 247-8
Straw, Jack 8, 13, 83, 85, 93, 106-8, 113ff., 125ff., 178, 215, 223, 226ff., 242, 277, 294, 316-18
structure, MI5 59-60
Stuart-Smith, Lord Justice Sir Murray 86, 299-300
Subversion 25, 27, 36, 58, 94, 100, 233
Sun 123, 277
Sunday Telegraph 190-93, 241
Sunday Times 7, 106, 189, 241, 251, 253-5, 288, 301
surveillance 25, 35, 44, 65, 74-5, 97, 101-2, 133, 206, 266, 285, 318; A4 section 65, 146-7; 'ABC' system 146-7; Brittain 195; bugging devices 59, 77-9, 87, 195; City of London bombing 141; Clark, Alan 114-15, 125; concept 73-5; 'dodgy holidays' 146; IRA 146, 148, 162; Mandelson 300; monotony 74; Scargill 134; tracking 146-7, 162; see also telephone tapping
Sweden 129
Swissair flight 211 explosion 257
SWP see Socialist Workers Party

T Branch 55, 60, 131, 136, 141, 148, 241, 289
TABnet 247
Taylor, A.J.P. 25
Taylor, Lord Justice 89
Taylor, William 141
telephone tapping 34-5, 50, 59, 73, 80-92, 120, 148, 154, 285, 296, 299, 308, 318; Brittain 194; Clark, Alan 115; Fielding 255; Mandelson 108, 113; Scargill 134
telephone warnings 150, 161
terrorism 3-15, 37, 59, 78, 132, 136, 165-8, 281-2, 318; vetting 118; *see also* bombings; IRA, Al Quaeda
Thames House vi, 10, 51-2, 80, 84, 95, 207, 282-3
Thatcher, Margaret 35, 42, 134, 137, 139, 226, 296,298
Thirkell-White, Jestyn 3-4, 14, 2755-6
Thompson, Marjorie 124
The Times 40, 44, 72, 131, 163, 232
Tomlinson, Richard 252-7
Tottenham Court Road 210
Tracking 146-7, 162
trade unions 77-8, 87-8, 103, 115, 133-4
training 41, 59, 67-8, 75, 142
Trevor-Roper, Hugh 26
Trotsky, Leon 97
Tsikata, Kojo 194, 196-9

Tumbledown (television) 90
Tunworth 185-7, 190

unfair dismissal *see* grievance procedures
United States (US) 97, 129, 171, 177, 257, 286, 305, 307-8, 315
universities 28, 40, 42-4, 100, 109, 313
Urban, Mark 37, 53, 74, 101, 185-6, 249-50, 289

Vansittart, Sir Robert 26
vetting 27-8, 43-4, 49-50, 52, 55, 71, 95, 114, 116-25, 205, 230, 267, 276, 316; BBC 117; character defects 28, 122; failure criteria 118-21; file access 96; historical background 28; levels 118; types 28, 59-60
voicemail 55-6

Wadham, John vi, 213,228-9, 232-5, 237-9, 241-3, 245-6, 248-9, 253, 259-60, 264, 270, 274-6
Waiting for Godot (Beckett) 46
Walker, Sir Patrick 44, 101, 134, 298-9, 301
Wallace, Colin 31, 108
Walpole, Robert 31, 108
Warner, Gerry 139
warrants 76, 79-86, 89, 91,

102-3, 108, 148, 194, 284, 294, 299, 308
Warrington bombing 151
weapons of mass destruction 313-14
Wells, Paul 166
whistleblowing 3-4, 233-9, 266
White, Dick 40
White, Ronnie 72
Williams, Lord 251
Willis, John 198-201
Wilson, Harold 30-31, 88, 109, 115, 296
Wilson, Michael 123
Woodfield, Sir Phillip 6
Woolsey, James 308
Workers Revolutionary Party (WRP) 98-9
World in Action (television) 90, 293
World Trade Center attack 171, 177
Wright, Peter 30-31, 40, 47, 74ff., 87, 106, 293
WRP *see* Workers Revolutionary Party

Y-boxed files 96-7
Yemen 168-9
Young, Eddy vi
Young, George 296
Young Turks 29-30

Zainulabin, Sulayman Bilal 170-71
Zinoviev letter 24-5